Eighteenth-Century Britain, 1688–1783

Palgrave History of Britain

Now available:
Eighteenth-Century Britain 1688–1783   *Jeremy Black*

In preparation, volumes covering:
Britain in the Early Middle Ages
Britain in the Later Middle Ages
Sixteenth-Century Britain
Seventeenth-Century Britain
Nineteenth-Century Britain
Britain, 1865–1939
Britain since 1931

Eighteenth-Century Britain 1688–1783

JEREMY BLACK

palgrave

First published 2001 by
PALGRAVE
Houndmills, Basingstoke, Hampshire RG21 6XS and
175 Fifth Avenue, New York, N. Y. 10010
Companies and representatives throughout the world

PALGRAVE is the new global academic imprint of
St. Martin's Press LLC Scholarly and Reference Division and
Palgrave Publishers Ltd (formerly Macmillan Press Ltd).

ISBN 0–333–53830–7 hardback
ISBN 0–333–53831–5 paperback

This book is printed on paper suitable for recycling and
made from fully managed and sustained forest sources.

A catalogue record for this book is available
from the British Library.

Library of Congress-in-Publication Data

Black, Jeremy.
    Eighteenth-century Britain : 1688–1783 / Jeremy Black.
        p. cm – (Palgrave history of Britain)
    Includes bibliographical references (p.) and index.
    ISBN 0–333–53830–7 – ISBN 0–333–53831–5 (pbk.)
        1. Great Britain–History – 18th century. I. Title: 18th century Britain.
II. Title. III. Series.

DA480 .B555 2001
941.07–dc21   2001019439

10   9   8   7   6   5   4   3   2   1
10   09 08 07 06 05 04 03 02 01

Printed by Creative Print and Design Wales (Ebbw Vale)

Contents

Preface

'Like a well-steered big boat'. That was how Britain was described by a Dutch commentator in 1708.[1] The nautical comparison was appropriate. The British Isles in this period can be discussed primarily in terms of landed interests and attitudes, but on the global scale Britain was important as a maritime state and the British as trading and colonising people. It was these features that were most important to other parts of the world, and this maritime and colonial trajectory that was to be most important for the following century.

It is necessary to balance or reconcile different priorities when writing British history in this period. To concentrate on the average would entail an emphasis on the poor, who were the majority of the population, and also, alongside any discussion of transformation, a stress on elements of life that did not change. There would necessarily be much on rural Britain for that was where the majority of the population lived. These aspects are considered in this book, but it is also written from a perspective that asks what about Britain was important and distinctive in this period; and thus seeks to explain why its history should be studied. This stance recreates the approach of contemporary foreign commentators and confronts the risk that it may mislead in its emphasis as they frequently did in their analysis.

Yet, although English is now the closest the world has to a universal language, it is misleading to assume that the history of Britain will be of interest, especially to foreigners, unless its broader significance is grasped. This then is not a history that centres on the details of political manoeuvre. Politics is deliberately confined to part of the book, and the emphasis there is on the wider resonance of political developments. There is an attempt to understand the history of Britain and its role in the world in a period when the state grew to become the strongest maritime power in the world. Such a study is not embarked on in any triumphalist or teleological sense, but it is important that Britain became the major European power in North America and South Asia and on the oceans of the world, and that the unity of the English-speaking world was shattered by the creation of an independent United States of America.

There is a wealth of good literature of this period and more appears each year. There are also serious historiographical debates about how best to understand the period. In the allocated span of words, it is only possible to glance at some of these debates and to refer to certain interpretations. Readers therefore are referred to the Selected Further Reading. They are also encouraged to read some of the wealth of original material that survives in print from this period, much of which is available in modern editions.

Nomenclature is a problem. For ease, the British Isles are referred to as Britain because they were a unit as far as international relations and war were concerned for most of this period. England, Ireland, Scotland and Wales are employed when specific reference is made to those areas, although, as a description of the area represented in the Westminster Parliament prior to 1707, England is sometimes taken to refer to England and Wales.

In writing this book, I have benefited from my earlier work on the period, but have also rethought problems and looked at much new material. I feel that work on archival sources helps an author appreciate the complexity of the subject, and I hope I have communicated this. In addition to my own research, I have been fortunate, as editor since 1989 of *Archives*, the journal of the British Records Association, and as general editor of the Macmillan (now Palgrave) series *British History in Perspective* and *British Studies Series*, to have kept in touch with first-rate work in many fields.

Endnotes have been kept to a minimum. Aside from the value of the individual sources cited, the endnotes are also intended to show the range and variety of material available. The citation of published work focuses on books appearing in recent years, as earlier works can be followed up both in their endnotes and in those of earlier general works.

There are already a number of first-rate treatments of this period. This study does not seek to supplant them, but rather to engage in a debate about a most fascinating period. In doing so, I am most grateful to Grayson Ditchfield, Bill Gibson, Murray Pittock and three anonymous readers for commenting on earlier drafts of sections of this work. In developing ideas, I have benefited from invitations to speak to the Société d'Études Anglo-Américaines des XVIIe et XVIIIe siècles, the Horace Walpole bicentennial series at St Mary's University College, and Friends of Devon Archives, and at the Huntington Library, the Jefferson on the Lawn Symposium at the University of Virginia, the External Studies departments of the Universities of Cambridge, Oxford and Virginia, Stillman College, and the Manorial Society conference on the history of crime in Britain.

It is a great pleasure to dedicate the book to an old friend and valued fellow-historian.

JEREMY BLACK

For Robert Peberdy

NOTE

1. Henri Abraham Châtelain, *Atlas Historique*, III (Amsterdam, 1708), preface.

Abbreviations

AE   Paris, Ministère des Affaires Etrangères
Add.   Additional Manuscripts
BL   London, British Library
Cobbett   W. Cobbett, *A Parliamentary History of England* (36 vols, 1806–20)
CP   Correspondance Politique
CRO   County Record Office
HL   San Marino, California, Huntington Library
LO   Loudoun papers
MO   Montagu papers
ns   new style
PRO   London, Public Record Office
SP   State Papers
NeC   Nottingham, University Library, Clumber papers

Introduction

Periodisation is always a problem in history, a subject that struggles with the complex identities and relationships of change and continuity. To choose dates is to define a period and to confer an apparent identity and thus unity on it. To periodise the past is to suggest frontiers in time that necessarily complicate issues of change and continuity by implying an apparent basis for them.

The period of this book is no exception. Why 1688 to 1783, and what might these dates suggest as opposed to other possible limits? The book, like others of the type, is designed to serve within a series. That has implications both in terms of the need to divide the whole of British history and also because this volume has to sit well next to others. The choice of 1688 to 1783 also reflects the importance of political divisions. The first is the date of the 'Glorious Revolution', the overthrow of the last Catholic ruler of the country, James II, by William of Orange, William III. This is seen to have led to major constitutional and political changes, and to particularly important shifts in the history of Scotland and Ireland.

In some respects, the period 1688 to 1783 can be seen as one of the workings out of the 'Glorious Revolution'. This was particularly true in the fields of state formation, parliamentary government, political ideology, public finance, foreign and imperial policy, dynastic conflict, and religious politics, and in Scotland and Ireland. Furthermore, links have been made between the radical ideas that were encouraged by the 'Revolution' and those that inspired, or at least were associated with, opposition to George III in North America in the 1760s and 1770s. In 1783, Britain acknowledged the independence of the Thirteen Colonies that had rebelled in 1775 and declared independence in 1776. This end to the War of American Independence, or American Revolution, marked a major transformation in the history of the British empire.

Yet, in other respects, both 1688 and 1783 can be queried as delimiting dates. Other dates that were important in political history, for example 1660 and 1800, the restoration of Charles II after the Republican Interregnum, and the Act of Union with Ireland – might seem more appropriate. As far as focusing on the fall of James II in 1688 is concerned possibly the creation of the Bank of England in 1694 was more important, as it was central to what has been seen correctly as a financial revolution in public finances, although that, and other aspects of the Revolution Settlement, can be seen as stemming from the events of 1688.

In addition, the value of choosing 1783 can be queried. It suggests a note of failure that was to be rapidly reversed, with the recovery of political stability during the long ministry of William Pitt the Younger whose initially precarious hold on power was consolidated by victory in the general election of 1784. By the end of 1787 both public finances and Britain's international position had appreciably improved, and by the end of 1792 the British empire was notably stronger and more extensive than in 1783. More broadly, is it appropriate to focus on political 'turning points'? Instead, should the note be one of continuities and/or should the focus be on non-political circumstances and developments?

These questions will be revisited in the Conclusions but they are posed now because they remind us that periods are not fixed, and that continuities as well as changes play a major role. In reading what follows, it is as well to be reminded of these points. They also help explain why the discussion of political changes is not put first. To do so would be to imply the dominant position of such changes in explaining developments, an approach that should be questioned.

It would be misleading to offer such a discussion without mentioning the historiographical context. It is of course possible to write about a period without such a discussion and many books do so, not least because a large number of readers find historiography uninteresting or a distraction. However, such an approach can lead to a misleading suggestion that the analysis of developments is without controversy and indeed that there is only one way to approach the subject, invariably that of the author. Such an approach is misleading. It insults the intelligence and interest of readers who are entitled to expect not only an avoidance of simplicity but also an explanation of the major themes of debate. It is also wrong to slight the work of others by omission.

Yet, historiography is both difficult to summarise and can date very rapidly. The following survey seeks to isolate the major debate and also to introduce readers both to the complexity of the period and to issues that will be revisited in the chapters and, more particularly, in the Conclusions. Although the contents of historiographical debate can date rapidly as new works are published and new issues come to the fore, historiography as a process does display major continuities in theme. Questions as to how best to relate economic developments to social structures, or both to political changes, as to how to integrate the general with the specific, or whether (and how) to focus on change and continuity, remain of abiding concern. They also help locate more particular questions of interpretation. Furthermore, by reminding readers of the controversial nature of historical discussion and analysis, historiography does not date.

The essential divide in treatments of this period has, in accordance with standard historiographical divisions, come between readings of the period that emphasise change and those that stress continuity. The former offer essentially a modernising account that places a focus on what are seen as the agencies of transformation. Emphases vary, but these classically include economic change, especially the 'financial revolution', 'agricultural revolution', the growth of oceanic trade, and industrialisation, with related social changes. Generally, these changes are related to the political and constitutional changes that stemmed from the 'Glorious Revolution', which is held to have freed more enterprising and liberal groups and tendencies in English and Scottish society. More recently, there has been an emphasis on the development of a 'public space' in which democratising tendencies, and aspirations that previously were little heeded, particularly those of women, could jockey for expression in a world shaped by entrepreneurship and by capitalist forces that channelled the demands of many, and thus brought a measure of empowerment.

There has also been an emphasis on the development of a more effective state, sometimes termed the 'fiscal military state'. This state is seen as devising fiscal means to tap the taxation and lending resources of society without causing economic harm. The resources were employed not for programmes of state-directed economic growth or social welfare, but rather to give force to the expansion of Britain as an imperial state.[1] Thus, shifts in her global position are directly related to her domestic political ethos and practices and to government institutions in a dynamic relationship. The domestic consequences of international competition included a concern with social harmony and this encouraged public initiatives, often at the local level, that undermine any account of government as passive.

Thus, the general theme is of change in all respects, of a society remaking its image and embracing the future. This has led to suggestions that it was Britain, not France, that was the real centre of the Enlightenment, the term applied to eighteenth-century progressive tendencies.[2]

Against this has come an emphasis on continuity. This is based on two linked approaches. The first minimises the factors cited above, for example by arguing that economic growth was qualified until the nineteenth century, and that factory methods remained peripheral to much of the economy. The second focuses on particular aspects of continuity, in particular the ideological framework of the period, a subject of considerable importance but one that is not easy to evaluate. In the most prominent exposition of the theme of continuity, Jonathan Clark's *English Society, 1688–1832* (Cambridge, 1985), Anglicanism, divine right monarchy, aristocratic paternalism, and a belief in the value of stability are seen as dominant throughout the period in England, and indeed as more challenged by the need to adapt to the expulsion of James II in 1688–9 than by subsequent radicalism. This interpretation was reiterated in the second edition, *English Society 1660–1832* (Cambridge, 2000).

Clark provided a theme for what had hitherto been somewhat mechanical accounts of political activity by asserting that continuity was the result of an active conservative ideology, rather than of the political calculation which had dominated the works of Sir Lewis Namier, and those influenced by his methods.[3] Clark put religion at the centre stage of English conservatism, and, by seeing this conservatism as vigorous and successful, not merely reactive, he put religious faith at the centre of English stability and identity.[4] In his book, England was presented as an Anglican church-state, an *ancien régime* society buttressed by the hierarchical ideology of a popular established religion. The Anglican church, no

mere religious establishment but the repository of widespread religious observance, supported the political system by, in particular, propagating an ideology of
obedience, while the state sustained the church. Clark argued that John Locke's
role in spreading rationalism had been overstated. In addition, according to Clark,
there were few radicals and the heart of radicalism was not secular notions of
earthly redistribution of power, but religious heresy, specifically Socinianism.
Though stimulating, this was a work based on printed material – sermons, books
and pamphlets, and thus provided evidence of ideology rather than practice.

The active role of religion was also prominent in another influential work,
Linda Colley's study of Georgian national feeling, *Britons*.[5] The stress that both
Clark and Colley placed on religion reflected a move from earlier interpretations
that had been inclined to adopt a more materialist approach to people's posi-
tioning and motivation, and a more secular attitude, to ideological stances and
political divisions.

Far from presenting nations as organic, historic phenomena, characterised by
cultural and ethnic homogeneity, Colley saw them as imagined communities, culturally and ethnically diverse, and requiring artificial construction. Her account
of Georgian loyalism was a study of how an idea of Great Britain was created
and how it was superimposed onto older alignments and loyalties. In this story,
Protestant identity (along with success in war and the profits of empire) was central. Colley argued that the sense of Britain as an elect nation, and the perception of
a contrast between a godly island and a popish continent, gave eighteenth-century
Britons one of their strongest self-definitions.

Where Clark's vision was traditionalist, constantly emphasising survivals
rather than origins, Colley's ideas of Protestantism was dynamic, modern and
more compatible with the notion of an emerging 'fiscal-military' state than with
Clark's confessional society. Another important difference was that Clark had little to say about anti-Catholicism. His 'other' against which majority identity was
defined was Protestant non-conformity, and especially Unitarianism. For Colley,
in contrast, Protestantism seemed at times to be little more than anti-popery.
Although she did argue that the gap between differing Protestant denominations
has been overstated, Colley underrated the challenge posed by Dissenters
(Protestant Nonconformists who believed in the Trinity), and the need on the part
of the national church to respond to it.

Yet, although Clark and Colley are notorious for providing contrasting
views of the eighteenth century, there are in fact surprising structural similarities
in their accounts of religion and nationality, which are shared by much of the
other recent work on this field. At base, both offer views of the period centred on
a sort of *Zeitgeist*, or spirit of the age. For each author, religion played the defining role in the *Zeitgeist*, and was crucial to the creation and maintenance of
ideology. For both historians, religion was both structure and agency: practice
and discourse. In their work, religious faith reflected and sustained a largely
unquestioned and hegemonic ideology. Faith dominated action and the possibilities of discussion, and tended to maintain the population in one particular vision
of themselves.

There are methodological and empirical problems with this approach. First, the dangers of treating religion as a hegemonic ideology must be recognised. Historians may stress the power of particular sets of ideas, but, to go beyond this, to suggest that one vision became a dominant discourse runs considerable risks. It may become self-validating; it has severe limitations in describing what was generally a diverse situation; it may neglect the complexity and compromises within discourses itself; and it may miss the extent to which supposedly hegemonic worldviews were actually divisive and polemical.

The Protestant-centred patriotism described in much of the literature may have been less effortlessly dominant than is sometimes suggested. James II's removal by William III in 1688–9 was an advance for particular views of England, Scotland and Ireland, but they did not secure these views instant dominance. Alongside praise for William as a Protestant and providential blessing on the nation, were Jacobite [supporters of the exiled James II], Tory and 'Country' views of him as a usurper, and of England, Scotland and Ireland as suffering depredations under his tutelage. These views are perfectly viable and attracted considerable support in the 1690s. They were marginalised not because of any inherent absurdity but because William was able to defeat his opponents swiftly and conclusively. His military victory, won without any compromise with his opponents, enabled him to exclude them from power and to condemn the critics of his vision of nationality as disloyal.

Yet the 'Glorious Revolution' of 1688 in fact led to a deep anxiety about the very character and future of the political system. This was not based on concern about the longevity of any particular ministry; nor did it relate to anxiety about the stability of the social system. Instead, dynastic conflict posed a more traditional anxiety. The legitimacy of the sovereign, and thus of the political system, was absent for many, and their continuation uncertain for all, until the crushing defeat of the Jacobites at Culloden in 1746 and the subsequent governmental reorganisation of the Scottish Highlands, the core area of Jacobite resistance.

The earlier military victory, for what were termed Revolution Principles, by William III coincided with a dramatic expansion of public politics. In the 1690s, the advent of annual sessions of Parliament, the ending of pre-publication censorship in 1695, and the development of a considerably more active press, meant that polemical politics began to produce more, and different, kinds of sources. As a result, the particular patriotic discourse associated with the victors of the revolution was widely disseminated and gained the highest profile in the culture of print, as well as on government record. Over the years after 1688, this discourse displaced rivals, both in the respectable discussion of the time, and in the records, especially the most-consulted metropolitan and printed texts, which historians would use to reconstruct that discussion; although those who were defeated also poured forth in print. Among opponents of William III, non-jurors and those who asserted passive obedience were prolific.

However, much of the scholarship dealing with the century after 1688 has been soaked in the sort of Whiggism promoted by that event, with the result that many of the ambiguities and complexities of the period, and the coherence and potential persuasiveness of alternative views have been obscured. Until recently, historians of the period were almost as effective as Williamite politicians in marginalising the Jacobite and other dissonant voices which were unsuccessful in the political struggles of the period.[6]

Similarly, too little attention has been paid to the exclusivity and polemical nature of the eventually dominant patriotism. Its victory has hidden the fact that it was directed against those critical of William, that it was therefore necessarily divisive, and that (far from uniting the nation in a universal ideology), it derived much of its early drive from its partisan character.

Again, William's victory in 1689–91 has been made to appear desirable because it was necessary for national development. It has been seen as the opportunity to move into the first rank of European powers. As part of this interpretation, discussion of national interest has shared the Williamite assumption of the need to oppose France (in contrast to the policies of Charles II and James II), and has neglected the problematic nature of the concept. Ideas of national interest in fact are inseparable from ideologies which seek to define and shape, role and destiny – so, in reality, enmity with France was only 'natural' to people certain not only that Catholicism, and Bourbon domestic and international policies were antitheses of Englishness and Britishness and threats to them, but also that Britain must take the lead in resisting them. Anti-Catholicism indeed ran deep before 1688, but the political consequences of this were less clear-cut. Finally, Williamite insistence that Jacobite and Tory opponents were bigoted dogmatists led to the construction of religious tolerance as a cardinal English/British virtue. Later commentators accepted this vision, but, in fact, under what is better known as the Toleration Act of 1689, Unitarians, Catholics and non-Christians did not enjoy rights of public worship in England and Wales, and Catholics were subject to penal statues; as were anti-Trinitarians under the 1697 Blasphemy Act. In denying rights to Catholics, the Toleration Act confirmed an existing trend seen in the Test Act of 1673.

This analysis of the Revolution Settlement and of eighteenth-century patriotism demonstrates the danger of accepting an influential ideology on its own terms. Once a particular view dominates the historical record (particularly the printed record of metropolitan political culture) it is too easy to forget that other views were, and still should be, available. Most dangerously, the easy hegemony which this process of self validation bestows can discourage historians from looking for opposition to, and weaknesses in, the *Zeitgeist* they discern. Particularly with the religiously-centred ideologies which have played a major role in scholarly discussion, too little attention has been given to the divisions of faith which undermined any effortless ideological dominance; or to the messy compromises which were often made once the discourse met complex conditions on the ground.

The division between Anglicans and their opponents can be seen behind some of the other fissures in society, as it was by contemporaries, although the equations Anglican = Tory and Dissenter = Whig are too stark, for many Anglicans were Whigs. Nevertheless, it is possible that a religious foundation to electoral behaviour went beyond politics, and was related to the embryonic ideas of class and the cultural influences brought by economic development. This is related to the important question of the level at which people primarily identified their concerns and interests. Religious-party allegiance was very different from localised loyalties based on landed estates or clientage. By linking people who perceived common interests in different parts of the country, it may have been central in the emergence of more 'national' – but more divisive – consciousnesses such as class.

Obviously, there is a danger that tension between Church and Dissent can be exaggerated. Divisions were sometimes less clear-cut and comprehensive than might be suggested; and people at all levels of society worked to avoid differences growing into dangerous ruptures. As a result, open conflict between the two communities was generally avoided; and intense rivalry was usually limited to specific localities.

Despite these caveats, there was no easy Protestant consensus, and Protestant identity was a contested area. Civic culture was also an arena for active debate, and, in so far as there was a common idiom in behaviour and debate, it was used to promote different views and was an expression of genuine pluralism. Religious diversity suggests that there was no underlying Protestantism on which a strong feeling of 'Britishness' could be based, while the degree of open religious debate must question any easy notion of a confessional church-state. However, it could also be argued that self-conscious knowledge of the importance of religion to national identity was the reason why some contested it as hotly as they did.

The tension between Church and Dissent poses a problem for historians trying to establish any easy link between a prevailing faith and a dominant identity. Yet there are more difficulties, including divisions within the different denominations. For example, English Presbyterians argued over the scriptural basis of doctrine, early Methodists divided over predestination, and Anglicans debated a wide range of religious issues. Moreover, close examination of particular neighbourhoods reveals that bold statements of religious identity in metropolitan print culture, for example vigorous anti-popery or Anglican ascendancy, were often not reflected in local conditions, in part because of a widespread wish to avoid disrupting local communities. The religious homogeneity assumed or called for in much eighteenth-century rhetoric was neither unchallenged, nor rigidly enforced.

A lack of such homogeneity must question any simple notion of religious hegemony, and the possible role of confessional solidarities serving as the basis for national ones. It can, in contrast, be argued that hegemony does not require absolute conformity. Religious attitudes can dominate by setting the grounds for debate, or by governing the assumptions used in argument, far more easily than by forcing total acceptance. However, the religious basis for national identity must have been more ambiguous, complex and confusing than is often suggested; historians need to check the solidity of the ideologies they describe.

Variety also extended to other aspects of religious experience. The call for Christian living made for example by Howell Harris (1714–73), a formidable itinerant missionary preacher for the revived Christianity that was to become

Welsh Methodism, was not always popular. In 1739, a sympathiser reported:

> Mr Howel Harris has been an instrument under God of raising about 30 reli-
> gious societies who all pray extemporary and from what we can see of them
> are filled with the spirit. He goes from place to place and preaches or exhorts
> on a place like a stage, which they raise for him, and he often appoints his
> meetings at such times and places where revels, cockfightings, etc. are
> appointed, whereby he has been a mighty instrument of reformation and of
> pulling down Satan's strongholds which, you may be sure, makes him rage
> horribly, so that he, Mr Howel Harris, has been often openly assaulted like our
> blessed Master.[7]

At the Monmouth races in 1740, Harris attacked 'balls, assemblies, horseraces,
whoredom and drunkenness' and provoked a riot. Whatever the confessional
background, there were different levels of commitment and piety.

More generally, variety in circumstances can also be linked to ambiguity on the
part of contemporaries (and historians) about the extent to which change equated
with a transforming pace of development. This uncertainty was particularly pronounced prior to the mid-eighteenth century. In part it was a product of a sense of
the mutability of achievement that reflected the widespread mentality of the period
which was focused on cyclical change, not steady growth. In his *A Tour through
the whole island of Great Britain* (1724–6), a book whose publication indicated
widespread interest in the nature of the country, Daniel Defoe noted:

> The fate of things gives a new face to things, produces changes in low life, and
> innumerable incidents; plants and supplants families, raises and sinks towns,
> removes manufacturers and trades; great towns decay and small towns rise;
> new towns, new palaces, new seats are built every day; great rivers and good
> harbours dry up, and grow useless; again new ports are opened, brooks are
> made rivers, small rivers navigable, ports and harbours are made where none
> were before, and the like.[8]

In his travels, Defoe noted that there was a geographical as well as a temporal
dimension to change. This theme has been underplayed in much work, but there
are interesting examples of a willingness to engage with the fundamental and formative character of regional and local differences, for example in Susanna Wade
Martins and Tom Williamson's *Roots of Change, Farming and the Landscape in
East Anglia, c. 1700–1870* (Exeter, 1999) and Steven King's *Poverty and Welfare
in England, 1700–1850. A Regional Perspective* (Manchester, 2000).

Any reading of studies of different communities and areas reveals a wealth
of contrasts, albeit common themes and changes, such as greater economic
integration with other parts of the British Isles. Thus, County Tipperary was
underdeveloped economically but, as it was drawn more fully into the market
economy, its agricultural sector experienced growing diversification and commercialisation. The essentially semi-feudal character of society still apparent in
the seventeenth century changed.[9] Even so, Tipperary remained very different to
Norfolk or Fife. So also did other areas where traditional agrarian practices

remained important, for example the Orkney and Shetland Islands.[10] Nevertheless, such distant areas were also changing as new tenurial relationships replaced older values and traditions.[11]

An emphasis on similar changes affecting different localities does not mean that they developed in the same way, either economically or socially. As Chapter three makes clear, the character of and response to enclosure varied greatly, and this underlines the need for 'well grounded and deeply contextualised local studies'. This issue should not be seen in terms of a contrast between traditional, and thus varied, rural societies and more progressive, and thus homogenous, urban counterparts.[12] Indeed, a study of Halifax has argued that middle-class culture originated in the local, rather than in the national, context, and that no single middle-class culture existed. Rather, a variety of local cultures developed, each a specific response to local context, and, in particular, to the particular ways in which capitalist relations of production emerged in that locality. In Halifax, economic change was accompanied by a cultural transformation that brought into being entrepreneurial attitudes and new social relations.[13] The local nuances and impact of these processes varied considerably.

The most basic and obvious point is that writers should beware of overly simplistic accounts. To turn again to the example of religion and national identity, whilst Clark alerted historians to the centrality of religion in politics and society, and there is much in Colley's suggestion that national identity was an artificial creation which needed some other emotion (such as anti-popery) around which to crystallise, it is necessary to build on these insights without suggesting that any neat pattern or elegant thesis can be advanced. Instead, it is more appropriate to emphasise the contingent and multiple nature of identities when looking at the relationship between faith and nationality.

Monolithic views of the church and national identity are unsatisfactory because they ignore the choices available to people, a point that is also of wider applicability in the economic, social, political and cultural history of the period. Men and women had a number of ways in which they could think of themselves; and they might adopt different, even contradictory, ones according to circumstance.

For example, a recent study of Catholics and Presbyterians in Lancashire suggests that stereotypical views of 'Papists' and subversive 'Dissenters' may have created sectional divisions in society, but may simultaneously have allowed vertical cohesion between social strata. A *national* identity overlaid on top of these denominational and class identities would have added yet a further dimension, and permitted people to adopt ideas and values selectively from the range of ideologies on offer. In this situation, nobody would have identified exclusively with denomination, class, or country. Their values and ideas would have been drawn from each, like a patchwork, and not come from one wholesale.[14]

Future scholarship will emphasise the diversity and flexibility of identity. It should also probe the danger in concentrating on themes found in metropolitan print culture. Writers and legislators tended to describe or advocate ideals. Modern stress on such ideals can unnecessarily reify them [turn them into things, i.e. treat concepts as if they described an active reality], and can lead scholars to ignore the far less clear-cut conditions of actual life. These conditions reflected both governmental activity and popular attitudes. In practice, regimes made messy compromises when trying to enforce legislation or national/religious allegiances; people implementing policy on the ground found the situation more complex than had been envisaged; and populations sought accommodations. Nevertheless, often pragmatic solutions were clothed in principled justifications.

If variety and complexity are major themes in this book, and there is also a stress on the importance of religion, not only in its own right but also for its impact in other fields; it is important to return to the historiographical dimension and to make brief mention of a number of important alternatives. An important strand of scholarly work focuses on the search for the roots of what is presented as modern political culture. This is especially illustrated by a quest for eighteenth-century radicalism, an assertion of the significance of the period in the perspective of a fashionable teleology that emphasises growing radicalism, and the location of the period between the mid-seventeenth century crisis and that of the French Revolutionary period. Thus, scholars focus on radical or progressive ideas and actions, especially signs of a popular political consciousness. The paraphernalia of mass action, essentially riots, crowds and demonstrations, attract particular attention, and their methods are scrutinised to establish a language of action. A key book in this approach was John Brewer's *Party Ideology and Popular Politics at the Accession of George III* (Cambridge, 1976), which deliberately rejected the focus of Namier's study, its assumptions and methodology. Instead, Brewer argued that politics was more ideological, more open to wider political and social currents, and more modern in the sense of reflecting a degree of mass participation. These themes were subsequently taken forward in a number of studies.[15]

The late 1990s witnessed the appearance of a number of studies that sought to offer a new synthesis. Douglas Hay and Nicholas Rogers' *Eighteenth-Century English Society: Shuttles and Swords* (Oxford, 1997), has a non-political focus and largely ignores religion. They are also very disapproving about the practices and ethos of the political world. Frank O'Gorman's *The Long Eighteenth Century: British Political and Society History, 1688–1832* (1997) and Wilfrid Prest's *Albion Ascendant: English History, 1660–1815* (1998) essentially adopt middle-of-the-road positions on issues of political structure, but each is inclined to emphasise the middling orders and to take a progressive, even teleological, stance. Prest also detects a decline in the importance of religion, suggesting that, under the early Hanoverians, it became increasingly concerned with individual rather than communal reformation, more a matter of willed decision than unconscious culture, and less integral to almost all aspects of life and thought than hitherto. Richard Price's *British Society 1680–1880: Dynamism, Containment and Change* (Cambridge, 1999), has much to offer on the social dimension of politics, although he also slights religion.

Mention of these works should not be left to, an often unread, 'Selected Further Reading' because it is important from the outset to see individual studies within a wider context. Such an approach both illuminates their distinctiveness and directs attention to other work.

In emphasising diversity, this book seeks to question any synoptic model, let alone teleological analyses that regard developments as inevitable. Yet, it is also reasonable to look if there is a general pattern underlying the variety. This is surveyed in the individual chapters and discussed in the Conclusions.

At this point, however, it is necessary to offer the wider context of the assessment of European developments as a whole in this period. In essence, views of the eighteenth century focus on the changes in the last half, especially the rule of the so-called Enlightened Despots, and, subsequently the French Revolution, which broke out in 1789 and is often given a wider span by locating it as part of an Atlantic Revolution. This approach can be misleading if the century as a whole is characterised in this fashion, because the governmental and political ethos and practices, as well as the demographic regime, and the religious and cultural world prior to mid-century were different, and, in many senses, closer in character to those of the late seventeenth century. Any account of the period in both Britain and on the Continent needs both to give due weight to these decades and to avoid treating them as a prelude for what was to follow.

This context offers a valuable dimension for considering the process of change in Britain. Paul Langford concluded his major study *A Polite and Commercial People: England, 1727–1783* (Oxford, 1989) by writing 'the polite and commercial people of the 1730s was still polite and commercial in the 1780s: it did not, in any fundamental sense, inhabit the same society'. Although this might appear to be hyperbole, Langford captured an important series of shifts. What is less clear is whether they should be seen as destructive of stability or as both the product of it and conducive to it. This will be a problem to return to in the Conclusions. Suffice it to note, that a dynamic *ancien régime* is not a contradiction in terms. Commentators frequently underrate the capacity of such societies to foster, adapt to, and benefit from change. The state created in the aftermath of the 'Glorious Revolution' did not always do so successfully, as the American Revolution amply showed, but it was more successful than is sometimes appreciated.

NOTES

1. J. Brewer, *The Sinews of Power: War, Money and the English State, 1688–1783* (1989).
2. R. Porter, *Enlightenment: Britain and the Creation of the Modern World* (2000).
3. L. Namier, *The Structure of Politics at the Accession of George III* (2nd edn, 1957) and *England in the Age of the American Revolution* (2nd edn, 1963).
4. For support for this view, J.J. Sack, *From Jacobite to Conservative: Reaction and Orthodoxy in Britain, c. 1760–1832* (Cambridge, 1993).
5. L. Colley, *Britons: Forging the Nation, 1707–1837* (New Haven, 1992).
6. See, for example, D. Cannadine, 'British History: Past, Present and Future?', *Past and Present*, no. 116 (1987), p. 189.
7. G.C.G. Thomas (ed.), 'George Whitefield and Friends: the correspondence of some early Methodists', *National Library of Wales Journal*, 27 (1991), p. 175.
8. D. Defoe, *A Tour through the whole island of Great Britain*, edited by P. Rogers (1971), p. 44.
9. T.P. Power, *Land, Politics and Society in Eighteenth-Century Tipperary* (Oxford, 1993).

10. W.S. Hewison (ed.), *The Diary of Patrick Fea of Stove, Orkney, 1766–1797* (East Linton, 1997).
11. F. Ramsay (ed.), *The Day Book of Daniel Campbell of Shawfield 1767 with relevant papers concerning the Estate of Islay* (Aberdeen, 1991).
12. C.E. Searle, 'Cumbria's Parliamentary Enclosure Movement: a comparative case study in rural quiescence', *Transactions of the Cumberland and Westmorland Antiquarian and Archaeological Society*, 95 (1995), p. 266.
13. J. Smail, *The Origins of Middle-Class Culture: Halifax, Yorkshire, 1660–1780* (Ithaca, 1994).
14. J. Albers, '"Papist Traitors" and "Presbyterian Rogues": religious identities in eighteenth-century Lancashire', in J. Walsh, C. Haydon and S. Taylor (eds), *The Church of England c. 1689–c. 1833: from Toleration to Tractarianism* (Cambridge, 1993), pp. 317–33.
15. See, for example, K. Wilson, *The Sense of the People: Politics Culture and Imperialism in England, 1715–1785* (Cambridge, 1995).

Life and death

It is as necessary to be wary of finding signs of modernity in the social and domestic life of the period as in its politics or culture. Watching works written in the period, such as John Gay's *The Beggar's Opera* (1728), or visiting houses from the age, it is all too easy to assume that life was in many respects similar to ours. This process has been taken further with film and television adaptations that stress the accessibility of fictional characters, such as Moll Flanders and Tom Jones, and of real counterparts in order to help make their lives of interest and concern to modern viewers. The furnishings and clothes are different, but there are few signs for the superficial viewer of more profound contrasts, contrasts that assure us that the very experience of life was totally different.

To start with the facts of life, is to begin with the fact of death. This was universally present to a degree that cannot be grasped in a modern age in which death is hidden from view, and, in large part, from consideration, while life expectancy is considerably higher than in the eighteenth century. Then, the impact of death took many forms. One of the most important was that of average life expectancy. Individual and collective responses are affected by the age of the individual observer and the average age of groups. The average experience of life for people in the period necessarily came at a younger age than for the average modern person.

Furthermore, this experience was shaped within a context of the ever-present threat of death, disease, injury and pain. There was still joy and pleasure, exultation and exhilaration, but the demographics were chilling. Alongside long-lasting individuals, there were lives quickly cut short. This was particularly true of infancy. Those who survived were stronger and luckier than the birth cohort, and this may have strengthened the genetic pool, but, even so, life remained vulnerable. This was as true of wealthy individuals with some chance of quality living as of the 'lower orders', although the life experience and demographic expectations of the latter were, on average, bleaker.

The aggregate results were as blunt. After the growth of 1500–1650, Britain's population did not rise greatly for a century. In England, it fell between 1660 and 1690, probably due to enteric fevers and gastric diseases, and in Ireland and

Scotland in the 1690s, a decade that was parlous throughout most of Europe. Declining fertility was important in causing the fall between 1671 and 1691, but death rates were of greater significance thereafter. The death-rate crises of 1696–9, 1727–30, and 1741–2 wiped out the growth of the intervening years in many areas. In Warwickshire, in 1727–30, 21 per cent of the population died in Alcester and 30–35 per cent in Stratford and Bidford.[1] In contrast, in Scotland, the crisis of 1727–30 was far less acute.

Despite these crises, life expectancy at birth showed an important trend from an average lifespan of about 30 for those born in the 1680s to 42 by the 1750s, a major increase but to a level still well below that of today. There was no official census until 1801, and figures are approximate, but the population of England and Wales probably rose from 5.07 million in 1666 and 5.18 million in 1695 to only 5.51 in 1711, 5.59 in 1731 and 6.20 in 1751. This was a rise of only one million in sixty years, although that rise posed serious problems, not least for the availability of food and work. Thereafter, as the demographic regime changed, the population of England and Wales rose rapidly, to reach 8.66 million in 1801.[2]

The same pattern can be seen in particular communities and areas, although there are difficulties with the accuracy of pre-1801 figures. For example, in Sussex the population rose from about 80,000 in 1676 and the same figure in 1724 to over 159,000 in 1801. The population in Cornwall rose from about 98,000 in 1660 to 108,000 in 1690, 116,000 for 1745, 123,000 for 1765 and 139,000 for 1779, the last the steepest period of growth.

England dominated the British Isles demographically, although less so than today. In 1689, the English population was about 4.9 million compared to about 2.0 million for Ireland, about 1.2 million for Scotland and about 0.3 million for Wales. The Scottish population fell in the 1690s to about 1.07 million, before beginning to rise to 1.265 million in 1755 and 1.608 million in 1801. Growth rates varied between the parts of the British Isles. Whereas Scotland and England both averaged annual increases of 0.3 per cent in 1700–1755, between 1755 and 1801 the figure for Scotland was 0.5, for England 0.8, and for Ireland 1.3–1.6.[3]

There was no census in Ireland until 1821, but the population probably rose from about 1.7 million in 1672 to between 2.0 and 2.3 million by 1712, about 2.3 million in 1754 and nearly 2.9 million in 1785, before rising rapidly to about 4.4 million in 1791. Within Ireland, the distribution of population was varied, with Ulster and north Leinster the most densely populated and Connacht less so.

There are problems with assessing population. For example, the baptisms recorded in parish registers under-recorded births due to the number of Catholics. The limitations of Scottish parish registers limit the use of the family reconstitution and aggregate back-projection techniques employed in England in order to establish population numbers. Trends are still clear. Although the bulk of the population lived in villages, hamlets and farmsteads, a growing percentage lived in towns. The role of agriculture ensured that much of the population lived in the most fertile areas, such as southern and eastern England, the fertile lowlands of South Wales, for example the Vale of Glamorgan, and the central lowlands of Scotland. Nevertheless, the role of agriculture also ensured that a greater percentage than today lived in areas that were less attractive for farming but where a living could still be earned from the soil. This was true for example of upland pasture areas.

There was also change in the distribution of population stemming from industrial growth. Industrial areas grew more rapidly than rural regions that lacked industry. In Scotland the population of the industrial zone near Glasgow grew greatly, whereas growth rates were far lower in much of the North-East and the eastern Borders. In the countryside, parishes that attracted immigration tended to be those that offered opportunities for cottage industry. The availability of common land could be very important here, not least in providing scope for the increased population.[4] Yet, throughout Britain at the local level there were important variations, reflecting the extent to which a national demographic regime was both superimposed on and mediated through local patterns of activity.

The relationship between population and household structure was very different from that in modern Britain. Barring occasional bigamies, wife sales and aristocratic Bills of Divorce, marriage was irreversible. As a consequence, it ended only with the death of one of the partners, or with a desertion that involved flight from the community. Marriage was also central to sex, procreation and the upbringing of children, a matrix that has been greatly changed in modern Britain. Most childbearing was within marriage. Despite the absence of effective contraceptives and of safe, let alone legal, abortion, recorded illegitimacy rates were low. They were very low by modern standards, although it is impossible to say how much illegitimacy was concealed by infanticide.

In contrast with modern Britain, many people never lived in a sexual relationship, although some of those who did not do so would have relied on casual sex. In the eighteenth century, this overwhelmingly meant prostitution. Many men and women never married, including nearly a quarter of those aged 40–44. Furthermore, marriages were generally late. At the end of the seventeenth century, English men married at about twenty-eight and women at about twenty-seven. Childbearing was thus postponed until an average of more than ten years past puberty, which itself occurred later than in modern Britain.

However, this situation was not static. The demographic regime was a composite and interaction of millions of events. These existed in a dynamic situation, prone, for example, to the impact of epidemics. Migration also had a powerful impact on the distribution of population and thus of childbearing cohorts. The readiness of large numbers of young people to travel in search of work had a major impact on the Scottish population, as did emigration, which increased after the Seven Years' War (1756–63) led to the conquest of Canada; about 45,000 Scots emigrated to North America in 1760–75. Emigration had an impact on the fertility of the remaining population, as there was a disproportionately high percentage of young men among permanent and, even more, short-term emigrants. Maybe half a million Irish emigrated during the eighteenth century. Emigration from England appears to have been particularly significant in the second half of the seventeenth century, when it was partly responsible for a fall in the population. As annual net emigration from England was reasonably constant, while the population rose its impact diminished. Across the eighteenth century, emigration accounted for about 20 per cent of England's natural increase. By the 1760s, the numbers emigrating from England were considerably less than those from Scotland, and, even more, Ireland. The majority of the latter were Protestants, especially Ulster Presbyterians of Scots descent, who suffered both political and religious disabilities under the 1704 Test Act and were affected by downturns in the local economy.[5]

The overall demographic situation also changed in the period, helping to ensure that population figures rose. By the start of the nineteenth century, there had been major changes. The link between marriage and childbearing became less powerful as the recorded illegitimacy rate rose from 1.8 to 5 per cent. On the other hand, marriage had become more common and thus normative. Fewer than 9 per cent of people remained unmarried. In addition, less of adulthood was now spent in the unmarried state. The average age at marriage had fallen to 25.5 and 23.7 for men and women respectively, with the fall being particularly pronounced from the 1730s to the 1770s. This also had an impact on the birth-rate.

This fall reflected a number of developments that focused on the increased freedom of labour and living arrangements, not least the process by which members of the 'familia' withered to 'employees'. For example, farm servants increasingly did not live in with their employers, and thus a restraint on early marriage diminished. In addition, the rise of urban employment and living broke the link between marriage and the availability of land which had been an important restraint. Marriage rates continued to be affected by real wages, but economic growth in the second half of the century created both opportunities and a sense of opportunity that encouraged marriage.

Disease remained a constant presence during the period. It was particularly serious in infancy. Thirty-eight per cent of the children born in Penrith between 1650 and 1700 died before reaching the age of six.[6] Very high child mortality figures continued to be recorded across Britain throughout the eighteenth century. Nevertheless, if childhood was survived, it was possible to live to a considerable age. Over 22 per cent of the congregation of Holy Trinity, Whitehaven who died between 1751 and 1781 were over sixty. More generally, infant mortality rates fell in the second half of the eighteenth century, maternal rates fell throughout the century, and adult rates particularly in the first half of the century. Marital fertility among women aged thirty-five and over rose from mid-century. The rise in marital fertility was probably the consequence of a fall in stillbirths, and this can be seen as evidence of rising average living standards. In Ireland, a major fall in mortality, particularly infant mortality was probably responsible for the rise in population from the 1750s as marriage ages were already fairly low.

Despite improving average conditions, those who survived infancy were well aware of their vulnerability. John Evelyn (not the famous diarist, but an office-holding relative) recorded in 1702 'On Thursday the 5th of November this year my cousin John Evelyn of Nuttfield a proper handsome young gentleman very promising in all respects and member of Parliament for Bletchingley in Surrey was taken ill of the smallpox of which coming out very thick, and not filling he died on Friday the 13th of the same month in the 24th year of his age'. This was followed by a Latin tag from Horace that translates as 'Why should our grief for a man so loved know any shame or limit?'.[7] This tag is an apt comment on the inaccurate argument that because the death of the young was common it was not grievously felt by those who remained.

Defences against disease remained flimsy, not least because of the limited nature of medical knowledge. There was no comparison to modern suppositions that there should be a medical cure for everything. Instead, folk cures and prayer were the remedies open to most people. Modern attitudes towards holistic approaches to medicine, suggest that these would have been far from worthless, and indeed they might have been more potent than today given contemporary belief in their appropriateness, if not efficacy. This is a topic that is difficult to analyse. However, the popularity of patent medicines suggests that confidence in folk remedies and prayer should not be exaggerated. Equally it is probable that many people sought to rely on a range of treatments, rather than on the more 'scientific' approach.

There were advances in the latter, especially in the prevention of smallpox, one of the most serious diseases. Among those it claimed was Queen Mary in 1694. Smallpox replaced bubonic plague as the most feared disease; the last attack of the latter had been in 1665 when about 56,000 people died in London. Immunity was low, not least because a more virulent strain began to have an impact in the second half of the seventeenth century. Both the virulence and the case fatality rate of smallpox continued to rise thereafter. As smallpox was airborne, it was far more contagious than plague had been, although the fatality rate was lower.

Smallpox was also found in the countryside as well as in towns, although it was most serious in London. It was particularly easily transmitted in the family or the household group as proximity was important. Growing urbanisation and a rise in population therefore increased vulnerability to the disease. In major urban areas, the disease became endemic as well as epidemic, and this proved particularly deadly to infants and children. It was also socially selective. The poor lived at a higher population density than the wealthy. In addition, smallpox viruses remained viable for up to a year and could be contracted via clothing or bedding. The poor were less able to afford to destroy clothing and bedding after a death, and this increased their vulnerability.

Initially, inoculation (ingrafting) as a bar to a serious attack of smallpox, introduced from Turkey by Lady Mary Wortley Montagu, wife of the Ambassador there, was of only limited value, not least because those treated, when not isolated, were a source of infection. Lady Mary had her daughter inoculated in London in 1721. Inoculation became safer after the Suttonian method of inserting only the smallest possible amount of infectious matter was widely adopted from about 1768. Sutton (1707–88) claimed to have inoculated 40,000 people. Vaccination, a safer method, was not performed until 1796, but inoculation lessened the potential breeding ground for smallpox.[8]

No comparable progress was made in fighting other serious problems. These included diseases that would not now be fatal to healthy Westerners with access to good medical care, such as intestinal diseases. In the eighteenth century, however, typhus, typhoid, influenza, dysentery, chicken-pox, measles, scarlet fever, and syphilis were all serious problems. Mobility and international trade increased the ease with which epidemics could spread, although with some diseases exposure also brought a measure of resistance. Other conditions, that can now be cured or held at bay, were debilitating. Alcohol and opium were the only painkillers, and cheap laudanum was a universal panacea and the basis of standard medicines.

There was no system of health provision. Skilled practitioners were few, generally concentrated in the town and expensive, although most parishes were within reach of a medic. Medical training could be very good, especially at Cambridge and Edinburgh, and the latter's medical school became particularly impressive. Nevertheless, medical treatments, such as blistering or mercury, could be inappropriate, and were often painful, dangerous or enervating. They were also no respecter of class. In 1737, Queen Caroline had an operation for a rupture while fully conscious. Some patients refused treatment. Surgery was primitive and performed without anaesthetics.

Trust in quack medicines and herbal remedies reflected the sense that something could and should be done, and there was no simple acceptance of the grim will of God, but there was no real pressure for any sweeping improvements in public health. In some respects this deteriorated as there were signs of a problem that was to become more urgent in the nineteenth century: the human and environmental costs of urban and industrial development. In 1714, the French envoy complained repeatedly about the effect on his breathing of the coal smoke that enveloped London. An essay, 'Observations on the method of burying the Parish poor in London, and on the manner in which some of the capital buildings in it are constructed and kept, as two great sources of the extraordinary sickliness and mortality, by putrid fevers, so sensibly felt in that capital; with hints for the correction of these evils', published in the *Annual Register* for 1776, criticised the dangerous stench from corpses that were buried in shallow graves, the hazards of crowded hospitals and public buildings, and the general lack of pure air: 'In this city, where coal fires are principally used, with the inflammable, mephitic, and other matters thrown out, probably an acid is decomposed, and exhaled from the sulphur in the coal.'[9]

Many industrial processes were dangerous to others besides the workers. Dressing and tanning leather polluted water supplies and was therefore kept outside cities: in London on the banks of the River Wandle south of the Thames. The kilns of brick and tile works produced smoke and fumes. There were restrictions on individual noxious practices, for example the pollution of water supplies by some industrial processes, but there was no systematic scrutiny or drive for improvement. Nevertheless, some of the urban improvements of the period reflected a desire to improve the quality of public health.

The virulence of diseases and the potency of crippling problems were more than a consequence of a lack of knowledge and treatments, especially antibiotics and anti-inflammatory drugs. Living conditions were also a major problem. Crowded housing conditions, particularly the sharing of beds, helped spread diseases, especially respiratory infections. Most dwellings were neither warm nor dry, and it was very difficult to get clothes dry. This discouraged the washing of clothes, and also led to the wearing of layers of clothes, many of them thick, so that exposure to the wet should not lead to wet skin. The prevalence of work out of doors and of transport on foot or horseback greatly increased exposure to adverse weather.

Sanitary practices were also a problem. The privies developed by Alexander Cummings and Joseph Bramah, patented in 1775 and 1778, were used by few, and people tended to urinate and defecate in corridors and alleyways. There were few baths, washing in clean water was limited, and louse infestation was serious. Although outer clothes were worn for long periods, and were not washable, those who could afford it wore linen and cotton shifts next to their skins, and these shifts could be regularly laundered. It has been suggested that the availability of relatively cheap cotton clothing, which was washable, combined with an increased use of soap to raise an awareness of cleanliness in the eighteenth century. However, most people wore the same clothes for as long as they could. By modern standards, breath, teeth and skin must have been repellent, and houses would have been smelly.

Humans were also very much at war with the animal world, although animals capable of inflicting death – bears and wolves – had long been wiped out. However, foxes attacked farm animals, rabies was a problem among the dog population, rats were a serious issue, in country houses as well as hovels, and bed bugs were another real horror that did not respect rank. Lice, fleas and tapeworms were also problems. John Wesley frequently suffered from the first two. Straw-thatched buildings provided attractive environments for numerous pests. Predators attacked farm animals, while mice and rats destroyed crops and stored food. Opposition to hostile animals could be linked to hostility to what were seen as their habitats, whether old buildings with earthen floors and walls, and thatched roofs, or areas of the countryside that were referred to as 'waste'. The latter was a standing reproach to improving landowners, such as Denys Rolle (1725–97) who disliked Dartmoor and Exmoor, was keen on enclosure and soil improvement by manuring, and sought to cultivate Woodbury Common.[10]

It is difficult to recreate an impression of the smell and dirt of the period. Ventilation was limited, drains blocked. Humans lived close to animals and dunghills, and this damaged health. Manure stored near buildings was hazardous and could contaminate the water supply. Effluent from undrained privies and animal pens flowed across streets and also into houses through generally porous walls. Privies with open soil pits lay directly alongside dwellings and under bedrooms. Many streets had their 'own' midden at the end. Pump water was affected by sewage and river water in towns was often contaminated. Refuse collection and disposal was a growing problem. In Leeds, public sewers passed effluent downstream to water-collection points. Glasgow had no public sewers until 1790 and the scavengers paid by Lancaster Corporation only cleaned the major streets. This unhealthiness was a cause and facilitator of disease, especially typhus.

Poor nutrition lowered resistance to disease and to the psychological impact of adversity. Fruit and vegetables were both seasonal and expensive. They played only a minor role in the diet of the urban poor, whose diet was therefore low in vitamins; and who were also generally ill clad. The poor ate less meat and, outside southern England, less wheat and more oats. Rising population put pressure on the supply of animal produce (meat, fish, milk), ensuring that a greater percentage of the population ate grain, rather than foods rich in proteins. The spread of the potato also helped feed the growing numbers.

Bad harvests increased vulnerability to disease, leading to higher death rates, as in Worcestershire in 1708–12 and the five year child mortality cycle in Penrith,[11] although there were no actual famines, unlike in Scotland and Ireland where there were severe crises, especially in Scotland in 1696–9 and Ireland in 1740–1. Scotland and England were also badly hit by dearth in 1740–1. In that crisis, poor harvests and very cold weather that killed livestock led to rises in the price of food, that helped to produce food riots in Edinburgh, Newcastle and elsewhere. Problems with food availability and weather accentuated the impact of disease in 1740–1. There was no effective system of provision during such crises. In 1740, John Couraud, an Under Secretary, claimed, 'the poor must have suffered greatly during this rigorous season had it not been for the charitable benefactions of the nobility and gentry etc. which has exceeded anything of the kind that I ever heard of.'[12]

In practice, such assistance was inadequate, as the paupers who sought help in towns during years of hardship showed. However, the agricultural growth discussed in the next chapter ensured that more food was available, and also acted as a restraint on its cost. In addition, the infrastructure of trade and communications, helped move food within the British Isles, although, again, many could not afford adequate food. Furthermore, the situation was placed under greater stress as the population rose. Periodic crises had not been abolished, and there was a serious one in northern Scotland in 1782.

Housing also varied greatly by social type. Evelyn reported in 1702, 'Truro a very pretty neat town built of stone and covered with slate as most of the houses in this country [Cornwall] are excepting those which belong to the poor sort which generally consist of mud walls covered with thatch.'[13] Such dwellings were often damp, cold and dark.

Accidents were a serious problem as well as dearth, and it was frequently difficult to deal with their consequences. Accidents were common at birth, and there were many crippled men and women who had been mangled in childbirth. One of the most important differences between modern life and the eighteenth century was the striking number of crippled people in the past: problems in childbirth, bone disease and fractures meant that many people limped.

For those who survived to adulthood, life could be very difficult and precarious. This became more of a problem when the population rose from the 1740s. The rise led to increased pressure as more sought land, employment, food and poor relief, disrupting local economies and hitting living standards.

Agricultural labour was arduous, generally daylight to dusk in winter, and 6 am to 6 pm in summer. The need to be out in all weathers, and the lack of shelter, encouraged high levels of rheumatism. Industrial employment was also hard – up to sixteen hours daily in the Yorkshire alum houses – and often dangerous. Notions of health and safety at work were barely understood. Millers worked in dusty and noisy circumstances, frequently suffered from lice, and often developed asthma, hernias and chronic back problems. Disorders could result from the strain of unusual physical demands or postures, such as those required of tailors and weavers. Many places of work were damp, badly ventilated and/or poorly lit. Work frequently involved exposure to dangerous substances, such as arsenic, lead and mercury, or was dangerous in itself, particularly construction, fishing and mining. Miners suffered death and injury from floods, falls, and underground explosions while working by candlelight. Although the hazards of many industrial processes were not appreciated by contemporaries, lead smelting was known to be poisonous.

Domestic service was far less dangerous, but was still arduous. At least 12,000 female domestic servants were probably employed in the four largest Scottish towns in the late seventeenth century, possibly 10 per cent of the 16–25-year-old women in Scotland. In 1785, George Home wrote from Edinburgh about a tax on servants: 'The operation of it in this country at least will be equal to a tax upon the female children of the poorer labourers.'[14] In England also many girls from poor backgrounds went into service.

When visiting the stately homes of the period, it is as well to remember the unpleasant tasks such as the disposal of excreta. Water-carrying, generally a female task, could cause physical distortion. Cleaning and drying clothes involved much effort. As surviving laundries suggest, the dirt had to be pummelled out of clothes with the use of lye, and early mangles required much muscle-power.

The world of work of the late seventeenth century was to be transformed as a result of the technological transformations, industrialisation and urbanisation that were to be associated with the Industrial Revolution, but this change took over a century, and much that was common in 1688 was still customary in 1860, despite railways, telegraphs and the expression of confidence in the future proclaimed with the Great Exhibition of 1851. This was especially true of domestic work.

A sense of beneficial change, improvement, even perfectability was present in some circles and became more important in the closing decades of the century. Yet, although this shift was significant in the development of reforming policies and radical aspirations, it would be mistaken to describe the mental world of the period in such terms. Instead, this mental world is best discussed and explained in terms of the impact of what we have been considering in this chapter. At the level of the individual and of the community, the emphasis was on precariousness, and of human vulnerability in the face of a hostile and unpredictable environment, and of forces that could not be understood, prevented or propitiated. This vulnerability has to be seen alongside the emphasis on improvement, and thus of improvability, that we will be discussing.

In general, the climate may have become more favourable, with warmer and drier summers improving crop yields and limiting damage to the harvest. What has more recently been termed the 'little ice age' of the seventeenth century came to an end, after a particularly malign bout of bad weather in the 1690s. In the first quarter of the eighteenth century, average August temperatures were a full degree centigrade higher than in the previous quarter-century. Aside from helping with crop yields and permitting a movement of growing zones into more upland areas, this may also have helped health, not least by being responsible for a marked decline in deaths due to 'griping in the guts': bacillary dysentery.

Although the general trend may well have been beneficial, there were still serious problems with individual harvests, not least in the late 1690s, late 1720s and early 1740s. Furthermore, the climate could show its potency and unpredictability, and the limited capacity of communal action, in a number of ways. Flooding was one such. Most rivers were not canalised and their flow was unregulated by any system of dams or reservoirs. In addition, coastal defences were often inadequate or non-existent. There were serious floods on the Somerset coast in 1696 and again in 1703, with the sea water reaching as far inland as Glastonbury. The 1703 flood led to William Diaper's poem 'Brent' which included the lines

> And soon the waves assert their antient claim,
> They scorn the shores, and o're the marshes sound,
> And mudwall cotts are levell'd with the ground.

The Steart peninsula began to be eroded in about 1783.

Inland, flooding could interfere with transport, both along and across rivers, hit fishing, disrupt industries dependent on water power, such as milling, and submerge the most fertile agricultural areas. Winter ice was another problem. Blocking rivers and canals, it hit transport and milling, causing unemployment and flour shortages. Wind was an alternative power source, but windmills were affected by storms. Storms also hit coastal areas, blowing sand over cultivated lands. As a result, an Act of the Edinburgh Parliament of 1695 forbade pulling up plants by the roots, as that left areas vulnerable to the advance of sand.

Agriculture was naturally vulnerable to weather and disease. There were few improved crop strains, and rainy winters produced diseased and swollen crops, while late frosts attacked wheat. There were few defences against animal diseases. The primitive nature of veterinary science ensured that preventive medicine was not possible. Instead, as with the cattle plague in 1749–50, animals had to be slaughtered or their movements prohibited. Wild animals, especially hares, partridges, pheasants and moorfowl, fed on crops; while rats and mice attacked grain stores. Urban life was also vulnerable, with spectacular fires that brought great devastation, as at Warwick in 1694 and Blandford Forum in 1731. Lightning was a particular problem and its dramatic destructive powers made a powerful impact, as when the spire of St Andrew's, Worcester was destroyed in 1733.

A sense of insecurity contributed to a widespread belief in an animistic world. Spirits were felt to play a prominent role, with death no bar to their intervention. Fairies – the 'little people' or, in Ireland, 'the gentle folk' – were seen as having a capacity for good or ill. It was necessary to avoid offending them.

Such concerns were an aspect of belief in a world that was more mysterious than subsequent generations were to credit. The world outside people's dwellings, especially after dark, seemed more hostile than is comprehensible today, when electricity offers illumination and clarification, and is sufficiently persistent to lead to criticism of light pollution. Night-time then offered different sensations, experiences and dangers. The role of moonlight was much more important than today. In the absence of the moon, the night was pitch dark, especially in rural areas. Within houses, it was shadowy when candles were lit and dark when they were snuffed. People stared into the flame of candles and fires, and this made their eyesight less accustomed (momentarily) to the dark and therefore made it more fearsome.

Popular religious beliefs were often removed from the teachings of the churches, but they did not amount to an alternative religion. Practices that derived their origins from pagan beliefs were not the same as paganism. Instead, such beliefs and practices coexisted or were intertwined with Christian counterparts, with only limited awareness of any incompatibility. This was particularly the case for ordinary lay people in the countryside.

The devil continued to play a major role in Christian consciousness, and also in 'folk' religion. This led to persistent concern about diabolical agents, particularly witches. Although now illegal, popular attacks on witches continued. There was an execution of an alleged witch at Dornoch in northern Scotland in 1727 following an illegal local trial. There were also attacks on alleged witches in England. Traditional astrological beliefs and practices also continued.

At the popular level, hostile external forces were blamed for intractable illness, and superstitions retained their role, for example the belief in lucky and unlucky days. Articles of clothing from unwell persons were left at 'clooty' burns and wells in Scotland, to produce a cure.

As old superstitions persisted, it has been suggested that the cultural gap between popular and elite beliefs had grown wider than in the previous century, and that hitherto general views and activities, such as belief in astrology, had been driven down the social scale. Indeed, most of the wealthy and well-educated lost their faith in magical healing, prophecy and witchcraft. The last legal execution of a witch in Scotland was in 1706. The Witchcraft Act of 1736 banned accusations of witchcraft and sorcery.

However, this thesis has to be advanced with care. Fashion played an important role in elite culture, and increasingly so as the growth in the quantity of printed works, and the increased frequency of their appearance, spread knowledge of what was seen as appropriate. It is difficult to assess the significance of the changes in fashion. The popularity, for example, of suspect medical cures, or of pseudo-paganism associated with Hell-Fire clubs, such as those started by the Earl of Wharton in 1719 and by Sir Francis Dashwood in the 1750s, and the vogue in the 1780s for the theory of animal magnetism all suggest that it is dangerous to regard the culture of the elite as clearly better-informed. Rather, their 'superstitions' were faddish.

It is more helpful to note that at all levels of society there was a wish to understand the hostile environment and to cope with the fears that it inspired. There was a search for stability in an essentially unstable world, that involved an attempt to reconcile divine justice with human suffering, and to order experience in a way that reflected the hard and apparently arbitrary nature of life. Religious world-views provided the most effective explanatory model, the best psychological defences, and the essential note of continuity. Faced with calamities, individuals and communities maintained their belief in religion. It is difficult to assess private conviction, and the propagation of heterodox beliefs encountered barriers, but it is still striking how little evidence there is of any widespread questioning of the notion of divine justice.

The hostile environment was understood in terms of retribution, with the possibility of winning remission by good actions. This marked out England from the Calvinism that dominated much of Continental (and Scottish) Protestantism with its emphasis on predestination. However, understanding of good works varied and could include both religious services and satisfying the demands of the occult and spirit world.

It is possible to point to an increasing questioning of the notion of direct divine intervention in the fate of individuals and communities. For example, there was growing scepticism that earthquakes reflected divine displeasure. Yet, this was not a secular society, and the contemporary notion of progress was not inherently sceptical. Instead, it rested in part on a diluted millenarianism, as well as on the traditional conviction that God provided means to cure all ills if only they could be discovered. This was a benign view that presented knowledge and science as part of the divine plan, and not as solvents of religious faith (see also Chapter 9).

There was also much criticism of new ideas, criticism that is all too easily neglected. For example, inoculation was condemned by those who championed the doctrine of providential affliction: the notion that God was responsible and that His reasons should not be questioned or defined. Probably for most people, every disease and accident had a cause arising from the travails of the soul and the temptations of sin. Moral behaviour would be rewarded with health, and thus restraint in personal conduct was prudent as well as virtuous.

This combination had moral and practical as well as religious consequences, or, looked at more accurately, reminds us of the artificial nature of such categorisation and of the extent to which what might be seen as separate analyses and strategies were, instead, seen as parts of a whole. Thus the religious views outlined above also influenced medical theory. In his lectures, in the 1750s and 1760s, William Cullen, the leading Scottish medical academic, related health and virtue in arguing that health was to be preserved by preventing disease through a rational lifestyle.

The search for divine support did not necessarily lead to worldly passivity. If the environment was understood as hostile, there was also much activity aimed at surmounting the challenge or coping with the consequences. Developments in life insurance and improvements in institutional medical care provide important examples. Life insurance took a long while to develop because the basis for assessing risk was absent. In the absence of comprehensive mortality statistics, actuarial knowledge and a sound grasp of probability theory, it was difficult to assess risk and there was a powerful element of gambling, rather than risk avoidance. More than sixty companies were formed in the period 1690–1720, an age of speculation or, as it was termed, 'projects', and life insurance was then very risky. However, knowledge, regulation and institutionalisation all developed. Richard Price, a radical Dissenter and an able mathematician who advised the Equitable, which was founded in 1762, provided reasonable guides which were of greater value because they were published, especially his *Observations on Reversionary Payments* (1771). The Gambling Act of 1774 sought to regulate life insurance, while the industry became more coherent as offices such as the Amicable, the London Assurance and the Royal Exchange developed. The growth of the life insurance industry had little affect on the bulk of the population, but it reflected an attitude to risk and to the threat of calamity that was removed from fatalism. There was a strong demand for insurance, particularly among the clergy.[15]

Medical care was another activist response. Infirmaries were built in many large towns from the early eighteenth century, and the practice spread. In 1720–80, four voluntary hospitals opened in London, twenty-three elsewhere in England, and three in Scotland. Each had the potential for marking and making a major shift in local attitudes and expectations. Provision was inadequate, but each new hospital was a change on the past.

In addition, the process was cumulative. Hereford gained a new hospital in 1709–10 and an infirmary in 1776. Jonathan Labray's hospital for decayed framework knitters, opened in Nottingham in 1726, was followed by 1782 by a public infirmary or general hospital provided by public subscription. The Royal Infirmary in Edinburgh opened in 1729, an infirmary in Bristol was erected by public subscription in 1737, the Bath Infirmary received its first patients in 1742, the Devon and Exeter Hospital opened in 1743, the first medical hospital in Worcestershire, the Royal Infirmary, was established in 1745, Addenbrooke's General Hospital was built in Cambridge in 1763–6, and in Birmingham the workhouse gained an infirmary wing in 1766, while a general hospital, with forty beds, opened in 1779. The Birmingham musical festival was founded in 1768 in order to raise funds for the hospital. Jacques Tenon, a leading French surgeon, who visited southern England in 1787 and discussed hospitals as far north as Birmingham and Worcester and as far west as Plymouth, making very detailed notes, especially on accommodation, menus, and administrative arrangements, was very impressed by what he saw.[16]

Dispensaries, institutions that provided out-patient care, were founded in numbers from 1770. They were used to inoculate the poor against smallpox. By 1793, there were nineteen alone in provincial England and annual admissions were probably in the tens of thousands.

Alongside the benign impression created by a discussion of such developments, it is also appropriate to point to the scale of the problem. The purposes of medical and other charitable foundations revealed the poor state of social welfare, the failure of family networks to care for all the destitute, the grim nature of much of life, and its harsh unpredictability at the individual level. In London, charitable donors sought to provide adequate care for lying-in women and their babies, to rescue the all-too-frequently orphaned and abandoned children, and to rehabilitate those driven into prostitution by poverty.

The pattern of care was a response to serious inadequacies, but was itself deficient in many particulars. The mentally ill and those with disabilities suffered especially, in part because they were seen as in some way lacking God's grace and because there was a lack of hope as to the possibility of helping them. George III's treatment in 1788–9 during his supposed madness was, by modern standards, harsh. The first institutions seeking to provide employment for the blind were not founded until 1791 (Liverpool) and 1793 (Edinburgh). In addition, the notion of a distinction between 'deserving' and 'undeserving' poor served as the basis for a harsh treatment of the latter. This reflected the ability of those with authority to categorise others.

The paternalism that conditioned care and charity was hierarchical, not democratic, in character. It owed much to religious notions, although there were also more secular readings of social obligation which stressed the responsibilities of those with wealth. A conflation of moralism and sensibility encouraged a culture of volunteerism expressed through charitable activity, not least the creation and support of hospitals. However, the reverse of this was an attitude towards poverty that led to the treatment of many of those in need of charity as miscreants.[17]

This was still a society that showed great cruelty to animals. Those that were used for work could be treated harshly, while cruelty was often seen as fun. This was captured in Hogarth's engravings *The Four Stages of Cruelty* (1751). In the first, animals are being tortured, by, for example, pushing an arrow into a dog's anus. In the second, a tired coach-horse is being beaten, while a tired lamb that has been driven too harshly to market is clubbed to death (and, as a reminder of man's inhumanity to man, a child playing in the street is being run over by a cart driven by a drayman who has fallen asleep). In his *Autobiographical Notes*, Hogarth wrote that the 'cruel treatment of poor animals makes the streets of London more disagreeable to the human mind than any thing what ever'.[18]

All this derived from a sense of cheapened life, both literally and figuratively. Cock-throwing, cock-fighting, and bear-, bull- and badger-baiting were all cruel sports. In his *Persian Letters*, George Lyttelton referred to people taking pleasure in seeing 'the animals worry and gore one another ... I had great compassion for the poor beasts which were forcibly incensed against each other.'[19]

There was, however, some action to restrain what was judged inappropriate with local bans on cock-throwing in a number of towns, and a county-wide ban in Essex from 1758. Each sport also had a particular social imprint, and each was affected by growing entrepreneurial activity. Other sports did not suffer the degree of prohibition directed at cock-throwing, although in 1772 Birmingham banned bull-baiting.

CONCLUSIONS

As so often in this book, and, more generally, with historical judgements, the question of whether to place the emphasis on change or on continuity invites different answers. In some areas, progress was definitely made and the idea of progress was expanded. For most people in England by 1780 the circumstances of life were more favourable than in Poland or Portugal, although the situation looked less benign from the perspective of Ireland. Attempts to ameliorate conditions in Britain reflected a search for improvement, and for a wide distribution of its benefits. These attempts ranged from friendly societies with their collective emphasis on self-help, and increasingly generous poor relief to advances in medical science. Scientific developments opened up the prospect of a changed relationship between man and the environment, and also brought improvement in many particulars. Several attracted particular attention. Lightning was tamed by lightning conductors, while smallpox was resisted.

Yet the constraints and catastrophes that affected individuals and communities continued to be grievous. In his first *Essay on the Principle of Population* (1798), Thomas Malthus, a cleric then living in Surrey, pointed to the effects of malnourishment on growth, and had to advocate celibacy and delayed marriage as the means to cope with over-population.

Mental health provided evidence of other stresses. Suicide was known as the 'English disease', and was regarded as more common than elsewhere in Europe, although the statistical basis for any modern comparison is lacking and religious teachings probably helped limit its impact. Suicide was seen as the culmination of the melancholia that was regarded as characteristic of the nation.

The environment helped to sustain a sense of fatalism, albeit one restrained by religion. It is difficult for a modern, predominantly urban, readership to understand a world in which the calamities of environmental mischance were matched by the incessant pressures of trying to scratch a living in adverse circumstances. Electricity, the internal combustion engine, and selective crop- and animal-breeding, had not yet conquered the countryside and transformed both agriculture and agrarian life. Power was limited to human and animal muscles. Furniture, utensils and foodstuffs were basic and rough, and crop and animal breeds improved only by the watchful care of generations. And, everywhere, the awful extremes of climate and disease could always lessen or annihilate the prospects of crops, livestock, and the humans who depended on them.

The limited progress that was made in improving the circumstances of life is understandable in light of the restricted technology of the age and the scanty resources of government, both national and local. It was the same across Europe. This limited progress also reflected contemporary attitudes. Alongside the confidence of some in the possibility of human progress through communal action, much of the population lived in a precarious fashion, fearful of the future and possessing only limited aspirations. This popular conservatism was to play a major part in affecting plans for change.

NOTES

1. A. Gooder, 'The population crisis of 1727–1730 in Warwickshire', *Midland History*, 1 (1972), pp. 1–22.
2. E.A. Wrigley and R.S. Schofield, *The Population History of England, 1541–1871: A Reconstruction* (1981), pp. 208–9.

3. R.E. Tyson, 'Demographic change', in T.M. Devine and J.R. Young (eds), *Eighteenth-Century Scotland: New Perspectives* (East Linton, East Lothian, 1999), p. 195.
4. R. Churchley, 'Population growth and industrialization in a rural Warwickshire community – Sambourne, 1675–1800', *Warwickshire History*, 11 (1999), pp. 23–4.
5. B. Bailyn, *Voyagers to the West: Emigration from Britain to America on the Eve of the Revolution* (1987); I. Whyte, *Migration and Society in Britain 1550–1830* (2000), pp. 103–35.
6. S. Scott and C.J. Duncan, 'Smallpox epidemics at Penrith in the 17th and 18th centuries', *Transactions of the Cumberland and Westmorland Antiquarian and Archaeological Societies*, 93 (1993), p. 159.
7. BL. Evelyn papers vol. 49 fol. 33.
8. G. Miller, *The Adoption of Inoculation for Smallpox in England and France* (Philadelphia, 1957); P. Razzell, *The Conquest of Smallpox* (Sussex, 1977); J.R. Smith, *The Speckled Monster, Smallpox in England 1670–1970* (Hunstanton, 1987).
9. AE. CP. Angleterre 265 fols 18, 24; *Annual Register*, 19 (1776), pp. 119–22.
10. R. Legg, *A Pioneer in Xanadu: Denys Rolle, 1725–1797* (Whitchurch, 1997).
11. Scott and Duncan, 'Penrith', pp. 158–9.
12. Couraud to James, 1st Earl Waldegrave, 28 Jan. 1740, Chewton House, Chewton Mendip, papers of 1st Earl Waldegrave.
13. BL. Evelyn papers, vol. 49 fol. 29.
14. George to Patrick Home, 14 May 1785, Edinburgh, National Archives of Scotland, GD 267/1/10/63.
15. G. Clark, *Betting on Lives: the Culture of Life Insurance in England, 1695–1775* (Manchester, 1999).
16. J. Tenon, *Journal d'Observations sur les Principaux Hôpitaux et sur quelques Prisons d'Angleterre, 1787*, edited by J. Carré (Clermont-Ferrand, 1992).
17. A. Borsay, *Medicine and Charity in Georgian Bath: A Social History of the General Infirmary c. 1739–1830* (Aldershot, 1999), p. 242.
18. J. Burke (ed.), *William Hogarth, The Analysis of Beauty, with the rejected passages from the manuscript drafts and autobiographical notes* (Oxford, 1955), pp. 226–7.
19. Lyttelton, *Letters from a Persian in England to his friend at Ispahan* (4th edn, 1735), p. 7.

3

Agriculture

Whether or not the eighteenth century saw an industrial revolution, or even the Industrial Revolution, tends to dominate discussion of the economy then, both in the years of supposed Revolution and in the preceding decades in which roots and causes are scrutinised. Here, however, we will start with agriculture, because the period of this book is generally seen in terms of an Agricultural Revolution, and because the impact of agricultural development was clearly important in preparing the grounds for industrialisation. Furthermore, the majority of the population lived in and on the countryside. Agriculture was the principal source of employment and wealth, the most significant sector of the economy, the basis of the taxation, governmental, ecclesiastical (tithes) and proprietorial (rents), that funded most others. Land, and its products, provided the structure of the social system and the bulk of the wealth that kept it in being.

Before proceeding it is, however, crucial to stress the diversity of agricultural circumstances in this period. At one level, this was a matter of the commonplace that the land was used in different ways. The most pronounced contrast was between regions that concentrated on arable (crops) and on pastoral (livestock). In crude terms, this was a difference between 'highland' and 'lowland' Britain. The former was not only higher, but also, on average, wetter, colder and with less good soils. The slopes of mountainous and hilly regions were difficult to cultivate. The prevailing westerly winds also ensured that rainfall was related to relief; coming off the sea, they were also salt-laden, as well as strong, which affected growth near the coasts. Steep slopes led to a high run-off of water, ensuring that valley bottoms were often affected by rivers and streams in spate. Much of the rainfall in upland areas fell as drizzle and there were prolonged cloud conditions. Cloud, mist and drizzle restricted sunlight and thus lessened the growing season, while the length of the frost-free season was also related to relief.

Over the centuries, heavy rainfall had helped wash soil from the uplands. This ensured that they had poor, frequently acidic, soils which lessened their suitability for continuous or intensive cultivation, especially in the absence of fertilisers. Poor soils, however, could also be found in lowland areas, many of which had been affected by erosion, especially that of glaciation, or had their nutrients leached out by heavy rainfall. The removal of natural cover and over-cultivation had also led to the deterioration of many lowland areas.

The combination of poor soils, steep slopes, a limited growing season and high relief encouraged dependence on animal rearing. In steep areas this meant sheep, in flatter (and lower) regions cattle. Neither, especially sheep-rearing, offered a form of agriculture that could support the population levels of arable regions, or encouraged their nucleated (village) settlement. Instead, dispersed settlement was the norm, frequently in the form of isolated farmsteads. Thus, different usage of the land led to contrasting settlement patterns, which had consequences in terms of social dynamics and socio-cultural patterns.

The detailed pattern of land-use variation was far more complex than might be suggested by upland pasture and lowland arable. Indeed, there was no such monoculture in either upland or lowland. In upland areas, grain was grown in small quantities as a subsistence crop, while livestock was kept in lowland areas to provide meat, milk, manure, wool and motive power. At the level of the individual farmstead and again of the village, there was a degree of self-reliance that is totally alien to modern farming. This reflected the relative difficulty of preservation and transport in an age before refrigeration and motor vehicles, but also the density and intensity of local systems of exchanges as well as the degree to which self and local reliance made more economic sense than in the modern age of specialization through comparative profit margins. Self-sufficiency was encouraged by the extent to which minor roads did not benefit from the turnpiking of major routes described in Chapter five. Alongside the widely dispersed nature of livestock and grain production, there was also more extensive cultivation of fruit and vegetables than today. Thus, apples were widely grown, both for eating and for cider. Again, the pattern was similar on the Continent.

Aside from the divide of terrain already referred to, there was a major contrast between areas with heavier soils, such as the Midlands and much of western England, and those with lighter soils, such as much of East Anglia. The latter were easier to work, and proved appropriate for root crops, such as turnips. Agricultural patterns were closely related to soil types; although drainage factors also played a major role. Thus, flood plains were used for meadowland, downland for sheep, and poor sands or difficult clays also served as pastureland.

The links between agriculture, industry and trade were close. The limited advances in the state of technological and scientific knowledge ensured that manufacturing was based on natural products. The synthesised goods which characterise the present age had not yet arrived. Much manufacturing involved the processing of agricultural goods, particularly if forestry is included. It was a continuum that included the recipes of the household economy for food preservation: curing, bottling and making vinegars. The staple industrial activities were concerned with the production of consumer goods: food, drink, clothes, shoes and furniture. The production of all of these was widely dispersed. For example, there were tanyards, producing leather, throughout the livestock-rearing areas.

Though some processing involved agricultural products from outside Europe, principally cotton, sugar-cane and tobacco, the source of most goods was British.

Thus, much industrial activity, whether urban or rural, was closely involved with the agricultural hinterland. As the bulk of the population lived in rural areas and engaged in agricultural activities, it is not surprising that these activities played a significant role in determining the level of purchasing power. Rural consumption created a market both for industrial goods and for agricultural products, such as meat; conversely, poverty limited both. Any rise in the cost of agricultural products, particularly grain, affected the urban population, reducing the purchasing power for goods there.

The general fall in grain prices between 1670 and 1750 freed income for the purchase of manufactured goods. On the other hand, illustrating the nature of an economic system where the benefit of one was frequently the loss of another, this fall put pressure on the rural economy. It led to heavy rent arrears and requests for rent abatement, the consequences of which are not generally grasped when modern visitors look at the stately homes of the period. For example, on the widespread estates of the Duke of Kingston rent arrears rose in the 1730s and 1740s.[1] A report on London prices carried in the *York Courant* on 20 February 1739, itself a sign of the growing national integration of the economy, reported:

> Last Monday [12th] ... the best shipping wheat for £6 [a load] which is so low, that it is impossible farmers can live and pay their rents at such prices; and as wool likewise bears so low a price, unless some care be speedily taken, and the people eased of the present heavy taxes, most of the lands of the kingdom will be flung up into the landlords hands.

More generally, wheat, barley and oats prices all reached their lowest level in the period in 1743–7, falling by more than 15 per cent relative to the prices of the 1720s. Price falls hit the agricultural sector, but they eased the burden on consumers. In 1741, one of the Under Secretaries wrote to a colleague, 'by all the letters I receive from the country, there is a good prospect of a plentiful harvest, and indeed provisions of all kinds begin to abate in their prices considerably; which is a good thing now we have so many mouths to feed.'[2]

There were great regional variations in the nature and impact of the agricultural depression of the second quarter of the century. The open-field farmers on the heavy Midlands soils of Warwickshire, Leicestershire and Northamptonshire fared particularly badly. The rising relative profitability of animal-rearing encouraged the farmers of this region to switch to it. This process involved enclosure, which transformed land management and led to a rise in the production of meat and dairy products.

Population growth from the 1740s led to greater demand on the rural economy. This increased the prosperity of farmers, especially as agricultural wages did not rise greatly. Greater demand affected both Britain and Ireland. From the 1760s, English demand for Irish grain, beef and dairy products helped in the commercialisation of Irish agriculture. However, pressure on rents encouraged agrarian discontent in Ireland. Britain was self-sufficient in food until the 1760s, from when grain prices rose sharply and imports from elsewhere in Europe, especially the Baltic, began.

In the second half of the nineteenth century, the demands of the rising population for food were met from North America, Argentina and Australasia, but this was not possible in the eighteenth century. Dried cod could be imported from Newfoundland and rice from South Carolina, but neither was central to the British diet and it was more profitable to import other goods from the New World. South Carolina rice was generally exported to southern Europe. Large-scale imports of grain and meat did not develop until refrigeration, steam-powered iron ships, and tin canning created new possibilities in the late nineteenth century. Prior to that, all parts of Britain had to devote considerable attention to agriculture. This reflected the nature of agriculture, which was characterised by uncertain production and, by modern standards, low productivity. The limited nature of specialisation (by modern standards) was also a product of the high cost and low speed of transport.

There were many signs during the period, especially from the mid-eighteenth century, of an improvement in agricultural output and productivity. This reflected the dissemination of new ideas and techniques, and a greater role for the production of crops and livestock for the cash economy, and for specialisation (not that any of them was new). However, farming was diverse, and there were also signs of continuing traditional practices, not that these were necessarily inappropriate.

Before pressing on to consider farming, it is important also to mention fishing and forestry, both of which are too easily overlooked. The first was an important source of food and employment. Given the concentration of fishing on the coasts, its local importance was even greater. Fishing was central to the economy of many small ports, but also important in bigger centres such as Hull. Aside from serving domestic consumers, producers, such as the Cornish pilchard industry, were important to British exports. Large quantities of fish, particularly salted or smoked herring, were exported to the Mediterranean and the West Indies. Fishing also benefited from the infrastructural developments that aided so much economic growth. The system of markets became more sophisticated, and the creation of turnpike roads helped in the development of long-distance trade. However, fishing did not grow at the same rate as agriculture, not least because the nature of transport – both costly and slow – affected fish more seriously: pannier ponies and fish vans were no equivalent to the droving of animals. The high cost of moving fresh fish ensured that the poor in inland regions could not afford it. Fish could be cured to preserve it but that increased the cost. The situation was not to change until the speed of rail traffic made fish a cheap and accessible foodstuff.[3]

Due to the earlier depletion of the most accessible woodlands and to the rising use of coal, forestry was less significant than in the past. Nevertheless, it was still important not just on the national scale but also in the myriad of interacting local economies that were both part of, and yet also in part separate to, the national economy. Furthermore, this was not just a case of depletion: tree planting could be locally significant and there was extensive replanting in the late seventeenth century.[4] There was also a new literature, as so often in a period that looked to publications for encouragement and advice. John Evelyn's *Sylva, or a Discourse of Forest-Trees and the Propagation of Timber in His Majesties Dominions* (1664) passed through several editions and was used by Batty Langley in his *A Sure Method of Improving Estates, by Plantations of Oak, Elm, Ash, Beech and Other Timber Trees, Coppice Woods* ... (1728). Wood provided fuel for industry and timber for construction. Indeed, wood was also important for agriculture. Aside from its use for the construction of barns and sheds, wood was also important for the construction of gates and fences, not least for newly-enclosed fields. In turn, elm and ash were grown in hedgerows. Wood was also used for the manufacture of many household items, including handles, chairs, bedheads and baskets. The value of wood helped ensure that landowners used the courts to try to prevent its theft. The Leicestershire parson and planter William Hanbury (1725–78) insisted that planting trees was a gentleman's patriotic duty and in his *Essay on Planting, and a Scheme for making it conducive to the Glory of God and the advantage of Society* (1758) castigated politicians for 'treacherously selling [trees] to our enemies' while 'eagerly buying up timber from Norway'.

The use of wood was part of the intensive pattern of utilisation that reflected the determination to achieve maximum benefit from resources. This can be seen in *The Duty of a Steward* (1727), in which Edward Lawrence claimed:

> As a steward should know the quantity and quality of every parcel of land occupied by the several tenants, so likewise he should have a map of the whole drawn out in the most perfect method; which may show ... the true figure of every parcel ... nearby that he may detect any tenant from alienating the least parcel of any land from his lord.

Most of what could be readily farmed was so already. This was a serious problem because it was difficult to maintain soil quality in the face of degradation through the leaching of mineral nutrients by rainfall from land once forest cover had been removed and through the impact of standard agricultural techniques. This helps to explain the appeal of the uncultivated soils of North America.

In Britain also, increases in production owed something to an extension of the cultivated area. This was true both of areas of 'reclamation', such as the Lincolnshire Fens, the peat bogs and mosses of Scotland and north-west England, and in the mountain valleys and along the lough shores of Ulster. Upland 'waste' lands were brought into more intensive use. Thus, in Durham, settlements such as Hamsterley, Witton-le-Wear, Eggleston and Wolsingham expanded as a consequence of squatting on the waste lands of Railey Fell. In upland Perthshire, poorer, marginal lands which had traditionally served as summer pastures were brought into cultivation.[5]

In common with much of the change in the period, the bulk of the reclamation of 'waste' lands occurred late in the century. For example, between 1660 and 1760, the only new works in the Lincolnshire Fens were the draining of the 10,000 acres of Holland Fen by Earl Fitzwilliam in 1720 and smaller reclamations in the Nene estuary in 1720 and 1747. After 1760, there was more activity including the Witham Act of 1762 and the Black Sluice Act of 1765, the construction of the Grand Sluice at Boston in 1766, the extension of Vernatt's Drain in 1774, and the draining and enclosure of about 25,000 acres of the Witham Fens between 1777 and 1797.[6] In north-west Suffolk, after a Drainage Act of 1759, a large area of fen was reclaimed. This process was not always welcome to local people whose traditional way of life was endangered. Richard Locke, lord of the manor of Highbridge, a farmer who pressed for drainage improvements, was stoned and beaten when he carried out a survey of moorland near Wedmore in Somerset. His attackers feared that if the land was improved, their rents would rise.[7]

In addition, in every agricultural area, opportunities were found to extend the cultivated area, a process encouraged by the payment of bounties on grain exports until 1766. The improvement in average temperatures after the 1690s helped by extending the growing season and thus the possibilities of growing crops at given altitudes.

There were also important qualitative advances. These deserve greater attention because they made more of an impact. They affected much of the already cultivated land, which was the area of prime agricultural importance. These advances reflected changes in inputs, land use and agricultural organization. In the first category, the increased use of lime as a fertiliser helped to raise agricultural productivity. This was important because the range of fertilisers was far less than today, but soil fertility was a problem because the same fields were used: there was no equivalent to the shifting cultivation and slash and burn techniques of some areas of low population density in the world. Lime helped to counteract the acidity of many soils and allowed other manures such as dung to work. Calcareous sea-sand derived from limestone or shells was used as a substitute, as was marl, a chalky sub-soil substance. By 1750, the use of lime was virtually universal among the better Devon farmers.[8] Limekilns were fired by coal and helped ensure widespread demand for it.

New stock was also an important input. Individual landowners and farmers were very important in this respect. The Leicestershire grazier Robert Bakewell (1725–95) produced the Dishley cattle, the Leicestershire breed of sheep, and a breed of black horses for farm work. Bakewell reflected the inventiveness, entrepreneurship, sociability and politeness of the century. He used double floors in his stalls in order to collect dung, which he turned into liquid manure. He collected skeletons and carcasses in order to further his studies of animal breeds, established the trade of ram-hiring on a large scale, founded the Dishley Society to maintain the purity of the breed, and insisted on treating his animals well.

Aside from new stock, there was also a shift towards a greater use of horses rather than oxen for ploughing, a process that had been going on for centuries. Horses were more efficient and adaptable, and faster. This process is a reminder of the need to appreciate the different speeds of agricultural change.

There were also inputs in the shape of improved machinery, although this was less important than over the following two centuries. Jethro Tull, a Berkshire landowner, invented a seed drill and horse-hoe in about 1701 and 1714 respectively. Furthermore, he published *Horse-Hoeing Husbandry* in 1733, an example of how the culture of print could provide information on new techniques.

In land-use, there was a spread of fodder crops, both 'artificial grasses' and root crops, for example sainfoin, clover, coleseed and turnips. These helped to eliminate fallow and to increase the capacity of the rural economy to rear more animals. Clover is a member of the legumes, a family of nitrogen-fixing plants that enhances soil fertility. More fodder allowed heavier stocking. These animals were the sources of crucial manure for arable farming. They also provided capital: animals were the most significant 'cash crop' in the economy. They provided both the 'roast beef of old England' and woollen cloth.

Charles, 2nd Viscount Townshend, a leading Norfolk landowner and former Secretary of State, popularised the idea of incorporating turnips in his crop rotations in the 1730s. Known as 'Turnip Townshend', he carried out experiments on his estate at Rainham.

The spread of convertible or 'up and down husbandry' was also important. In this, land alternated between pasture and arable after a number of years. This was beneficial in several respects. It resulted in increased yields when the land was cultivated, and improved grass at other times. Such husbandry in a sequence on different fields in one estate could ensure a range of products. Mixed farming reduced the impact of bad harvests or animal diseases. The nature of up and down husbandry and mixed farming varied with regard to particular local circumstances, but the effect was to improve productivity. For example in Thanet in the first half of the eighteenth century, the widespread cultivation of sainfoin, rotations, and the intensive stocking of barley lands with sheep controlled by folds, boosted agricultural productivity.

ENCLOSURES

Changes were aided by the practice of enclosing land. Consolidated, compact and enclosed holdings were not an innovation of the period, and parts of the country, cspccially much of the South-East, North and West had long had many enclosures, in part in order to control livestock. By 1500, much of Devon and Cornwall was enclosed, while, by the end of the seventeenth century, most of the lowland east of County Durham had been enclosed so that it could be more easily farmed and adapted to new agricultural methods to provide food for a local population that had grown greatly with the expansion of coal and lead mining.

However, enclosures became far more common in the eighteenth century, particularly in the Midlands. During the century, about 21 per cent of England was affected by enclosure Acts of Parliament, although there were relatively few prior to mid-century. They were particularly common during the 1760s and 1770s (and again during the French Revolutionary and Napoleonic Wars). In the 1760s and 1770s, the heavy clay soils of the Midlands were enclosed, and, in a linked, but also separate, process, there was widespread conversion from arable to pasture. In the same period, the Vale of White Horse in Berkshire was enclosed, both the pastoral zone and the arable areas.

Over a longer time span, the counties that had the most Acts were, in order, the West Riding of Yorkshire, Lincolnshire and Norfolk. However, the number of

Acts is not always a measure of the importance of the process. For example, in Norfolk the majority of Acts simply 'tidied up a process of abandoning open-field agriculture which had been ongoing for some centuries, or they finally brought small commons and wastes into cultivation'.[9]

The process of obtaining Acts reflected the social politics of the period. Once the major landowners were convinced of the value of such a process they would petition Parliament for an Act. The Acts named Commissioners responsible for effecting the enclosure, and these were the choice of the socially prominent. The Commissioners organised a detailed land survey, determined who owned land or enjoyed common grazing rights, arranged their valuation, and then replanned the enclosed area. This entailed determining what would be the new plots of land, as well as the routes of roads and water-courses. The new plots were allocated to those whose rights of ownership had been accepted. Once the process was complete, the Commissioners had to draw up a detailed written record of their work,[10] an aspect of the determination of official and other bodies to record their activities that was increasingly common in this period.

Enclosure entailed either the reorganisation of fragmented holdings in open fields or the subdivision of former common pastures and wastes. It was often accompanied by revision in tenure, by the replacement of tithes by land or grain rents, and by a series of expensive changes including improved land drainage, farm buildings and roads, and new agricultural methods. Enclosure played a major role in the literature of agricultural improvement.

Enclosure, however, did not necessarily increase efficiency. There are examples of unenclosed areas that witnessed agricultural improvement, the introduction of new crops and techniques, and better crop strains. For example, north-east Cheshire retained its four-field open system until the late seventeenth century at least 'but that was because it was very adaptable to new systems of husbandry, and exchange renting of lands meant that people had consolidated holdings without tenanting them on long-term leases or owning them outright (which also meant that they could adapt their holdings to suit their family's needs)'.[11]

More generally, on the whole, those who farmed the land were more interested in such improvements than those who owned it, and often minor changes at the level of the farmer could be crucial, irrespective of whether the estate was enclosed.

The agricultural politics of enclosure should not be neglected. Enclosure appears to have made it easier to control the land. It was often accompanied by a redistribution of agricultural income from the tenant farmer to his landlord as rents rose more than output. Landlords supported enclosure because they anticipated a major rise from rents, as well as the increased control that stemmed from the end of open-field farming with its communal practices. More generally, enclosing landlords alarmed much of the rural population and created wide disruption of traditional rights and expectations, common lands and routes.

The controlled character of the enclosed landscape was shown in the rectilinear character of the new plots. The role of the surveyors could be seen in new straight-edged fields. These also led to straight roads, often with sharp right angles when they went round plots. Older enclosures were different, and their boundaries were more responsive to the local topography. New plots were also hedged and fenced, an expense that had to be met by their new owners.

Enclosure was helped by the extent to which land ownership in Britain was relatively concentrated by European standards. Peasant ownership of the land was limited and the system of tenure helped to perpetuate landlord control. However, the social context of enclosure varied. In some areas, such as Hampshire and Sussex, enclosure was mostly by private agreement. This caused less tension than in others, such as Northamptonshire, where landlords secured Acts of Parliament to further their interests. In Sussex, indeed, there was some pressure for enclosure from commoners, concerned about over-stocking and over-cutting, and seeking security and better returns in private allotments.

The same was true of Cumbria. There the opportunities arising from increased integration with national livestock markets led to heavy pressures on commons and 'waste' and to the breakdown of collective regulation through the manorial courts. Instead, the customary tenants, who owned much of the land in a county where landownership was much more evenly spread than in the Midlands, decided that absolute ownership of hitherto communal lands best served their interests. As a consequence, opposition to enclosure in Cumbria was limited and tended to focus on attempts to ensure that its detailed implementation served particular interests.[12]

Nevertheless, in general, enclosure produced much hardship for the largely subsistence economies of small farmers and others who had relied on access to common land, and, as a result, helped to encourage migration from the land. Whether landholders or not, English peasants had enjoyed common rights. The right to use common pasture land was particularly valuable to many small occupiers. Prior to enclosure, a large number of families in areas with common fields lived, in part, off the income from working or letting very small amounts of land. At least a third of the population of the open-field (unenclosed) Midlands did so. The more extensive unenclosed common 'waste' of upland regions supported others. Combined with rents generally lower than those in enclosed villages, and with comparatively ready access to land, common rights had offered a degree of insulation against general movements of prices and wages. This contributed to the vitality of a peasantry that relied on shared land use. Common rights also made it possible to gather fuel in the shape of wood.

As a result, enclosure, especially of the common lands, could be very detrimental to small farmers. When in 1759, Revered John Loder, the lord of the manor of Hinton Waldrist in Oxfordshire, informed his tenants that he wanted to enclose the land, they replied that it would create much hardship for those who only had short tenure, that it would be expensive to grow and maintain hedges, and would be divisive: ''tis likely to create uneasiness amongst us as long as we live and one will be ever thinking another's land better than his'. Despite this, an enclosure Act was passed the following year.[13] Customary practices such as wood gathering and gleaning were now defined as crimes, and convictions became more common, for example, in Berkshire in the 1770s and 1780s.

The response to enclosure was generally anger, although rural protest was directed at more than enclosure. In Galloway, the enclosure of pasture land for cattle-grazing led in 1724 to the Levellers Revolt in which the local peasantry knocked down the dry-stone dykes.[14] Troops were used to suppress the revolt. On the Cromartie estates in northern Scotland in 1766, the small tenants attacked the tacksmen's sheep and broke down dykes in order to pasture their own cattle illegally. In Ireland, the Hougher outbreak in Connacht in 1711–12 was a movement of agrarian protest that led to attacks on livestock. The Whiteboys resisted the enclosure of Irish commons and the payment of tithes during 1761–5 in counties Cork, Kilkenny, Limerick and Waterford, by attacking agents, destroying fences, hedges and walls, and maiming cattle. The Whiteboys re-emerged in 1769–76, affecting Tipperary, Kilkenny, Carlow, Kildare, Wexford and Queen's country, while in Antrim, Derry, Down and Tyrone opposition to increased rents led to the Hearts of Steel agitation in 1769–72. In Northamptonshire, an alliance of small occupiers and landless commoners resisted parliamentary enclosure with petitions, threats, attacks on gates, posts and rails, and other crimes.

This was not a rural society simply of deference and order, but one in which aristocratic hegemony was also seen as selfish and disruptive. Benign accounts of the agricultural revolution have to take note of its social politics and consequences.[15] At the same time, by driving labour from the land, the reorganisation of agriculture increased the amount available for industry, although some of those who left the land emigrated. This was true for example of many Scots-Irish who left Ulster for the West Indies and North America. The precondition of economic growth was the ability to maintain agricultural development whilst shedding labour from agriculture. British agriculture did so, and was efficient by European standards.

Nevertheless, it would be mistaken to suggest that agricultural improvement and shedding labour were co-terminous. In practice, the situation was far more complex, and also differed with reference to various patterns of land use. Enclosure could lead to rural depopulation, but the replacement of pasture land by tillage required more labour. So also did many of the tasks that were important to raising crop yields, for example underdraining. Where industry was absent, static or in decline, which was the position across much of East Anglia and the south, plentiful labour was available, especially in the second half of the century as the population rose. Thus, it was possible to obtain more labour without having to pay higher wages. Of these areas, East Anglia was most suited for developments in arable husbandry. Yet, in the context of a rising population, agricultural reorganisation, especially in pastoral regions, could lead to a decline in the share of the workforce whose labour was required, or could lead to a harsh casualisation of working conditions. The net effect was to exacerbate social relations, and to look towards the widespread rural violence of the early nineteenth century.

AGRICULTURAL IMPROVEMENT

In Scotland, enclosure was less of a factor, but the rotation of crops also helped to raise agricultural productivity. Scottish improvers, such as John Cockburn,

William Cullen, Sir Archibald Grant of Monymusk and Alexander Murray, advocated sowing grass seeds to improve grazing and growing root crops and criticised overstocking, poor ploughing, insufficient manuring and run-rig farming with its interspersed strips of land. Grant was planting leguminous crops by 1719 and turnips by 1726 and was active in reafforestation, drainage and enclosures. The 1st Earl of Cromartie recruited Dutch experts to reclaim low-lying land and in the 1690s was interested in turnip cultivation and enriching rotations. In the 1730s, the 3rd Earl introduced new rotations on his estate.[16] In 1695, the Scottish Parliament passed two Acts relating to the division of commonalties and lands lying run-rig, that aided the processes of consolidation of holdings and enclosure. The use of lime in lowland Scotland greatly increased.

Britain was prominent in the field of agricultural literature. Works such as Timothy Nourse's *Campania Foelix, or a Discourse of the Benefits and Improvements of Husbandry* (1700) and Thomas Hale's *A Compleat Body of Husbandry. Containing rules for performing, in the most profitable manner, the whole business of the farmer, and country gentleman, in cultivating, planting, and stocking of land* (1756), and John Houghton's periodical *A Collection for the Improvement of Husbandry and Trade* (1692–1703) offered practical suggestions. *The Short Treatise on Forest Trees, Aquatics, Evergreens, Fences and Grass Seeds* (1735) by Thomas, 6th Earl of Haddington, assessed the relative value of clover and other fodder crops. Haddington played a major role in spreading the popularity of clover. Henry Home, Lord Kames (1696–1782), a prominent Scottish jurist and intellectual, was also a great agricultural improver, who brought into cultivation part of the moss of Kincardine, winning much favourable attention. In 1776, Kames published *The Gentleman Farmer; being an attempt to Improve Agriculture by subjecting it to the test of Rational Principles*. The popularity of such a work led to a fourth edition appearing in 1798. Arthur Young acquired fame as a publicist of agricultural improvement. His many works included the foundation and part authorship of the monthly *Annals of Agriculture* (1784–1809). Relevant material also appeared in the press. For example, the *Original Ipswich Journal* of 17 December 1774 included a piece on the raising of seedling potatoes.

The practical nature of much agricultural literature and its basis in long experience were indicated by works such as *A Treatise on Watering Meadows* (1779) by the Dorset farmer, George Boswell, and *Observations on Livestock* (1786) by the Northumberland farmer George Culley, an improver who bred the new Border Leicester or Culley sheep, drained marshy land and introduced new crops and rotations. Numerous agricultural societies, such as the Glamorgan Society for the Encouragement of Agriculture, were founded. The Bath and West Society was established in 1777.

The continued growth and integration of the market economy, as transport links improved and the growth in population fostered demand, encouraged change. As national markets developed, so the relative importance of local consumption declined and regional variations in price became less pronounced. For example, the first shipload of Cheshire cheese reached London in 1650, but by the 1680s over fifty cheese ships were sailing from the north-west. Increased sales of Cheshire cheese drove land prices up and led to the creation of new businesses, while return cargoes helped to transform the regional economy.[17] Cheese also came to London from Somerset via Bristol, while the Bristol market itself was supplied with butter and meat from South Wales, cheese from Cheshire and Somerset, milk, eggs and poultry from the West Country, and, by the close of the eighteenth century, potatoes from south Gloucestershire.

This process of growth and specialisation in the market economy was intense near major centres, for example in Essex, which served London. Fruit and vegetables from Berkshire, especially apples, pears and cherries, supplied London, Bath and Oxford, especially in the second half of the century. No longer known for its agriculture, Middlesex was then a major centre of market gardening for London. The development of the market economy also affected more distant places, whether producing for the market economy or organising the movement of crops and livestock. Portsmouth, for example, acted as a growing market for the grain and livestock of West Sussex and Hampshire. Cattle were driven south to London from Yorkshire, while Welsh cattle were driven to Kent to be fattened for the London market: Stockbridge in Hampshire still has the Welsh lettering on houses left by eighteenth-century drovers. Scottish linen and cattle exports to England rose after the Union of 1707: cattle from about 30,000 yearly to perhaps 80,000 a year in the 1750s. Irish dairy and livestock production developed in response to external demands, with substantial exports of beef and butter to England, and of salted pork to colonies such as Newfoundland. In Wales, Henry Herbert, 1st Earl of Powis of the 2nd creation, benefited in the 1750s and 1760s from demand for Powis oaks for the Royal Navy.

Demand for distant markets helped transform local agriculture and also encouraged improvement in transport links. In Cleveland, enclosure of both open field and commons owed much to the increase in arable and pastoral farming for the London market. Cleveland produced good quality wheat. After 1769, when the Tees was bridged at Stockton, large quantities were shipped from there to London. Good quality butter was also moved to London by sea: from Malton via Scarborough, Whitby and Hull.

Many movements of goods reflected long-established economic links, especially the driving of animals from upland pastures to lowland fattening areas and markets, for example from the Scottish Highlands to the fair at Crieff. Greater knowledge recently of economic links, monetarisation and commerce in the Middle Ages has ensured that subsequent developments appear less stark. Nevertheless, there was still a difference in scale and in the intensity and infrastructure of commerce. Furthermore, political changes, especially the Union of England and Scotland in 1707, greatly affected the trading world.

The pattern of production and market was a complex one, but its overall development was dynamic, especially once the population started to rise. Manufacturing and mining areas, where there was substantial immigration and only limited agricultural production, were of growing importance as markets. For example, the linen manufacturing area of east Ulster provided a market for the barley and oatmeal of neighbouring counties, such as Monaghan, and for the young stock reared on nearby hills. This stress on markets suggests that, rather than seeing agriculture and agrarian developments as an external force, provoking and making possible other changes in the economy and society, it should be seen as a part of a more complex interactive system.

The parameters of this system were affected by government action. Legislation was contentious and important for example in issues such as the free movement of Irish agricultural products to Britain, and the export of wool and grain from Britain. Henry Pelham, both First Lord of the Treasury and MP for Sussex, stressed the importance of corn bounties for local rentals in the early 1750s. However, agricultural development owed little to positive action on the part of successive governments. Indeed Arthur Young told the Count de la Bourdonaye in 1788:

> he knew very little of our government, if he supposed they would give a shilling to any agricultural project or projector; that whether the ministers were Whig or Tory made no difference, the party of the plough never yet had one on its side ... our husbandry flourished ... by the protection which civil liberty gives to property.

This was true, at least in so far as the properties was concerned. Continuity among the tenant farmers through regularly renewed leases was crucial in assisting the development of agriculture as it encouraged investment by safeguarding its benefits.

There was less continuity at more humble levels. In the Scottish Lowlands, the cottars or subtenants with smallholdings, the majority of the population before 1750, had been partly eliminated by 1820, in order to increase the size and efficiency of farms. Agricultural improvement between 1755 and the 1790s was responsible for a fall in the population of most Scottish rural parishes. This process was helped by the brevity of tenancies – from four to nineteen years – and this encouraged emigration to America. In England, yeoman farmers – small-scale owner-occupiers – were in part displaced to make more room for landlords and tenant farmers.

AGRICULTURAL REVOLUTION?

Yet it is also appropriate, as with industrial development, to consider how revolutionary changes were. Enclosure, and the opportunities and discontent it could create, were not new: there had been much unrest about agricultural change in the sixteenth century. Claims about an agricultural revolution have to take note of the importance of long-term developments. This was true for example of regions at the forefront of new techniques, such as Norfolk. There, some of the changes commonly associated with the eighteenth century, such as the introduction of fodder crops, had occurred during the Middle Ages. On the other hand, the proportion of Norfolk and Suffolk farmers growing turnips or clover rose dramatically from the 1660s to the 1720s: probate inventories suggest a rise in the percentage of farmers growing turnips from 1.6 to 52.7. The Norfolk four-course rotation, of wheat, turnips, barley and clover, was established on many farms by mid century.

Improvements in agricultural productivity in East Anglia were not solely a matter of new crops. There were also important improvements to the soil, particularly in marling and underdraining. By changing the chemical and physical structure of the soil, these processes improved its productivity, although they required much labour. Thus, the agricultural revolution, like its industrial counterpart which it fed, 'rested – in the final analysis – on the exploitation and impoverishment of rural workers, especially those in East Anglia and adjacent regions'.[18]

Continuity in change can also be emphasised for less 'advanced' regions, such as Aberdeenshire. There, many of the measures taken by the agricultural improvers of the mid-eighteenth century had already been tried in the seventeenth. These include attempts to encourage tenants to plant trees and to sow legumes. Similarly, organisational changes, such as the reduction of multiple tenancies and the commutation of rents in kind, had begun in the seventeenth century and accelerated in the eighteenth.

Just as the time span was longer than the term revolution might suggest, it is also important not to exaggerate the scale of change. For example, in 1771, Arthur Young praised Charles Turner who, on his Cleveland estate at Kirkleatham, had created compact farms, constructed new farm buildings, and introduced cabbages, clover and improved breeds of cattle. However, most Cleveland farmers did not use clover, and Young criticised the failure to reclaim much of the moorland. Across the country as a whole, extensive commons persisted into the nineteenth century, and there was still land for a major wave of enclosures in 1793–1815 during the French Revolutionary and Napoleonic Wars.

Many areas showed only limited signs of agricultural improvement. Cornish agriculture remained fairly stagnant until about 1780, although the earlier spread of potato cultivation was a sign of change. Visiting his Cardiganshire estate, Hafod, for the first time in 1780, Thomas Johnes was angered by the poor condition of the estate and tenantry. The timber had been denuded, transport was by ox-sledge, there was little rotation, ploughs were poor and fertilisers were primitive. Agricultural improvement was also limited in north-east Scotland until after 1790: there was only a limited use of fallow and nitrogenous crops, and of the light but effective ploughs that could be pulled by two horses, rather than a larger team, usually of oxen. On the Isle of Man, clover was introduced in 1770 and turnips in 1772, while threshing mills had arrived by 1793 and rotations by 1800, but much agricultural practice on the island remained conservative, not least in the farm implements used.[19]

More generally, the demand side was critical in agricultural improvement. Price movements did not reward the improvers until after 1760, while local urban markets were often too small to act as a spur for specialised agriculture. Many farms were small, and the legacy of established practice pressed hard. It was not easily possible to alter the size, shape or nature of fields, nor the farm buildings and yards. Most British small farmers lacked the necessary capital and willingness to accept risk for a programme of improvement. Illiteracy also limited receptiveness to agricultural innovations.

At the end of Chapter 5, we will turn to the general question of where best to place the emphasis on the economy: change or continuity. As far as agriculture is concerned, there was much continuity, and the rate of agricultural change should not be described as revolutionary. Nevertheless, the ability to raise production was important, as were the organisational developments that are summarised in terms of enclosure.[20]

NOTES

1. G.E. Mingay, 'The agricultural depression, 1730–1750', *Economic History Review*, 2nd series, 8 (1955–6), p. 326.
2. Couraud to Edward Weston, 17 July 1741, PRO. SP. 43/105.
3. R. Robinson, 'The fish trade in the pre-railway era: the Yorkshire coast, 1780–1914', *Northern History*, 25 (1939), pp. 222–34.
4. T. Williamson, *Polite Landscapes: Gardens and Society in Eighteenth-Century England* (Stroud, 1995), pp. 124–9.
5. A. Bil, *The Shieling, 1600–1840. The case of the Central Scottish Highlands* (Edinburgh, 1990) and 'The formation of new settlements in the Perthshire highlands, 1660–1780', *Northern Scotland*, 12 (1992), pp. 35–66.
6. D. Robinson, 'Drainage and reclamation', in S. and N. Bennett (eds), *An Historical Atlas of Lincolnshire* (Hull, 1993), p. 72.
7. P.M. Slocombe, *Mark. A Somerset Moorland Village* (Bradford-on-Avon, 1999), p. 78.
8. M. Havinden and R. Staves, 'Agriculture and rural settlement 1500–1800', in R. Kain and W. Ravenhill (eds), *Historical Atlas of South-West England* (Exeter, 1999), pp. 287–8.
9. M. Turner, 'Parliamentary enclosure', in P. Wade-Martins (ed.), *An Historical Atlas of Norfolk* (Norwich, 1993), p. 124.
10. M. Turner, *English Parliamentary Enclosure* (Folkestone, 1980).
11. J. Groves, *Piggins, Husslements and Desperate Debts: a social history of north-east Cheshire through wills and probate inventories, 1660-1760* (Sale, 1994), p. 67.
12. C.E. Searle, 'Customary tenants and the enclosure of the Cumbrian commons', *Northern History*, 29 (1993), pp. 126–53.
13. P. Keene (ed.), *The Parish of Hinton Waldrist* (Kingston Bagpuize, 2000), p. 13.
14. J.W. Leopald, 'The Galloway Levellers Revolt of 1724', in A. Charlesworth (ed.), *Rural Social Change and Conflicts since 1500* (Hull, 1984), pp. 18–41.
15. K.D.M. Snell, *Annals of the Labouring Poor: Social Change and Agrarian England, 1660–1900* (Cambridge, 1985); J.M. Neeson, *Commoners: Common Right, Enclosure and Social Change in England, 1700–1820* (Cambridge, 1993).
16. See also T.C. Smout, 'Landowners in Scotland, Ireland and Denmark in the age of improvement', *Scandinavian Journal of History*, 12 (1987), pp. 79–97.
17. C. Foster, 'Cheshire cheese: farming in the north-west in the seventeenth and eighteenth centuries', *Transactions of the Historical Society of Lancashire and Cheshire*, 144 (1994), pp. 1–46.
18. S.W. Martins and T. Williamson, *Roots of Change. Farming and the Landscape in East Anglia, c. 1700–1870* (Exeter, 1999), p. 209.
19. R.E.C. Forster, 'Aspects of Manx emigration: 1750–1850', *Proceedings of the Isle of Man Natural History and Antiquarian Society*, 10 (1989–91), p. 25.
20. A useful overview is provided by J.V. Beckett, *The Agrarian Revolution* (Oxford, 1990).

4

Industry

The developments in the economy and society that contributed to, and comprised, what was subsequently termed the Industrial Revolution, arose from an economy and society that were far from static. For centuries, the pressures of an increasingly insistent market economy had encouraged change, a process facilitated by the availability of investment capital and the absence of internal tariffs. What is generally understood by the term Industrial Revolution, particularly steam-driven power, specialised factories, and associated social changes, such as widespread urbanisation, were not typical in this period, but rather of the nineteenth century. Nevertheless, there was a substantial shift in the occupational profile of the population. Furthermore, it would be foolish to present the important developments of the period in terms of a failure to achieve such a revolution, as if they were supposed to be heading in such a direction and should only be judged appropriate if they reached it.

Aside from diversity, it is also, as elsewhere in this book, important to note the problems created by the nature of the surviving evidence. It is difficult enough for modern economists, able to draw on the records of a highly regulated and fully monetarised economy, to assess and analyse trends. Both tasks are much harder for a period that was essentially pre-statistical, and where the regulatory regime was much more patchy and did not lead to series of data in central government records. Aside from making it difficult to probe the economy as a whole, this situation also makes it difficult to assess the situation in particular areas or industries, other than by turning to contemporary descriptions that were largely impressionistic. Excise records survive for several industries, but their value is affected by the degree of evasion.

Manufacturing was affected by factors of supply and demand. The former generally command attention, but it is also worth noting the latter. Although an increasing quantity of manufactured goods was exported, especially to Britain's North American colonies, Britain was not the exporter to the world that she was to be in the mid-nineteenth century. Manufactured goods were less important to international trade in the earlier period. Instead, demand was principally domestic, and was therefore affected by domestic population, purchasing power and consumer attitudes. Thanks to the rise in population from the mid-eighteenth century, there was an important increase in domestic demand.

Most industrial production was able to serve existing and developing demands profitably without seeking to alter its supply-side capability. However, supply-side factors were of importance and there were significant changes in them. These included the quality of entrepreneurship, the supply of skilled labour, technological developments, and changes in industrial organisation and location that permitted the cutting of costs. There were also particular supply-side factors in individual industries. For example, the crucial woollen textile industry was dependent on factors, especially disease and weather, that might affect the number of sheep.

The balance of emphasis between individual supply-side factors in the economy as a whole is a matter of controversy. Classically, the stress was first on new technology, and this was indeed significant not just for the individual changes in manufacturing capability it brought, but also for the sense that continuing change was not only possible but in progress. Textile manufacturing was a sector that witnessed technological development in which Britain led the way and that subsequently attracted the attention of commentators. A series of inventions were learned by subsequent students, although the information provided no guidance to the difficulty of the process. John Kay's flying shuttle of 1733 increased the productivity of handloom weavers by making it possible both to weave double-width clothes and to weave more speedily, although it was not in general use in Yorkshire until the 1780s, and was only slowly spreading elsewhere in England twenty years later. The early machinery of woollen textile manufacturing, such as James Hargreaves's hand-powered spinning jenny (1764), and scribbling and carding machines, greatly raised labour productivity; but the spinners saw it as a threat to their livelihood, and Hargreaves's machines were destroyed by rioters in Blackburn in 1768–9.

The 1760s–1780s saw a series of developments that permitted the manufacture of machine-spun cotton yarn strong enough to produce an all-cotton cloth, especially Richard Arkwright's water frame (1768), which applied the principle of spinning by rollers, and Samuel Crompton's mule (1779) with its spindle carriage. The history of Arkwright's invention provides a good indication of the potential and problems of machinisation. The yarn produced by Arkwright's water frame was of a firmer texture than that spun by the jenny. The smoothness and evenness of the yarn ensured that stockings woven from it were much better than those woven from hand-spun cotton. Unlike with the spinning jenny, the process of manufacture was continuous. In 1773, Arkwright produced a cloth solely of cotton, an innovation in England, and in 1775 he brought out a patent for a series of changes allowing the entire process of yarn manufacture to be performed on one machine.

Arkwright and his partners built a number of water-powered cotton mills in Lancashire and the Midlands, the first in Derbyshire in 1771. These displayed the characteristics of the factory system, including the precise division of labour and the continual co-operation of workers in the different manufacturing processes.

In 1772, his Nottingham mill employed over 300 people, some children from the parish workhouses. Yet, there was also much discontent. In 1776, Arkwright's new factory at Birkacre, near Chorley in Lancashire, was burnt down by rioters angered by the offer of work at lower rates. Over 100 machines were destroyed in the Lancashire riots of that year. This reaction against the move to a more controlled working environment was not supported by Parliament, which in 1780 responded to a petition by the cotton-spinners by supporting the use of machines.

In 1790, Arkwright installed a Boulton and Watt steam engine in his Nottingham mill. These machines were powered by coal. A readily transportable and controllable fuel, certainly in comparison with wood, the traditional fuel source, coal, was useful even in the preparatory stages of traditional manufacturing processes, such as soap-boiling, let alone in factories. In contrast, wood, with its greater bulk for calorific value and less readily controllable heat, was a poor basis for many industrial processes, as well as for the development of large new industrial populations, with attendant demand for bricks, pottery and all the other fuel-consuming ancillaries of towns. Coal could be mined throughout the year, whereas water mills were affected by ice, flooding, and summertime drops in water flow.

Unlike wood, however, coal had to be mined. Furthermore, despite centuries of cutting down trees, wood was still more widely available than coal. As a result, the accessibility and movement of coal played a large role in its use. Both mining and transport acted as spurs for innovation and activity, particularly the construction of canals and of railways. Along these, horse-drawn barges and wagons respectively moved large quantities of coal from pits.

One major route was the movement of coal from County Durham to the banks of the river Tyne, where it was used in manufacturing or shipped to London, for domestic or industrial use. In 1725–6, the first railway bridge in the world, Causey Arch, was built for the movement of Durham coal across the Causey Burn towards the Tyne. It had the largest span of any bridge built in Britain since Roman times, and the architect had to work from Roman models. The system of wagonways developed greatly during the period as techniques improved. The wagons ran on wooden wheels, which were later flanged. By the 1730s iron bindings were being tried, and by the 1780s cast-iron wheels were in general use. After the formation of the Grand Alliance of leading coal-mining families in North-East England in 1726, a process of sharing and rationalising existing wagonways and of improving the system led to an increase in the length of wagonways and thus in their efficiency. New links included the New Western Way opened in 1739, and the extension of the Wear system to Pelton Fell by 1746. Wagonways developed to link other coalfields to riverside wharves and to ironworks, for example from the East Shropshire field to wharves on the Severn.

Without transport, coal was of scant value, but coal with transport could serve as the basis for the creation of buoyant mixed-industrial regions with large pools of labour and demand, and specialist services. For rapid industrial growth, the essentials were capital, transport, markets and coal.

Coal was used to power steam engines, potent symbols of a new world. The first engine was developed by Thomas Savery in 1695. It was improved by

Thomas Newcomen with his Atmospheric Engine in 1712. In this, the injection of water condensed steam in the cylinder, causing the piston to descend under the weight of the atmosphere. The piston was then returned to the top of the stroke by the weight of the beam. The beam transmitted power by moving a chain attached to the pump rod, but on the down stroke only. Newcomen's engine was progressively improved during the century, not least with better cylinders and valves which increased its energy efficiency. The boring machines introduced by John Wilkinson in 1774 and 1781 improved the casting and boring of cylinders. This allowed the steam engine to become more efficient in its fuel use and more regular in its operation.[1]

The Newcomen engine was eventually superseded by James Watt's engine. Watt (1736–1819) invented the separate condenser which greatly increased the fuel efficiency of steam engines, and also patented in 1769 the steam jacket round the cylinder. Watt also developed an engine that could transmit power on the up as well as the down stroke. Watt's first full-size steam engine was installed in 1776, and six years later he patented the double-acting rotative engine, which gave a comparative uniformity of rotary motion, and thus increased the capacity of steam engines to drive industrial machinery. Greater energy efficiency made steam engines less expensive to run.

Steam engines were expensive to purchase and not free from problems. They were best suited to enterprises, such as large mines, where substantial quantities of energy were required for a long period. They were particularly useful for pumping water out of mines, first in the important Cornish tin industry and later in coal and iron ore mines, and in recycling water and in ironworks. Steam power replaced water power, such as the 'two vast engines' seen by John Evelyn in a Cornish tin mine in 1702: 'consisting of several wheels in the nature of pumps to draw the water out of the places they intend to search, they are continually going by the force of water which passing through several peoples grounds costs a great deal before it can reach the engines to which it is conveyed in a wooden trough very high'.[2]

From Cornwall, steam engines spread first to the coalfields. The first Newcomen engine in the Cumbrian coalfield was completed in 1717, and the use of another made possible the sinking of the important Salton Pit there in 1730. The first one in the East Shropshire coalfield was in operation in 1719 and by 1733 there were apparently four on the coalfield.[3] By 1733, there were about 100 in operation across the country. Although Ayrshire contained five by 1734, progress was slower elsewhere in Scotland.

The introduction of such engines required investment and accentuated distinctions within coal mining. In contrast to the deep mines which used steam engines, smaller bell pits and slants required much less investment. They also had a far shorter life.[4] It is necessary to remember such pits alongside the deep mines. Again, while some pits used rails and horses to haul the coal others relied on haulage by humans. Again, while some pits used ventilation by fire baskets others did not. Similarly, some coalfields were affected by insufficient investment and poor transport. These were problems for the Fife coalfield.[5]

Steam engines were also used for winding and, by the end of the century, for driving machinery. In 1779, James Pickard, a Birmingham button-manufacturer, fitted a crank and flywheel to his Newcomen engine in order to use its power to drive a mill that could grind metals. This innovation greatly enlarged the market for steam engines which was exploited by the partnership of Watt and the Birmingham industrialist, Matthew Boulton. Steam engines were also to be important for the development of canals as they filled their reservoirs and wound their inclined planes.

Mining benefited not only from the use of the steam engine for pumping and winding, but also from a number of innovations including the introduction of explosives, better methods of lining shafts and supporting roofs, and improved underground transport, especially with the adoption of rails along which wagons could be pulled. Improvements above ground in the transportation of bulk goods by water and, to a lesser extent, road, cut the price of coal and thus expanded demand. The first coal barge arrived in Birmingham on the new Birmingham Canal in 1772.

In 1700, the British production of about three million tons of coal had been largely for domestic heating, and the north-east of England had been the most important coalfield, accounting for nearly half the national output. (East) Shropshire, (South) Yorkshire and (South) Staffordshire, in that order, were then the most important other coalfields.[6] Output rose by just over 1 per cent per year to 5.2 million tons by 1750, and then by over 2 per cent per year for the rest of the century: to 8.8 million tons by 1775 and 15 million by 1800. There was par-ticularly important expansion after 1750 in Lancashire and South Wales. This growth was far greater in both absolute and relative terms than that in any other country, and this helped to make the British economy distinctive. It opened up a powerful comparative advantage over the Continental economies. However, although mining was developed at Coalisland in Tyrone, there was very little coal in Ireland.

The expansion of coal-mining was both the product and the cause of economic development. It interacted with the transformation of the metallurgical industry. Here Britain led the way. The smelting of iron and steel using coke, rather than charcoal, freed an important industry from dependence on wood supplies, and was an important instance of the process by which mineral sources of power increasingly supplanted organic sources. This 1709 innovation by Abraham Darby at his blast furnace in Coalbrookdale was not widely applied at first, due to initial difficulties with the process, cost and quality considerations. The first known coke-fired furnace in County Durham, at Whitehill, was not established until about 1735. From the 1750s, charcoal costs rose and the process spread rapidly, although improvements in furnace technology may also have played a role.[7] Henry Cort's method of puddling and rolling, invented in 1784 but not adopted until the 1790s, produced malleable iron with coal more cheaply than the charcoal forge and refinery. Industrialisation created business. The Coalbrookdale ironworks benefited from demand for steam engines, and by 1748 over 77 cylinders had been cast there.

Combined with the application of steam power to coal mining, blast furnaces, and the new rolling and slitting mills, this led to a concentration of the iron industry on or near the coalfields, as in South Wales. By 1796, there were 25 furnaces in South Wales, including three at Dowlais, where development had begun in 1759. The largest town in Wales in 1801 was Merthyr Tydfil, no more than a hamlet in 1750, but now the leading centre of the coke and blast-furnace-based iron industry of South Wales, and the leading centre of iron production in the world.[8] Its development showed the potential importance of industry to population movements, an importance that was to be clearly displayed over the following century.

Other areas of iron production declined. The long-established iron industry in the Weald had been based on its woodlands (as had the glass industry there), but this declined as coal-based production became more economic. The steel industry also developed on and near the coalfields.

Iron spurred the demand for coal. The development of the South Staffordshire coalfield owed much to the construction of ironworks, the first, outside Dudley, in 1772, and fourteen in all by 1794. Copper smelting also came to be located on coalfields, as in south and north-east Wales. The Swansea Valley dominated the non-ferrous smelting industry in Britain. Jabez Fisher, a visiting American Quaker, noted in 1776 that the Forest Copper works there 'vomit out vast columns of thick smoak, which, curling as they rise, mount up to the clouds'.[9]

While copper-mining developed rapidly during the period, there was also more mining of lead deposits. Lead smelting was affected by the introduction of the reverberatory furnace which was about five times larger than the earlier ore-hearth and could melt and refine the ore to produce both lead and silver of higher purity. These larger furnaces involved more extensive buildings, including long flues. To take a major lead-smelting region, County Durham, smelt mills began operation towards the end of the period in, for example, Gaunless in 1770 and High Eggleston in 1771, but there were also earlier works, for example at Jeffries from 1713, Rookhope from 1736 and Burteeford from 1743. Metallurgy could produce great profits. The lead deposits at Llangynog in north Montgomeryshire, discovered in 1692, produced a profit of £140,000 for the Earls of Powis in 1725–45.

The production of iron rose from an annual average of about 27,000 tons in 1720–4 and 1745–9 to 80,000 tons in 1789. This iron was used in the expanding industries of the period. The spread of mining led to greater interest in railroads, and thus to more demand for iron. Metallurgy and sophisticated engineering were developed by the innovations of men such as Boulton. The first rolling mill in Birmingham was opened in 1740. From the first half of the century, the rolling mill was applied to tin-plate, giving the tin-plate industry a major international competitive advantage.

Although developments with steam-powered machinery were more dramatic, there was also important progress with hand tools and small machinery, particularly in the metal trade, which benefited from improvements in drilling equipment, and innovations in batten making. Metalworking was crucial to what was termed 'toymaking', the manufacture of small metal objects, such as buckles, buttons and snuffboxes. The great expansion of such manufacture was part of the growth of the world of goods in this period, and also provided goods for export.

Several other industries also saw major growth. One of the most dramatic was the consequence of developments in ceramic technology, which led to hard, high-fired and commercially successful British china. Josiah Wedgwood (1730–95) turned a craft into an industrial process, creating a major export industry in the process. A skilful entrepreneur, Wedgwood helped make his ware fashionable and knew how to translate this into a mass market. The Staffordshire pottery industry needed cheap transport, for clay and for finished products, and benefited greatly from new canal links. There were also important organisational changes in the Staffordshire Potteries, especially the development of large-scale production which provided economies of scale, opportunities for division of labour and a quality control lacking in earlier smaller-scale, often domestic, works.[10]

The glass industry also needed fuel, and thus developed in areas where it was readily available such as on Tyneside. Newcastle produced about 40 per cent of all the glass made in England in the seventeenth century: the Lemington glass-houses, started in 1760, joined those in Closegate and Skinnerburn. The chemical industry also developed on Tyneside. In 1778, Losh opened an alkali plant at Low Walker that used cheap coal and spoilt salt. On the Wear, local coal helped to encourage the development of salt-boiling, glassware, pottery, and other industries. More generally, coal was the major fuel in sugar refining, brewing, salt-boiling and brick making by 1700.

Most crucial new technological inputs were British in origin, but there was also some important borrowing from abroad. Building on the pioneering efforts of Thomas Cotchett, Thomas Lombe, who imported Italian silk-throwing machinery and patented it in 1718, erected a large water-driven factory on the river Derwent at Derby in 1721. The first silk-throwing mill in north-west England was opened at Stockport in 1732.

The transformation of the 'Potteries' into a specialised manufacturing region is a reminder that industrial change had a powerful geographical impact.[11] In England, industry was becoming especially important in the North and the Midlands, especially on and near coalfields. Lancashire, Yorkshire and the West Midlands were the principal centres of industrialisation. This was particularly important in metallurgy. In addition, there was great growth in textile production in Yorkshire and Lancashire. Furthermore, urban manufacturing was very important: towns such as Derby, Newcastle and Nottingham became major centres of activity, and London remained a major centre of production, especially catering for the needs of its population, by far the largest individual market in the British Isles.

Yet, in part, such growth was achieved at the expense of regions that declined, while, more generally, due to varying rates of growth, the development of particular regions led to a shift in relative importance. For example, the growth in textile production in Lancashire and Yorkshire was in part achieved at the expense of traditional centres of production such as Colchester, Exeter and Worcester. Labour was cheaper in Lancashire and Yorkshire and the textile industry less restricted by corporatist traditions than in long-established centres, such as Norwich. There, the manufacture of worsted stuffs remained important and its output rose until the 1780s, but the industry remained essentially domestic and quasi-domestic, no factories of any size were built, and competition from the West Riding of Yorkshire had passed it by the mid-century. Partly as a consequence, population growth in Norwich was limited: the number of inhabitants rose from nearly 30,000 in 1752 to 41,000 in 1786, before falling to 37,000 in 1801. Due to competition with the uniform quality and lower prices of machine-spun yarns from the West Riding, the Suffolk yarn industry had collapsed by 1800.

The exports of serges, a type of cloth popular on the Continent as well as in Britain, from Exeter, the leading fulling and finishing centre in the West Country, rose from 120,000 pieces in the 1680s to 365,000 in 1710, a quarter of England's entire cloth exports, before falling to 162,802 in 1745. Thereafter, thanks to demand from the East India Company, exports revived to peak at 390,000 in 1777, although British and European markets had been largely taken by East Anglian and Yorkshire competitors. Nevertheless, this is a reminder that the chronology of industrial and commercial activity cannot be explained simply in terms of the heartlands of the Industrial Revolution.[12]

In contrast to an annual average population increase for England and Wales in 1750–70 of 0.75 per cent, that for the West Riding was 1.7 per cent. By the 1790s, industrial change had a clear regional pattern that was reflected in indicators such as expenditure on poor relief per head of population. In 1801, the average figure for England and Wales was 9 shillings 1 penny (45 pence) but in the industrial counties it was far lower: 6s 7d in the West Riding and 4s 4d in Lancashire. In contrast, counties with hardly any industry, such as Sussex, or with declining industries, such as Essex, Norfolk and Suffolk, had to pay far more than the average.

Some cities that were not at the forefront of rates of economic growth still saw important developments. Bristol's dominance of trans-Atlantic trade was successfully challenged by Liverpool and Glasgow, but Bristol still saw important industrial growth, some of it in the processing of colonial goods. It had a tobacco industry, for example milling snuff, as well as sugar-refining, with a peak of sixteen refineries. In 1731, chocolate and cocoa-making began there. In the second half of the eighteenth century, there were at least three cotton mills in Bristol, while the city benefited from coal from the nearby Forest of Dean in the development of industries such as zinc and copper smelting, iron founding, lead works, gunshot making, salt refining and soap making. The first English brass-making foundry was established there.

The Scottish economy changed greatly. Prior to mid-century, it had been relatively backward, with limited long-distance trade and an economy dependent on England, to which cattle and linen were exported and from which manufactured goods were imported. The Act of Union of 1707 admitted Scotland to a free-trade area that comprised Great Britain and the colonies. Complementary and competitive Scottish industries, such as linen, benefited greatly, as did the west of Scotland, which could now trade freely with the West Indies and North America. Conversely, less competitive industries, such as fine woollens, collapsed.

From mid-century, the availability of capital in Scotland interacted with the investment opportunities provided by new technology. Although the extensive sugar and tobacco trades based on Glasgow had little direct effect on the rest of the economy, their profits helped to stimulate activity. For example, tobacco profits funded the development of the chemical industry and increased the liquidity of banks such as the Edinburgh-based Royal Bank. The chemical industry developed using coal in the mid-century, and from the early 1750s there was also growth in paper mills, printed linens, and metallurgy. By 1761, the Carron Company at Falkirk, which concentrated on ironmaking, had 615 employees. Output in Scotland's largest manufacturing industry, linen, more than doubled in 1740–80, and cotton manufacture developed in Lanarkshire.

Scotland remained poorer than England, and the credit system had an inadequate cash basis. However, the growth in the economy of central Scotland showed what was possible. It also contrasted with the situation in Ireland. Scotland had a more self-sufficient and mixed agricultural sector, coal, and more favourable political, financial and social circumstances than Ireland. Apart from Ulster, where linen-weaving developed strongly from mid-century in much of the east and south, Ireland had comparatively little industrial growth, although the linen economy also affected other regions, including Cork, Mayo and Roscommon. The capital and skill of Dublin merchants was crucial to the development of Ulster's linen industry.

Hitherto the emphasis in this chapter has been on development, machinisation and the growth of large concerns. It is necessary, however, to look also not only at contrary indications, but at the full range of industrial activity and organisation. Thus, alongside coalfield manufacturing, even factories, it is necessary to consider proto-industrialisation. This term is widely ascribed to the development of rural areas in which a significant portion of the population became dependent on income from the industrial production of goods. This process has been presented as the consequence of the expansion of traditional rural domestic craft production without any matching technological advance.

There were a number of reasons for the expansion of rural industry. Labour was more flexible and cheaper than in the towns. A lower wage economy stemmed from the absence both of alternative non-agricultural employment and of a tradition of organised labour. Labour costs were also affected by the presence of both grinding poverty, which made people accept low returns, and of income from farming, which reduced dependence on income from manufacturing and thus again made people accept low returns. The employment of outworkers in rural areas permitted an effective integration of different labour resources. Some cottage workers were wage-earners, while others were self-employed.

Energy costs may also have been significant. Water-power was easier to utilise in areas of rapid flow, and wood supplies were more plentiful in the countryside, as was coal in mining regions. Raw materials could also be found in rural areas. Thus the leather industry depended on cattle hides for tanning.

However, despite the general availability of cheap rural labour, most rural areas, for example much of Ireland, did not become centres of industry.

Entrepreneurial activity was a crucial factor in producing a symbiotic relationship between rural activity and urban funds, markets and, frequently, stages in manufacture. This enabled rural industry to move from the stage of direct sale by domestic craftsmen to that of sale to distant markets. For example, the merchant-hosiers who controlled the knitting of worsted stockings in rural Aberdeenshire, provided the wool and collected the stockings.

Textile production lent itself readily to rural industrialisation. Power could be supplied by rivers, traditions of rural domestic textile manufacture were strong, wheels and looms could be found in the countryside, and textiles could be transported without much risk of damage. The rural and urban aspects of textile manufacture were intimately linked, with finishing processes usually concentrated in the towns. Merchants organised the system of outwork and the marketing of the final product. West Yorkshire was an important site of the rural manufacture of woollen cloth, and Ulster became one for linen. By 1770, John Flounders, a bleacher and linen manufacturer, had four sites for collecting linen in Cleveland and sixteen receiving agencies between Newcastle and York. Such a system encouraged local as well as distant trade and transport. In Scotland, the spinning of linen yarn spread to remote districts, such as Highland Perthshire, the Moray Firth, Ross and Orkney. Putting-out systems developed considerably in scale during the century.

The development of rural industry should not necessarily be seen as a stage, whether successful or not, on the path to 'full' industrialisation. Proto-industrialisation is a term that is often used with implications of a continuing process of development and growth, but in many senses rural industrialisation was a stabilising factor both for industrial production and for rural economies. Such industrialisation made it possible to deal with the demands of a rising consumer population without increasing costs excessively and thus squeezing demand. It also brought more prosperity to rural zones, limiting emigration and supporting marriage at an early age. For example, in Aberdeenshire, where individual households were the units of production, women and children prepared and spun the wool which the men wove. For families making a livelihood with perhaps a small-holding and weaving, the local product made in the traditional way was all they had time to produce.

Most rural industry was not mechanised to any significant extent. Often products were for a local market only, techniques were limited, and the capacity for innovation low. This was true for example of much, but by no means all, production in Devon, Somerset, Dorset, Wiltshire, Essex, Norfolk, Suffolk, Worcestershire and Aberdeenshire. The important hand-knitting of stockings, gloves and caps that provided much employment for women and girls in the western dales of North Yorkshire lacked capital and fuel for steam power, and lost ground to mechanised industry at the end of the century.

Yet, within such areas, there was also expansion thanks to entrepreneurial activity and, in places, experimentation in dyeing and new technology. Large-scale concentration of textile production in factories did not really begin until the 1790s. Prior to that, rural textile production grew in quantity and range. The attractions of combining industrial and agricultural activities and the importance of already-established traditions helped offset any process of national concentration. However, there could be a process of local concentration as centralised workshops developed in some rural communities.

Thus, industrial development did not only lead in one direction. Furthermore, it faced many problems. The technological level of most industries was fairly low, and innovations often spread only very slowly. Some processes were 'trial and error' and, even when successful, the reason might not be understood. Much industrial plant was primitive, prone to climatic disruption, a particular problem with mills, and dependent on an often poorly-educated labour force. The provision of fuel was often erratic, fuel economy was limited, and mechanical working parts were prone both to break down and to become less efficient. This affected product quality. Most industrial plant was fairly simple and there was rarely an opportunity or need for the costly retooling that might have encouraged innovation. Poor communications also affected many individual enterprises, as well as the aggregate efficiency of the industrial system.

The small size of most industrial units helped ensure that there was very little specialisation, either in machinery or labour. Skilled labour was frequently in short supply. Skills frequently took years to develop, and were often not readily transmissible, except by acquiring the men who had them: books or blueprints would not suffice; although 'pattern books' in fields like furniture design and architecture became widely used.

The limited skill-base made change more difficult, but there was also a culture of continuity. Artisanal mentality included a sense of the importance of traditional values and communal stability. There was a general disinclination to innovate, understandably so in a culture where training was largely acquired on the job and where tradition determined most industrial practices. The apprenticeship system did not encourage new values. Uncertainty about likely returns as well as psychological rigidities helped ensure that technological possibilities were not grasped in many sectors. The limited and precarious financial resources of most entreprises also discouraged innovation. Most contracts were short-term, hindering the development of a relative security that might encourage often expensive investment in new plant.

As yet, technological transformation was selective and change often slow, firm size was generally small and organisation personal, labour markets were frequently local, outwork was common and factories were rare. Ayrshire, although a major coal-mining county, was typical at the end of the period in having most of its manufacturing carried on in small hand-, horse-, and water-powered units. Similarly, most of the tasks in the important linen industry were performed by hand. Flax-spinning and linen-weaving were cottage-based. Larger, factory-type units serving wider areas were created only for the finishing processes of bleaching and bettling. The important Warrington file-making concern of Peter Stubs relied mostly on outworkers at the end of the century. Over much of the British Isles, industry was still far less important than agriculture as a source of wealth and employment at the end of the century.

In addition, if attention is focused on 1783 as the close of our period, rather than the eighteenth century as a whole, then it can seem even more appropriate to stress the limited transformation that economic change had produced. Steam did not become the major energy source for manufacturing until the 1870s, and, prior to that, much industrial growth came from the unmechanised sectors of the economy. Furthermore, although many innovations that attract attention occurred before 1783, nevertheless, their working out in production processes and diffusion frequently followed that year. Furthermore, the economic expansion that followed the coming of peace in 1783 brought fresh demands and opportunities that encouraged growth. Thus, it was after 1783 that the West Riding woollen textile industry and its marketing really changed and developed, and the industry acquired a price advantage over competitors.[13]

Even focusing on the period prior to 1783, there was still much development. To take some of the factors already mentioned, entrepreneurs brought innovation and there was an openness to new technology in crucial sectors. Thanks to the increasing specialisation of labour functions in many sectors of the economy, there was also an extension and intensification of the skill-base.

Problems with investment and working capital were lessened by borrowing and also by the role of investors with substantial disposable funds. Although they tended to spend more on building and enhancing stately homes, major landowners played a crucial role in the expensive business of developing coal mines and attendant transport facilities, for example in Ayrshire, Cumbria, Lancashire and north-east England. Such activity was not restricted to mining. Earl Gower, later 1st Marquis of Stafford (1721–1803), was actively involved in coal, lime and iron ore extraction, and the development of canals and mineral railroads. Scottish landowners played a prominent role in harbour construction, salt-boiling, the production of coal-tar, glass and lime, and canal and turnpike development. Property rights made investment a safer prospect than in some Continental countries.

The importance both of outside and of aristocratic investment was clear in Wales. Bristol financiers developed copper works near Swansea from 1717, as well as iron and coal workings in south Wales. Mineral development in Anglesey and, to a lesser extent, Caernarvonshire owed something to Charles Roe from Macclesfield. Reinvestment of profits from Jamaica was important in the development of slate quarrying at Penrhyn.

CONCLUSIONS

In addition to an emphasis on developments in the decades prior to 1783, it is also appropriate to note the importance of earlier growth, growth that underlines the need to see industrialisation as a long-term project. There is evidence of significant change in the first half of the eighteenth century. This was true of aggregate economic growth. Although that is difficult to measure, it has recently been suggested that English industrial output may have grown by about 15 per cent in the first quarter of the eighteenth century.[14] Such figures underline the work of scholars who have stressed long-term changes in the economy rather than a late eighteenth-century 'big bang'.[15] Aside from growth at the national level, there was also important development in particular areas prior to the mid-eighteenth century. For example, in north east Lancashire, where the local economy was already fairly dependent on the manufacture of woollen, linen and fustian cloth by the mid-seventeenth century, there was a gradual, rather than revolutionary, development over the following century that reflected a shift towards a more integrated and specialised economy.[16]

In addition to growth in output, there was within industry a process of change in which profit opportunities were sought and enhanced, and many inefficiencies that could be overcome were challenged; while, as indicated in Chapters two and four, improvements in the agricultural and transport situation created more helpful circumstances for industrial activity. At the same time, although this might have been true on the national scale, it could be less so on the regional, and, still more, local scales. Thus, opportunities in agriculture and transport might deprive industry of labour and investment. The relative availability of both labour and investment may have played a role in the higher industrial growth rates in the North East, South Yorkshire, and the Midlands, compared to southern and eastern England where agricultural opportunities were greater. In relative terms, London became less important as a manufacturing centre, in part because of opportunities there in commerce and the service sector.

However, the situation was more complex, not least because industrial growth created opportunities for local farmers, while rural (or at least landlord) prosperity could provide investment capital. Furthermore, changes in land use, such as enclosure and/or a switch from arable to pastoral could lead to a movement of people from the land. Thus both agricultural and industrial growth could occur in the same area. Issues of entrepreneurial activity, artisan culture and a more general willingness to accept often unwelcome aspects of changes, such as investment risk and new working arrangements, were also important.

Technological innovation and a large percentage of the national income coming from non-agricultural activities, were distinguishing and advanced features of the British economy, although organisational improvements in much of industry were as, or more, important than technological shifts. Alongside agricultural improvement and the construction of canals and better roads, industrial growth led to a rise in national wealth and a new economy, that was different to that across most of the Continent. The percentage of the male labour force employed in industry rose from 19 in 1700 to 30 in 1800, and, as the total population rose, this represented a considerable increase. Nevertheless, machine-based manufacture was in most of the country overshadowed by handicrafts. Agricultural productivity increased, and the percentage of the male labour force employed in agriculture fell from 60 to 40, a drop not matched anywhere else in Europe. By 1750, those employed in industry and commerce exceeded those who worked in farming. The British economy developed powerful comparative advantages in trade and manufacturing, and greatly interested and impressed informed foreign visitors.

A sense of new possibilities was not only seen in the supply side of the economy. There was also significant change in the demand, which encouraged developments in production. An active culture of print, especially newspapers and magazines, and the availability of images (mezzotinting made this an 'industrial' process) helped to sustain and disseminate fashions in a society in which fashion and social emulation played a growing role in creating a consumer market attuned to new developments. This was essentially the market of the 'middling orders', greatly concerned about social status and aspiration, who, by 1725, had seen an appreciable increase in the scale of their material possessions, such as pottery and furniture, an increase that was to continue during the century, and to be spread to less affluent groups. The enhanced purchasing power of the bulk of the population in the first half of the century also helped industrial growth, for example with the rise of gin distilling, a new industry.

Industrial development powerfully contributed to a sense of progress that was experienced by many commentators in the second half of the century. It could be glimpsed visually in the depiction of potent industrial scenes, such as the Iron Bridge and ironworks at Coalbrookdale. In the Frog Service designed by Josiah Wedgwood for Catherine the Great of Russia, and finished in 1774, the contemporary British scenes displayed included not only landscapes such as Stowe but also the Prescot glass works on Merseyside. The country as well as the life of its people was changing.

NOTES

1. L.T.C. Rolt and J.S. Allen, *The Steam Engine of Thomas Newcomen* (Hartington, 1977).
2. BL. Evelyn papers vol. 49 f. 23.
3. B. Trinder, *The Industrial Revolution in Shropshire* (3rd edn, Chichester, 2000), p. 48.
4. R.N. Cooper, *Higher and Lower An Illustrated History of the Higher and Lower Division of Llanrhidian* (Llandrindod Wells, 1998), pp. 73–6.
5. C.A. Whatley, *Scottish Society 1707–1830: Beyond Jacobitism, Towards Industrialisation* (Manchester, 2000).
6. J. Hatcher, *The History of the British Coal Industry, I: Before 1700: Towards the Age of Coal* (Oxford, 1993).
7. L. Ince, *The Knight Family and the British Iron Industry 1695–1902* (Birmingham, 1991); E. Thomas, *Coalbrookdale and the Darby Family* (York, 1999).
8. L. Ince, *The South Wales Iron Industry 1750–1885* (Birmingham, 1993).
9. K. Morgan (ed.), *An American Quaker in the British Isles: The Travel Journals of Jabez Maud Fisher, 1775-1779* (Oxford, 1992).
10. L. Weatherill, *The Pottery Trade and North Staffordshire, 1660–1760* (Manchester, 1971).
11. P. Hudson (ed.), *Regions and Industries: A Perspective on the Industrial Revolution in Britain* (Cambridge, 1989).
12. W.G. Hoskins, *Industry, Trade and People in Exeter, 1688–1800* (Manchester, 1935).
13. J. Smail, *Merchants, Markets and Manufacture: The English Wool Textile Industry in the Eighteenth Century* (1999).
14. J. Hoppit, *A Land of Liberty? England 1689–1727* (Oxford, 2000), pp. 324–5.
15. M. Berg, *The Age of Manufactures, 1700–1820* (Oxford, 1985).
16. S. Schwartz, 'Economic change in north-east Lancashire, *c.* 1660–1760', *Transactions of the Historic Society of Lancashire and Cheshire*, 144 (1994), pp. 47–93.

5

Transport and trade

Infrastructure was crucial to agricultural and industrial development. Without effective transport systems and viable financial structures, regions could not benefit from the diffusion of new methods or from new demands. Economic activities had different requirements, and the spread of competition brought by improvements in infrastructure did not benefit all, but most of the country was affected by changes in communications and by improvements in banking facilities.

Whether in terms of the movement of people or of goods, of transport with speed or in bulk, of regular or of intermittent links, poor communications were a serious problem. They magnified the effects of distance and imposed high costs on economic exchange. Land communications were generally slow, variable and unreliable to an extent that it is difficult for modern readers, accustomed to modelled roads and mechanised transportation, to appreciate.

The quality of the roads reflected the local terrain, in particular drainage and soil type. Road construction and maintenance techniques were of limited effectiveness in marshy regions or in areas with a high water table, such as the heavy clays of the English Midlands, South Essex and the Vale of Berkeley in Gloucestershire. Travelling into Cornwall in August 1702, John Evelyn found 'dirty or stony lanes'.[1]

Mountainous terrain increased the need for draught animals and limited the speed of transport. The need to travel up or down added greatly to distance, and thus increased the time and cost of travel. Even in lowland areas, a small hill often affected road and rail routes. Steep climbs limited the value of wheeled vehicles. Furthermore, many mountains were difficult to cross. It was not until the nineteenth century that advances in transport engineering, especially bridge-building and the use of dynamite, nitro-glycerine and gelignite in tunnel construction, helped overcome some of the problems posed by the terrain.

Marshy areas were particularly hazardous, as were fords. Between Chester and Hawarden in 1698, Celia Fiennes 'crossed over the marshes, which is hazardous to strangers'. On her return from Wales, she

> forded over the Dee when the tide was out ... the sands are here so loose that
> the tides do move them ... many persons that have known the fords well, that

have come a year or half a year after, if they venture on their former knowledge have been overwhelmed in the ditches made by the sands, which are deep
enough to swallow up a coach or wagon.[2]

The roads of North Wales were a major obstacle to moving goods speedily from
southern and midland England to Ireland. The coastal town of Conwy incurred a
stunted local economy for most of this period as travellers to Holyhead took an
inland route rather than be conveyed across the Conwy estuary by boat. More
generally, poor roads led to long and unpredictable journeys that strained individuals, damaged goods and tied up scarce capital in goods in transit. A wagon
drawn by four horses pulling 4,000 lbs could rarely cover more than 20 miles
daily. Poorly-constructed roads led often to a reliance on light carts with only two
horses. This increased the number of carts necessary to move a given load, with
resulting costs in manpower and forage. Still more often, burdens were limited to
280 lbs or so, which could be carried in panniers on a horse or mule, against the
1,120 lbs which could be drawn by a single horse over good roads. The construction of good roads could therefore offer a fourfold increase in loads.

Pack-horses were still very common in Britain's advancing areas, even in the
1800s, and were even more so elsewhere, and this contributed greatly to a ubiquity of horses that is all too easy to forget. Pack-horses represented a decision not
to rely on wheels. Wheeled vehicles were not widely used in many areas. It was
not until the late 1760s that the first coach in Falmouth, the most important
Cornish port, was recorded. Even when roads were improved, there were still
major problems. Wagons and carts often provided merchandise only inadequate
shelter, and the methods of packing and of moving heavy goods on and off carts
were primitive.

Due to limitations in transportation methods, droving was the principal way
of moving livestock, although it was both slow and the animals used up much
of their energy on the move. Cattle from Scotland and Wales and turkeys (shod
with tarred feet) from East Anglia all walked to London. Other settlements were
similarly served so that at any one time large numbers of animals were on the
move.

The ability and determination of local communities to keep the roads in good
repair was important because, under the Statute for Mending of Highways of
1555, each parish in England and Wales was responsible for road upkeep.
However, as the resistance of the surface, usually loose and rough, to bad weather
or heavy use was limited, there was a need for frequent repair. Expensive in
money and manpower, this duty was generally not adequately carried out, certainly not to the standards required by heavy through-traffic, let alone for any
increase in traffic. Nevertheless, it would be mistaken to ignore the extent of the
pre-turnpike road system.

There was no technological or engineering innovation to transform the road surface. Because narrow wheels dug ruts, commentators from the 1750s advocated
broader wheels for carriages and wagons, and an Act of 1753 stated that wheel rims
on wagons had to be at least nine inches wide. In the 1770s, James Sharp pressed

for rollers sixteen inches wide, rather than wheels, claiming that they would consolidate the road surface. Despite parliamentary support, such rollers were impracticable as they were cumbersome and expensive. There was no significant improvement until the early nineteenth century when the Scots John McAdam and Thomas Telford improved road surfaces with new construction techniques.

Instead, in the eighteenth century, major road improvements occurred as a result of organisational changes, specifically the role of turnpike trusts. These were bodies authorised by Parliament to raise capital in order to repair and build roads and to charge travellers to these ends. The capital was raised as loans which were to be repaid through income from tolls. Initially, trusts were given powers and responsibilities for twenty-one years, but this was subsequently extended. The decision to establish trusts reflected confidence in the financial return, and thus in the economic prospects, of transport links. The availability of investment capital was crucial. In many respects, therefore, turnpike trusts were a consequence of economic health and a testimony to a confidence in the future that came from local communities. As later with canals and railways, not all turnpike schemes were implemented, while some that were were not effective. Nevertheless, turnpiked roads benefited from more expenditure than their counterparts, and were therefore generally better, and often far better.

The co-operation of parliamentary authorisation and local charge-levying bodies, reflected the absence of a national road policy, let alone a transport ministry. Unlike elsewhere in Europe, for example France, Prussia, Russia and Spain, the government played only a small direct role in road construction. This role was particular to the Scottish Highlands, where the army built about 250 miles of road between 1726 and 1738 to aid a rapid response to any Jacobite rising. The possibility of creating turnpike trusts was thus a permissive national policy, not a prescriptive one. Rather than following some master plan, the road system came in large part to reflect the degree of dynamism of individual trusts, and the ability of particular routes to produce revenue. The last was essentially a consequence of the strength of the regional economy and the role of the route in intra-regional communications. Although trusts reflected local initiatives, a national turnpike system was created, but this was due to commercial opportunity in defining necessary and profitable links, not national planning.

The desire of local merchants and manufacturers for growth was important, but turnpikes were not just commercial ventures: the trusts were dominated by noblemen and the squirearchy, and the turnpikes were seen as a form of social improvement. Parliament oversaw the system through renewal and amendment Acts that reflected the strength of local interests.

The first turnpike trust was created in 1663, and the first section of the London–Norwich road was turnpiked under an act of 1696. Early trusts dealt largely with repairs, rather than the construction of new roads. Many trusts, such as the Bath Trust, which was established in 1707, had considerable success in improving the situation.

By 1750, a sizeable network of new turnpikes, radiating from London, had been created. London and north-west England were well linked, with the road to

Chester and both roads to Manchester turnpiked for most of their length. A spur from the Chester road had been turnpiked to Shrewsbury in 1725. By 1750, three routes from Yorkshire to Manchester were also turnpiked, as were the routes from London to Bath, Canterbury and Portsmouth. In Lincolnshire, the Great North Road was turnpiked from Grantham northwards in 1726 and from Grantham to Stamford in 1739; the year in which a trust was also authorised for the road from Lincoln to Baumber.

Nevertheless, compared with what was to come, the 1730s and 1740s were decades of limited progress. For example, at that point, the already bad communication system in Wales arising from the limited nature of inland waterways looked as though it would receive no improvement by road. In contrast, there was substantial expansion in the 1750s and 1760s, so that by 1770, when there were 15,000 miles of turnpikes in England, most of it was within 12.5 miles of one. After 1751 it became easier to obtain Turnpike Acts.

By 1770, a network of turnpikes radiated from major provincial centres.[3] Birmingham benefited from the convergence of improved routes: the Bromsgrove (1726), Hagley (1753) and Dudley (1760) turnpikes. The first from Chichester was begun in 1749, and by 1779 the city was the junction of four turnpikes. This led to an increase in overland trade from West Sussex to London, and a relative decline in the longer sea route. The first Devon trust, the Exeter Trust, was established in 1753, and was rapidly followed by many others, leading to major improvements. The first in Cornwall, to turnpike the Falmouth–Truro road, was in 1754. In 1756–65, thirteen new turnpike trusts were formed for Lincolnshire and two others were enlarged. The first road in north Lincolnshire to be turnpiked was that from Lincoln to Barton on Humber in 1765. This was part of a system for north Lincolnshire laid out in 1765, that also saw the turnpiking of side-roads to Caistor and Melton Ross, as well as of a road from Louth to Gainsborough and then into Nottinghamshire, that crossed the Lincoln–Barton road. Following an Act of 1764, two turnpikes improved the road links to the East Shropshire coalfield. Most roads between Norwich and rural Norfolk were turnpiked between 1760 and 1800.

Improved roads were not restricted to England. Important routes in Wales included Hereford to Brecon (1757), and on to Haverfordwest (1787), and Cardiff to Neath, and on to Carmarthen. In Montgomeryshire, a turnpike trust was authorised in 1769, as part of a route from Newtown to Aberystwyth, and the first turnpike was in use from the early 1770s.

In Ireland, an Act of 1729 established turnpike trusts, and they constructed a number of new arterial routes in the 1730s–50s, while local landlords sponsored a widespread turnpike system in the linen region of Ulster. Aside from turnpikes, there were important legislative initiatives that created the possibility for better roads in Ireland. A Road Act of 1765 allowed county grand juries to levy a charge per acre on all farming households for the repair of roads and bridges, or the construction of new ones, which had to be at least 21 feet wide. This helped lead to a major expansion and improvement of the rural road network and a welcome measure of standardisation. Further Acts in 1771–2 allowed parishes to raise an extra tax for roads and grand juries to raise funds to construct roads through unimproved regions.

The Irish road system, however, was worse than that in Britain, with less extensive turnpiking than in England, while roads in Scotland and Wales were not as good as the English system. The development of turnpikes in Scotland was slower than in England and Wales. The first trust in north-east Scotland was not formed until 1795. Throughout the British Isles, many roads that were not turn-piked, for example those on the Isle of Man, remained inadequate. There were deficiencies in many parts of England. For example, north Devon had poor land links and was largely dependent on shipping. In his play *She Stoops to Conquer* (1773), Oliver Goldsmith wrote of a rural journey 'it is a damned long, dark, boggy, dirty, dangerous way'.

From the mid-eighteenth century, the road system was further enhanced by a marked increase in the number of bridges, the most marked for several centuries. Stone bridges replaced wooden ones and ferries, improving the load-bearing capacity and reliability of the system. Existing bridges were widened, and new and wider bridges erected with large spans. The importance of London and the availability of resources was shown with the building of bridges there and nearby. Several replaced ferries. Across the Thames, bridges were built at Datchet (1706), Putney (1729), Westminster (1738–50), Walton (1750), Hampton Court (1753), Kew (1758–9), Blackfriars (1769), Battersea (1771–2) and Richmond (1774–7).

Bridge building was not restricted to the London area, although the second half of the century was far more important than the first. In Cambridge, the Great Bridge was rebuilt in stone in 1754. The Old Bath Bridge was rebuilt in 1754, and Pulteney Bridge added between 1769 and 1774. A wide three-arched bridge over the Avon was opened at Bristol in 1768, while a stone bridge built at Stockton between 1764 and 1768 replaced ferries and fording points and supplanted Yarm Bridge as the lowest bridging point on the Tees. In 1774, a new crossing over the Exe provided a bridging point below Exeter. No new bridges had been built across the Severn between 1540 and 1772, but, thereafter, six more were built by 1850, including at Stourport (1775) and the Iron Bridge at Coalbrookdale (1779, opened for traffic 1781).[4] The New Bridge, the second across the Clyde in Glasgow, was built in Glasgow in the 1760s, and a new bridge at Worcester in 1780. In Carrickfergus in Ulster, the wooden bridge was replaced in stone in 1740.

However, many bridges did not come until after the period closed; for example the bridges over the Trent at Gainsborough (1790–1) and Dunham (1830–2). As a consequence, ferries remained important, for example over the Trent north of Newark, or the Witham between Lincoln and Boston. They also remained very important across estuaries, such as the Humber and the Tamar. This led to a continued focus on earlier routes, and thus transport nodes, that should not be forgotten when new developments are discussed. Ferries across the Bristol Channel – from Sully near Cardiff to Uphill in Somerset and from Beachley to Aust – continued to move cattle and other products. Many settlements were best approached by sea. Water – both the sea and inland waters – had far more of an impact on people's lives than is the case today. Many towns that now lack quays were ports.

Furthermore, where bridges already existed they were often poorly maintained. Alongside lists such as those above that suggest steady improvement, it is worth noting episodes that lead towards a different conclusion. Thus, the group of bridges over the watercourses of the River Otter at Fenny Bridges on the major route east of Exeter, were reported as in a poor state of repair to the Quarter Sessions in 1704. The parishioners of Gittisham were able to show that the parish was too poor to carry out the necessary repairs, and when the Sessions provided £15, requests from other parishes for their bridges led the court to rescind the money. A report was ordered, but none was made until 1711 when the court was told that a nearby landowner, Lady Kirkham, had conveyed nearby land in trust to provide funds for bridge repairs. However, the trustees declared that the profits from the land were insufficient and claimed to be responsible for the bridges in Feniton parish and not in Gittisham, an interpretation that was challenged. The court took the charity into its hands, but it was not until 1723 that the trustees provided the accounts ordered in 1714. Deciding that they had money in hand that should have been used for bridge repairs, the magistrates ordered the trustees to pay it into court, but the trustees refused and the administration of the trust was not settled by the High Court of Chancery until 1750, the year in which Dr Richard Pococke recorded being delayed several hours by the road flooding. A new brick arch bridge was built at Fenny in 1769, but it had to be rebuilt in 1809 after complaints in 1797 and an indictment of the county in 1806 for not keeping the bridge in repair.[5]

This could be repeated elsewhere for bridges, roads and other transport improvements. Such problems have to be recalled rather than the uncomplicated account of progress that is too often offered. The focus on action after 1750 is also instructive.

Allowing for deficiencies, it is still appropriate to stress change. Within towns, access and routes were improved, although not with the purposefulness that was to characterise the Victorians. In order to improve access, Nottingham's last surviving medieval gate was pulled down in 1743, and the North Gate in Exeter in 1769. Three new openings were made in Exeter's city walls.

Better links were used to transport both people and goods, and it became easier to move between major centres. Travel was made faster by the cross-breeding of fast Arab horses, while further improvements came from the replacement of leather straps by steel coach springs and the introduction of elliptical springs. The first coach service between Limerick and Dublin was established in the 1750s, although only as a summer service. Travel was also made easier by the improvement of facilities. Old inns were rebuilt or extended, and new inns were built.

There were very important improvements in carrying services. The first regular Norwich to London coach service taking less than a day started in 1761, and by 1783 there were 25 departures a week from Norwich to London, as well as two departures of stage wagons. The same year, about 150 places within 30 miles were visited at least once weekly by a carrier from Norwich. Thus, the improved carrying system both served to link regional centres with each other (and with the metropolis), and also strengthened their position within the region.

The increased speed and frequency of deliveries also improved the integration of production and consumption, and furthered the development of the market; it became easier to dispatch salesmen, samples, catalogues, orders and replacements. The development of the turnpikes was central to the creation of regular long-distance horse-drawn wagon services, which also benefited from the construction of bridges. Whereas Kendal in Cumbria had been served by regular packhorse trains moving goods as far as Bristol, London and Southampton from the fifteenth century, in the eighteenth horsedrawn wagon services with their greater capacity for moving goods took over long-distance and regional routes to and from Cumbria. Similarly, wagon access to Liverpool began in the 1730s and a direct coach service thence to London in 1760.

These improvements did not prevent a major development in water transport. The difficulties and costs of road transport had for long helped to ensure that much was moved by river or sea, or both. Water routes were particularly favourable for the movement of heavy or bulky goods, for which road transport was inadequate and expensive. Thus, the Severn was the major north–south route for freight in the West Midlands, and was particularly important for the movement downriver of coal from the East Shropshire coalfield. Goods carried upstream included products from outside Britain, such as wine, Baltic timber and, from further afield, tea, sugar, spices, tobacco and citrus fruit, most of which had been transhipped at Bristol (although Gloucester was also a transhipment point), as well as those from elsewhere in Britain. Tributaries, such as the Warwickshire Avon, extended river systems.

However, the river system had many deficiencies. Many rivers were not navigable, transport was often only easy downstream, rivers did not always supply the necessary links, and many were obstructed by mills and weirs. The un- or poorly-controlled flow of water ensured that spring thaws and autumn floods could bring problems, by sending rivers into spate. Conversely, in the summer, they could be too shallow to use; this was a particular problem in the upper parts of rivers. In the North Riding of Yorkshire, the navigable rivers – the Tees, Ouse and Derwent – were all on its boundaries, while the Swale, Esk and Rye were too swift, shallow or liable to flood for navigation. As a result, lead from the western dales had to be moved overland to the Tees ports, an expensive process.

The response to such problems – the canalisation of rivers and the construction of canals – represented a determined attempt to alter the environment and to make it operate for the benefit of man. As with the turnpikes, and again unlike elsewhere in Europe, private enterprise and finance were crucial. The result was a costly and inflexible transport system, but it cut the cost of moving bulky goods, increased the comparative economic advantage of particular areas or interests, and was therefore actively supported.

Until the 1750s, when a period of canal construction began, the improvement of rivers took precedence, with peaks of activity in the late 1690s and in 1719–21. The improvement in the Aire and Calder navigation to Leeds and Halifax in 1699–1700 was a major step. The Yare was made navigable for quite large ships between Great Yarmouth and Norwich, helping Norfolk's grain exports and the movement of coal from north east England to Norwich. Work on the Mersey to improve navigation to Manchester began in 1724, the Avon was fully navigable between Bath and Bristol by 1727, the Douglas between Wigan and the sea was opened to navigation in 1742, and improvements in the Weaver helped Cheshire's economy. The Fossdyke between Lincoln and the Trent, built by the Romans, was restored in 1740–4. The improvement of the Witham to Lincoln was largely complete by 1770.

There were also setbacks. The Avon was improved from 1675 to enable commercial navigation from Salisbury to the sea at Christchurch, but the link was not possible after 1715 and by 1744 two unsuccessful attempts had been made to re-establish the route.[6] Aside from work on rivers themselves, for example dredging, towing paths were constructed along them to permit the replacement of human bow haulers by horses.

Canal construction was more impressive than river improvement because it created completely new links. It was also expensive, as large numbers of 'navigators' or navvies had to dig canals by hand. As a result, the construction of canals can be seen as a response to deficiencies in existing transport arrangements, to powerful new demands, and to the availability of considerable resources. Landlocked counties found their relative position transformed, while the movement of bulk goods by new links created important new economic opportunities. The first canal in the South West in this period, opened east of St Austell in about 1720, was designed to serve clay pits, although it was only short and ended in 1731 when the tunnel collapsed. Far more significantly, the Sankey Brook Navigation, completed in 1757, carried coal from St Helens to Liverpool, and stimulated the development of coal-consuming industries on Merseyside and the expansion of Cheshire's salt industry, which depended on coal-fired salt pans. The Duke of Bridgewater had a canal completed in 1763 to move coal from his Worsley mines to nearby Manchester. Two years later, Wedgwood turned to James Brindley, who had made his reputation planning this canal, to link the Trent and the Mersey. Brindley did this with the 'Grand Trunk Canal'. The building of the 46 mile long Staffordshire and Worcester Canal from the Trent and Mersey Canal between 1766 and 1772 added a link to the Birmingham Canal and to the Severn at the new port of Stourport, so that Staffordshire's coal, iron and pottery could be readily transported to the major English cities. The system was amplified with additional links and spurs, for example the Dudley and Stourbridge canals opened in 1779 which improved links between the Severn and the Black Country.[7] Aside from the development of canal systems, there was also the digging of individual canals to create or improve particular links. For example, 1770 saw the opening of the Louth Canal, which made Louth a port.

Canals were important in developing inter-regional links, especially between the West Midlands and Lancashire, and cutting transport costs. The industries benefited from cheaper transport costs and more reliable links than French counterparts. The potential for regional specialisation increased, because regions that could produce goods cheaply were now better able to compete in areas with higher-cost local production. This was to be crucial to economic development, because division of labour was only effective with a high volume of production and this required a large market.

However, it would be foolish to neglect the limitations of the canal system in this period. The network was sparse, fragmented, and especially limited in Scotland, Wales and Ireland. Bar an abortive attempt by George Dixon to construct a canal on Cockfield Fell in the 1760s, the North East was scarcely affected. In these areas, the terrain was unsuitable for canals. After the failure of the short canal near St Austell in 1731, none was opened in the South West until 1794, although such points underrate interest in new links in the intervening period, and the sense of profitable change that this reflected or created. For example Beavis Wood, Town Clerk of Tiverton, recorded on 24 October 1768:

> A subscription is set on foot here to raise a sum of money to bring down Mr Brindley to take a survey of the country in order to make a navigable canal through part of Somerset and down by way of Taunton and Tiverton or Cullompton to Exeter or Topsham. Subscriptions have also been opened for this purpose at Exeter, Cullompton and Uffculm and other parts of this neighbourbood ... people in general (gentlemen and others) seem in earnest and to believe such a scheme very practicable and advantageous.[8]

The reliance on subscriptions for the survey reflected the voluntarist, rather than governmental, nature of local activism. A canal craze or mania did not hit much of the country until the 1790s.

Construction problems included the provision of an adequate water supply and preventing leaks. As later with the railways, numerous canals that were planned were never completed and many other schemes were never even pursued. Others took much longer than had been intended. Due to financial problems, the Forth and Clyde Canal, begun in 1768, was not finished until 1790, although it reached the outskirts of Glasgow in 1777. The transport of grain to the city was one of the purposes of the canal.

Many major canals were only built or completed after 1783. This was particularly true in Ireland, although the Newry Navigation, linking Carlingford Lough with the River Banna at Portadown, and opening up links between mid-Ulster and Dublin, in order to take coal to the capital from east Tyrone, was built in 1731-42. This system was expanded when the Newry ship canal was finished in 1769, making Newry an important port. The Tyrone navigation, finished in 1787, linked Coalisland to the river Blackwater, and the Lagan navigation from Belfast to Lough Neagh was completed in the 1780s.

A focus on canals and turnpikes has led to a misleading lack of attention to coastal trade and unturnpiked roads. Coastal trade was important for a whole series of local and regional economies. It also grew with the developing economy. For example, Cornish, Irish and Anglesey copper was brought by sea to the works near Swansea, while Bristol received copper for smelting from Anglesey and Cornwall, china clay from Cornwall, and iron, coal and naval timber from the Forest of Dean. Ports were also developed for exporting raw materials. Slate was dispatched from Snowdonia via Bangor, Caernarvon, and Port Penrhyn, which was developed by

Richard Pennant, 1st Lord Penrhyn, who was responsible for the systematic working of local slate deposits from 1765. Mineral owners developed ports in order to ship coal, for example in Cumberland: the Curwens at Harrington and Workington, the Lowthers at Whitehaven, and the Senhouses at Maryport, which was founded in 1749. Milford Haven was developed to serve Pembrokeshire.

The widespread improvement in docks and harbour facilities benefited domestic as well as international trade. For example, an Act of Parliament of 1717 established the River Wear Commissioners in order to develop harbour facilities on the lower Wear. In place of a hazardous anchorage made difficult and dangerous by rocks, sandbanks, the passage of a difficult bar, and exposure to north-easterly gales, came buoying, dredging, lighting, pier-building and controls over the dumping of ballast. The result was a much-improved harbour entrance and navigable channel that permitted a major growth in trade with the Wear, and thus aided the development of Sunderland. This was an important example of what could be achieved, and also indicated the importance of a legislative framework. Another Act, of 1749, enabled the new Port Commission of Lancaster to develop St George's Quay (1750–5), and this was followed by a Custom House in 1764 and the New Quay in 1767. The Port Commission, in which slave traders played an active role, also promoted Lancaster's representation in commercial issues of national importance.[9]

Nevertheless, there was scant improvement in the condition of marine transport. It still remained heavily dependent on the weather. The seasonal variation of insurance rates reflected the vulnerability of wind-powered wooden ships, which had not reached their mid-nineteenth century levels of design efficiency and seaworthiness. By modern standards, they lacked deep keels. Sea travel was very slow compared with what it was to become the following century. However, it was the cheapest method for the movement of goods, and the sea brought together regions such as south-western Scotland and eastern Ireland, whose road links to their own hinterlands were poor. Inland towns might be most accessible via their nearest ports rather than by long-distance overland routes.

The east coast, where Captain Cook acquired his nautical skills, was an important route, especially for the shipment of coal from Newcastle to London and intermediate ports such as King's Lynn and Great Yarmouth, the ports for East Anglia. The average annual amount of coal shipped from the Tyne rose from just over 400,000 tons in the 1660s to well over 600,000 by 1730–1, and to nearly 800,000 tons in the 1750s. Seventy per cent of this coal went to London in 1682, and King's Lynn and Great Yarmouth took half of the rest.

The Irish Sea also formed an economic zone held together by marine links based on major ports, such as Belfast, Bristol, Dublin, Lancaster, Liverpool, Milford Haven, Wexford and Whitehaven, as well as now-forgotten or tiny ports, such as Parkgate in Wirral,[10] and Aberaevon. These links provided crucial supplies. Ireland's fuel shortage was met by coal from Cumbria and, to a lesser extent, Ayrshire and Lancashire.

Non-turnpike roads were also important, crucially so in local economies. In the British Isles as a whole, however, although Arthur Young's works suggest that even local roads were improving from the 1770s, much of the dense network of local routes changed little during the century, in quality, direction or use. Many roads essentially remained bridleways. When new roads were constructed they usually followed existing routes.

Overall, changes in transport were limited during the period, certainly compared to the following century. The balance between land and sea transport did not alter significantly. Nevertheless, as indicated, there was important change, and this affected the rest of the economy. The reduction in transport costs helped to increase and extend consumption and markets. These benefits were fully understood and encouraged investment. New and improved transport links required large amounts of capital.

TRADE

Developing international trade also posed challenges for the transport system. The volume of British trade rose significantly, leading some scholars to refer to a commercial revolution, and Britain became the major trans-oceanic trading nation, dominating the North Atlantic trade as well as becoming the leading trader to India and China. Average annual exports rose from £4.1 million in the 1660s to £6.9 m in 1720, £12.7 m in 1750, £14.3 m in 1770, and £18.9 m in 1790, and that during a period of only modest inflation. Imports rose from £6 million in 1700 to £6.1 m in 1720, £7.8 m in 1750, £12.2 m in 1770 and £17.4 m in 1790. These figures exclude the extensive contraband commerce imported by smugglers, who tended to focus on high-dutiable commodities such as alcohol and tea. There were also contraband exports, such as wool, although they were less important. Given the difficulties that merchants encountered, including political disruption, natural disasters, such as typhoons, the dishonesty of ships' captains and agents, difficulties in ensuring and receiving payment, and the weakness of legal redress, the growth in trade was particularly impressive.

More important than the aggregate growth in trade was the diversification of markets and products. The relative importance both of woollen exports and of trade with nearby areas of Europe declined, while that of oceanic trade increased. Average annual exports to North America rose from £0.27 million in 1701–5 to over £2 million in 1786–90.

Trade increased Britain's world presence. British goods were exported across large areas of the world. When Peter Macskásy, a Transylvanian landowner but not an aristocrat, died, in 1712, his effects included 'fourteen measures of English cloth with collars of marten ... a fine saddle blanket made of English cloth ... a pair of London summer gloves, and a lined black English mantle'.[11]

Thanks in large part to the protective system created by the Navigation Acts, British-owned shipping tonnage grew appreciably: English shipping tonnage rose from 340,000 in 1686 to 421,000 in 1751, 523,000 in 1764, 608,000 in 1775, and 752,000 in 1786; largely due to more rather than bigger ships. The number of Glasgow's ships rose from 30 in the late 1680s to 70 by the 1730s.

The expansion of trade helped to transform the economy. Exports helped to raise the demand that led to technological developments and diffusion. Trade encouraged industry. It also helped ensure that the British economy benefited from comparative advantages. Thanks to imports, industry, for example, was able to benefit from Baltic and North American timber, hemp and iron. Trade led to the integration of numerous areas and groups into a global economy, as suppliers or consumers. It also helped win support for Union in Scotland and Ireland.

Ideas of free trade had little currency until the end of the century, Adam Smith's *Inquiry into the Nature and Causes of the Wealth of Nations* only appearing in 1776. Economic regulation promised government protectionism and this was further encouraged by the notion that the volume of trade was essentially constant, so that an increase in that of one power would necessarily lead to a reduction elsewhere, and also by the weakness of currency mechanisms which led to a stress on bullion and therefore on a favourable balance of trade that would maintain bullion inflows. Economic attitudes thus looked back to the protectionism of seventeenth-century mercantilism, and not forward to nineteenth-century free trade. Trade entailed competition with foreign powers. This was a matter not just of pessimism about the prospects of economic growth, but also of an inherently competitive approach to trade and the economy.

The government sought to create a protected home market, to restrict imports, and to encourage a positive balance of trade in manufactured products. The export of raw materials, such as raw wool, and thus sheep, was prohibited, as was that of textile machinery and the emigration of artisans. Manufactured imports were restricted or prohibited, for example silks and printed calicoes in 1700, and all manufactured silks and velvets in 1766, a great advantage to the British silk industry. The 1721 ban on the wearing of imported printed fabrics, passed in order to protect native manufactures of wool and silk stuffs from the competition of Indian calicoes imported by the East India Company, stimulated the growth of a British cotton industry. This issue continued to embitter relations between the Company and British manufacturers throughout the period. As yet, British producers did not enjoy the advantage over Indian rivals that machinisation was to bring the following century, but they were able to profit from printing the imported fabrics.[12]

The Irish and colonial economies were regulated and restricted in order to make them assist, not rival, that of Britain. The Cattle Acts of 1666–7 hit Irish exports until they were suspended in 1758–9, giving the Scots an advantage in English markets. Irish trade was dominated by the British market, which absorbed about 75 per cent of Irish exports in the late-eighteenth century, but the terms of this trade were set in London. Irish exports of wool and woollen textiles to foreign and colonial markets were banned in 1699, although the percentage of Irish exports going to the New World colonies, as a percentage of total Irish exports, rose from about 6 per cent in 1698 to nearly 20 per cent in 1784. Nevertheless, most of this trade depended on English intermediaries and Irish expatriates, especially in London. Irish manufacturing was increasingly affected by British exports as its largely domestic and quasi-domestic structure was unable to compete with cheaper and better-finished goods produced by new methods. The Irish silk industry collapsed between 1775 and 1783. Colonial trade and industry were also affected by regulation. In 1750, the making of steel, the refining of iron and the manufacture of finished articles from iron were prohibited in the North American colonies.

Economic interests in general supported regulation, especially protectionism. Smugglers, the major practitioners of free-market initiatives were a surreptitious, not a vocal, group, their services used by many of the elite, including Walpole, but their profits dependent on protectionism and their activities widely decried on the grounds that they purveyed foreign non-essentials, such as brandy and lace, and exported bullion.

The rising importance of trade entailed the greater significance of merchants and mercantile lobbies. This ensured that the appropriate organisation for trade remained controversial. Privileged companies that possessed monopolistic rights in particular areas, such as the Royal Africa Company, the Hudson's Bay Company and the East India Company, aroused anger in those excluded from their benefits, principally the merchants of ports outside London, which were known as outports. In 1698, hostility to the East India Company led to the establishment of a New East India Company, but the two united in 1708. In 1752, the Steadfast Society of Bristol agreed to spend up to £200 in lobbying Parliament against the monopoly of the Levant Company in the trade with Turkey.[13] Some critics claimed that these companies were too concerned with their profits to risk them by expansion, either by increasing the volume of trade, and thus lowering prices, or by adding to their overseas territorial interests and thus increasing costs. However, such companies operated in areas where a measure of organisation was required either because, as in India, West Africa and northern Canada, bases, often fortified, had to be supported, or, as with Turkey and Russia, trade was heavily dependent on negotiations with a foreign power. Many efforts were made to break the trading monopoly of the East India Company, but the Indian trade was not thrown open till 1813 and the Chinese till 1833.

Most British trade was not controlled by such companies. This was as true of trade which saw major expansion, such as that with the Thirteen Colonies that became the USA, the West Indies, and Portugal, as of trade with areas where growth was less spectacular, especially north-west Europe. Government-backed regulation, which focused on protectionism and the Navigation Acts, was generally supported, even if particular details might arouse opposition. Ministerial policy and parliamentary decisions were influenced greatly by mercantile pressure groups. The 1726 Act against importing foreign plate was drawn up by the Goldsmiths Company, and the government sought the advice of the Russia Company on the progress of the Anglo-Russian commercial negotiations in 1733–4, which led in 1734 to a trade treaty. In the 1720s and 1730s, Walpole's personal links with the directors of the major chartered trading companies and of the Bank of England were close, and helped to explain his sound grasp of financial matters and his ability to manage the government's fiscal interests. They also played a major role in enabling these groups to influence the ministry. Other mercantile groups, such as the merchants trading to the West Indies, did not enjoy the same links with the government. However, their pressure-group tactics, a well-organised petitioning and propaganda campaign, were very successful in persuading Parliament to pass a series of measures in their favour, such as the Molasses Act of 1733 and to influence other legislation such as the Sugar Act of 1764.[14]

Lobbying reflected the sense of Britain as an economic space, and also the extent to which Parliament and print were part of the same process. In 1769, George Chalmers wrote to George Grenville MP seeking his support, and also throwing light on links between industrial and landed interests.

> We are to make an application to Parliament this winter for several new matters regarding the table linen which is a staple in this part of the kingdom ... I have much personal interest in one branch of the application viz the laying of an additional duty on foreign diapers or table linen having an estate here surrounding Dumferline which manufactures more of that species than any other place in Great Britain or Ireland ... The principal manufacturers assure me that they are in a condition to supply a great part of the English consumption if they have proper encouragement and have no doubt but the laying on of a small additional duty on foreign diapers will at least double or triple the value of the manufactures of this place ... I shall ... send you sometime before the House [of Commons] meets a state in print of what they propose to apply for.[15]

Commercial developments led to a new economic geography of Britain in which proximity to the Atlantic was most important. Initially, this benefited Bristol, especially after some of the regulatory framework that had maintained London's control over certain trades was dismantled. The freeing of the African trade from the control of the Royal Africa Company in 1698 legalised the position of interlopers. This helped Bristol merchants develop the triangular trade in which they took goods to West Africa and used them to purchase slaves who were then taken to the West Indies and North America. Textiles, alcohol, metal goods, guns and gunpowder were exported to Africa and offered on credit in order to obtain slaves. Private enterprise was crucial to the growth of the slave trade.

In 1725, Bristol ships carried about 17,000 slaves and between 1727 and 1769 thirty-nine slavers were built there. Bristol's mercantile standing and prosperity were reflected in the rebuilding of the Council House in 1704 and in the New Exchange of 1743 which was designed by John Wood the Elder, the leading architect of elegant gentility in Bath. By 1750, Bristol had replaced Norwich as the second most populous city in England.

However, although the volume of Bristol's shipping rose, its relative importance declined. The city suffered from congestion in the docks, a lack of industry in the hinterland, entrepreneurial failure in the tobacco and slave trades, and an over-specialisation in the profitable sugar trade. Bristol's trade was not sufficiently linked to export industries that would probably have given a greater boost to industrial and demographic growth in its hinterland and, as a result, foreign and domestic demand were not effectively linked. More specifically, Bristol's trade was hit by the War of American Independence, especially as it was more exposed to French privateers than its principal rivals, Liverpool and Glasgow.[16]

Glasgow increasingly dominated the import of tobacco and Liverpool the slave, American and Newfoundland trades. By 1752, Liverpool had 88 slavers, with a combined capacity of over 25,000 slaves. In 1750–79, there were about 1,909 slave trade sailings from Liverpool, compared to 624 from Bristol and 869 from London.[17] Liverpool also had better port facilities, not least the sole wet dock outside London. The Old Dock was followed by the Salthouse Dock (1753), St George's (1771), and Duke's (1773). Lancaster and Whitehaven also benefited from the growth of the Atlantic economy.

In contrast, inland towns that lacked good communications were very badly placed to benefit from the growth in foreign trade, and some, such as Athlone and Hereford, stagnated badly. Even long-established inland river ports, such as Gloucester, could not compete with sea ports.

By supplying new products or providing existing ones at a more attractive price or in new forms, oceanic trade both satisfied and stimulated consumer demand. In 1702, John Evelyn had at Falmouth 'a small bowl of punch made with Brazil sugar'.[18] This process was not restricted to ports, but was spread by mercantile activity that responded to markets encouraged by both demand and emulation. If the falling prices and greater availability of trans-oceanic goods such as sugar or calicoes, were significant, so also were the varied means, including the development of the press and other advertising media, by which fashions could be encouraged and retail services publicised. Publications spread news of new fashions and encouraged the idea that it was better to drink tea or coffee than alcohol. In order to boost the industry, Queen Caroline encouraged by Jonathan Swift wore Irish linens. She also tried the same with silk from Georgia.

Trade interacted with changing domestic demand, especially the growth in consumption of goods designed to stimulate: groceries such as sugar, tobacco, and caffeine drinks: tea, coffee and chocolate. As none of these were 'necessary', this was very much consumerism. Foreign trade was central to what has been termed the 'consumer revolution'. From 1717, English ships began a regular cycle of trade direct to China in order to obtain tea, and, whereas in the 1720s almost nine million pounds of tea were landed, by the 1750s more than 37 million pounds of tea came to Britain, the price falling roughly by a half over that period.[19] The diet was changed by the import of sugar, which was added to jam, cakes, biscuits, chocolate and medicine. Between 1663 and 1775, the consumption of muscovado sugar in England and Wales increased twentyfold, while British rum consumption rose from the 207 gallons imported in 1698 to an annual average of two million gallons in 1771–5.[20] Such increases led to great demand for shipping.

Critics decried what they presented as the enervating effects of luxury and the emphasis upon consumption rather than conduct. Criticising tea consumption and smuggling, Joseph Danvers told the House of Commons in 1734: 'I wish we would or could be made all to return to the good old way of our ancestors, in breakfasting upon good English ale and bread and cheese.'[21] This was a fruitless cause, but Danvers was correct to note a major change in attitudes. Earlier,

Addison and Steele had presented the spice trade as a foreign threat. Spices were seen by critics as both symbolic of, and a means to, a luxuriousness that threatened national order and the moderation that was held up as a virtue.

Consumerism related to things as well as stimulants. Tea and coffee had to be prepared and drunk from utensils, such as teapots, although the geographical and social spread of such novelties varied. Hot drink utensils were appearing in Kentish inventories by 1685, but not in Staffordshire until 1725.[22] The rooms where tea and coffee drinking occurred were more likely than hitherto to have clocks, curtains and other goods. Wallpaper became fashionable, carpets more common, and furniture more plentiful.

Demand for goods interacted with the development of shops and provided the latter with crucial profit margins. The development of a retail infrastructure transformed the nature both of the domestic market and of townscapes. Shops complemented, and competed with, markets, and also with other settings for trade, such as private dealings in inns and peddlars and chapmen. The latter, like the traders who went round markets, were part of the traditional itinerant character of commerce which was increasingly transformed by the growth of facilities offering continuous transactions, both shops and also week-long markets. The first Exchanges in Manchester and Liverpool were built in 1729 and 1749–54 respectively. New covered markets were constructed in many towns. Bristol gained a new Market-House in 1745 and St James's market in 1776, Gloucester the Eastgate market in 1768, Lancaster the Shambles in 1774.

The growth of new retail outlets, and the improvement in transport links that came with turnpike roads, ensured that less successful markets ceased activity or were transformed into monthly, quarterly or annual markets or fairs. Thus, the long-standing process by which a hierarchy of markets was shaped continued. The more successful markets were able to remain as centres for a considerable hinterland, but others became simply markets for local exchange or for the supply simply of the town itself. This was part of the process by which towns were increasingly differentiated from what were to become villages. Contemporaries were aware of a transformation in commercial links, and discussed its consequences. The *Glocester Journal* of 12 March 1792 noted:

> It is observed, that the decline of Bristol fair, together with all great periodical fairs, for the staple commodities of this kingdom, affords a striking evidence of the diffused general intercourse, that subsists in every direction between the manufacturers and tradesmen to their mutual benefit by means of the facility of credit, and the increased opportunities of conveyance, by land and water, through every part of the country. Of late years an immense quantity of business, heretofore transacted at the great regular local marts of the kingdom, now goes on, by frequent and immediate correspondence, between the manufacturer and the vendor of the shop.

The 'consumer revolution' benefited producers; the retail network served them as well as merchants importing goods from abroad. Thus the Coalbrookdale ironworks sold its pots, kettles and firebacks through fairs in market towns such as

Bishop's Castle, Congleton, Oswestry and Wrexham, as well as to shops including, in 1718, in Birmingham, Bromsgrove, Evesham, Gainsborough, Ludlow, Macclesfield, Manchester, Newtown, Shrewsbury, Stone and Welshpool. Such networks helped to finance manufacturing.[23]

Advertising reflected and sustained a pattern of changing retail patterns, as well as underwriting the prosperity of the press; while trade directories provided information. From 1755, lists of Dublin merchants and traders were published annually in *Wilson's Dublin Directory*. The first Birmingham directory appeared in 1767. Bailey's *Western and Midland Directory* was published in 1783.[24]

The 'consumer revolution' was part of an expanding world of goods. There were more material goods, a rising demand for all types of goods, and a slowly-changing material fabric of life. This was most obvious in the cities, but itinerant retailers also took goods throughout the British Isles, and this helped to increase the penetration of the commercial system in areas where the money economy co-existed with barter.

Clothes reflected new developments. The cotton fabrics imported by the East India Company were both attractive and could be used to provide for a mass market the styles that were otherwise restricted to more expensive silks and brocades. People consumed more medicaments, a process encouraged by longer average life-spans, and, more generally, accumulation and expenditure both rose with life expectancy.

The expanding world of goods was matched by an increasing number of trades. Wills and inventories reveal that specialist trades were spreading in many communities. For example, in the Devon town of Uffculme both a gunsmith and a clockmaker appeared.[25]

The probate inventories of the Warwickshire village of Stoneleigh indicate that around 1700 goods appeared there which were produced for mass distribution, such as Ticknall ware for the dairy and tin dripping pans for the hearth. In addition, dining rooms emerged in the same period, while new furniture meant new fashions: court cupboards or dressers replaced aumbries, falling tables superseded trestle tables.[26]

More generally, furniture reflected social changes, including the rise of 'politeness' (see Chapter 6) as well as of sedentary activities such as card-playing and drinking tea. These were not restricted to the towns but were part of a developing national culture. However, as that term has to be understood both to exclude those too poor to participate and to note similar processes in comparable milieux abroad, both in Europe and in the European colonies, it is possibly best to refer to a material culture, that can be termed class-based if class is understood in loose terms and as a description of relative prosperity.

The production and sale of furniture also reflected the entrepreneurial character of the period. Much furniture was fairly simple, and was designed for those who were not particularly affluent. It was produced in the neighbourhood out of local wood and used alongside inherited pieces. At the same time, the more affluent consumed as part of a fashionable world, in which designs changed and were popularised by books of designs, exotic woods such as mahogany were imported, decoration was enhanced by inlaid woods and veneers, and pieces were designed to complement each other and other items in the room.[27] The whole effect was of a designed environment and a completeness in which material culture and aesthetic values were linked.

Although average real wages were roughly stationary in England between 1760 and 1790, the rapid rise in population ensured that total demand rose. In Scotland, average real wages themselves rose as the rate of population growth was less than that in England and Ireland. Scotland, Wales and Ireland shared in the improvement in commercial facilities. In Ireland, there were relatively few new markets in the first half of the century, but, in the second half, 200 market centres were granted patents, so that little of Ireland was more than twelve miles from a market. The number of fairs also increased. Hitherto remote areas, such as much of West Mayo, were, for the first time, provided with markets and roads. In County Tipperary there were market-houses in Fethard by 1712, Carrick by 1726, Tipperary by 1737, Thurles by 1743, Clonmel and Nenagh. In Carrickfergus in Ulster a new market house was constructed in 1775.

Commercial activity in part depended on the nature of the financial and regulatory systems. By European standards, the British Isles both constituted a relatively uniform economic system, especially as links between the English and Scottish economies developed, and had sophisticated capital markets. Scottish law differed from that in England and Wales, but, within each country, there were neither significant legal variations nor internal tariffs.

The Act of Union decreed that English standards of weights and measures were to be used throughout Britain, but Scottish weights and measures were retained, and two bills introduced in 1765 to establish uniform weights and measures were not enacted. More generally, there was considerable variety in weights and measures. Within Scotland, the old Scottish Trone weights, abolished in 1617 when Scottish Troy weights were made standard, were, nevertheless, still used. In parts of Scotland, such as the Hebrides, the standard weights and measures were not used. The Linlithgow boll, a unit for the dry measure of grain, abolished in 1696, remained the general measure, but was variously defined. Within England, each region had its own variants of such customary measures as acres, tons, chaldrons, and bushels. For acres there were 'statute acres', 'estimated acres' and local measures. In some cases, old men with long memories were called in to guess boundaries and acreages.

The Act of Union also provided for a uniform coinage, though Scottish currency remained in circulation until the nineteenth century. The British coinage was based on specie, although complications were created by a general shortage of specie, which led to the circulation of coins from foreign countries. Portuguese gold and Spanish silver coins circulated in England. Spanish dollars, overstruck as worth 4s 9d, were common in Scotland in the second half of the century. There was a particular shortage of small copper coin, which encouraged the use of tokens.

The availability of bullion was reduced because of the need to finance negative trade balances, particularly with China and India, thus helping to explain widely-held concern about balances and about these trades. Bullion was also reduced through use in non-monetary forms and through the continuous loss of metal from coins due to processes such as wear, reminting and fraudulent clipping. These shortages encouraged the use of paper money, and the period witnessed the spread both of banking and of banknotes. Progress in development in the provision and means of credit was not, however, obtained without a cost in terms of periodic crises and instability. The precarious nature of most banking firms and the vulnerability and short-term nature of most credit created difficulties. For example, there was an exchange crisis between England and Scotland in the 1760s. The dependence of the economy and confidence on credit helps to explain the severity of laws against fraud. The provision of long credit for transoceanic trade created many problems. As today, banks were affected by political crises. In 1745, during the Jacobite rising, the Bank of England only prevented a run on the pound by ordering clerks to work slowly.

Yet, by European standards, the British banking system was reasonably stable. The Bank of England, founded in 1694, operated successfully as a source of government credit, and this helped to bring relative stability and growth to the banking system. The Bank of Scotland was founded in 1695, although, unlike the Bank of England, it did not lend money to the government. The Royal Bank of Scotland followed in 1727, as a second Scottish public bank. In Scotland, by mid-century, there was a third public bank, the British Linen Bank, which began issuing notes in 1750 and specialised in credit for the linen industry, as well as nearly twenty important private banks in Edinburgh. Despite earlier discussion, a Bank of Ireland was not established until 1783.

There was a major transformation in banking. A variety of informal lending and notarial activities developed into a banking system with the emergence of distinct banking functions, although earlier practices also continued. For example, in Wales many drovers also acted as bankers. Banking houses, single-unit partnerships with unlimited liability for their losses, developed in London and the provinces, especially in the second half of the century. The first bank in Norwich was opened in 1756, in Exeter in 1769, and in Chichester in 1779. Furthermore, there were no local monopolies: individual banks were rapidly followed by others. Thus, in Exeter, the Exeter Bank (1769) was followed by the Devonshire Bank (1770), the City Bank (1786), the General Bank (1792) and the Western Bank (1793). By the end of the century, there were several hundred provincial banks in England, highly local in their operation, helping to keep the money supply buoyant and circulating, and to spread credit.

An inter-regional credit structure based on London developed, ensuring that local economies were very much linked to national financial developments, and also thus to each other at the national level. The establishment of a bank clearing house in Lombard Street in London in 1775 led to a great improvement; banks were allowed to balance credits and withdrawals by a ticket system. The first Scottish provincial banking companies were established in Aberdeen in 1747, Glasgow in 1749, Dundee in 1763, Ayr in 1763, Perth in 1766, and Dumfries in 1766. By the mid-1760s, four banks had been founded in Glasgow. There was similar expansion in Ireland.

Banks were a part of increasingly complex commercial mechanisms, including growing insurance and stock markets. The 1690s saw a major expansion in the establishment of joint-stock companies, and the emergence of the stockjobber as a figure for criticism. This was taken further when the South Sea Bubble, a great, and corrupt, speculation in trading opportunities, government finance, and speculation itself, burst in 1720.[28] The crash led to a deep sense of unease that focused earlier anxieties about joint-stock companies and paper credit. It also led to the Bubble Act, which limited the flotation of small joint stock enterprises. In 1773, a group of brokers subscribed towards the acquisition of a building which became known as the Stock Exchange.

London was emerging as the powerful financial centre of the world's leading commercial empire. Stock prices were reported in the press. In 1696, Edward Lloyd, a coffee-house keeper, published a tri-weekly *Lloyd's News*, which contained much shipping news. In Anne's reign, *Proctor's Price-Courant*, the *City Intelligencer*, *Robinson's Price-Courant* and *Whiston's Merchants Weekly Remembrancer* were all published, and, in the 1720s, the *Exchange Evening Post*, *Freke's Price of Stocks* and the *Weekly Packet with the Price Courant*.

The insurance industry developed, particularly to offer protection against fire and shipwreck. London companies included the Sun Fire Office, established in 1708, Royal Exchange Assurance (1719), and Phoenix Assurance (1782). These and other companies founded provincial agencies, but there was also competition from elsewhere, especially Edinburgh, where the first fire insurance office was founded in about 1719.

The spread and greater intensity of the money economy affected other aspects of life. Crime, for example, reflected the process. Forging notes became a more profitable activity. The game trade, although illegal under the Game Laws, flourished in the second half of the century as game that had been poached reached urban markets, especially London, in increasing quantities, in part through the developing network of coach services. Alongside poaching for the pot (for the poacher), there was therefore also a national business. The government responded with an Act of 1707 imposed fines on innkeepers and carriers who bought, sold or possessed game, but this failed to stop the trade. As a result, an Act of 1755 made the sale of game illegal by both those allowed to hunt and by others. This Act also failed, but it made those who wanted game dependent on poachers.[29]

The spread in tea and brandy consumption from the social élite to the middling orders encouraged, and was facilitated by the development of large-scale smuggling, especially, by mid-century, in tea. Merchant capital financed much of the smuggling and the latter was insured in London. Allegedly, half the tea and tobacco consumed were provided by smugglers.

More mundanely, the spread of pawn shops provided opportunities for fencing. Smuggling and fencing supplied goods to a population with greater aspirations. This can be seen as an aspect of the consumer revolution, and it troubled commentators. Morality and order were both at stake. Thus gin, a new consumer product, was seen as a cause not only of a new kind of drunkenness, but also as a threat to morality, health and social order, with people trying to do everything to get it bar work. Both Fielding and Hogarth criticised the quest for gin.

Profit was also made from the struggle against crime. Thief-takers were paid a bounty, while sites near the London gallows at Tyburn were let out to spectators.

The so-called Financial Revolution also helped underwrite British participation in the Atlantic economy by providing the funds and instruments for long-term credit. The Atlantic economy ran on borrowed capital. This was important both to the expansion of sugar production in the British West Indies and to the development of the slave trade to provide the necessary manpower. British success in gaining access to South American bullion, especially Portuguese gold, and the stabilisation of financial markets in London after the foundation of the Bank of England were crucial in developing the finance and infrastructure for credit.

Finance was also important to the development of tobacco production round the Chesapeake, although this was less significant as a source of wealth than sugar. The percentage of slaves in the Chesapeake population rose, as most slaves to British North America were shipped between 1720 and 1770, but in the eighteenth century, Jamaica, a sugar colony, received eight times the number of slaves that the Chesapeake got. Between 1691 and 1779, British ships transported 2,141,900 slaves from African ports, and colonial ships took another 124,000.[30] By 1775, there were about 1,800 sugar plantations in the British West Indies.

At the level of the individual who was transported, the reality was of the trauma of capture and transportation, shock, hardship, violence and disruption. The labour regime in sugar and rice (grown in South Carolina) cultivation was particularly deadly. Hacking down sugar cane was backbreaking work. This was crucial to the profitability of the industry. Slaves were more malleable than indentured servants from the British Isles. The growing prosperity of the plantation economies of the West Indies, Georgia, the Carolinas and the Chesapeake helped to finance their import of British goods, such as Irish textiles, as well as trade within the colonies that increased their value as a market.

A CHANGING ECONOMY?

To suggest that the situation was one of both change and continuity, innovation and conservatism, is to draw attention to the variety in economic activity and regional fortune that characterised the British Isles. There are also major problems in measuring activity, in assessing how far change was feasible, and in considering what was most likely to contribute to sustained economic growth. Any discussion was, and is, affected by limitations in the evidence. In part, there was only a limited consciousness of the value of collecting statistical, or indeed any, information on the economy, but, in addition, the surviving data is incomplete and poses problems. There was no national census until 1801, and information on land ownership and agricultural productivity was limited.

Assessments in part depend on the basis for analysis. A theme of growing economic activity, specialisation and sophistication, and, specifically, of industrial specialisation, that might appear appropriate for much of England and the

Scottish lowlands, seems less well grounded if Highland Britain and Ireland are also to be considered. Much of Ireland's economy remained basically pre-industrial, and many economic transactions took place outside the market context.

Yet, there was also major change in Ireland, reflecting many of the developments seen in England and Scotland. Touring Ireland between 1747 and 1760, Richard Pococke, a Church of Ireland bishop, noted much that was new to praise, including fertilised fields and new industries, as well as other signs of change, such as charity schools and new stately homes.[31] As it was drawn more fully into the market economy, Ireland's agricultural sector experienced growing diversification and commercialisation. Agricultural prices and rents rose substantially in the second half of the century, for example in County Wexford where a malting barley economy developed, largely supplying the Dublin market. In County Tipperary, there was a major expansion in cereal cultivation from the 1760s, reflecting and encouraging a more capitalised agriculture, and leading to the spread of flour mills. More productive English strains of cattle, sheep and pigs were introduced into Ireland in the second half of the century. Textile production developed, and turnpiking improved communications.

Thus, it would be inappropriate to suggest that areas not at the forefront of economic change were in some respects static. Instead, these areas were affected by the currents of change elsewhere. If the regional dimension is to be stressed, then it is clear that the industrialising regions such as South Wales and North-East England were at the forefront of economic change in the world. On the other hand, emphasis can be placed on socio-economic-political fundamentals that operated at a national scale. These included a relatively stable political system, legal conventions that were favourable to the free utilisation of capital, especially secure property and contracting rights, a social system that could accommodate the consequences of economic change, and an increasing degree of integration and interdependence. Belief in the stability of political and economic arrangements encouraged the long-term investment that was crucial in many spheres, including transport. Taxes on manufacturing industry and transport were low or non-existent.

The role of economic affairs can be seen in the press. Newspapers stressed their economic information. For example, the *London Evening Post* of 30 March 1762 devoted much of its attempt to publicise its contents to its economic news, offering:

> an exact table of the current price of merchandize ... an account of the arrival of British ships at, and their departure from, the several ports of the habitable world ... the several courses of exchange, the prices of gold and silver, of stocks of corn at the Corn Exchange ... and of their articles of a like nature.

It was generally accepted that such information was of importance to many readers. In Fanny Burney's novel *Cecilia* (1782), the opinionated, practical man of business Mr Hobson declares, 'for as to not letting a lady speak, one might as well tell a man in business not to look at the Daily Advertiser; why, it's morally impossible.'[32] The press helped to make many of the processes of economic exchange more fluid and public. For example, major regional newspapers were the chief medium for advertising that a country house was to let.[33]

Visiting Helston in Cornwall on a very busy fair day in 1702, Evelyn noted, 'where we dined was the Royal Oak Lottery which one could hardly have expected to have found in a country town so remote from London.'[34] Another sign of greater national integration can be seen in the rise of Post Office revenues, from £116,000 in 1698 to £210,000 in 1755. This reflected the foundation of new routes, such as Exeter–Bristol–Chester in 1700, and others that became more frequent, as the London to Bristol and Birmingham services did in the 1740s. The national distribution of London newspapers depended on the mail service, initially horse-mail and then the mail-coach. All contributed to a sense of change in which the past partly ceased to be the reference point for human potential and activities.

NOTES

1. Evelyn journal, BL. Evelyn papers 49 fol. 21.
2. C. Morris (ed.), *The Illustrated Journeys of Celia Fiennes c. 1682-c. 1712* (1982), pp. 157–9.
3. W. Albert, *The Turnpike Road System in England 1663–1840* (Cambridge, 1974).
4. D.F. Harrison, *Bridges and Communications in Pre-Industrial England* (DPhil, Oxford, 1996).
5. D.L.B. Thomas, 'Fenny Bridges in Feniton and Gittisham', *Devon Historian*, 50 (Apr. 1995), pp. 5–10.
6. Alderbury and Whaddon Local History Research Group, *Alderbury and Whaddon* (Alderbury, 2000), p. 110. See, more generally, D. Hussey, *Coastal and River Trade in Pre-Industrial England. Bristol and its Region, 1680–1730* (Exeter, 2000).
7. C. Hadfield, *The Canals of the West Midlands* (Newton Abbot, 1966).
8. J. Bourne (ed.), *Georgian Tiverton: The Political Memoranda of Beavis Wood 1768–98* (Exeter, 1986), p. 5.
9. M. Elder, *The Slave Trade and the Economic Development of Eighteenth-Century Lancaster* (Preston, 1992).
10. G. Place, *The Rise and Fall of Parkgate, Passenger Port for Ireland, 1686–1815* (Chetham Society, 3rd ser., vol. 38, 1993).
11. K. Verdery, *Transylvanian Villagers* (Berkeley, 1983), p. 157.
12. M. Morineau, 'The Indian Challenge: seventeenth to eighteenth centuries', and D. Rothermund, 'The changing pattern of British trade in Indian textiles, 1701–1757', in S. Chaudhury and M. Morineau (eds), *Merchants, Companies and Trade: Europe and Asia in the Early Modern Era* (Cambridge, 1999), pp. 243–86.
13. Bristol, Society of Merchant Venturers, Minutes of the Steadfast Society, pp. 56–7.
14. R.B. Sheridan, 'The Molasses Act and the Market Strategy of the British Sugar Planters', *Journal of Economic History*, 17 (1957), pp. 62–83.
15. Chalmers to Grenville, 1 Nov. 1769, HL. STG. Box 21 (28).
16. D.H. Sacks, *The Widening Gate. Bristol and the Atlantic Economy, 1450–1700* (Berkeley, 1991); K. Morgan, *Bristol and the Atlantic Trade in the Eighteenth Century* (Cambridge, 1993).
17. D. Richardson, 'The British Empire and the Atlantic Slave Trade, 1660–1807', in P.J. Marshall (ed.), *The Oxford History of the British Empire. II. Eighteenth Century* (Oxford, 1998), p. 446.
18. BL. Evelyn 49 fol. 37.

19. J. Walvin, *Fruits of Empire. Exotic Produce and British Taste, 1660–1800* (1997), p. 16.
20. A.J. O'Shaughnessy, *An Empire Divided. The American Revolution and the British Caribbean* (Philadelphia, 2000), p. 72.
21. Cobbett IX, 261.
22. K. Wrightson, *Earthly Necessities. Economic Lives in Early Modern Britain* (New Haven, 2000), p. 298.
23. Trinder, *Industrial Revolution in Shropshire*, p. 27.
24. J. Norton, *Guide to the National and Provincial Directories of England and Wales, excluding London, published before 1856* (1950); K.H. Rogers (ed.), *Early Trade Directories of Wiltshire* (Trowbridge, 1991).
25 P. Wyatt (ed.), *The Uffculme Wills and Inventions 16th to 18th Centuries* (Exeter, 1997).
26. N.W. Alcock, *People at Home. Living in a Warwickshire Village, 1500–1800* (Chichester, 1993).
27. C.D. Edwards, *Eighteenth Century Furniture* (Manchester, 1996).
28. J. Carswell, *The South Sea Bubble* (2nd edn., Stroud, 1993).
29. P.B. Munsche, *Gentlemen and Poachers: The English Game Laws 1671–1831* (Cambridge, 1981).
30. Richardson, p. 442.
31. J. McVeagh (ed.), *Richard Pococke's Irish Tours* (Dublin, 1995).
32. F. Burney, *Cecilia* (1904 edn.), p. 857.
33. H. Colvin, *Essays in English Architectural History* (New Haven, 1999), p. 287.
34. BL. Evelyn 49 fol. 36.

6

Society

INTRODUCTION

Any chapter under this title faces the problem of definition, not least because prominent historians have treated the subject very differently over the last two decades. Society cannot be divorced from such categories as economy, politics, religion and culture, and indeed arrangements and developments in each of them can be treated as aspects of the social history of the period. In this book, points that might be considered 'social' indeed occur in chapters devoted to those categories. Without any suggestion that the topics exhaust the definition of social history, this chapter focuses on social organisation understood as issues of gender, family structure, and the orders of society.

The basic framework is clear. Social relationships and attitudes reflected a clear cultural inheritance and the prevalent economic and technological environment. The Judaeo-Christian inheritance, clearly enunciated in the laws and teachings of the churches, decreed monogamy, prohibited marriage between close kin, stipulated procreation as a purpose of matrimony while condemning it outside, denounced abortion, infanticide, homosexuality and bestiality, made divorce very difficult, enforced care of children, venerated age, and ordered respect for authority, religious and secular, legal and law-enforcing. Other issues that would be more regulated today, such as spousal abuse and rape within marriage, were ignored.

The economy was technologically unsophisticated and much of it was agrarian. Economic productivity was low, there was little substitute for manual labour, and the value accrued through most labour was limited. Most of the population neither controlled nor produced much wealth, and the principal means of acquisition was by inheritance. The dominant ethos was patriarchal, hierarchical, conservative, religious and male-dominated, although each involved both tensions and a variety of means of expression.

WOMEN

It would be difficult to guess from many textbooks that women made up half the population, and, indeed, that before the later eighteenth century the gender balance of the population was weighted towards them. Clearly women faced ecological challenges similar to those of men, but that is no reason for neglecting them as a separate category. Furthermore, women's biological role brought specific problems, while their treatment by society differed from those of men. Many women faced gruelling labour and debilitating diseases identical to that of the men at their sides, but they were also in a society that awarded control and respect to men, and left little independent role for female merit or achievement.

The economy of the poor was such that employment was the essential condition for most women. The arduous nature of most of the work, and the confining implications of family and social life, together defined the existence of the majority of women. Social and economic pressures helped drive women towards matrimony, and, whether married or not, also towards employment. Employment in agriculture and textiles was very important, although, by the end of the period, female agricultural service was declining significantly in south and east England.

Domestic service was a common form of work for unmarried men and women. Service was the life of many in a society where household tasks were arduous and manual, and the contribution from machines minimal. Jobs such as the disposal of human excreta were unpleasant. Many servants were immigrants from rural areas. Generally not members of collective groups, and lacking guilds, they were largely at the mercy of their employers. It was possible to gain promotion in the hierarchy of service, but, in general, domestic service was unskilled and not a career. Wages were poor, and pay was largely in kind, i.e. food and accommodation. This made life very hard for those who wished to marry and leave service, and married servants were relatively uncommon.

For girls saving for a dowry, domestic service was far from easy. In addition, they were often sexually vulnerable to their masters. This was a central theme in two important early novels, Samuel Richardson's *Pamela* (1740) and, with a male servant pursued by a female employer, Henry Fielding's *Joseph Andrews* (1742). The notorious Colonel Francis Charteris was convicted of raping Ann Bond, a servant, in 1729, only to be pardoned by George II. The Chelsea bastardy examinations of claimants before a Justice of the Peace included

> the voluntary examination of Sarah Powell, single woman, taken 15 Oct. 1754, before Thomas Lediard esq. ... Who upon oath saith that she is pregnant of a bastard child or children which was or were unlawfully begotten on her body by one James Silvester of the parish of Chelsea ... with whom this examinant lived as a hired servant ... James Silvester in the month of June last, about two o'clock in the morning (being just after her mistress was gone to market) came to this examinant's bedside in his dwelling house and her waked out of her sleep, and did take the advantage of getting to her in bed.[1]

Service was not only domestic, although that was the area in which female labour was most important. Agricultural servants were also vital. Generally living with their employers, they gave many nuclear families the quality, in part, of an extended family. The need for both men and women to go into service, and also the need for servants, varied geographically, seasonally and socially. The contradictory needs led to difficulties, such as dismissals, and migration in search of employment, producing a labour market filled with uncertainties. More generally, servants, labourers and women could not aspire to the 'independence' so valued by political theorists.

Domestic manufacturing was another important source of employment for both married and unmarried women. Clothing was the biggest, though not the sole, form of employment in this area. Spinning-wheels featured frequently in British household inventories. Domestic manufacture could be a crucial contribution to family income, especially in areas where agriculture was poor and in households that had limited agricultural resources. The women involved either formed part of a family in which all members worked in domestic manufacturing or supplemented family income derived from other activities. As the value added by their work and that of children was generally greater than that derived from comparable labour in the fields, women and children generally made a greater contribution to family incomes if they engaged in domestic manufacturing. However, their opportunities were limited by the restricted nature of market-oriented domestic manufacture in many areas, and, to a *lesser* extent from the second half of the century, by the growth of factory-type employment.

By taking the worker out of the home, such employment made it difficult to care for children. Particularly if combined with a move in the location of manufacturing, the development of such employment could destroy the basis of the family economy by lessening the chances of married women obtaining remunerative labour. It has been suggested that these economic changes had social consequences, including a rise in marital separation. Nevertheless, in some spheres, job opportunities for women improved. In the north of England, for example, the production of women's outer garments was increasingly handled by local mantua-makers.

The most striking aspect of the female contribution to the labour force was its variety. Although women had only a relatively small role in the churches, save with the Quakers, as Methodist preachers and in charitable works, and none in the armed forces (save the important informal role of camp-followers), they were found in most spheres of employment, including those involving arduous physical labour. Thus women were employed as coal-heavers, taking coal to the surface, and as fish- and salt-carriers, and many worked in agriculture. Much of this employment reflected the expediency economy of the poor, and female opportunities were limited by the nature of the economy as well as the particular problems and restrictions that affected women. Literacy rates were lower for women in England, Ireland, Scotland and Wales; a result of the limited attention to their education. Women were generally given the worse-paid jobs. In many industries, such as glove-making, women were given the less skilled jobs or their employment was defined as less skilled and therefore was paid less. The majority of the poor were women. That was certainly true of lists of resident parish poor in Scotland, and reflected the impact of widowhood, spinsterhood, unwanted pregnancy, and differential job opportunities.

Not all women were confined to poor jobs. A tiny minority had interesting careers, some benefiting from the expansion of the commercial economy. The Swiss-born painter Angelica Kauffmann was one of the founding members of the Royal Academy in 1768. The political pamphleteer Catharine Macaulay, in her initially successful *History of England* (1763–83), advanced a radical Whig agenda of parliamentary and constitutional reform, including the extension of the franchise and annual Parliaments. She applauded the execution of Charles I, criticised the Glorious Revolution for failing to be revolutionary, and always refused to retire with the ladies after dinner. Women played an important role in the debating societies that developed in London from the late 1770s, although less so in enlightened societies in Scotland.

In the theatre from the late-seventeenth century, actresses took over female roles and this led to a more realistic presentation of women and of gender relationships. Both became more relevant to women play-goers. However, women writers faced difficulties, in part because they were objects of a cultural anxiety directed at 'empowered' women outside their proper roles and at 'feminized' men led by their emotions. Thus, Eliza Haywood, who offered frank discussions of female desire in *The City Jilt* (1726) and *The Mercenary Lover* (1726) could be seen as a threat. Haywood's *Anti-Pamela* (1742) was less successful than Samuel Richardson's *Pamela* because it was more disturbing and less didactic, and because Richardson was better able to capitalise on the market for fiction thanks to his authorised role in the print trade.[2]

Women's reading troubled many (male) commentators. Even biblical and devotional reading were not always considered safe for female readers. Imaginative literature was seen as potentially exacerbating the female imagination, and drama also raised the perils of sensibility. Reading works about science became increasingly acceptable for women, but, for many commentators with conservative inclinations, science, especially botany, remained problematic. It was less so, however, than fiction and philosophy, both of which led to persistent reading bans for women and girls. Women were thought especially vulnerable to new philosophical ideas. The danger to women of reading radical texts was repeatedly imagined in fictional works such as novels in terms of sexual transgression leading to illness, breakdown and death.

Despite, and, at times, because of, such strictures, many women enjoyed reading, and explicitly commented on its pleasurableness. Reading permitted critical engagement with issues of authority, although that could help accentuate the anxiety that reading could give rise to. Where though were women to read? Private libraries were generally seen as male domains. They were frequently identified with patriarchal power. In novels by women, the male authority and rationality figured by the library was likely to have a dark side which became explicit in Gothic fiction. There, the ruined library recurred as a symbol for the bankruptcy of male authority and literary culture.

Women, in contrast, favoured subscription and circulating libraries, which were crucial to the 'democratization' of literature. Women writers were also dependent on them as a reliable market for their writing. The image of libraries dominated by the works of women for female readers, and, more generally, the ubiquity of the female reader as an icon, increased. Female novel-reading gave women writers a series of potent images to deal with their anxieties about, or even to fight for their rights to, literary authority.[3]

Women played only a minimal role in politics. Personal relations were such that, at the individual level, the influence of women over their husbands or lovers could be considerable. Nevertheless, public practice and theory were male-centred. There were no women in Parliament, although some played a role in the management of constituencies. Women also acted as political hostesses. The image of justice might be female, but its formulators and executors were all male: there were no women judges, JPs or councillors. A few individuals were prominent because of their royal position. This was particularly true of William III's wife and co-ruler Mary II (1689–94), Queen Anne (1702–14), and the wives of George II and George III, Queens Caroline and Charlotte. Caroline played an important role in Walpole's retention of power in 1727 and was formally proclaimed regent on four occasions when George II visited Hanover.

Several other women were also influential because of their spouses or connections. Sarah, Duchess of Marlborough (1660–1744), Groom of the Stole to Anne and an influential advisor to her, who became a Duchess, as wife to John, 1st Duke of Marlborough, was left the effective head of the family on his death in 1722. Intelligent and obsessed with politics, Sarah was committed to the Whig cause. Unusually for the period, she was allowed by her husband to manage her dowry and retain her salaries from court posts. She died the wealthiest woman in the country, but with the conviction that her sex had deprived her of political influence.

The use of the household as the basis for social organisation led to an emphasis on the role of men, because they were regarded as heads when they were present. The legal rights of women were limited, not least their rights to own and dispose of property. Legal devices circumvented common law rules of inheritance that would otherwise have left more land inherited or held by women. The Strict Settlement was a device that encouraged patrilineal inheritance and primogeniture. It preserved estates by limiting charges for subordinate members of the family; although that did not imply that landowners lacked concern for the members of their nuclear families nor that children and wives were casually or indifferently treated.[4] Thanks in part to the Strict Settlement, land that had been added to a great estate was likely to remain with it.[5]

Yet it would be mistaken to minimise the role of women. For a start, it would be wrong to imagine that they lacked political consciousness. For example, women frequently participated in riots. This may have reflected the crucial role that women played in the purchasing of foodstuffs and the sense that women would receive more lenient punishments than men, but it also reflected political awareness. If this primarily took the form of hostile responses to changes in the price or availability of foodstuffs that were believed to be unfair, that was the politics of the poor in general. Women were also of great importance as consumers. The need to satisfy the demands and fashions of women in the middling orders comprised a major aspect of the consumer revolution. This was also true, more generally, of their role. Rather than being subordinate agents, women played an important part in influencing developments. For example, the major shift from women-only midwifery to a situation by the 1770s in which increasing numbers of children were being delivered by male midwives reflected the choices of mothers, not the imposition of male structures of control.

There were also instances of women playing a role as officials. Thomas Coram's Foundling Hospital in London placed the children it accepted with rural wet-nurses for the first five years of their lives. The system depended on the voluntary inspectors who identified suitable wet-nurses and then supervised them. The majority of the women inspectors had the necessary skills of literacy, numeracy, and administrative ability. The role of those women in the 1750s was striking. There was no precedent for the management and supervisory activities undertaken by women for the Foundling Hospital; neither had there been any previous recognition by a national organisation of women working for it on equal terms with men.[6]

Poverty was an experience to which women were particularly vulnerable. This was different from that of men for a number of reasons, particularly the responsibility of women, both unmarried and married, for children. It was the women who were commonly held responsible for the birth of illegitimate children, while married men had a greater propensity than their spouses to abandon their families.

Seduced girls often had recourse to prostitution. The absence of an effective social welfare system, and the low wages paid to most women, ensured that prostitution, either full- or part-time, was the fate of many. The diseased prostitute, her hair and teeth lost in often fatal mercury treatments, was a victim of the socio-economic and cultural circumstances of the period. More generally, an economic system that bore down hard on most of the population, was linked to a social system in which the position of women, whether relatively fortunate or unfortunate, was generally worse than that of men. The breakdown of marriage and desertion by the spouse frequently featured in accounts of women vagrants.

It has been argued that male attitudes to women softened and became more sympathetic to female feelings, as a crucial part of the process by which more 'polite' and genteel social norms were encouraged. The good manners implied by the term 'gentleman' were thus redefined. An aspiration towards politeness was certainly a keystone of various public discourses. It fostered particular ends of moral improvement, Christian purpose, and social order. Propriety and the developing cult of 'politeness' were used to help manage the symbolic authority of fathers and husbands. In their periodicals, the *Tatler* and the *Spectator*, Addison and Steele fostered and glamorised heterosexual sociability, thereby raising the prestige of those spheres which offered women a place beside their men and also the profile of the cosmopolitan gentleman who could do a woman honour.[7]

Politeness in part meant female passivity. It is no accident that whereas much late-seventeenth-century literature presented women as manipulating sexual relationships, a century later women were seen as passive foils, and victims of a pattern of seduction that had to be contained by changing male behaviour, not by increasing female assertiveness.[8] An emphasis on female restraint can be seen in much of the reporting of the theatre published in magazines and periodicals. Thus, the column 'The Theatre' in the *Town and Country Magazine* of December 1782 referred to one actress: 'She seems to have imbibed too strongly the rantings of a strolling company, to figure in a capital part upon a regular stage ... she does not seem calculated for the soft feelings of tender passion.' Another actress, that month, had 'a powerful voice; but it is destitute of the pathos. Her action is not graceful, but rather violent.'

Descriptions of the culture of the period in terms of a 'polite society' are insufficient. In fact, the culture was highly ambiguous. Politeness was part of the century's self-image, but a coarseness of utterance and indeed of thought was equally part of its image. Frequent campaigns against swearing, lewdness and profanity, and the insistence on sabbath observance were of a piece with sexually explicit and forthright language, and prurience. The stress on sobriety and restraint can be seen as a comment on drinking levels. There was much matter-of-fact acceptance of prostitution, casual sex and venereal disease, although it is generally necessary to go back to archival sources for evidence, as, until recently, printed editions generally omitted such matter. For an example from a more recent edition, on 2 February 1702, George Hilton (1674–1725), a Westmorland Catholic gentleman, recorded in his journal 'went to Geo Dix at the Sandside with Geo Wilson broake 3 of my resolutions vizt eate flesh laid with a woman up till 2 o'clocke in the morning'.[9] An explicit sexuality was hardly remote from a society in which large quantities of self-education sex literature was printed, while prostitution was also very important. Many men may not have 'internalised' the politeness that they apparently valued in public. Possibly this presaged the public morality and private vice of the Victorians.

Yet, this public morality was important. If politeness was a public act, it tells us something about changes in society that such a show was thought necessary, although politeness itself could be seen as far from virtuous. Engine, a maid in Edward Ravenscroft's play *The London Cuckolds* (1681), explained:

This employment was formerly named bawding and pimping, but our age is more civilised and our language much refined. It is now called doing a friend a favour. Whore is now prettily called mistress. Pimp; friend. Cuckold-maker; gallant. Thus the terms being civilised the thing itself becomes more acceptable. What clowns they were in former ages.

There was also a class dimension. Politeness and gentility, or at least a discourse of their value, can be seen as 'middle-class' virtues and the discourse as characteristic of 'middle-class' writers. Eighteenth-century public restraint can thus be presented as evidence of the emergence of values which defined the 'middle class', and of their greater importance within society. There were also ideas of moral and social superiority implicit in the attitudes to vulgarities and the vulgar.

The idea of equality between men and women was increasingly approved of, but the general notion of equality was one of respect for separate functions and development, and the definition of the distinctive nature of the ideal female condition did not entail equality by modern standards. This was true of sexuality. Women, but not men, were expected to be virgins when they married, and chaste thereafter. When in 1779, Parliament discussed the 'more effectual discouragement of adultery', it was of course an all-male body.

The extent to which there were changing meanings and styles for masculinity and femininity is unclear. By European standards, British social conventions were not rigid. The Comte de Gisors was surprised, when visiting England in the 1750s, to find young women of quality paying visits alone without loss of reputation, but the French ambassador told him that it was the English habit to trust daughters to do this. In 1763, a later French ambassador was described as 'not yet been long enough in England to learn that the ladies here had much rather trudge up and down the stairs by themselves, than be escorted by anybody'.[10]

The fluidity of gender practices and the complexity of gender relations undermines efforts to present a simple pattern of 'separate spheres' in which the public world had a male complexion while women were largely restricted to private and domestic spheres and roles. This may well have been the pattern in parts of social life, but it is unclear that this represented an intensification of earlier trends, not least because recent scholarship has been sceptical about the degree to which pre-industrial/eighteenth-century British women had more economic and political liberty. For the eighteenth century, notions of 'public and private' and 'separate spheres' have also been questioned in order to suggest that the public profile of privileged women was important and advancing. These women were employers and consumers, who made their devotions and took their pleasures in public.[11] Furthermore, within the domestic sphere, women were also able to assert independence and self-control, for example in music-making, and this assertiveness was not contained by that sphere.[12]

Nevertheless, by modern standards, the situation was far from benign. The emotional position of many women was difficult. The portrayal of marriage to a callous husband as imprisonment, offered in Thomas Southerne's play *The Wives' Excuse* (1691) was not fanciful: Mrs Friendall, the perceptive and wronged protagonist, declared 'But I am married. Only pity me,' and later spoke of the 'hard condition of a woman's fate'. This was not fanciful. In 1712, Mary Pierrepont, was intended by her father, Evelyn, Marquess of Dorchester, for Clotworthy Skeffington, heir to Viscount Massereene. She felt she 'had rather give my hand to the flames than to him', whom she described as Hell, but Dorchester, 'the disposer of me', refused to accept her decision for a single life. To escape, Mary eloped.[13]

Prior to 1750, the majority of actions for divorce brought in the London Consistory Court were brought by women against their husbands for cruelty, not for a lack of love or compatibility. Expectations about what women should obtain from marriage rose and after mid-century the notion of romantic marriage and domestic harmony came to prevail among the prosperous, and the practice of divorce for incompatibility arose. However, the custody of any children was generally invested in the father and divorced women commonly lost touch with them.

In Scotland, where parental consent to marriage was not made compulsory by law, as in England, there appears to have been more sexual equality. There was a general availability of divorce at all levels of society and, at least in law, it was recognised that adultery was equal grounds for divorce for both sexes.[14]

Gender issues were also affected by what appears to have been a greater assertiveness on the part of homosexuals or a stronger consciousness of their role. This is a controversial field in which, due to the character of the relatively scanty sources, the analysis is necessarily impressionistic. Nevertheless, certainly in London, there was the development about 1700 of a more overt homosexual subculture whose participants, known as 'mollies', were regarded as distinctive in clothes, mannerisms and speech. 'Working-class' men played a major role, although there were also prominent homosexuals.[15] It has been suggested that this subculture affected attitudes to relations with women as most men sought to prove that they were not bisexuals or with homosexual tendencies but, instead, were clearly heterosexual. This has been seen as leading to a greater acceptability of prostitution, and thus to a different attitude to women and to marriage.[16] Such claims are difficult to substantiate, and it is not always clear whether relevant documents, such as court records, note more than the keeping of more records.

FAMILIES

It has been argued that the period witnessed the rise of a pattern of family life that placed more weight on the wishes of individual members and in which affection rather than discipline, and emotion rather than patriarchalism, bonded families together.[17] This shift has in part been explained by a rise in the life expectancy of children and women allegedly encouraging a greater degree of emotional commitment. In turn, these changes have been linked to a range of developments, including the rise of distinctive clothes and the toy industry for children, the literary cult of the sentimental family, and new pedagogic fashions that placed greater weight on the individuality of children and the need to socialise them without treating them as embodiments of original sin.

Discussion of these suggestions is complicated as the overwhelming majority of the population did not keep journals or leave correspondence. Furthermore, it is unclear how to assess, let alone measure, affection and changes in it. It is important not to mistake changes in style, such as modes of address within the family, for changes in substance. Certainly, if marital experiences and expectations were related to economic circumstances, then it is difficult to see much reason for major change.

In addition, recent work on sixteenth- and seventeenth-century family life has revealed that many of the suppositions supporting the ideas of subsequent periods as different were actually false. The idea that romantic love as a reason for, and aspect of, marriage was an eighteenth-century invention, whether a consequence of modernisation or not, has been rejected, as has the notion that children were brutally treated until then as a matter of course. Rather, it seems clear that in this period, as earlier, parents of all social and religious groups loved their children. In bringing them up, they saw the need to teach them basic skills, but regarded this, correctly, as for the benefit of children as much as parents. This was particularly the case when children were to follow the occupations of their parents, a tendency that was made desirable by the nature of inheritance practices and by the limited opportunities faced by most people. Furthermore, the absence of state-provided education placed a burden of responsibility on parents and, failing them, other relatives. The same was also true of health, housing and social welfare.

The degree to which the individual family lived together in close proximity led to a need for co-operation and mutual tolerance that necessarily affected the nature of patriarchal authority. The inculcation of deference, discipline and piety by authoritarian parents was not incompatible with affection, and the tension between individual preferences and family pressures was scarcely new. The basic unit of society was the nuclear family: a married couple and their generally non-adult children, although nuclear families were also nodes within closely connected networks of kin. Other than those headed by widows or widowers, there were few one-parent families. The structure of individual families was not constant. Birth, ageing and death ensured that the life-cycle of families was continually changing. It was necessary to adapt in order to survive periods when the family altered to include dependants, young children and invalid adults. As these groups consumed without working, they posed a challenge to the economy of individual families, just as they created formidable problems for society in general, and for many other functions, such as education.

The responsibilities of social welfare were left to families, communities, and private and religious charity, but communal and charitable support focused on families rather than single adults. There was also the question of safety: an isolated individual could be in a vulnerable position.

Families coped with the problem of feeding children by defining childhood so that it included employment as far as possible and in so far as it was necessary. Many agricultural and industrial tasks, such as tending livestock, were undertaken by children, and were part of a family economy. Thus, in the Cornish pilchard industry, which was dominated by self-employed fishermen, curing was generally a family affair with wives and daughters carrying out the curing. Publicists approved of child labour, arguing that it prevented idleness and begging, educated children to useful employment, and, through a system of domestic apprenticeship, accustomed them to work. Most families needed no such encouragement; their problem was to find employment for the children and to feed them until they were able to work.[18]

The employment of as many family members as possible was essential not only to its well-being, but also to its very existence as a unit. Parents who could not cope left children to foundling hospitals, which were established from mid-century. Unmarried mothers sometimes turned to abortion and infanticide,[19] but both were treated as crimes and the former was hazardous to health. The women, often very young, who were punished as a result of these desperate acts, suffered from the limited and primitive nature of contraceptive practices; as did those exhausted from frequent childbirth. Unwanted children were not only an economic liability, but also, when born to unmarried mothers, the source of often severe social disadvantages, moral condemnation and legal penalties. In a society where women sought marriage as a source of precarious stability, the marital prospects of unmarried mothers were low, with the significant exception of widows with children of a first marriage, especially if they possessed some property. As a consequence, unmarried mothers frequently became prostitutes or were treated as such.

THE ORDERS OF SOCIETY

To move from gender relations and family dynamics to consider the orders of society is not to move to the static and the structural, because social patterns were more the product of dynamic relationships, especially the daily reiteration of status and the continuous interaction between and within groups, than of any fixed caste-like rigidity that left no role for social mobility. Nevertheless, the weight of the past was very apparent in the distribution of wealth, status and power. The influences that affected this distribution were similar to those of the previous century, and there was little change in the methods by which the social position of individuals was determined or could be altered, although there was also considerable diversity of views about the nature of hierarchy in the eighteenth century. Furthermore, certainly in comparison with the following two centuries, the rate of social change was low, although that does not imply that there was little social change. In addition, although it cannot be measured with precision, social mobility was greater than on the Continent.

Status and power were linked to wealth, although not identical with it. This was generally regarded as appropriate, although there was a degree of tension over the definition of wealth. In particular, the legitimacy of money as opposed to landed wealth was a matter of controversy. Great wealth could be made in London. Sir Francis Child, a goldsmith banker who came from a clothier family in Devizes, became Lord Mayor in 1698 and an MP, and was able to purchase the Osterley estate in 1713. His grandson, Francis, was able to spend £17,700 buying Upton as a country seat for hunting in 1757, as well as £1,200 on his election as an MP in 1761. His brother Robert was estimated to earn at least £30,000 per annum from the bank. Frances Bankes, daughter of a London merchant, brought £100,000 when she married Sir Brownlow Cust in 1775.

Many saw such wealth as disruptive. Jonathan Swift offered the classic Tory critique of financial activity and speculation. In his pamphlet *The Conduct of the Allies* (1711) he referred to

> undertakers and projectors of loans and funds. These, finding that the gentlemen of estates were not willing to come into their measures, fell upon those

new schemes of raising money, in order to create a moneyed interest, that might in time vie with the landed, and of which they hoped to be at the head.[20]

Similarly, in his pamphlet *Thoughts on the late Transactions respecting Falkland's Islands* (1771), Samuel (Dr) Johnson referred to 'the sudden glories of paymasters and agents, contractors and commissaries, whose equipages shine like meteors and whose palaces rise like exhalations'.[21] This looked back on a rich tradition, but was in many respects outdated in a society where such activity and wealth were of growing importance. Legislation was passed to ensure that only those with a certain amount of land could become Justices of the Peace (JPs), but this reflected the failure to maintain such criteria. Acts of 1732 and 1744 decreed that JPs posess freehold or copyhold land with an annual value of £100 above all encumbrances, or other land of a yearly value of £300.

The relationship between capital and income greatly favoured the former, and the ability to create income without capital was limited. Nevertheless, opportunities for self-advancement from imperial expansion or industrialisation existed and towards the close of the period grew. In some cases, this led to massive wealth-epitomised by Robert Clive, the conqueror of Bengal, who became an aristocratic landowner, and by such manufacturers as Josiah Wedgwood and Samuel Crompton. Such newly minted wealth was still uncommon, sufficiently so for there to be grave suspicion about the wealth produced by 'nabobs' who had made their money in India. Nevertheless these men began to make their mark. Francis Sykes, who had done so, had a splendid Palladian mansion built for him by John Carr at Basildon Park in Berkshire in 1776–83, and James Dawkins from Jamaica, purchased the Oxfordshire estate of Over Norton in 1726, spent at least £1,000 standing, unsuccessfully, as MP for Oxford in 1734, and was elected unopposed for New Woodstock on the interest of Sarah, Duchess of Marlborough, sitting for the constituency from 1734 until 1747.

Such new wealth offended many, but the care taken by the newly-affluent to buy status helped ensure that they did not undermine notions of social hierarchy. The very existence of social distinctions was seen as obvious, and as arising from the natural inequality of talents and energies. Egalitarianism found favour with few writers on social topics, and social control by the elite was a fact, not an issue, in politics.

These assumptions pervaded society, encouraging ranking by birth and snobbery. They affected the choice of friends and marriage partners. Though he was the son of a Wakefield linen-draper, John Potter, Archbishop of Canterbury from 1737 to 1747, disinherited his eldest son for marrying a domestic servant. The desire to preserve family status and wealth in part lay behind Hardwicke's Marriage Act of 1753, which increased the power of parents, by outlawing clandestine marriages in England, although not in Scotland. There, a woman over twelve and a man over fourteen who agreed to marry and then had sex were considered legally married, whether or not they had parental consent, the calling of banns, or a licence.[22] Social differentiation, or at least an awareness of distinctions of rank and status, may have become more acute in response to social mobility and to the pressures of commodification that commercialism created. Hereditary and stability were regarded as intertwined. At the same time, there was a strong sense that status should be a matter of conduct not lineage. This stress on civil, rather than social, virtue was particularly evident in urban settings, and contributed to the importance of conduct judged polite.

Social differentiation was reflected in a range of activities and spheres, such as sport and dress. Although there was elite participation in popular recreations, such as bull-baiting, horse-racing, cock-fighting and fishing, hunting was restricted by the Game Laws. The Game Act of 1671 gave the exclusive right to hunt game to freeholders worth £100 a year, or leaseholders worth £150 a year. This substantial landed property qualification restricted the sport to wealthy landed gentry. There was supplementary legislation in 1707, 1771 and 1773. The Acts of 1771 and 1773 were directed at night-time poaching. Such Acts were supported by gamekeepers and mantraps, and both the legislation and its defence helped to make clear the nature of hierarchy and power in the rural community. Hunting was not only restricted by legislation. In addition, keeping horses was expensive. Furthermore, sports where there was little elite participation, such as dog-fighting, were less favourably viewed than cock-fighting where there was gentry sponsorship.

Those with pretensions to social status wore wigs, while the poor wore their own hair. The seating arrangements in churches and the treatment of the dying and their corpses also reflected social status and differences, as did the provision of health. Wealthy subscribers recommended poor dependants for admittance to infirmaries. Patterns and practices of crime and punishment, credit and debt also reflected social distinctions. The hanging of Earl Ferrers in 1760 for the murder of his steward John Johnson, and of the cleric Dr William Dodd for forgery in 1777, were cited as evidence of the universality of the law, but it was rare for members of the elite to suffer execution or imprisonment unless involved in treason. Aristocratic debtors similarly escaped the imprisonment for debt that was a frequent consequence of the role of credit in society. The impact of social differences was also clear at the hiring fairs where employers scrutinised the men and women who sought employment, and in housing where there was increasing social segregation.

For example, in Edinburgh, thanks to the economic expansion of the Central Lowlands of Scotland in the third quarter of the eighteenth century, there was money to invest in building in order to cater for new demand and new tastes, not least in the form of the New Town. Economic differentiation and social division became more pronounced. The New Town set the seal on this process. The poor became more closely delineated as urban space in Edinburgh was redefined. The Old Town became the more crowded, less healthy and poorer part of Edinburgh.[23] Similarly, in Newcastle, there was a growing social segregation in residential areas.[24]

Religion offered a degree of contrast, because the churches remained a career open to the talent of the humbly born, as was demonstrated by several bishops of the Church of England. Nevertheless, connections and patronage generally worked to the benefit of the well born. Clergy from a gentry background received a disproportionately high share of the good livings.

Educational access and provision also reflected social power and assumptions. Because so many children worked, their access to formal education was limited, even if it was available free. Attendance at school was far lower in summer, the highpoint of agricultural work, than in winter. Education in England had to be paid for by the pupil's family, which was generally the case in grammar schools, or by a benefactor, dead or alive. There were many 'petty' charity schools, often known as 'dame schools', though most were small. However, some took more children in return for payment. Thanks to benefactions, some grammar schools were also free. Education was not supported by taxation, central or local.

Educational provision expanded. The Society for the Promotion of Christian Knowledge (SPCK), established in 1698, encouraged the foundation of charity schools; and 63 schools were founded in Lincolnshire alone in the first quarter of the eighteenth century. However, the situation remained very uneven. The vicar of the Yorkshire rural parish of Brandesburton reported to a diocesan visitation in 1764:

> Mrs Frances Barker of York left the interest of £100 to this parish towards the maintenance of a schoolmaster, who should teach poor children to read and write *gratis*, till a convenient purchase could be made with the principal. This sum is now laid out in lands at Sutton. Besides these poor children there are about 30 taught from this and the neighbouring villages in reading, writing and arithmetic by Thomas Ryley. Care is taken to instruct them in the Christian religion according to the Church of England and to bring them to church.

But, for every child who acquired some education, there were many others who received none. Girls and the rural population had fewer educational opportunities than boys and town-dwellers. In 1706–12, there was schooling only in about 60 parishes in Buckinghamshire and a surprising number of the county's parishes had no regular charitable endowments. The replies to the episcopal visitations of Surrey in 1725 and 1788 reveal that by explicit statement or implication more than a third of the parishes responding had no educational provision.[25] In 1778, only about 5 per cent of the children in Cheshire attended school.

More generally, literacy levels reflected the degree of economic freedom enjoyed by families and their occupational aspirations. Illiteracy in the rural parishes of Dorset in 1750–1800 appears to have been an average of 56 per cent, with Worcestershire as 50 per cent and Cambridgeshire and Huntingdonshire as 58 per cent. Male was higher than female literacy. In a sample of communities in West Sussex, the general literacy level for brides was between 15 and 25 per cent lower than that of the grooms in the second half of the century. In the Sussex towns surveyed 'totally illiterate marriages' seldom formed more than one fifth to one quarter of the total in any decade, but literacy levels were lower in the rural parishes. The highest rates of illiteracy were to be found amongst those without land, trade or skill.[26]

The poor who were educated were offered less. Reading, writing and arithmetic were provided in the 'dame schools', where free or inexpensive teaching was provided by widows and elderly women, although sometimes only the reading was provided free. The classical teaching offered by the grammar schools was not available in most schools, but nor also in many was free mathematics. There was a general assumption in charity schools that the pupils should be provided with a vocational education, which meant teaching employable skills as well as the morality that contributed to good conduct. These requirements were laid out in the terms of the bequests under which charity schools operated. Thus, spinning, weaving and knitting was taught to girls. Morality was provided by discipline and by the teaching of the fundamentals: the catechism, the creed, the commandments and the Lord's Prayer. Local worthies and the clergy played a major role in the foundation of schools. Land was donated as sites, money provided for construction, and rentals were used to guarantee the salary of the schoolmaster (most schools had just one). In 1720, the SPCK offered premiums to towns to set up charity schools and workhouses. In 1723, the Workhouse Test Act was sponsored by the SPCK, so that the worship and schooling offered was Anglican. The London workhouse school was established in 1698 and the *Account of the Workhouse* (1725) indicated that schools were an integral part of workhouses. Besides charity schools, probably the biggest number of ordinary (not those from an affluent background) children were educated in workhouses.

Education and printing exacerbated social divisions and gave an extra dimension to the flow of orders, ideas and models down the social hierarchy. The limitations on the poor expressing themselves was accentuated. Printing and books emphasised the dependence of the poor and illiterate on the literate.

The social elite favoured boarding schools for boys. Eton and Westminster were the most popular. Pupils who wished could move on, without difficulty to Oxford and Cambridge, the only universities in England and Wales. Most of the elite did not bother to take degrees, while some had the right to a degree based on status. Degrees were generally taken by students who hoped to follow a career as clergymen in the Church of England, although members of the elite taking degrees rose steadily after about 1740 encouraged by reforming heads of colleges, such as William Markham, Dean of Christ Church 1767–77. Girls from this background received far less formal education. Most were educated at home, and universities were not an option.

In Scotland, there was a stronger tradition of obligation to provide education for all. After the Reformation, schools and universities there came under the control of local authorities. Under an Act of 1696, which ratified earlier Acts, heritors (landowners) were supposed to build a school in each parish, half the cost of which they could recoup from their tenants. As a result, many parishes in the Lowlands had both school and schoolmaster funded by fees and landowners. Many heritors, however, did not build schools, for example in Galloway and the Highlands, so that educational provision and access partly depended on the presence of charity schools or those of the Society in Scotland for Propagating Christian Knowledge (SSPCK). Established in 1709, in order to found charity schools in the Highlands, the SSPCK had opened 176 schools by 1758. Free education was available to only a minority of Scottish schoolchildren, but free or low cost education in Scotland was perhaps more widespread than is generally allowed.[27] In Ireland, the absence of a system of parochial schools for the native population ensured that education did not serve to anglicise the people, nor to convert them to Protestantism.

Medical attention, poor relief, philanthropy and moral admonition can be considered as forms of control, 'the body' for example being 'subject to cultural policing' by 'professionally-oriented forms of illness-interpretation and healing'.[28] Thus, the Reformation of Manners movement has been seen as an attempt to control popular pastimes and mores, as well as vice and impiety. This movement, which flourished from the early 1690s to the late 1730s, with later revivals in the late 1750s and late 1780s, led to the foundation of reformation of manners societies that raised funds to bring prosecutions for offences such as breach of the Sabbath regulations and streetwalking.

However, the idioms and symbols of reformation provided a rhetorical theme that could be used by a variety of groups, and to varying ends and in different contexts. Far from being restricted to, or in some respects defining, a middle-class consciousness, the theme of the reformation of manners had a longer tradition, back to Puritanism and beyond, that was not exclusive to the middling sort, and a powerful religious dimension that looked forward to reforming and evangelical movements at the close of the century.[29] Similarly, although philanthropy reflected social norms and hierarchies, its ideology was more complex than any focus on social ordering and policing might suggest.[30]

'Politeness' was more socially exclusive as a concept than the reformation of manners, with its religious dimension; although it would be misleading to separate the two too clearly. 'Politeness' had a public and a private side, but both were characterised by an emphasis on an orderly sociability that was defined in a socially excluding way that contributed to a sense of shared values and identity among the middling orders. Two social institutions that developed in this period, the male club and the mixed assembly, have been seen as spheres for an important redefinition of social consciousness that led towards the idea of a middle-class culture.[31] The political equivalent to politeness was the distinction between appropriate and dangerous activism:

> 'I believe there is no sober man doubts but there is a difference, a very material one, between liberty and licentiousness, and that the latter ought to be restrained ... the ruin of free governments has been owing to nothing more than to the degenerating of liberty into licentiousness.[32]

The distinction generally had a social dimension: those who pursued liberty were polite, while the 'mob', to use a contemporary term, were licentious.

It would be mistaken to assume that individuals and groups should be seen in terms of a simple and single position. As with social positions, actions and aspirations, those focused on culture reflected multiple interests, possibilities, commitments and anxieties. Analysis in terms of social groups is only helpful if their openness to many and varied cultural pressures is understood. For example, it is possible to present landscape gardening in terms of social control and display and as a 'landscape of exclusion'.[33] Queen Caroline's expansion of gardens at

Richmond, Hampton Court, Windsor and Kensington, meant that rather than a team of royal gardeners circulating round the royal palaces, a separate garden staff was employed at each palace. At the same time, a 'commercialisation of botany and gardening' with many 'working class enthusiasts' has been emphasised, and it has been argued that 'a horticulture of aristocratic ostentation had developed to such an extent that it now encompassed the leisure time of the middle classes and the hobbies of working men and women. Gardening had been democratized as well as commercialized'.[34]

There is no reason why such developments should be seen in terms of conflict or subversion. Any consideration of stylistic shifts has to be cautious in assuming social causation, and too much contextualisation has depended on older, static models such as class conflict and cultural conflict. The social context was more complex than many of the sources suggest. In 1746, Thomas Harris, a London lawyer, wrote to his brother James,

> This has been one of the most entertaining weeks for the mob that has happened a great while ... yesterday (which was the top of all) Matthew Henderson was hanged, at whose execution all the world (I speak of the low-life division) were got together; and he died to the great satisfaction of the beholders, that is he was dressed all in white with black ribbons, held a prayer book in his hand and, I believe, a nosegay.[35]

In fact, there was no clear divide in such audiences. Executions and other spectacles attracted the 'beau monde' as well as the 'low-life division'.

In Ireland, Scotland and Wales there was another dimension to social difference captured by the linguist William Jones in Wales in 1775: 'It was market-day at Llandilo, and I could not help fancying myself in a Flemish town; it was at least wholly unlike an English one, as the language, manners, dress and countenances of the people are entirely different from ours; I speak of the lower sort, for the gentry are not in any respect distinguishable from us.'[36]

THE SOCIAL ELITE

Power and wealth were concentrated. The hierarchical nature of society and of the political system, the predominantly agrarian nature of the economy, the generally slow rate of change in social and economic affairs, the unwillingness of governments composed of the social elite to challenge fundamentally the interests of their social group or to govern without their co-operation, and the inegalitarian assumptions of the period, all combined to ensure that the concentration of power and wealth remained reasonably constant. The old order was under scant threat from popular protest. Furthermore, despite Tory claims to the contrary, the Whigs were a party of great landowners, as well as of bankers, Dissenters and the urban interest.

Across Europe, those who enjoyed power and wealth tended to be nobles by birth or creation. In Britain, however, the ownership of a significant amount of land was not an indication of noble rank, though those of the (non-aristocratic/noble) gentry who did have much land enjoyed considerable social status. The major landowners are the most appropriate point of comparison with the continental nobilities, although special privileges (and relatively few of these) were attached only to the peerage. Creations helped to keep the number of peerages up: there were 43 by William III, 42 by Anne, 66 by George I, 74 by George II, and 197 by George III between 1760–1800.[37] The size of the peerage was far smaller than on the Continent, but gradations in the peerage remained vital to individual and family status and aspirations. Although affected by political divisions, the relatively small size of the English aristocracy helped make it far more socially coherent than Continental counterparts.

There was an active land market, and status could be readily acquired, but marriage and inheritance remained the crucial means by which land was transferred. The pattern of estates also did not alter. Thus in Oxfordshire, the estate of the Dukes of Marlborough could be created only because there was a royal manor – Woodstock – to use. This affected the nearby parliamentary constituency of New Woodstock. The Dukes became the hereditary high stewards, claimed the right to appoint the Recorder of the borough (an influential figure at election time), and selected many of the MPs, including family members, such as the heir, the Marquess of Blandford, in 1727, John Spencer, grandson of the 1st Duke in 1732, 1734, 1741 and 1744, and Lord Robert Spencer, 3rd son of the 3rd Duke in 1768. Robert's brother, Lord Charles, sat for the county from 1761 until 1801. Such individuals regarded membership of the Commons as a right. They were also the prime catches in the marriage market and thus best able to preserve and increase their wealth by marriage.

A remodelling of the local power hierarchy comparable to that produced by the creation of the Churchill estate was unusual in England where there were no changes comparable to those suffered by Catholic landowners in Ireland. The Tories suffered political proscription under George I and George II, but were not driven from the land, although, denied access to office, Tory landowners could find it harder to hang on to their existing estates.

The small size and relatively closed nature of the peerage helps to make aristocratic/noble rank too narrow a specification for any analysis of the elite. The inheritance of noble status only by the eldest son was an important limiting factor, although other children were not released destitute into the world. All adult, male, non-Catholic English peers were members of the House of Lords. The parliamentary representation of the Scottish peerage, however, was limited after union with England to sixteen, chosen by election among their own number. In 1719, the Peerage Bill sought to change this to 25 nobles who were to inherit their position. The Bill also included a provision for fixing the size of the English nobility. This measure was defeated, in part because of the heavy representation in the Commons of gentry who aspired to ennoblement.[38]

The absence of serious tension between nobility and gentry was an important feature of British society, and a crucial aspect of stability. They formed a homogeneous group that intermarried and socialised together. There were moments of tension, for example in 1745 when there was some opposition to the idea that peers receive government pay for the volunteer regiments they were raising and officering, and in the Berkshire by-election of 1776 when it was claimed that wealthy peers were trying to override the gentry.

However, an absence of contention was far more common. The divide between peers and gentry did not operate as a political fault line and did not reflect political or social divisions. The nobility had great influence in many areas, but this partly depended on their numbers. In Wales they were less numerous and important than in Northamptonshire, in part because of the exclusion from power of the Catholic and High Tory aristocrats whom Charles II and James II had favoured, because the Welsh peerage was relatively sparse, and because relatively few of the Welsh gentry were promoted to the peerage.

Central and local government were dominated by the elite of nobility and gentry, although not in the major towns. Command of local government reflected supremacy in local society. Justices of the Peace (JPs) were the crucial figures in local government and law and order, and the Bench of JPs was dominated by the gentry. As commissioners, they were also the crucial figures in the local allocation of the Land Tax. This was paid by all landowners, including peers, unlike the considerable tax immunities of much of the Continental nobility.

The dominance of both centre and localities by the landed elite was expressed by enclosure Acts which facilitated a reorganisation of the rural landscape to enhance the control and profits of landlords (see also Chapter three). As freehold tenure became more important, the sense of place and identity of others who worked on the land was challenged. This was taken furthest where settlements were moved. Enclosure Acts were part of a more general process by which in parts of the country landholding was concentrated in fewer hands.[39]

The gentry could use their resources and the law to harm other groups. Sir George Downing (*c*. 1685–1749), a Suffolk landowner and MP for Dunwich, used his wealth to buy most of Dunwich, took a lease of the right to collect taxes for the Crown there, had the freemen who could not pay imprisoned for debt, and allowed his tenants to fall into debt while requiring them to enter into bonds on the understanding that they would support him at elections. If most of the landed elite preferred to gain their ends in a more consensual fashion and managed their localities in a more reciprocal manner, they, nevertheless, did so in their own interest. Consensualism and reciprocity were only taken so far, and many were excluded from its scope.

THE MIDDLING ORDERS

Those who can be variously termed the 'middling orders', 'middle class' or 'bourgeoisie' are not easy to define. They tail off into the elite and the poor, and were far from uniform. As a whole, the middling orders were a distinct social group. They tended to emphasise values of professionalisation, specialism and competence that helped to define their social function and presence. A stress on such factors was necessarily one of the individual, rather than the family or dynasty.[40]

Yet the latter were also very important. It would be mistaken to focus on function, for example as doctors or lawyers, and to ignore the concern of the middling orders with hierarchy and background. Such considerations also played a major role for them, and snobbery as much as function helped to define social presence. Furthermore, there was a widespread aspiration to gentry status.

The expansion and growing profitability of the commercial and industrial sectors of the economy led to a growth in the middling orders,[41] although, at the individual level, there was much fragility in status and position. The protection offered today by reliable systems of insurance and pensions and by relatively secure investment and credit was absent. Attempts to associate together in order to provide a measure of security could offer only limited protection.[42]

This fragility was also captured by novelists with their emphasis on prospects and on turns of fate. In Daniel Defoe's *Moll Flanders* (1722), wealth comes and goes, it is difficult to find emotional and financial constancy, and crime, marriage and inheritance are ways to acquire capital. The sense of precariousness was unsurprising given the financial crash of 1720, the South Sea Bubble. Moll's third husband 'finding his income not suited to the manner of living which he had intended, if I had brought him what he expected, and being under a disappointment in his return of his plantations in Virginia, he discovered many times his inclination of going over to Virginia to live upon his own.'[43]

Nevertheless, at the general level, and in a period of only modest inflation, the percentage of households with annual incomes between £50 and £400 rose from 15 in 1750 to 25 by 1780, and that in a period of growing population. The middling orders were increasingly difficult to locate in terms of a social differentiation based on rural society and inherited position. Many lived in the towns, which shared the inegalitarian and hierarchical nature of the rest of society. The wealthy and prominent in towns derived their power from their ability to organise others, generally economically and often politically. The oligarchical nature of urban government corresponded to that of the countryside, although there was less of an emphasis on lineage. Rural commentators might group townsmen above the rank of artisan in terms of 'trade', but in fact there were many distinctions in terms of wealth and status.

There was also an important middling order in rural society: tenant farmers, the agents of landlords,[44] and rural professionals such as parsons. This entire group were greatly affected by the movements of the agrarian economy. Many encountered particular problems during the agrarian difficulties of the 1720s and 1730s, although the fate and fortune of tenant farmers varied greatly. From mid-century, the rise in grain prices due to the growing population brought more wealth into the rural economy, but its distribution within rural society was very uneven.

The middling orders played a considerable role in public affairs, generally co-operating with the landed elite to achieve their socio-political objectives. Their property and interests were as much protected by the general emphasis on liberty and property, and by the ethos and direction of parliamentary government, as were those of the landed order. Property qualifications for many posts were relatively low, enabling the lower middling orders to participate in the government of the localities.[45] Subscription associations also gave them an important role, as, more generally, did the full range of public politics.

The middling orders did not seek political change to benefit themselves collectively, although lawyers, merchants and others were capable of lobbying hard for their professional and commercial interests. Rather than seeing themselves as the flag-bearers of a 'rising middle class', they displayed little sign of what would later be termed class consciousness. It has been argued that there were signs of a new ethos, especially in books and plays that portrayed a way of life emphasising the value of industry and discipline, in contrast to supposedly aristocratic habits of self-indulgence, but it is important not to exaggerate the significance of such ideas. They were neither new, nor politically pointed and significant, and much of the landed elite would have accepted them.

The middling orders were affected by a porosity of social boundaries that was greater than that on the Continent, although less than in Britain's North American colonies. Social mobility was helped by primogeniture (undivided inheritance by the eldest son), and the consequent need for younger sons to define and support their own position, and also by the relative openness of marital conventions. Despite snobbish disdain for 'trade', these allowed the sons of land to marry the daughters of commerce, and, less frequently, led to the daughters of land marrying the sons of commerce. Partly as a result, the social elite in England was far less exclusive and far more widely rooted in the national community than was the case in most Continental countries or in Ireland. In some counties, such as Durham, land estates were frequently acquired by purchase, and acquisitions by previously non-landed men were frequent. More generally, there was an active land market, and status (though not peerages) could also be readily acquired.[46] The notices in the *London Journal* of 27 November 1725 included one for Thomas Rogers 'Agent for Persons that Buy or sell Merchandises, Estates etc', who was willing to meet customers at the Rainbow coffeehouse in London, and that very much presented a society where land and money were easily exchanged:

> Any person that has twenty thousand pounds to lay out, may be informed where a good estate in land very improvable, may be purchased at a price considerably less than land now usually sells for ... A person wants to buy a large estate with a seat, fit for a gentleman in any pleasant healthy country. Another an estate from about £6,000 to £8,000 value not far from Bath. Another a good house with some farms near Reading of from £200 to £500 a year. Another an estate of £2,000 value, or upwards, in Middlesex, Essex or Hertfordshire ... '

The market that was discussed was not particularly place specific. Many sought the right property rather than a specific location.

Marriage and land purchase were not the sole links. Urban and rural groups also shared cultural and leisure interests, such as visiting spas, and were linked by myriad patterns of subscription and other forms of social intercourse. For example, the Birmingham Bean Club acted as a dining society to bring the town's leaders and the local gentry together. Towns were a social focus for the surrounding countryside. Chester had important race meetings in midsummer and autumn, and the Lent and summer assizes. Towns competed to make themselves attractive to wealthy country visitors, this competition being another stage in that which had led them to compete as centres of the rural economy with rival fairs.

At the same time, the urban/rural divide could remain strong, and there was rural resistance to urban influences.[47] Differences remained, not least in politics and religion, and the landed magnates visited towns on their own terms. It is too easy to assume that rural society responded rapidly or evenly to urban developments, or that rural values and opinions were determined by those of the towns. Yet, there was a degree of interchange based on shared values that was arguably greater than that of the previous two centuries.

The pattern which has emerged from studies of education is suggestive. Towns, especially market towns, advanced in the early-eighteenth century, while the village poor had few educational resources. By the late century, country education was generally much better, while the industrialising towns fell sharply back. The countryside was not cut off from the towns; the latter played a major role as markets for the countryside, and as centres of, and for, consumption, while road links improved with the spread of turnpikes. Peddlers from towns brought wares, while rural readers read newspapers, acquiring information about urban opinions, fashions and products. Alongside signs of tension between urban and rural interests and consciousnesses, it is also possible to present the two as different aspects of the life of the elite, and as related or unified in a new sensibility.[48]

More generally, fashions were rapidly transmitted between social groups and made accessible and affordable. This mobility strengthened, rather than weakened, the social hierarchy. There were fewer signs of social tension than at the close of the nineteenth century.

THE POOR

There are problems with describing all those not in the social elite or the middling orders as the poor. That term was used in broader and narrower ways, but quite often quite restrictively for those on relief or dependent on charity. When the phrase 'labouring poor' began to catch on in the second half of the century, some commentators, such as Edmund Burke, attacked it as new-fangled cant. The vast mass of the population, both urban and rural, was in the category. The 'labouring poor' was a very varied group. Forms of status and security were attainable for some, although they were precarious. Commentators distinguished between the 'mob' and the 'people'. The former comprehended the bulk of the poor; while many of the latter had a more settled income and were artisans, their economic interests and social cohesion frequently expressed through membership of fraternities of workmen.

Occupational descriptions of the population were infrequent and affected by terminological variations. To take Northamptonshire, the surviving militia lists are the nearest approach to an occupational census prior to the table of occupations included in the printed abstract of the 1831 census. Of the 13,741 men recorded on the lists for 1777, the occupations or status of 87 per cent, only perhaps two-thirds of the males aged 18 to 45 in the county, were recorded by the parish constables. The majority of those whose occupations were listed were employees. To take the countryside, 11.1 per cent were farmers, but 19.2 per cent were labourers and 20.8 per cent were servants, mostly 'servants in husbandry'.[49]

In the countryside, where the bulk of the population lived until the mid-nineteenth century, rising demand for foodstuffs benefited landlords and tenant farmers, not the landless poor. Agricultural wages remained below fifteenth-century levels in real terms. The rural population was dominated by an economy of proprietary wealth: a system built around rent and poor remuneration for labour in the context of a markedly unequal distribution of land. The rural poor were badly affected by enclosure, by the decline in some rural industries, especially textiles, and by any factor, short- or long-term, that pressed on real wages.[50] Demographic and economic change led both to a substantial increase in the numbers of those working for wages and to a growth in what would subsequently be termed the 'underclass'. Thus a recent study of four Cheshire townships in the 1740s, while noting that each had its own distinct character, found a 'general movement from a society in the middle of the seventeenth century with a large number of small farms occupied and run by their owners without the assistance of labourers (except living-in young people) towards one at the end of the eighteenth century with fewer but larger farms run by less well capitalised rack-rented tenants employing growing numbers of families of labourers. This may partly explain the well-known and relentless rise of the poor rates and the appearance of a rural proletariat'.[51]

Heavy rent rises led to the emigration of about 20,000 Scots to North America between 1769 and 1774. The Reverend William Thom claimed in his *Candid Inquiry into the Causes of the Late and Intended Migrations from Scotland* (1771) that 'in whatever country the whole property is engrossed by a few, there the people must be wretched'.

Social welfare provisions for the poor were limited. By modern standards, the Elizabethan Poor Law, which provided the framework for social welfare, was unacceptable, but it was more generous than provision in most of the world in this period. Nevertheless, the poor were generally treated as objects, or a problem, not as equal participants in the community. As the *Citizen* pointed out on 5 April 1757, 'They are called the vulgar, the mob, the rabble ... and treated as if they were of some inferior species, who are designed only for labour'. The poor were particularly harshly treated or regarded if they could not earn their keep. Thus, John Locke proposed to the Board of Trade that the poor should be made to work, and that those who refused should be whipped and, if necessary, mutilated. His suggestions were not adopted, but should not surprise us from an individual and society that profited from the slave trade. Wesley conspicuously adopted a different viewpoint, seeing the poor as industrious and a source of spiritual renewal, and the beggar as an image of the suffering Christ. However, in order to try to avoid the birth of children who would be a burden on the rates, parish vestries sought to dissuade the poor from marrying.

The largest urban group was the poor, who tended to lack political weight. Their poverty stemmed from the precarious nature of much employment in even the most prosperous of towns. Most workers lacked the skills that commanded a decent wage, and many had only seasonal or episodic employment. Day-labourers, servants and paupers were economically vulnerable and often socially isolated. A large number were immigrants from the countryside.

Due to poverty, the poor, both rural and urban, were very exposed to changes in the price of food and generally lived in inadequate housing. As they could not afford much fuel, the poor were often cold and wet in the winter, and were more commonly in the dark. The circumstances of their life made them prone to disease, though disease was also a social leveller. Malnutrition stunted growth, hit energy levels, and reduced resistance to ill-health. Poor diet encouraged colon parasitic infection, hepatitis and salmonella.

There was scant understanding of the problems posed by unemployment and under-employment, and such hardships were treated as self-inflicted and thus deserving of neglect or punishment. The standard precept of care was that it should discriminate between the deserving and the undeserving. This religio-moral principle tended to be applied on grounds of age, health and sex, rather than on socio-economic criteria relating to income and employment. The sick, elderly, young and women with children were the prime beneficiaries of relief, while the able-bodied, whether in low-paid employment or unemployed, were denied it.

A well-established system of poor relief was available through the Poor Law. Compulsory poor rates had been introduced in England and Wales in 1572, and in 1598 the relief of poverty was made the responsibility of the individual parish, but able-bodied men unable to find work were treated as rogues and vagabonds. The financial and administrative system organised in the Elizabethan Poor Law Acts remained until the 1834 Poor Law Amendment Act, although supplementary legislation was of importance. The Poor Relief Act of 1662 made the right to relief dependent upon the pauper being settled in the parish, a practice that led to the expulsion of paupers deemed non-resident. Individuals could only remain in a new parish if they had a settlement certificate stating that their former parish would support them if they became a burden on the poor rate. The rest were liable to be driven away unless they could find work. They were generally harshly treated and were frequently whipped as vagabonds. The removal orders from Bradford-on-Avon, a leading centre of the West Country cloth industry, show the expulsion of married men with families, together with single women, wives, and a small number of widows. Clearly there was concern to limit the number of dependent children in the community. The chances of removal from Bradford increased considerably from the 1750s.

In many English parishes a P stitched on clothes denoted those in receipt of poor relief. There was no equivalent to the Scottish licensed begging system, where a blue badge granted the right to beg in one's home parish. The general parish system of poor relief worked reasonably well in Scotland.[52]

A growing institutionalisation of poor relief was seen in the eighteenth century. It involved specific facilities and also taking forward the provision under the Elizabethan Poor Law Acts that 'overseers of the poor' should try to find them work. From 1696, 'corporations for the poor' were established in Bristol, Exeter,

London and other cities to distribute poor relief through a system of workhouses. The first was John Carey's central workhouse, established in the Mint in Bristol (1696) and later named St Peter's Hospital, which represented a major development in the treatment of the able-bodied poor. An increase in the number of the poor led Worcester in 1703 to establish a workhouse in which 'Beggars and idle people' could be compelled to work.

The Workhouse Test Act of 1723 encouraged parishes to found workhouses to provide the poor with work and accommodation. All Nottingham's parishes built workhouses under the Act in the 1720s, Lancaster built one in 1730, and Birmingham another in 1733. In 1740, the vestry of Nazeing in Essex decided that a workhouse should be built to control the costs of poor relief because there had been complaints from the parishioners that they were 'oppressed by the exorbitant assessments annually raised for relief and maintenance of the poor'.[53] Although proposed from the reign of Anne, Edinburgh's charity workhouse did not open until 1743. By 1757 it had 701 inmates, and other workhouses in the urban area were opened in 1761 and 1762. In addition, in 1747, the town council decided to build a new prison within the House of Correction under the control of the workhouse's managers.[54]

However, over the country too few workhouses were founded to deal with the problems of poverty, especially as the population rose from mid-century, and many workhouses were badly underfunded. In the second half of the century, as more workhouses were opened, a higher proportion were built in rural areas. Nevertheless, only 47 of Lincolnshire's 701 parishes claimed to have a workhouse in 1776, although some of these may also have served the poor in neighbouring parishes. Some workhouses were purpose-built, while others were converted from existing properties. The poor set to work in workhouses generally were given tasks involving textiles, such as combing wool, spinning and clothes making.

Growing public concern about the system was expressed in mid-century, and again after the Seven Years' War, and led the House of Commons to establish committees of inquiry into the state of the poor in the 1770s and 1780s. The returns made by the Overseers of the Poor in response to an enquiry in 1776 were printed in the Sessional Papers the following year. Defects in the system were recognised in Gilbert's Act of 1782, which gave JPs the power to appoint Guardians running Houses of Industry for the elderly and infirm.

Workhouses, however, remained less important than 'out relief': providing assistance, and sometimes work, to the poor in their own homes. This had the virtue of flexibility, not least in dealing with the seasonal problems of unemployment, under-employment and dearth that the variations of work in agriculture, industry and transport produced. A seasonal need for relief was best served through outdoor relief rather than through institutionalisation.

Instead of condemning the Old (pre-1834) Poor Law as ineffective or repressive, it is necessary to appreciate that it could be an adaptable system offering a satisfactory response to the needs of many communities.[55] As with the political and ecclesiastical institutions and practices of the period, it is important, alongside contemporary criticism and subsequent replacement, to note the longevity and general success of the system. Variety remained the keynote of the provision of poor relief, as more generally with administrative practice in Britain. Some parishes had 'poorhouses', but did not provide work. Others provided the poor as cheap labour for employers, but did not house them.

The situation was less favourable in Ireland. City corporations of the poor in the charge of workhouses were created in Dublin in 1703 and Cork in 1735. They were supported by local taxes and donations. The Dublin workhouse opened in 1706. In 1757, Belfast introduced a tax on all householders in order to fund out-door relief for the poor. Dublin's problems were alleviated by a subsidy on the movement of domestic grain to it. Legislation of 1772 extended these corporations of the poor and their workhouses to the entire country and decreed that they were to be supported by subscriptions and county grants. The impotent poor were to be maintained and the deserving poor were to be licensed to beg, but begging without a licence was made a criminal offence. However, the Act of 1772 was in general inoperative, particularly outside the larger towns. There were major problems even there; the Dublin House of Industry, established in 1772 to care for vagrants and beggars, was unable to cope with the level of distress when it began to rise in 1777.

The general problem was the same everywhere: an absence of resources not only to deal with the poor *in situ*, but also with problems created by migration. There was neither wealth nor tax income sufficient to provide a widespread and comprehensive welfare system. However, as the government was not seeking to abolish poverty, but rather to alleviate it, or at least allay the fears created by the depiction of the poor, it is perhaps anachronistic to criticise it for failing to create an adequate system or for treating the effects of poverty, rather than dealing with its causes.

Nevertheless, in the last quarter of the century, there are signs of growing pressure, as the poor of all ages came to rely more heavily on parish poor relief. Although it has been argued that paupers were becoming younger, recent work has suggested that a growing proportion of the parish population was being impoverished at the same phases of the life-cycle as always.[56]

It was difficult for the poor to improve their condition. Despite the development of charity schools, they had only limited access to education, especially if they were female. Although the political process was not impervious to public opinion and pressures, it was closed to any attempt to redistribute wealth and opportunities. Labour had only limited possibilities of improving its conditions, although there was widespread trade unionism, for example among the West of England clothworkers and the framework knitters of the East Midlands.

There were also many industrial disputes, frequently as a result of defensive action against unwelcome changes. In 1752, the combers in the Norwich textile industry struck in order to gain better wages and to prevent the employment of blackleg labour. In 1758, there was a major strike by check weavers in and near Manchester. They sought a return to the prices of the 1730s and recognition of the Manchester Smallware Weavers' Society, but the strike was defeated after a prosecution for illegal combination, a method also used to stop a worsted weavers' combination in Manchester in 1760. Four years later, the journeymen weavers of Carrick in Ireland conducted a five-month strike over the issue of substitute labour. New technology in the English textile industry was resisted by rioters, for example in Leicester in 1773 against improved stocking frames.

However, there was also a degree of dialogue between employers and workers, albeit not from a position of equality. This helped industrialisation in the West Riding, but there was less common ground in the West Country. There the introduction of machinery into the weaving industry led to much unrest. In the case of the violent London silk-weavers strike of 1768–9, peace was restored only after the Spitalfields Act of 1773 brought an unusual degree of outside regulation of wages.

There was also discontent and direct action in rural areas. Enclosures could lead to an angry, indeed violent, response, as with the riots of 1777–80 that accompanied the enclosure of the former Malvern Chase.[57] Evictions, as land was 'cleared' of much of the tenantry, with the introduction of large-scale sheep farming and substantial rent rises, led to tension between landowners and tenants in the Scottish Highlands in the second half of the century. Throughout the British Isles, poaching was a form of resistance that was crucial to the livelihood of many. The Game Laws were widely seen as unfair, while the gentry viewed challenges to them as theft and as threats to the preservation of the social order. In the late 1770s, game preserves were first protected by spring guns and mantraps. In the wider British world, slavery can be seen as an important aspect of British society, although it played no role in Britain and the Somerset case of 1772 established that a person could not be a slave in England.

CONCLUSIONS

If the political system maintained social inequality, that was very much what those with power expected. This was a society that took inegalitarianism for granted, although there was a certain amount of social criticism. In *The History of the Life of the late Mr Jonathan Wild the Great* (1743), Henry Fielding offered a satirical indictment of false greatness: 'the plowman, the shepherd, the weaver, the builder and the soldier, work not for themselves but others; they are contented with a poor pittance (the labourer's hire) and permit us the GREAT to enjoy the fruits of their labours.'

It would be misleading to suggest either that there was widespread criticism of the existence of a hereditary hierarchical society or that tensions were only, or more, apparent between, as distinct from within, social groups. Social tension is difficult to assess. It probably increased after 1760, but it was not until the crisis in Britain in the 1790s created by the French Revolution that a notion of class-based politics developed. In the meanwhile, a relatively open society, in which people sought to create their own identities, was noticeable. This openness can be seen in the clubs of the period. The numerous social clubs for the affluent were matched by many others for labourers. These fulfilled recreational functions, although some, the friendly societies, also offered welfare. Clubs for labourers were self-regulated and part of a world of sociability that was only lightly supervised by government, and then largely in the form of licences for public houses (pubs). Some women accompanied their husbands to pubs and there were female clubs, but the overwhelming complexion of organised sociability was male, and the same was true of sociability in public places, such as street activities. The openness of society (although not to the illiterate) was captured by the critical 'Lilliputian' in the *Newcastle Courant* of 24 December 1743:

> Your mathematical corespondents grow so numerous of late that, unless some task be assigned them, we shall know no end of their debates. It is but too common in these our days for a young student to commence pedant before he thoroughly understands his common arithmetic, and to fancy himself a philosopher as soon as he has gained a smattering of Euclid's Elements. To carry on an epistolary correspondence in a private manner, for the sake of instruction, or for finding out the truth is commendable enough; but to pester the public with common questions in navigation, which every school boy can solve, is most intolerable ... each of them seems to value himself upon his own abilities.

Such a situation was encouraged by the culture of print. At the same time, there was also a measure of popular resentment that should not be ignored, although it would be misleading to present successive governments as presiding uneasily over a seething mass of discontent. Food rioters appealed to biblical notions of charity as well as to ideas of what humans owed each other in time of need, rather than to a language of rights.[58] More generally, riots can be seen both as community politics – showing discontent with establishment practices – and as direct action. It is important not to overlook the element of desperation, seen most clearly in food riots. Seizing food was more important than staging a protest, let alone regulating markets.[59] Equally, it would be mistaken to ignore political currents in popular agitation. During the 1722 elections, the Earl of Egmont, a Whig, reported, 'The mob which is generally High Church have where they are strongest been insufferably rude, as at Westminster, Reading, Stafford etc.' In July 1736, when London workers rioted against the employment of cheaper Irish labour, and were dispersed by the militia, Walpole wrote to his brother:

> I sent several persons both nights to mix with the mob, to learn what their cry and true meaning was, and by all accounts their chief and original grievance is the affair of the Irish, and so understood by the generality of the mob, but in several others, the Gin Act was cried out against, in some few, words of disaffection were thrown out, and one body of men of about eight were led on by a fellow that declared for Liberty and Property.

Two months later, troops were deployed in London to prevent disturbances over the Gin Act, Walpole writing

> the murmurings and complaints of the common people for want of gin and the great sufferings and losses of the dealers in spiritous liquors in general have created such uneasiness that they will deserve a great deal of attention and

consideration, and I am not without my apprehensions that a non-observance of the law, in some, may create great trouble, and a sullen acquiescence and present submission in others, in hopes of gaining redress by Parliament, may lay the foundation of very riotous and mobbish applications when we next meet.[60]

The last did not occur, while, more generally, the absence of serious radical political pressure from the lower and middling orders in the 1740s, when the political nation was divided and the state was vulnerable, suggests a need to put such pressure in perspective. Had there been such a challenge from below, it is doubtful whether the non-Jacobite elite could have afforded the bitter political disputes that occurred. Instead, the absence of a social challenge on the part of the unpropertied allowed the elite to pursue their divisions.

NOTES

1. T. Hitchcock and J. Black (eds), *Chelsea Settlement and Bastardy Examinations, 1733–1766* (1999), p. 91.
2. C. Ingrassia, *Authorship, Commerce and Gender in Early Eighteenth-Century England: A Culture of Paper Credit* (Cambridge, 1998).
3. J. Pearson, *Women's Reading in Britain, 1750–1835: A Dangerous Recreation* (Cambridge, 1999).
4. E. Spring, *Law, Land, and Family: Aristocratic Inheritance in England, 1300 to 1800* (Chapel Hill, 1994).
5. B. English, *The Great Landowners of East Yorkshire 1530–1910* (1992).
6. G. Clark (ed.), *Correspondence of the Foundling Hospital Inspectors in Berkshire 1757–68* (Reading, 1994).
7. A. Vickery, *The Gentleman's Daughter: Women's Lives in Georgian England* (New Haven, 1998).
8. Hitchcock, 'Demography and the culture of sex in the long eighteenth century', in J. Black (ed.), *Culture and Society in Britain 1660–1800* (Manchester, 1997), pp. 74–5.
9. A. Hillman (ed.), *The Rake's Diary. The Journal of George Hilton* (Barrow, 1994).
10. Journal du voyage de M. le Cte de Gisors, AE. Mémoires et Documents, Angleterre 1 fols 25–6; George Villiers, 4th Earl of Jersey, to Lady Spencer, 2 Dec. 1763, BL. Althorp F101.
11. A. Fletcher, *Gender, Sex and Subordination in England 1500–1800* (New Haven, 1995); R.B. Shoemaker, *Gender in English Society 1650–1850: The Emergence of Separate Spheres?* (1998).
12. R. Leppert, *Music and Image* (Cambridge, 1993).
13. I. Grundy, *Lady Mary Wortley Montagu: Comet of the Enlightenment* (Oxford, 1999), pp. 46–8.
14. L. Leneman, *Alienated Affections: The Scottish Experience of Divorce and Separation 1684–1830* (Edinburgh, 1998).
15. R. Norton, *Mother Clap's Molly House: The Gay Subculture in England 1700–1830* (1992).
16. R. Trumbach, *Sex and the Gender Revolution, Volume I: Heterosexuality and the Third Gender in Enlightenment London* (Chicago, 1998).
17. L. Stone, *The Family, Sex and Marriage in England, 1500–1800* (1977).
18. T. Pawlyn, 'The Cornish Pilchard Fishery in the Eighteenth Century', *Journal of the Royal Institution of Cornwall*, 2nd series, 3 (1998), pp. 69–75; L. Pollock, *Forgotten Children: Parent-Child Relations from 1500 to 1900* (1983); H. Cunningham, *Children of the Poor: Representations of Childhood since the Seventeenth Century* (1991).

19. M. Jackson, *New-Born Child Murder: Women, Illegitimacy and the Courts in Eighteenth-Century England* (Manchester, 1996).
20. H. Davis *et al.* (eds), *The Prose Works of Jonathan Swift* (16 vols, Oxford, 1939–68), VI, 10.
21. S. Johnson, *Political Writings*, ed. D. J. Greene (New Haven, 1977), p. 371.
22. C. Flint, *Family Fictions: Narrative and Domestic Relations in Britain, 1688–1798* (Stanford, 1998).
23. R.A. Houston, *Social Change in the Age of Enlightenment: Edinburgh 1660–1750* (Oxford, 1994).
24. M. Barke and R.J. Buswell (eds), *Newcastle's Changing Map* (Newcastle, 1992), pp. 23–7.
25. J. Broad (ed.), *Buckinghamshire Dissent and Parish Life, 1669–1712* (Aylesbury, 1993); W.R. Ward (ed.), *Parson and Parish in Eighteenth-Century Surrey. Replies to Bishops Visitations* (Guildford, 1994); C. Annesley and P. Hoskin (eds), *Archbishop Drummond's Visitation Returns, 1764, I: Yorkshire A-G* (York, 1997).
26. G.J. Davies, 'Literacy in Dorset, 1750–1800', *Notes and Queries for Somerset and Dorset*, 33 (1991), pp. 21–8; D.E. Smith, 'Eighteenth-century literacy levels in West Sussex', *Sussex Archaeological Collections*, 128 (1990), pp. 177–86.
27. R.A. Houston, *Scottish Literacy and the Scottish Identity* (1985).
28. M.E. Fissell, *Patients, Power and the Poor in Eighteenth-Century Bristol* (Cambridge, 1992).
29. J. Innes, 'Politics and morals: the reformation of manners movement in later eighteenth-century England', in E. Hellmuth (ed.), *The Transformation of Political Culture: England and Germany in the Late Eighteenth Century* (Oxford, 1990), pp. 57–118.
30. D. Andrew, *Philanthropy and Police: London Charity in the Eighteenth Century* (Princeton, 1989); M.E. Fissell, 'Charity universal? Institutions and moral reform in eighteenth-century Bristol', in L. Davison, T. Hitchcock, T. Kiern and R. Shoemaker (eds), *Stilling the Grumbling Hive: The Response to Social and Economic Problems in England, 1689–1750* (Stroud, 1992), pp. 121–44.
31. J. Smail, *The Origins of Middle-Class Culture: Halifax, Yorkshire, 1660–1780* (Ithaca, New York, 1994).
32. Anon., *The Treaty of Seville and the measures that have been taken for the four last years, impartially considered* (1730), p. 30.
33. T. Williamson, *Polite Landscapes: Gardens and Society in the Eighteenth Century* (Stroud, 1995), esp. pp. 100–40, quote p. 100.
34. N. McKendrick, 'The commercialization of leisure: botany, gardening and the birth of a consumer society', in S. Cavaciocchi (ed.), *Il Tempo Libero Economia e Società. Seccoli XVII–XVIII* (Prato, 1995), pp. 599–600.
35. Thomas to James Harris, 26 April 1746, Winchester, Hampshire CRO. 9H73 G309/31.
36. Jones, 14 Ap. 1775, BL. Althorp papers G.
37. J.C. Sainty, *Peerage Creations 1649–1800* (1998).
38. J. Cannon, *Aristocratic Century* (Cambridge, 1984); J.V. Beckett, *The Aristocracy in England, 1660–1914* (1986).
39. C.F.Foster, *Four Cheshire Townships in the Eighteenth Century* (Northwich, 1992).
40. J. Barry and C.W. Brooks (eds), *The Middling Sort of People: Culture, Society and Politics in England, 1550–1800* (1994).
41. G. Holmes, *Augustan England: Professions, State and Society* (1982).
42. M. Hunt, *The Middling Sort: Commerce, Gender and the Family in England, 1680–1780* (1996).
43. D. Defoe, *Moll Flanders* (1722; 1978 edn), p. 98.
44. D.R. Hainsworth, *Stewards, Lords and People: The Estate Steward and his World in Later Stuart England* (Cambridge, 1992).

45. P. Langford, *Public Life and the Propertied Englishman 1689–1798* (Oxford, 1991).
46. L. and J.C.F. Stone, *An Open Elite* (1984).
47. C. Estabrook, *Urbane and Rustic England: Cultural Ties and Social Spheres in the Provinces 1660–1780* (Manchester, 1999).
48. L. Manley, *Literature and Culture in Early Modern London* (Cambridge, 1995), pp. 524–30.
49. V.A. Hatley (ed.), *Northamptonshire Militia Lists, 1777* (Northampton, 1993).
50. K. Snell, *Annals of the Labouring Poor: Social Change and Agrarian England, 1660–1900* (Cambridge, 1985).
51. C.F. Foster, 'The landowners and residents of four North Cheshire townships in the 1740s', *Transactions of the Historic Society of Lancashire and Cheshire,* 141 (1992), p. 148.
52. P. Hembry (ed.), *Calendar of Bradford–on-Avon: Settlement Examinations and Removal Orders 1725–98* (Trowbridge, 1990); R.A. Cage, *The Scottish Poor Law, 1745–1845* (Edinburgh, 1981).
53. Nazeing History Workshop, *Five Miles from Everywhere. The Story of Nazeing,* Part 1 (Nazeing, 2000), p. 91.
54. R.A. Houston, *Social Change in the Age of Enlightenment: Edinburgh 1660–1750* (Oxford, 1994).
55. M.A. Parsons, 'Poor relief in Troutbeck [Westmorland] 1640–1836', *Transactions of the Cumberland and Westmorland Antiquarian and Archaeological Society,* 95 (1995), pp. 169–86.
56. S. Ottaway and S. Williams, 'Reconstructing the life-cycle experience of poverty in the time of the old Poor Law', *Archives,* 23 (1998), p. 28.
57. J. Neeson, 'The opponents of enclosure in eighteenth-century Northamptonshire', *Past and Present,* 105 (1984), pp. 114–39; M. Turner, 'Economic protest in a rural society: opposition to Parliamentary enclosure in Buckinghamshire', *Southern History,* 10 (1988), pp. 94–128.
58. E.P. Thompson, *Customs in Common* (1993).
59. A. Randall and A. Charlesworth (eds), *Moral Economy and Popular Protest: Crowds, Conflict and Authority* (2000).
60. Egmont to Daniel Dering, 27 Mar. 1722, Robert to Horatio Walpole, 29 July, 30 Sept. 1736, BL Add. 47029 fol 110, 63749A fols 249, 262.

7

Towns

Urban life became more important in Britain, especially in England. The percentage of the population living in towns (settlements with more than about 2,000 people) rose from about 17 in 1700 to about 27.5 in 1800. This was a major increase, especially as it occurred when the population was rising. In 1700, London had more than half a million people, nearly 10 per cent of the English population and more than all the other English towns together; and only five of the latter had more than 10,000 people: Norwich, Bristol, Newcastle, Exeter and York. By 1800, there were more than twenty-seven such towns. These included important industrial and commercial centres in the north of England and the Midlands, such as Bolton, Leeds, Manchester, Sheffield, Sunderland, Birmingham, Stoke and Wolverhampton.

At the other end of the size spectrum, the situation was more complex, because contemporary ideas of a town cannot be readily summarised in terms of a settlement with more than 2,000 people. Indeed, many settlements that were recognised as a market town, or were incorporated or parliamentary boroughs, or were regularly referred to as towns, had smaller populations. The size criteria is also problematic, because population figures prior to the 1801 census are approximate, and are complicated by the lack of a clear equivalence of town and parish: many towns were either part of a parish or part of several. At the lower level, many towns grew considerably, but others were stagnant and some declined. As with the population as a whole, growth was most pronounced after 1750.

By 1800, London's population had doubled to make it the most populous city in Europe, or the Americas. It was over ten times larger than the second city in England, although London's share of the national population did not rise in the eighteenth century. This should be seen not as a sign of failure, for London continued to expand and to attract many migrants, but rather as a sign of its already large size, and of the growth of manufacturing and commercial centres that were central to industrialising regions and to the Atlantic economy. Despite the growth of the latter, the reiterated stress on the commercial importance of London ensured that its trade was generally seen as synonymous with that of the country. In the third edition of his influential *Universal Dictionary of Trade and*

Commerce (1766), a work that first appeared in 1751, Malachy Postlethwayt, an active writer on economic issues, added a dedication to George Nelson, Lord Mayor of London, and to the aldermen and councillors of the city, that included the passages

> London tradesmen appear to constitute the very active soul of the commerce of the whole British state; and they are an essential medium between the merchant, the country shop-keep, and the consumers ... Of such high concernment are the London tradesmen to the whole traffic of the nation, that all our native commodities and manufactures almost of every sort, more or less, center at first in London, and amongst the London tradesmen, brought to them from all the inland manufacturing and trading towns; and are afterwards sent again from London to the several different trading towns and cities throughout the kingdom, where those commodities and manufactures are not made or produced. The countrymen sheer their sheep, sell their wool, and carry it from place to place; the manufacturer sets it to work, to combing, spinning, winding, twisting, dyeing, weaving, fulling, dressing, and thus they furnish their numberless manufactures in the whole woollen branch. But what must they do with them, if London did not take them first off their hands, and the London tradesmen, warehousemen, factors, and wholesale dealers, did not vend and circulate them amongst the London merchants, as well as to all the remote parts of the nation? London is the grand central mart to which the gross body of all our native commodities are first brought, and from whence they are again sold ... this is the case be it Manchester for cotton wares; Yorkshire for coarse cloth, kersies etc. ...[1]

This was an exaggeration of London's economic centrality, but, nevertheless, the market and finance of London were central to economic activity.

London was significant in influencing notions of urban life (although there was also much provincial autonomy), and also posed the greatest problems of law and order and social conditions. London's dominant position owed something to the enormous growth of the city's trade, but also reflected the city's role as the centre of government, the law and consumption, and its dominance of the world of print, which became even more important as a shaper of news, opinion and fashion. Political programmes were conceived and debated in London, the seat of the Court, the legislature, executive and judiciary. Nevertheless, there were frequent opposition claims, especially under Walpole, that the government neglected London and was unpopular there.

London newspapers circulated throughout Britain and were also crucial sources for the provincial press. The turnpike and postal systems also centred on London. This dominance of communications reflected and sustained London's economic importance. Thus, London-based insurance companies, such as the Sun Fire Office, and banks were able to organise insurance and banking elsewhere by delegating the work to agents in other towns with whom regular contact could be maintained. Profits from trade and government helped bridge the gap between the city as a centre of production and as a centre of consumption.

London grew significantly, especially at the beginning of the century, when the West End estates of landlords such as Sir Richard Grosvenor and Lord Burlington were developed as prime residential property. Mayfair and St. James's became the select side of town and the streets there still bear the names of the politicians of the period, for example Harley Street and Oxford Street. Building and gentrification helped make the area safer. Leading aristocrats built or re-built grand London houses, such as Burlington, Carlton, Chandos, Chesterfield, Derby, Devonshire and Spencer Houses. Buckingham House was bought by George III.

Other areas further east, such as Clerkenwell and Hackney, became less fashionable, a process paralleled in Paris. Westminister Bridge opened a new route across the river Thames and helped development on the south bank. It was followed by Blackfriars Bridge, opened in 1769 after nine years' construction. The $\frac{1}{2}$d toll demanded from those who crossed led to a riot. London's squares were imitated in cities such as Bristol.

The different worlds of London co-existed on uneasy terms, and this was noted by commentators. The novelist Henry Fielding focused on London presented not as a predatory bourgeois environment, but as a world corrupted by Westminster. The city was atomized in terms of the corrupt Court and aristocracy of its west end, with their commerce in vice, and the more acceptable commercial metropolis.[2] Civic splendour was celebrated in the Mansion House, built in 1739–53, but the stability and growth of the City of London was not problem-free, but was affected by periodic crises. A pamphleteer wrote of London's freemen in 1722: 'as South Sea has stripped them of their superfluous riches, long wars, continued taxes, and high duties, impaired their stock, and shaked their credit.'[3] In addition, there were important political divisions within London. These led to the City Elections Act of 1725 which defined the freeman franchise as narrowly as possible and imposed an aldermanic veto on the actions of the more popular and Tory-inclined Common Council in order to limit the volatility and independence of popular London politics.

The creation of London was an evolutionary, not a revolutionary, process, with development out of existing housing types and traditional layouts. The ability to change and upgrade the structure of new houses, plus the high level of maintenance they required, particularly in the painting of woodwork, made them perfectly suited to a consumer society geared towards the continued renewal and replacement of products. Consumerism and class also interacted in open spaces. Squares tended to be public, rather than private, arenas until the 1720s. Then, London began to be shaped as a series of bounded spaces, both physically and socially, where enclosure ensured exclusion and exclusion provided exclusivity.[4] The designs of London's new houses were given wider impact through Richard Neve's *The City and Country Purchaser and Builder's Dictionary,* which first appeared in 1703, with a second edition in 1726.

London developed further as a centre of consumption and leisure. The amount of fixed specialised investment in the latter rose greatly with theatres, including the Theatre Royal, the King's Theatre and the Pantheon (a grand assembly room in Oxford Street completed in 1772), pleasure gardens, picture galleries and other facilities, ranging from gambling houses to coffee houses, auction houses to brothels. Although some facilities were or sought to be exclusive, most were readily accessible to anyone with money to spend. London, though large, was compact: it was still immune from the congestion and sprawl of the following century. The proximity of the countryside lessened the demand for private gardens. The social basis of London's development was not only that the rural elite increasingly came to spend part of the year there, but also that the 'middling sort' expanded considerably.[5]

This was moreover true of regional capitals, such as Norwich and Nottingham, county centres such as Warwick, and developing entertainment centres, particularly spa towns, such as Tunbridge Wells and Bath. 34 new spas were founded in England between 1700 and 1750, and even more in the second half of the century. Spas and resort centres, such as Moffat, were also founded in Scotland. The first Pump Room at Bath was built in 1706, followed in 1708 by Harrison's Assembly Rooms, and in 1730 by new rooms in the Palladian style by John Wood. The development of Bath as a city of orderly leisure owed much to Richard 'Beau' Nash, who in 1705 was appointed first Master of Ceremonies. His 'Rules' for the behaviour of visitors to Bath were first published in 1742, part of the process by which the codification of social propriety was expressed (and debated) in print.[6]

The 'middling sort' were largely professionals and gentlemen merchants. Doctors, bankers, lawyers, clergymen, and Customs and Excise men could all be found in major towns, and their numbers increased. They were largely responsible for new building and rebuilding, the replacement of timber-frame by brick in houses for the well to do, for example in Norwich from the late-seventeenth century and in Lancaster, although stone, rather than brick, continued to dominate Scottish building. Queen's Square begun in 1699 set the fashion for brick-built houses in Bristol, and was responsible for the growth of brickworks there.

The period is often associated with urban elegance, as in the squares of the West End of London. Brick buildings with large windows were built in a regular 'classical' style along and around new streets, squares, crescents and circles. The latter, even if not the invention of John Wood Senior, were first used on any scale in the suburbs he laid out north of Bath, one of the most influential towns for the establishment of urban forms. Wood began the King's Circus in 1754, and his son began the Royal Crescent in 1767.[7]

In west-central Glasgow, stone town houses in a neo-classical design, with balustraded roofs, entablatures and urns, were constructed from 1710. Genteel dwellings lined Charlotte Street (1779). In Bristol, the very spacious Prince's Street (1725), was followed by King's Square and Brunswick Square laid out between 1755 and 1769. The New Town proposals of Sir Gilbert Elliott and Lord Provost Drummond sought to make Edinburgh a fitting metropolis as the chief city of North Britain. In Dublin, the Wide Streets Commission began work in 1757.[8]

Alongside light, roomy and attractive private houses for the affluent, numerous public and philanthropic buildings were built. Theatres, assembly rooms, subscription libraries and other leisure facilities were opened in many towns, alongside public outdoor space: parks, walks and racecourses. The social world that fostered the demand for new buildings and spaces, was matched by entrepreneurial activity, artistic skill and the wealth of a growing economy. Provincial architects, such as Joseph Pickford in Derby, Richard Gillow and Thomas Harrison in Lancaster, and John Johnson in Chelmsford[9] were responsible for fine buildings in a large number of centres. However, not all towns moved at the same pace towards what has been seen as an urban renaissance.[10]

New buildings often marked a major change in local consciousness, not least as a replacement of past settings of authority, as with the new Guildhall in Worcester designed by Thomas White and constructed between 1721 and 1727. In mid-century, Nottingham replaced its medieval timber-framed Guildhall by a brick one with a colonnaded front. More generally, the image of towns altered. Timber and thatch were seen as dated, unattractive, non-utilitarian and, increasingly, non-urban, as were long-established street patterns. Furthermore, although some churches were rebuilt, new stone and brick buildings increasingly offered new definitions of town function, with an emphasis in particular on leisure and retail, and, more generally, on private space open to those who could pay (shops/subscription rooms) rather than spaces open to all (market places, churches).

New forums for sociability were created. The influential Assembly Rooms at York were largely built in 1731–2. Assemblies were first held in Newcastle in 1716 and new assembly rooms opened there in 1736 and 1776. Norwich gained assembly rooms in 1754. The townscape literally became brighter as street lighting was introduced. The main streets of Lancaster were lit from 1738. Human noise was also focused on towns. In his play *The Relapse* (1696), Vanbrugh referred to London as 'that uneasy theatre of noise'.

Service activities, rather than industrial expansion, were the basis of growth in many towns (see also Chapter 5). The economic basis of the shift was growing prosperity, especially in commerce, and this interacted with increased and differentiated consumption. Most of the non-food goods bought by affluent households were made in towns, and, even more, sold there or through them. Facilities for, and patterns of, service activity responded to the example of London, which was presented as the benchmark for conditions elsewhere, although it would be mistaken to ignore the provincial capacity to preserve local practices and to take initiatives, and, in part, London's impact was itself a product of its openness to influences from outside.

Towns also benefited from the strength of the rural economy, providing not only a commercial but also a social focus. A degree of urban–rural rapprochement and cohesion at elite level was an important factor encouraging stability, and possibly contributed to a degree of cultural merging. Joseph Pickford (1734–82), the London-born architect who designed the Derby Assembly Rooms, also designed the Riding School at Calke Abbey as well as Josiah Wedgwood's house and factories at Etruria.[11] It is important not to exaggerate: differences remained between urban and rural values, not least in politics and religion, and the landed magnates visited towns on their own terms. Yet there was a degree of interchange based on shared values that was arguably greater than that of the two previous centuries.

In addition, rather than displaying a coherent standpoint, the urban population shared in the spectrum of existing opinion, and was divided by confessional, economic and political views. This lack of urban homogeneity aided integration with the views of the rest of society, and also helped ensure that urban interests could be wooed by élite politicians.

The urban dimension of politics was important, especially thanks to the location of so many parliamentary seats in towns, albeit, often, small places, and also due to the very specific and important economic interests towns had, which could be furthered by political means. Purges of corporate government undertaken after the restoration of Charles II in 1660, and again in the 1680s had helped accentuate the politicisation of many towns, undermining attempts to present town life as harmonious and unified. This fed through into the so-called 'rage of party' of the reigns of William III (1689–1702) and Anne (1702–14), when party groups sought to use the tactic of removing their opponents from town councils in order to ensure unity. The political role of town corporations cut across their function as institutions of local government, and the co-existence of the two helped provide much of the character of town government.[12]

At another level of politics, a town's use of its MPs to advance or defend its local interests with government or in Parliament, particularly in relation to the passage of Acts of Parliament, provided the basis for a strong relationship, that required both parties to give and take. At that level, politics was reactive and consensual, with the search for compromise part of a dynamic relationship in which local issues were crucial. This relationship between MPs and towns, and the recognition on both sides that it had to be constantly nurtured, was a long-term structural feature of politics that added stability to the system.

There were, however, particular problems in managing large urban constituencies. 'Radicalism' as generally understood was particularly associated with large towns, especially London. In 1762, Elizabeth Montagu was shocked by the extent of critical sentiment in London,

> all mankind are philosophers and pride themselves in having a contempt for rank and order and imagine they show themselves wise in ridiculing whatever gives distinction and dignity to kings and other magistrates, not considering that the chains of opinion are less galling than those of law, and that the great beast the multitude must be bound by something. Alexander the Great was treated with contempt by a certain philosopher in a tub [Diogenes], but in this enlightened age the man who made the tub would use him with the same scorn.[13]

The presence of political or quasi-political institutions in major cities, most obviously Parliament [in London, Dublin and, until 1707, Edinburgh], and their potential interaction with popular urban tension, could serve to increase urban political volatility; disturbances in London were linked to parliamentary opposition in 1733, and again during the Wilkesite troubles in the 1760s. Edinburgh and Dublin were similarly centres of contention, but so also were other major towns. The malt tax riots in Glasgow in 1725 led to the despatch of troops, who killed

19 rioters, and food shortages led to major riots in Newcastle in 1740 and in Belfast in 1756. A number of towns were affected by food riots in 1766. The use of troops did not always overawe rioters. During a food riot at Dysart in 1720, the rioters attacked the soldiers and seized their weapons.

Any stress on towns as centres of culture, commerce and growth must take note of their variety. Urban growth was principally stimulated by external links: relations with other towns and with the countryside, and these varied. Improved communications were important to the integration of a urban system and the specialisation of activities in individual towns. A study of the urban system in Cheshire and southern Lancashire has suggested that 'what stimulated growth was not necessarily intrinsic to particular towns, but to do with their extrinsic relationships, their linkages with town and country. It was the system of towns and not the qualities of individual centres which drew together the productive forces of the region, facilitated economic specialization, and generated regional growth. Thus a fully integrated urban system was vital ... '[14]

Aside from the centres of provincial culture, there were also important industrial towns, although their growth, as with Birmingham, owed something also to their role as centres of trade and distribution. This role was particularly important for ports. In the South West, the ports became more important. Plymouth replaced Exeter as the region's largest town in the second half of the eighteenth century, while Falmouth, a small settlement in the mid-seventeenth century, was Cornwall's largest town a century later. Whereas the inland regional centre and manufacturing centre of Norwich was the second most populous town in England in 1700, Liverpool, an Atlantic port that was not a county capital, was in 1800.

Other oceanic ports had less spectacular or sustained growth, but, nevertheless, still saw a major rise in population. Whitehaven's population rose to 16,000 in about 1785. However, it was not only oceanic ports that saw major rises in population. On the east coast, Sunderland, North and South Shields and Tynemouth all benefited greatly from the export of coal, and from coal-based industries. Hull and Newcastle, both more established urban centres, also saw major population growth.

Some towns, such as Oxford and Hereford, were fairly static communities, and growth rates were relatively low in some formerly important centres, such as Worcester. Other towns were affected by adverse economic circumstances. Gloucester's trade, sugar refining and glass manufacturing could not compete with that of Bristol, and its cloth industry also declined. York was hit by the growth of Leeds, although it was able to benefit as a centre for the local gentry and also to profit from developments in the trade in food. York became in mid century the largest national collecting point of wholesale butter and the provincial source of London's butter. This reflected the prosperity of the Vale of York. The net effect of such shifts was to accentuate the long-established changing character of the urban network.

In Ireland, urbanisation was overwhelmingly concentrated in Dublin, the centre of government and services, but also a port. The other leading Irish towns – Cork, by far the largest after Dublin, Belfast, Drogheda, Limerick and Waterford – were ports, their prosperity dependent on the growing commercialisation of the Irish population. In Scotland, Edinburgh had about 30–35,000 people in 1700, more if the suburbs are included, and was the second city in Britain, while Glasgow had about 18,000 inhabitants. In mid-century, Glasgow had about 30,000 people, with 15,000 in Aberdeen, 12,000 in Dundee and 9,000 in Inverness. Wales was far less urbanised.

Towns, particularly the major ones, constituted the living space of the most articulate and informed members of society, and tended to have their associated paraphernalia, such as printing presses. The press indeed is one index of urban success. Excluding London, the number of English newspapers rose from about 24 in 1723, 32 in 1753, and 35 in 1760, to 50 in 1782. The presence of newspapers was important to political consciousness in towns. The provincial expansion was due both to the increase in the number of towns with papers and to more towns having more than one paper: this was particularly true of Bristol, Exeter, Newcastle, Norwich and York.

Yet there were also failures. After the *Union Journal: or, Halifax Advertiser* (1759–*c*. 1763) ceased publication, Halifax had no paper until the early-nineteenth century. After the failure of the *Darlington Pamphlet* (1772–3), the needs of Teesside continued to be met by the Leeds, Newcastle and York press, and no other paper was launched at Darlington until the *Darlington and Stockton Times* appeared in 1847. The *Hereford Journal* (1739) was also short-lived, but the *British Chronicle, or Pugh's Hereford Journal* launched in 1770, lasted into the twentieth century. In Cumbria the *Kendal Courant* (1731–6), *Kendal Weekly Mercury* (1735–47) and *Whitehaven Weekly Courant* (1736–43) all failed, but the *Cumberland Pacquet or Ware's Whitehaven Advertiser*, launched in 1774, was successful.

Other towns only acquired their first papers later: Montrose in 1793, Carlisle in 1798, Greenock and Arbroath in 1799, Falmouth – the first in Cornwall – in 1801, Ayr in 1803, Swansea – the first in Wales – in 1804, Inverness in 1807, Bangor – the first in north Wales – in 1808, and Barnstaple – the first in north Devon – in 1824. After two or possibly three failures in the eighteenth century, the continuous publication of papers in Plymouth began in 1808. This is a reminder that the character and fortune of towns varied.

Many towns saw graceful as well as profitable urban expansion. It was not only the large towns that expanded. Stockton, an important port for North Sea trade, acquired a new parish church (1712), customs house (1730), town hall (1735) and theatre (1766). Some towns were less fortunate. Lieutenant Richard Browne wrote to his father from Enniskillen in Ulster in 1765 that it had 'but a miserable aspect, being small, the houses mean and thatched with straw'. Yet, as ever, variety was the keynote. Browne had written from the Isle of Wight in 1757, 'Newport is a very clean pretty town regular and well built, the Bath players are in it and we have plays every night.'[15]

Overall, the growth in the numbers of schools, hospitals, dispensaries, infirmaries, theatres, reading rooms etc. in the British Isles may not have been massive, but it was significant and changed the institutional and cultural landscape of most of the well-populated regions. This was important to the period's self-image as an improving society. Such self-understanding should neither be taken at face value nor regarded as descriptively or analytically sufficient, but it did reflect something of the realities of eighteenth-century life.

In some respects, urban life offered freedom. If towns did not offer equality of opportunity, they did provide opportunity, and the sustained migration to them was a testimony to this. Each migrant represented an individual decision that life might be better in a town. For many, this proved illusory: rural penury translated into urban poverty. Towns contained impoverished, squalid and dangerous areas. Indeed, urban degradation was more pernicious, because of the absence of the social and community support that was more prevalent in rural parishes, although not without its own harshness and exclusions. Alongside consumerism and the middling orders, it is also important to remember the important role of manufacturing in towns, and the extent to which economic shifts could push artisans into what would today be called the 'underclass'.[16]

However, the social system was more fluid in towns: mobility was greater, traditional hierarchies weaker, and control laxer. Urban populations were not on the whole radical in their politics or beliefs, but town life did provide the context for most new ideas, both elite and popular, and offered new experiences. It was also easier to bridge the divide between elite and non-elite in towns, whether in the dissemination of fashions, such as tea drinking and the wearing of imported cloth, or of new political views. The concentration of people in towns, their higher rates of literacy, and more marked traditions of political autonomy and independence of attitude, helped to foster, at least in part, a consumer society, the consumerism of which went beyond goods and services.

CONCLUSIONS

A growing urban sector coexisted with landed society and this helped to ensure a two-way flow in social and cultural attitudes. Urban development altered the institutional and cultural landscape of well-populated regions, and was crucial to a growing self-image of Britain as an improving society. Towns were also the forcing houses of the commercial economy and culture of print through which Britain became not only a world power but also a political society that saw domination as its national destiny. The relationship between town development and urban politics has been presented very differently. It is possible to emphasise the way in which urban renaissance aided elite integration and thus growing stability,[17] but it is also reasonable to stress the resilience, and indeed vitality, of divisions within the urban community, including within the elite. As elsewhere in the book, the argument here is that both approaches are correct and that it is unhelpful both to isolate either stability or strife, continuity or change, and to treat them as in some way incompatible. Instead, as was only to be expected, in a complex society with a high degree of political awareness and participation, there was both change and continuity, division and unity, and their dynamic interaction provided much of the flavour of urban consciousness and politics.

NOTES

1. M. Postlethwayt, *Universal Dictionary* (4th edn., 2 vols, 1774), I, i–ii.
2. W.A. Speck, *Literature and Society in Eighteenth-Century England. Ideology, Politics and Culture, 1680–1820* (1998), pp. 107–8.
3. Anon., *Reasons against Building a Bridge from Lambeth to Westminster,* (1722), p. 6.
4. E. McKellar, *The Birth of Modern London: The Development and Design of the City 1660–1720* (Manchester, 1999).
5. P. Earle, *The Making of the English Middle Class: Business, Society and Family Life in London, 1660–1730* (1989).
6. P. Borsay, *The Image of Georgian Bath, 1700–c.2000: Towns, Heritage and History* (Oxford, 2000).
7. M. Reed, 'The transformation of urban space 1700–1840', in P. Clark (ed.), *The Cambridge Urban History of Britain, II: 1540–1840* (Cambridge, 2000), p. 634.
8. N. McCullough (ed.), *A Vision of the City: Dublin and the Wide Streets Commissioners* (Dublin, 1991).
9. N. Briggs, *John Johnson 1732–1814. Georgian Architect and County Surveyor of Essex* (Chelmsford, 1991); A. White, *The Buildings of Georgian Lancaster* (Lancaster, 1992).
10. R. Sweet, *The English Town 1680–1840: Government, Society and Culture* (1999).
11. E. Saunders, *Joseph Pickford and Derby. A Georgian Architect* (Stroud, 1993).
12. P.D. Halliday, *Dismembering the Body Politic: Partisan Politics in England's Towns 1650–1730* (Cambridge, 1998).
13. Elizabeth Montagu to George Lyttelton, 23 Sept. 1762, HL. MO. 1422.
14. J. Stobart, 'Regional structure and the urban system: north-west England, 1700–1760', *Transactions of the Historic Society of Lancashire and Cheshire*, 145 (1996), p. 73.
15. Browne to his father, 3 June 1765, 6 Aug. 1757, BL. RP. 3284.
16. L.D. Schwarz, *London in the Age of Industrialisation: Entrepreneurs, Labour Force and Living Conditions, 1700–1850* (Cambridge, 1992).
17. P. Borsay, *The English Urban Renaissance: Culture and Society in the Provincial Town, 1660–1770* (Oxford, 1991).

8

Faith and the churches

To the casual observer of today the period may not appear a particularly religious age. Urban building is not generally recalled for its churches, no more than the British painters of the period are remembered for religious works. Religious warfare is seen as largely something of the more distant past, and the period is viewed as one of growing toleration. It is seen as a period of enlightenment, and the Enlightenment is presented as a secular movement. Faith is generally ascribed to superstitious conservatism or irrational religious enthusiasm. The serious anti-Catholic Gordon Riots of 1780 are seen as an anachronism.

Though such inaccurate views are not found in most recent scholarly works, they are still widely held; and there are genuine problems of definition and methodology. The quality of the religious experience of the bulk of the population is difficult to assess, as is the source and depth of their faith.

It is similarly difficult to establish how far such personal and communal experience was affected by the politico-ecclesiastical changes of the period. The political crisis of 1688–92 had led to major changes that were important not only in themselves, but also, because of the role of the recent past in conditioning the understanding of developments which was influential in affecting attitudes. Religious antagonism provided a key to past, present and future. Such antagonism was also about society, politics and culture, but was rooted in the need to save souls.

In Ireland, the political crisis, indeed transformation, of 1689–91 reimposed and strengthened an Anglican ascendancy, completing a process that had begun in the sixteenth century. Catholic officials and landowners were replaced. Bishops and regular clergy were driven abroad under the Banishment Act of 1697. Transportations begun in 1698, and at least 444 priests were certainly expelled. Banning the bishops prevented the ordination of priests in Ireland. Parish priests were obliged to register under the Registration Act of 1704 and compelled to renounce loyalty to the Stuarts. Acts of Parliament forbade mixed marriages, Catholic schools and the bearing of arms by Catholics, although the need to re-enact them suggests that they were evaded. The culture of power in Ireland became thoroughly and often aggressively Protestant.

Yet, the Catholic percentage of the population did not decrease because serious repression was episodic; instead the ratio of Catholics to Protestants rose from about 3:1 in 1731 to 4:1 in 1800, and Catholics thus remained in the unusual position of being a persecuted majority. The draconian wartime legislation of 1697, 1703–4 and 1709 was inspired by fears of Catholic disloyalty and links with France, for example in response to the French invasion attempt on Scotland of 1708. Persecution slackened in peacetime. The Penal Code was designed essentially to destroy the political and economic power of Catholicism rather than the faith itself, although it was also an attempt to erode Catholic belief and practice.

The ability of the Anglican establishment to proselytise in Ireland was limited by its general failure to communicate with a still largely Gaelic-speaking population. There were few clerics such as John Richardson (1664–1747), who frequently preached in Gaelic in his parish, published several books in the language, including an attack on pilgrimages, and played a role in the Gaelic translation of the *Book of Common Prayer* which appeared in 1712.

In contrast, the Catholic colleges, such as the Irish College in Paris, stipulated a knowledge of the language as a requirement for priests in Ireland. The Catholics published many catechisms and devotional works in Gaelic. The Church hierarchy survived largely intact and the Catholic clergy, wearing secular dress and secretly celebrating mass, continued their work, sustained by a strong oral culture, the emotional link with a sense of national identity, by hedge-school teaching, and by a degree of tacit government acceptance. In 1719, for example, the government in London blocked an attempt by the Dublin Parliament to make castration a punishment for priests. The Convocation of the Church of Ireland meeting in 1711 planned to establish a system of free compulsory education for Catholics in order to teach children Protestantism and the English language. The children were to attend school until the age of 16 and to be regularly examined by the parish minister in English and the catechism. The scheme, however, was ineffective. No Church funds were forthcoming and the House of Commons was opposed to any plan involving higher taxation. A royal bounty, and from 1745 a parliamentary grant, finally financed a small-scale scheme, launched by Primate Boulter in 1731, that established a system of primary schools to encourage Protestantism and the English language.

Irish Catholics were not an amorphous mass of down-trodden victims whose destiny was to endure, but a group of socially-mobile individuals who struggled not only against civil disabilities, but also amongst themselves.[1] At the same time, it is inappropriate to regard the penal statutes as no more than a system of petty oppression. They did weigh heavily, although the situation improved in mid-century, paving the way for the emergence of the Catholic bishops into greater public prominence.[2]

Anglican religious tests for public office in Ireland also handicapped the large Presbyterian community in Ulster until 1780, when the Dublin Parliament abolished tests for Protestant Dissenters as a wartime concession, while Presbyterians and Catholics had to pay tithes to support the Church of Ireland. To Presbyterians, there was an Anglican, not a Protestant, ascendancy. Under the Test Act of

1704, they were banned from civil and military offices, and their churches and schools were closed. The Presbyterian church was not endowed like the Church of Ireland, but was linked to government by a small subsidy, the *regium donum* (king's gift), first paid in 1672. An Act of 1719 extended the 1689 Act of Toleration to Ireland.

Many Irish Presbyterians emigrated to America, where strong Congregational, Presbyterian and Quaker churches prevented the establishment of an Anglican hierarchy in the transatlantic colonies, and were eventually to form the core of the independence movement as they defended their autonomy from what they saw as an imperialistic English establishment.

In Scotland, the 'Glorious Revolution' led to a Presbyterian ascendancy. In 1689, the Scottish Parliament abolished Episcopacy and in 1690 a Presbyterian Church was established there. Episcopalian clergy were purged from their livings and from educational institutions. They created the basis of an Episcopal Church in Scotland, which received limited legal recognition by the Act of Toleration passed by a Tory government in 1712. An Episcopalian culture of loss and loyalty was to underpin Jacobitism in Scotland, particularly in the north-east, and also affected English Anglicans, some of whom, such as Bishop Samuel Horsley, championed the Scottish Episcopalians, partly because of their sense of isolation: they felt threatened by the Church of Scotland and by English Dissent.

The Presbyterian settlement was confirmed, not reversed, by the Act of Union (although lay patronage, abolished in 1690, was restored in 1712), so that 1707 led to the creation of a multi-confessional state. The establishment and continuation of Presbyterianism was in some respects crucial to the success of Union. The Act of Union contained a clause also safeguarding the privileges of the Church of England, and thus placed the Church of Scotland on a similar footing to the Church of England as an established church.

In 1779, when supporting the repeal of restrictions on Dissenters in England, Thomas Townshend MP told the House of Commons that he

> rejected the idea of so essential a connection between our church establishment and our constitution, that any alteration in one must endanger the other. If that position had been true, how could the same legal government support two distinct church establishments, that of England and that of Scotland, which differed so very essentially from one another?

The crown was represented at the General Assembly of the Church of Scotland by the Royal Commissioner.

The Episcopal Church in Scotland declined during the course of the century. About 40 per cent of the Scottish population were Episcopalians in 1700, but only 5 per cent in the 1780s; they remained under disabilities until the early nineteenth century.

Catholicism was the third most popular creed in Scotland and was particularly strong in the West Highlands and Banff and Buchan. Concern about the Jacobite threat led to action directed against the Catholics. The Scottish Society for the Propagation of Christian Knowledge was granted a royal charter in 1709 to 'eradicate error and to sow truth, to teach true religion and loyalty and to strengthen the British Empire by the addition of useful subjects and firm Protestants'. From 1710, the Society erected schools and supplied teachers who also acted as catechists for the Church of Scotland until 1758. In 1723 and from 1725, the crown gave an annual grant of £1,000 to the General Assembly of the Church of Scotland to assist in the struggle against Catholicism. The Royal Bounty was used to support catechists and missionary ministers. The Catholic mission in Scotland was badly affected by underfunding, divisions, political commitments and clerical shortcomings.

In England, the 'Glorious Revolution' ensured that the monarch would be a Protestant, but loosened Anglican hegemony. Under the 'Act for Exempting their Majesties Protestant Subjects, Dissenting from the Church of England, from the Penalties of certain Laws', the concessionary but restrictive formulation of what is better known as the Toleration Act (1689), Dissenters (Protestant Nonconformists who believed in the Trinity) who took the oaths of Supremacy and Allegiance and accepted thirty-six of the thirty-nine Articles, and made the Declaration against Transubstantiation could obtain licences as ministers or school-masters, although these had to be registered with a bishop or at the Quarter Sessions, tasks which posed problems for both. The Act was followed by the registration of numerous Dissenting meeting-houses: at least 113 in Devon by 1701. The Presbyterians, Independents (Congregationalists), Quakers and Baptists were the leading Dissenting churches. A Presbyterian chapel was opened in Nottingham in 1689, followed by another in 1690 for the Unitarians, who were very influential in the city, and one for the Baptists in 1724. In Exeter, two Dissenter meeting houses were opened in about 1687 (and others by 1715 and 1760), followed by a Quaker meeting house in 1715, a Baptist church in 1725, an Independent chapel by 1744, and a synagogue in 1763. An Independent meeting house was opened in Norwich in about 1693, followed by a Quaker meeting house in about 1699 and a Baptist chapel in 1745. In Coventry, a large Quaker meeting house was opened in 1698, a new Presbyterian chapel in 1701, and one for the Particular Baptists in 1724. Anglicanism declined in the city in the face of a strong challenge from the Presbyterians and the Unitarians.

Unitarians, Catholics and non-Christians (mostly Jews) did not officially enjoy rights of public worship under the Act of Toleration, and Catholics were subject to penal statutes, as were Unitarians under the Blasphemy Act of 1697. There was no Toleration Act for Unitarians until 1813 and in Scotland the death penalty existed for denying the Trinity. Trinitarian orthodoxy was strong and was shared by Catholics and Protestants.

Aside from clashes between different churches, there were also tensions within them, as with the Church of England. Some of its clerics were more hostile to other Protestant groups and inclined to see a threat in toleration, a threat not only to church attendance and religious orthodoxy, but also to the moral order and socio-political cohesion that the Church was seen as sustaining. The Toleration Act contributed to a sense of malaise and uncertainty. The lower clergy were frustrated that William III did not allow Convocation (the clerical assembly; there was one for each archdiocese) to meet until the last year of his reign. It was prorogued (postponed) continually from that of George I on (from 1717 with the exception of a brief session in 1741–2), as was the Convocation of the Church of Ireland. Dr Henry Sacheverell, a high Anglican Cleric and a Tory, felt able to argue controversially in 1709 that the Church was in danger under the Revolution settlement, as interpreted by the Whigs. Indeed, Thomas, 1st Earl Wharton, the Whig Lord Lieutenant of Ireland, was sufficiently pro-Dissenter in this period, that the Irish House of Lords, where the bishops were influential, complained to Queen Anne and he was recalled in 1710. The Occasional Conformity (1711) and Schism (1714) Acts, which had been designed respectively to prevent the circumvention of communion requirements for office-holding by Dissenters communicating once a year, occasional conformity, and to make a separate education for them illegal (measures both passed by Anne's Tory ministry of 1710–14), were both repealed by the Whigs under George I in 1719. The Reverend Benjamin Robertshaw, Rector of Amersham 1728–44, recorded the tension in Anglican attitudes to Dissent,

> About the year 1721 I was so unfortunate as to fall under the displeasure of my diocesan, Bishop Gibson [a Whig]... The occasion was my refusing to bury a Presbyterian's child, sprinkled in their unauthorised way, in my parish at Penn. Upon my absolute refusal the parents ... carried it to Wycombe, where it was buried by one who I suppose would have given Christian burial even to Pontius Pilate himself, provided he had but in his lifetime used to cry 'King George forever!'[3]

Nevertheless, attempts during the years of Whig ascendancy to repeal the Test and Corporation Acts failed. These Acts, of 1673 and 1661 respectively, obliged members of borough corporations and office holders under the Crown to take oaths of allegiance and supremacy and to receive communion in the Church of England, and these remained in force until 1828, although the Corporation Act was much diluted in 1719 so that many Dissenters were able to play a role in local government. The Test Act, however, remained much more effective at the national level.

The Tories retained their control of the University of Oxford, where many clerics were trained. The royalism of Oxford had been compromised during the reign of James II when the Catholic king's attempts to improve the position for his co-religionists led him to clash with Magdalen College over its statutes, and as a result to purge the fellowship. However, once the male line of the Stuarts had been driven out in 1688–9, the dynasty became a convenient symbol for conservatism and several prominent eighteenth-century Oxonians were Jacobites, including James, 2nd Duke of Ormonde, Chancellor 1688–1715, and George, 3rd Earl of Lichfield, Chancellor 1762–72. In 1719, on 25 May, Restoration Day, the anniversary of the restoration of Charles II in 1660, Thomas Warton, the Tory Professor of Poetry, preached a pointed Jacobite sermon on the text 'Oh Israel, thou hast destroyed thyself, but in me is thine help'. The University had two MPs, elected by its doctors and masters of arts. All the MPs elected were Tories, including such prominent Anglican champions as Henry Hyde, Viscount Cornbury

(MP 1734–50) and Sir Roger Newdigate (MP 1750–80); as the crown did not possess the power of creating honorary doctors, by which a Whig majority was secured at Cambridge.

The Whig party had traditionally been associated with Dissenters, although many Whigs were Anglicans and were sometimes referred to as 'Church Whigs'.[4] Whig Anglicans were mostly Low Church, and the bulk of the Presbyterians who were absorbed into the Church of England after 1689 swelled the numbers of the Low Church. From 1722, a small *regium donum* (king's gift) was given annually to trustees from the Baptist, Independent and Presbyterian churches, the funds used to supplement the incomes of their indigent clerics. Tory propaganda accused the Whigs of being anti-Church: 'The Church of England and her clergy were ever objects of my most implacable aversion', declared a Whig in a Tory pamphlet of 1724.[5]

However, the cautious Whig administrations of Sir Robert Walpole and his successors did not fulfil Tory fears and tamper with religious fundamentals, not least because of the considerable groundswell of opinion in defence of the Church. Nevertheless, government control of ecclesiastical patronage – the crown appointed the archbishops, the bishops and about a tenth of the parish clergy – greatly influenced the senior ranks of the Church of England, and ensured that it was in alliance with the secular power. It also greatly affected the Church of Ireland. Appointments of all of its bishops and of many of its plum livings was vested in the crown, and this led to the appointment of many Englishmen, including all the Primates of Armagh from 1702 until the Union. This was bitterly unpopular with Irish Protestants.

More generally, there was a close relationship between the Church of England and the landed elite. The appointment of the majority of the parish clergy, about 53 per cent, was directly controlled by the latter. In addition, one-third of English tithes were held by lay impropriators, while church properties tended to be rented on favourable terms by the laity. Most tenants were too powerful to be exploited, and resistance to episcopal rent increases was effective. In Ireland, opposition to the payment of tithes also affected the Protestant landowning class which, after a long and bitter legal struggle, passed a series of resolutions in the House of Commons in 1735 that, in effect, declared pasture land free from tithe.

There was a degree of anticlericalism in the early Whig ascendancy, for example on the part of Viscount Stanhope, who both brought in a bill to repeal the Schism Act in 1718 and wished to repeal the Test and Corporation Acts in 1718–19, while the Earl of Sunderland sought to increase government control over the English universities. However, from the 1720s, the hierarchies of Church and State moved closer together in England. Some prominent Whig politicians were personally devout. Thomas, 1st Duke of Newcastle, a Secretary of State from 1724 until 1754, and First Lord of the Treasury from then until 1756 and again in 1757–62, read a lesson every day and followed a course of theological reading. Lord Chancellor Hardwicke listened to daily prayers. High Churchmen moved towards the Whigs as they responded to the piety of Whig patrons. Newcastle, the minister who was most influential in ecclesiastical appointments in 1742–62, was concerned to ensure that effective and able men were appointed to positions of responsibility, although concern about the political consequences led him in the 1740s and 1750s to oppose the introduction of bishops into the American colonies. From 1726, Walpole obtained Indemnity Acts, protecting the Dissenters from malicious prosecution, especially office-holders who had failed to take communion, each year bar 1730 and 1732, and they were repeated frequently until 1757 and regularly thereafter. However, moves to repeal the Test and Corporation Acts were defeated in 1736, 1739, 1787, 1789 and 1790.

The division between Anglicanism and Dissent that had played such a major role in the dynamic of Whig–Tory struggle, especially in 1689–1720, was still important thereafter. For example, Dissenters played a major role in pro-American agitation in the 1770s. As the Test and Corporation Acts survived the 1689–1720 period of controversy and change, so Anglican prerogatives and privileges became a permanent feature of the Whig state; unlike in the mid-seventeenth century, it was possible to remove the Stuarts without overthrowing Anglicanism. It also proved possible to install a Calvinist King (William III), although he was careful to leave his wife a major say in Church patronage, and a Lutheran monarch (George I) without apparent danger to the Church of England. As a consequence of the Church's maintenance of its position, pressure for the repeal of the Acts, the prime political thrust of Dissent, itself came to denote opposition to the dominant system.

If the defeats of attempts to repeal the Test and Corporation Acts reaffirmed the identification of religion and state, in the form of government protection for the Church of England, they also sustained local tensions. In England and Wales, animosity between Anglicanism and Dissent and in Scotland between Episcopalianism and Presbyterianism, was a basic political axis, although the two rivalries were different in important respects and, in addition, there is much evidence that the fit between religious and political divisions was far from neat and uniform. In England, Dissenters tended to support more radical political positions, especially prior to the 1720s and after mid-century, and their urban locale ensured that their activism was predominantly middle-class and had only limited reference to aristocratic leadership and interests.[6] Whether the Church was in danger or not at the national level, Anglicans felt it necessary to protect it in the localities. Furthermore, in the absence of a modern structure of party organisation, ecclesiastical links provided the basis of community and sociability that was so important in the development of political alignments and the mobilisation of political support.

This was a society in which disagreements over how (not whether it was) best to worship God and seek salvation, how to organise the Church, and the relationship between Church and State, were matters of urgent concern. 'Polite' and 'religious' are not mutually incompatible, and the image of Hanoverian Britain as a 'polite' society is misleading if that is taken to imply the marginal nature of religious zeal. In fact, despite the claims of other Protestant groups, the established churches were not devoid of energy, and their congregations were not sunk in torpor. The Societies for the Reformation of Manners indicated the strength and social awareness of Anglican piety.

As a concrete example of religious activity, hundreds of churches were built, or significantly altered, during the century. Although few new parishes were created, new churches were built in areas of expanding population, including Manchester, Lancaster, Birmingham, Bath and Leeds, and the problem of providing for population growth did not become very serious for the Church until the 1780s. New churches included the new London churches of Queen Anne's reign, as well as Thomas Archer's baroque St Philip's in Birmingham (1711–24), and St Michael's (1734–42) and St James's in Bath (1768–9), All Saints, Gainsborough (1736–48), Holy Cross, Daventry (1752–8), and St Paul's in Liverpool (1765–9). Churches were built at new fashionable watering places, such as Bristol Hot Wells. Many churches were rebuilt, for example five in Worcester in 1730–72,[7] and St Nicholas's in Bristol in the 1760s. Most churches were kept in good repair. The creation of side aisles and the erection of galleries increased the seating in many churches, as at Saddleworth. In Ireland, the growing numbers and greater wealth of the Catholics led to the erection of new churches, six in Dublin during the reign of George I. Despite the construction of new churches, many growing towns, such as Leeds and Hull, lacked sufficient church accommodation. Nevertheless, the building of new churches is important, because all too often the impression created is of an age that only, or very largely, built secular public buildings. Furthermore, new churches made a major impact on communities. Economic growth and social challenges and changes also posed major problems for the churches as they affected both the population and particular congregations.

Much recent work has stressed the dedication and diligence of clergymen, and the relative effectiveness of the Church's ministry. Clerical diaries of the period indicate faith and an attempt at self-examination. There is also much evidence of clergymen fulfilling the standards of clerical life. For example, the diary of 1759–62 of James Newton, rector of Nuneham Courtney, shows his daily attendance at morning and evening prayer, his care to find replacement clergy when he was absent, and his concern to provide food for the poor.[8] Other sources provide similar evidence.

Thanks to toleration, the Church of England had to operate more effectively if it was to resist the challenge of other churches. Some bishops, such as Henry Compton and Gilbert Burnet, consciously responded to the idea of competition from Dissent. The duty of the Church to teach the faith was much emphasised: religious activism for clergy and laity alike was stressed in Anglican propaganda, not the soporific complacency of a stagnant establishment. The Church continued the themes established at the Reformation of strengthening piety and education. Reform was a major element. Correspondence with officialdom, or visitation returns might give an over-optimistic view on the part of incumbents, but they also reveal what the clergy wanted to happen.[9]

The range of religious practice was extensive. There were very few professed atheists, and they could suffer prosecution under the Blasphemy Act. Instead, there was no necessary dichotomy of enlightenment and faith, the secular and the religious, scientific and mystical. 'Freethinker' critics of the Church of England should not be seen in a secular context, but rather as advocates for a reforming civil theology.[10] Deism, which was influential in intellectual circles, was not anti-religious. Deism was not a clear intellectual position or a movement, for it had neither creed nor organisation; it was a vague term used by polemicists that had a wide range of religious connotations. Eschewing the notion of a God of retribution, deistic writers, such as John Toland, in his *Christianity not Mysterious* (1696), suggested a benevolent force that had created a world and a humanity capable of goodness, and a God not intervening through revelation or miracles. The universe therefore had origins, order and purpose, but there was no need for a priesthood.

Literacy, relative wealth and an urban environment enabled some to respond to new intellectual and spiritual currents, though it would be wrong to suggest that, in contrast, rural religion was necessarily unchanging. It is unclear how far shifts in religious sensitivity in intellectual and clerical circles affected popular Christianity. In some of these circles, actions based on scriptural authority alone were treated with suspicion, although scripture was the best guide to conduct for most people.

There was, as in practically every period, widespread concern about irreligion, which was exacerbated by the inability of the Church of England after 1689 to enforce church attendance. Concern about irreligion led to the foundation in 1698–9 of the Society for Promoting Christian Knowledge (SPCK), an Anglican missionary society. The preamble to its charter in 1699 claimed that 'gross ignorance of the Christian religion' was responsible for a threatening 'growth of vice and immorality', a situation the Church sought to combat by making active use of the Church courts. In 1738, John Hildrop, a country cleric, published *A Letter to a Member of Parliament containing a Proposal for bringing in a Bill to revise, amend, or repeal certain obsolete Statutes commonly called the Ten Commandments*, a satirical pamphlet that argued that they should be abolished because they were little regarded by fashionable society. An essay on preaching published in *Lloyd's Evening Post* on 2 February 1761 complained,

> it is very obvious that the Clergy are no where so little thought of, by the Populace, as here ... the vulgar, in general, appearing no way impressed with a sense of religious duty ... pretty much neglected in our exhortations from the pulpit.

The writer complained that Church of England preachers stressed reason, not passion, and sent their bored listeners to sleep. Instead, he praised Methodists for the passion of their preaching. Similarly, the Evangelicals of the Church of Scotland criticised the Moderates of the Church for lacking enthusiasm in their sermons.

Nevertheless, there is copious evidence both of massive observance of the formal requirements of the churches and of widespread piety. Sunday schools and devotional literature, such as the chapbooks read by relatively humble people, fostered sanctity, piety, and an awareness of salvation. Popular piety was internalised, and there was a high level of introspective or 'internalised' faith. Concerns over the frequency of receipt of communion were caused by feelings of unworthiness; one reason for the infrequency was that many people felt unworthy of it.

Devotional literature was extensively purchased. The *Whole Duty of Man* by Richard Allestree (1619–81), Regius Professor of Divinity at Oxford (1663–79), which was first published in 1658, appeared in its 25th edition by 1690, was revised by 1743, and was widely recommended, especially by Edmund Gibson in his *Pastoral Letters. The Church Catechism explained by way of question and answer, and confirm'd by Scripture proofs* (1700) by the Kent cleric John Lewis (1675–1747) went through 42 editions by 1812. Lewis also wrote a series of defences of the position of the Church of England. William Law's *A Serious Call to a Devout and Holy Life, adapted to the State and Condition of all Orders of Christians* (1728) enjoyed huge sales, and was influential in the development of Methodism. John Bunyan's *Pilgrim's Progress* (1678) was widely read, and was praised by the influential Dr Johnson.

The journey to an earthly perdition and a hellish end was extensively rehearsed by commentators, both the explicitly religious and the 'secular' – for example William Hogarth's popular mid-eighteenth century morality series of engravings, including *The Rake's Progress, Industry and Idleness,* and *Before and After*. Such works depicted and offered guidance on the routes of life from within a Christian context. This was even more true of explicitly religious admonitory prints, such as the Methodist *The Tree of Life* (*c.* 1770), which brought both the 'Heavenly City' and the 'Bottomless Pit' into the picture.

The Church of England, as always, faced serious problems, especially in the distribution of its resources, but was in a less parlous state than is sometimes suggested. Standards of pastoral care were as good as in earlier periods, and were encouraged by the vigilance of the hierarchy. The claim that Benjamin Hoadly, an influential Whig clerical polemicist, never visited his diocese while Bishop of Bangor (1715–21), has long been debunked. Thomas Herring, his successor in 1737–43, regularly toured it in order to ordain and confirm, and to exercise a pastoral ministry among the clergy. Translated to York, Herring was again an energetic and conscientious diocesan who ordained with regularity. More generally, the vigilance of the Anglican hierarchy in supervising clergy promoted pastoral commitment.

The non-residence of clerics could be a problem, and certainly became more common. Herring's visitation return indicated that 393 out of the 836 parochial benefices in the diocese of York in 1743 had non-resident clergy. Some 335 out of 711 of the clergy were pluralists. In 453 out of 836 parishes the required two Sunday services were not provided. In 1780, only about 38 per cent of English parishes had resident incumbents and 36 per cent of Anglican clergy were pluralists. Pluralism [holding more than one living] often arose due to lay impropriation or from clerical poverty arising from major discrepancies in clerical income and the inadequacy of many livings, but this did not necessarily lead to inadequate pastoral care. Non-resident incumbents frequently lived nearby and, in general, there were resident stipendiary curates. Pluralism was more common in areas where many parishes had poor endowments, for example on the Essex coast. In the diocese of London, there were many preachers, readers and lecturers, and a high level of clerical activity. Although there was non-residence and pluralism, levels of daily celebration and services were high, and the clergy had a pronounced view of their duty. The episcopal visitation of the diocese of Llandaff in 1763 showed that of 145 returns only 37 parishes had resident incumbents, but there was coverage by others, often curates. Furthermore, while only a minority of churches had both morning and evening services on a Sunday, an even smaller minority fell below one service a week.[11]

In general, increasing clerical income helped attract better educated clergy to the church: the rise in the social standing of the clergy and in their general educational standard was widely ascribed by contemporaries and historians to a rise in income from livings that resulted from the greater profits from agriculture from mid-century and to opportunities for pluralism.

Pluralism and non-residence were also common problems among Church of Ireland clerics, and gravely limited their ability to undertake missionary work among the Catholic population. Thomas Percy, best-known for his research on early-English poetry, was so frequently absent in England when Bishop of Dromore (1782–1808) that the Archbishop of Armagh felt obliged to complain.

In addition, the Churches were not averse to religious campaigns, such as that waged in Wales in the early decades of the century by the Anglicans and the Dissenters, against Catholicism, drunkenness and profanity, and for salvation and literacy. There was a major expansion of the printed word in Welsh and the majority of it was devoted to religious works.

In Wales, religious issues and renewal were linked with language. The schools founded by the Puritan Thomas Gouge's Welsh Trust in the 1670s used English as the teaching medium and were designed to teach the poor to read English. Gouge founded more than 300 schools and distributed copies of the Bible. The Society for the Propagation of Christian Knowledge, which drew on Gouge's Welsh Trust, followed from 1699, and provided charity schools and copies of the Bible. Another school-founder, Reverend Griffith Jones of Llanddowror (1683–1761), was much denounced as a secret spreader of Methodism because, from the 1730s, he stressed the need to use Welsh as the medium of a popular literary campaign and to catechise in it. He was partly responsible for the edition of the Bible and Prayer Book in Welsh issued by the SPCK in 1746, and encouraged its reading as a way to revive Christian life and to teach moral precepts. His educational sense of mission was indeed conducive to the spread of Methodism, which shared a tendency to think in terms of new possibilities and rebirth. In both Wales and Ulster, a vigorous religious tradition of evangelical Protestantism developed as part of the so-called 'Great Awakening'.[12]

More generally, and in no way restricted to the evangelicals, there was a stress on the public dimension of religion, or, in part, looked at differently, on the spiritual health of the community. Piety and worship became fashionable and, as such, were also public practices, with charity sermons, fashionable services and fashionable churches, such as St George's, Hanover Square and St James's, Piccadilly in London. The role of the Churches in worship was but part of a wider mission that helped to enhance their importance. Within England, the Church of England in particular played a major role in education and social welfare.[13]

The very nature of established churches that sought to minister to all, in an age when religion was a social obligation, as well as a personal spiritual experience, posed problems for some of those, both clergy and laity, who criticised anything that might compromise the latter. Believers sure of their faith could find the compromises of comprehension abhorrent, but the determination of clerics to ensure standards of religious knowledge and observance ensured that these compromises were not those of the lowest common denominator.

Dissatisfaction, however, reflected the importance of, and widespread commitment to, religion, the church and the clergy. Few believed that they could or should be dispensed with, or doubted the close relationships of faith and reason, church and state, clergy and laity, religion and the people.

Methodism was one consequence of religious enthusiasm. It was initially a movement for revival that sought to remain within the Church of England, supplementing the official parochial structure by a system of private religious societies that would both regenerate the Church and win it new members. However, after Methodism's institutional founder, John Wesley (1703–91), died, it broke away completely, and his decision to ordain ministers on his own authority in 1784 marked a point of real division between Methodism and the Church of England. Wesley had begun his evangelical campaign in England in 1738, although George Whitefield, Howell Harris and Daniel Rowlands were already preaching a similar message. They used the same methods as Wesley, but preached Calvinism while Wesley preached Arminianism.

Many 'Methodist' clergy and worshippers probably thought of themselves as Anglicans throughout the century, although Methodism can be seen as a revival movement within both the Church of England and Dissent. Although Methodists, until the 1790s, declared themselves to be Anglicans, they used methods and practices that were quickly adopted by (and thereby encouraged) other Dissenters. They also developed a theology that placed them closer to Dissent, for example Wesley's emphasis on conversion and the stress on the importance of works placed Methodism close to the Baptists. Wesley combined concern for the church establishment with first-hand contact with Continental Protestants, particularly the revived Moravian Brethren based at Herrnhut, a German religious community developed by the Pietist Count Zinzendorf, that established a permanent presence in England. Methodism, initially intended by Wesley as a means to reawaken Anglicanism, was thus part of the 'Great Awakening', a widespread movement of Protestant revival in Europe and North America, and it employed many of the organisational features of European Protestant revival, including itinerant preaching and love feasts.[14]

Seeing his mission as one of saving souls, Wesley urged men to turn to Christ to win redemption, and promised they would know that they had achieved salvation. Wesley's Arminianism led him to stress that salvation was open to all. He rejected the predestination of Calvinism, asserted justification by faith, and offered an eclectic theology that was adapted to a powerful mission addressing itself to popular anxieties. Wesley combined traditional religion with Enlightenment thought processes.

His belief in religion as an epic struggle, with providence, demons and witchcraft all present, and his willingness to seek guidance by opening the Bible at random, all found echoes in a growing popular following in many, though not all, areas. This was facilitated by the energy of the preaching mission, and the revivalist nature of Methodism, with its hymn-singing, watch-nights and love feasts. In his *Enthusiasm of Methodists and Papists Compared* (3 parts, 1749–51), the hostile George Lavington, Bishop of Exeter, claimed that Methodism imitated the enthusiastic excesses of medieval Catholicism, with visions, exorcisms and healing; although Wesley, in fact, argued against excessive emotionalism and enthusiasm. He was both flexible in his approach, and well-aware of the value of print, producing many tracts and much serial material. Wesley was also tolerant, accepting men and women of all denominations for membership, and, from the mid-1740s, using lay preachers because he could not obtain enough support from ordained ministers. The use of lay preachers helped to increase clerical opposition, as did unease about Wesley's theology.

Wesley had much sympathy for the poor, although not enough to allow them leisure time: he disliked the idea of the poor having time away from work or worship. Wesley criticised some aspects of society, but was loyal to the dynasty and the political system. Thus, Methodism did not pose a threat to the political order or elite. Wesley's loyalty, concern about personal and social disorder, and belief in divine intervention were reflected in a letter he sent Matthew Ridley, Mayor of Newcastle, during the Jacobite rising of 1745. He felt bound to write, by the fear of God, love of his country, and zeal towards George II, as he had been pained by 'the senseless wickedness, the ignorant prophaneness' of the city's poor and the 'continual cursing and swearing, and the wanton blasphemy' of the soldiers, and feared this would endanger divine support.[15]

Methodism was particularly popular among artisans and servants, and was responsive to the religious needs of such groups. In Nottingham, its following was mostly among artisans, particularly those working in the important stocking industry. Their first chapel in the city, the Octagon, was founded in 1764; it was replaced by a larger chapel in 1784, and again in 1798. Methodism was also very popular among Cornish tinners and fishermen, both dangerous jobs. It developed rapidly in England and Wales, especially among artisans (though not so much among unskilled workers), and in manufacturing and mining areas, such as the West Riding of Yorkshire, where the parochial structure was weak, but had little impact in Scotland or Ireland, especially among Irish Catholics. Wesley's Arminianism was resisted by the strong Calvinism of many Scots, although he made frequent visits there and there were independent Scottish revivals. Methodism was to be the characteristic creed of the Welsh-speaking areas of north and west Wales in the nineteenth century. The first two Methodist chapels in Caernarvonshire were built at Tg-mawr in 1752 and in Clynnog in about 1764. Methodism won more support among women than men.

Methodism was an important development, but it is necessary not to exaggerate its numerical significance. Although visitation returns in the diocese of York
in the 1760s suggest that the challenge of Methodism was developing, the Church
was maintaining its position, and the old High Church tradition was still alive.[16]
There were only around 100,000 Methodists in England and Wales by 1800.

The evangelical revival affected not only the Anglicans, but also the Dissenters,
for example the Particular Baptists, who increased their numbers by an active policy of evangelisation. The first new denomination was the New Connexion of
General Baptists. This was formed in 1770 by orthodox elements of the Arminian
wing of the Baptist movement who were motivated by conversionist zeal. Their
founder Dan Taylor (1738–1816), the son of a coal miner who had himself worked
in the pits, had been a Methodist preacher, who became a Baptist pastor. The foundation articles of faith of the New Connexion are a useful reminder of the extent
to which it is necessary to appreciate that the 'Age of Enlightenment' or of 'politeness' displayed a great variety of values. They were the natural depravity of man,
the obligation of moral law, the divinity of Christ, the universal design of atone-
ment, the promise of salvation for all the faithful, and necessary regeneration by
the Holy Spirit.[17]

Space devoted to religion is generally restricted in modern textbooks, which is
unfortunate given its importance to contemporaries. More particularly for the
eighteenth century, it leads to a relative neglect of the Dissenters. There is a focus
on the Church of England, on anti-Catholicism, and on the rise of Methodism, but
not on the Dissenters. Baptists, Quakers, Presbyterians and Independents (Congregationalists) were the major categories of Dissenters. Aside from theological and
organisational differences, not least over Trinitarian and predestinarian principles,
both of which came under increasing criticism in this period, and over baptism,
these congregations also varied socially and geographically. For example, Baptists
were more commonly rural and Presbyterians urban. The laity played a bigger role
in Quaker and Baptist worship than in that of the Independents and Presbyterians.
Anglican clergy regarded Quakers in a more hostile fashion than they treated
Presbyterians, some of whom partially conformed to Anglicanism.[18]

There were very strong continuities between areas where Dissent was strong
and those that had earlier been characterised as Puritan. Dissent itself appears to
have contracted and become increasingly urban from mid-century, before being
affected by a revival from the 1770s that owed much to itinerant and lay preaching. The complex pattern of Dissent was part of the variety of religious life in
Britain that undermines clearcut descriptions. At the same time, alongside the
conventional term for variety, a mosaic, it is important to note that the individual
pieces were linked, by organisational and other ties. The interaction between varied local circumstances and these links helped give the period much of its
dynamism.

Methodist meetings sometimes met with a violent response, as in Sheffield
(1744), Exeter (1745), Leeds (1745), York (1747), Norwich (1751–2), and
Birmingham (1764), although the degree to which the Church of England did not
respond to Methodist activity in an official fashion is striking. Wesley was not

expelled from the Church. Thus, there was an effective toleration of Methodism at the national level that was not always matched locally, although the local experience varied greatly. If Bishop Lavington of Exeter was very hostile in the 1750s, Bishop Ross was very friendly in the 1770s. By the 1770s it was rare for Methodist-minded clergy to be denied permission to preach when outside their own parish. Lavington, like Gibson, was also hostile to the Moravians, but the majority of Anglican bishops did not see them in the same light, and in 1749 supported the passage of the Moravian Act, which recognised the Moravian church.[19]

Nevertheless, the degree of toleration in religious life must not be exaggerated. Religious issues were 'real', indistinguishable from political and social issues, and worth fighting over, literally so as the riots against Dissenters in England in 1710, 1715 and 1791, and against Catholics in Edinburgh and Glasgow in 1779 and in England in 1780, indicated all too clearly. There was a major riot in Dingwall in 1704 over the choice of a new minister. The fear among non-Anglican colonists that Anglican episcopacy would be imposed in order to give effect to the apparent Anglican world view of George III's government helped to fuel American hostility towards the British link.

Anti-Catholicism was a powerful force, throughout the period at the popular level, and at least until mid-century, at that of the elite. Prior to then, it was widely believed that Catholicism was on the increase in the British Isles and on the advance in Europe; the latter was certainly true until Frederick the Great of Prussia's invasion of Silesia in 1740. Suspicions of Catholic disloyalty were increased by the Jacobite threat. There was an enormous amount of anti-Catholic material both in the culture of print-newspapers, pamphlets, prints and books – and in the public culture of anniversary celebrations, for example of the defeat of the Armada and the discovery of the Gunpowder Plot, and of other public rituals. The representation of Catholics was generally crude and violent: their intentions were seen as diabolical, their strength and deceit were frightening. The public ritual lent immediacy to the material in print, and both were further linked by sermons, as for the anniversary of the Gunpowder Plot. The wish of William Wake, Archbishop of Canterbury from 1716 until 1737, for closer Anglican relations with the French Catholic church (as well as with the Orthodox and Continental Protestants) was unrealistic, and evidence of divergence between popular and clerical religion.

It has been argued that anti-Catholicism diminished during the period, especially after the suppression of Jacobitism in the 1740s;[20] but it is unclear that this was so, especially at the popular level, although there is little doubt that, at the level of the elite, social relations between Protestants and Catholics improved. The stone with which the nave of York Minster was repaired in mid-century was the gift of a Catholic, Sir Edward Gascoigne. Catholic landowners, however, were hit by a double land tax.

Anti-Catholicism was not static, but an ideology that could be flexible and influenced by its local environment and by political developments. Where landowners were Catholic, as on some of the Hebrides, the Penal Laws against Catholics were generally not enforced, although the Jacobite rebellion in 1745 led to a serious upsurge in anti-Catholic activity. From at least mid-century, awareness of Britain's position as a great power encouraged a re-evaluation of attitudes to the religiously heterodox, and, by the 1770s, political elites were contemplating the emancipation of Roman Catholics. Rebellion in the American colonies in 1775, and the prospect of a broad European alliance against Britain, forced consideration of ways to allow the mass of the Irish population and Scots Highlanders to be recruited into the armed forces, and directed attention to the penal religious legislation which prevented this.

However, as a result of the 1779 anti-Catholic riots in Scotland, the concessions given English Catholics by the 1778 Catholic Relief Act were not extended to north of the Border, although John Wilkes told the House of Commons that 'when I am informed that the peaceable and loyal Roman Catholics of Scotland find no security, even in the capital, for their lives and property, I do not hesitate to assert, that there is a dissolution of all government'. Under the Act, officiating Catholic clergy were no longer liable to life imprisonment and the provision by which land must pass over any Catholic heir to the next Protestant in line was repealed, in both cases so long as the Oath of Allegiance was taken: Jacobitism and the temporal authority of the papacy had to be rejected. Catholics remained barred from public life until 1829. Nevertheless, there was a spread in open Catholicism, with the foundation of Catholic chapels. As a consequence, Catholic worship came to be less dependent on the gentry families that had sheltered priests.

The easing of the legislative code in 1778 may have been catching up with elite and, possibly, increasingly widespread popular attitudes, but pressure for the repeal of the Catholic Relief Act in England led to the activities of the Protestant Association, which culminated in the Gordon Riots in London and the provinces in 1780. The riots were a challenge to order in the centre of empire greater than anything hitherto seen that century. About 50,000 members of the Association marched on Parliament to present the petition for repeal. The JPs had only about 76 constables to control the crowds, but Parliament refused to be intimidated into repeal. The angry demonstrators initially turned to attack Catholic chapels and schools in Westminster and London, before threatening establishment targets, such as the homes of prominent ministers, politicians thought to be pro-Catholic, Anglican clerics, and those magistrates who sought to act against rioters. The prisons were stormed in order to release imprisoned rioters. Troops had to be used to restore order. Outside London, Catholic chapels were burned down, as in Bath.[21]

The riots reflected a popular Protestantism that was deeply suspicious of elite tolerant tendencies; and they helped to delay further Catholic Relief Acts until 1791 (England) and 1793 (Scotland). However, although anti-Popery may have been a key element of public discussion, its constant use did not result in a homogenous campaign of anti-Catholicism. In practice, anti-Popery was an extremely eclectic discourse, which could operate in different ways in particular social, political and cultural contexts, and could identify a multiplicity of varying evils according to circumstance. Rarely, did it advocate open hostility to British Catholics. Rather, the religious persecution and social disruption implied by such hostility were themselves often denounced as 'popish', so that the recognition of actual religious pluralism created an ambiguity within the ideology of anti-popery itself.

In Ireland, rising Catholic wealth in the second half of the century was important to the long-term process by which Catholics came to play a more central role in politics and a more active role in society. The legal position of Irish Catholics improved. In 1774, an Act allowed them to take the Oath of Allegiance. Four years later, the Catholic Relief Act for Ireland removed restrictions on Catholics holding lands.

Religious antagonism had other manifestations. The small Jewish community grew by immigration, but the strength of popular Anglicanism was demonstrated in 1753, when a vicious press campaign of anti-Semitic hatred, with popular backing, forced the repeal of the Jewish Naturalisation Act of that year, which had made it easier to be naturalised by private act of Parliament, dropping the phrase 'on the true faith of a Christian' from the Oaths of Supremacy and Allegiance. The *Salisbury Journal* of 7 January 1754 recorded the celebrations in Devizes,

> Last Friday the gentlemen and principal tradesmen of this borough, met at the Black Bear Inn to rejoice on account of the repeal of the Jew Bill; and though numbers of different persuasions were assembled on this occasion, yet party and prejudice were entirely laid aside, and all were unanimous in expressing their joy and highest approbation. The effigy of a Jew was carried through every street in town, attended with all sorts of rough music; several men had torches that the inhabitants might see the effigy, and read the paper that was stuck on his breast, containing these words
>
> NO JEWS!
> Reformations to the B--ps [Bishops];
> Christianity for ever.
>
> They made a halt two or three times in every street, drank and repeated the above, amidst the acclamations of a great number of people: a large fire was made, and they burnt the body of the Jew, and set his head on the top of the pillory; the bells rang, and beer was given to the populace; several loyal healths were drank by the gentlemen, etc. and likewise variety of toasts, applicable to the occasion. The Thursday following (being Market Day) the head was again put on top of the pillory, which gave great delight to the farmers and other country people.

Religious issues were also an expression or aspect of other disputes, ranging from that over the succession to the crown following the Glorious Revolution, to the town-country tension that played a role in Anglican–Dissenter rivalries. Towns were often centres of Dissent, challenging Anglican religious-cultural hegemony in the locality and region; just as they could seek to resist the attempts of the local gentry to control their parliamentary representation, and were also centres of a changing economy. Dissent was strongest in regions where the parochial structure was weak, particularly in the West Riding of Yorkshire where Quakers, Presbyterians and Baptists were numerous.

At the same time, it is necessary not to exaggerate the divide. Some Whig bishops preached moderation in dealing with Dissenters, as did Tories such as Compton and Sharp. Protestant unity remained a prominent theme in public polemic, and, during the Jacobite risings, Dissenters, in works such as Samuel Chandler's *Great Britain's Memorial against the Pretender and Popery* (1745), stressed their loyalty by emphasising a broad, Protestant patriotism which could include them as well as the established faith. There was no sustained or coherent crusade against Dissent. As in the case of Catholics, Dissenters found they could generally live peacefully among Anglican neighbours (despite the vigorous polemics, and occasional outrages against them), and Dissenters found many ways to integrate into mainstream politics and culture.

In local communities, such as Great Yarmouth, a workable accommodation was gradually worked out after the Toleration Act;[22] and the decline in church courts and ecclesiastical authority hastened by that legislation allowed a 'freedom' to diverge from orthodoxy. Clerical investigations into Dissenter numbers rarely challenged the right of people to worship outside the church in their homes or meeting houses, and, throughout the period, non-Anglicans found ways – especially through Occasional Conformity and Indemnity Acts – to evade the laws against them.

As with Catholics, the very discourses used by the religious majority to discuss the heterodox came to accept the realities of diversity. Whilst all Anglican polemic deplored schism from the Church, and the spiritual pride which allegedly prompted it, most rejected a return to enforced uniformity as counter-productive, or labelled it as an anti-Christian sin of uncharity that was as bad as schism itself.

Religious tension is difficult to measure, because its classic product was not the violence that might attract judicial and, possibly, political or even military attention, but the prejudice that was expressed in endogamy (marriage within the group), discriminatory political, social, economic and cultural practices, and the acid of abuse and insult. Religious minorities cohered not only in order to practice their faith, but also for protection, employment, commercial links, credit, and the maintenance of their identity. Endogamy also served to preserve their strength and, as a consequence, intermarriage led to criticism. Where today European religious groups generally face the challenge of the assimilation of their members into predominantly secular cultures, in the eighteenth century religious identity was maintained because assimilation on such terms was not an option. The role of clergymen and ecclesiastical and religious bodies in education, charity and social welfare furthered identification with confessional groupings, although it would be mistaken to give the impression that different religious groupings remained isolated from one another.

CONCLUSIONS

Methodism developed from the 1730s, but this, and other, aspects of religious enthusiasm reflected not so much a failure of the Church of England as the contradictions inherent in a national body that had to serve all, as well as enthusiasts.

In addition, there was an international dimension to Protestant evangelicalism, so that the development of Methodism is not explicable solely in English terms. Within the Church, alongside pluralism, non-residence, appointments due to patronage, and a very unequal system of payment of clerics, there was conscientiousness and the provision of regular services in most parishes.

As ever, contrasting images of religious commitment and life can be presented. The strongest one of my schooldays was of the copious meals of a Norfolk Church of England minister, James Woodforde, whose diaries had been published.

Another is suggested by an account Richard Browne sent his father in 1765. He had visited St Patrick's Purgatory, an island in Lough Derg in County Donegal where each year over 10,000 Irish Catholics made a pilgrimage, a practice expressly forbidden under the Popery Act of 1704. He found

> a multitude indeed of both sexes mostly indeed of the poorer sort ... in one place there are built seven small places of a circular form like pounds in which place the penitents are obliged to run so many times round bare foot on sharp pointed rocks repeating so many ave marias etc., in commemoration of the seven deadly sins ... in other parts they are obliged to wade to the middle in the water and stand there for a stated time repeating a certain number of prayers, when this is over the next penance is to retire to a vault made purposely, where they must remain 24 hours without eating, drinking, speaking or sleeping, for they are sure if they do either the Devil has a power of carrying them away, and to prevent sleeping, everyone that goes in there supply themselves with pins which they thrust into anyone they find dozing ... the last ceremony is washing in the lake, when they wash away all their sins.[23]

NOTES

1. G. O'Brien (ed.), *Catholic Ireland in the Eighteenth Century: Collected Essays of Maureen Wall* (Dublin, 1989); T. Bartlett, *The Fall and Rise of the Irish Nation. The Catholic Question 1690–1830* (Dublin, 1992).
2. I. Murphy, *The Diocese of Killaloe in the Eighteenth Century* (Blackrock, Co. Dublin, 1991).
3. G. Eland (ed.), *Shardeloes Papers* (1974), p. 50.
4. Edward Carteret to Viscount Townshend, 2 July 1725, PRO. SP. 35/57 fol. 9.
5. Anon., *The True Character of a Triumphant Whig both in his Religion and Politics* (1724), pp. 7–8.
6. S. D'Cruze, *Our Time in God's Hands: Religion and the Middling Sort in Eighteenth Century Colchester* (Chelmsford, 1991).
7. D. Whitehead, 'The Georgian churches of Worcester', *Transactions of the Worcestershire Archaeological Society*, 3rd ser. 13 (1992), p. 211.
8. G. Hannah (ed.), *The Deserted Village: The Diary of an Oxfordshire Rector* (Stroud, 1992).
9. J. Gregory, *Restoration, Reformation and Reform, 1660–1828, Archbishops of Canterbury and the Diocese* (Oxford, 2000), p. 8.
10. J.A.I. Champion, *The Pillars of Priestcraft Shaken. The Church of England and its Enemies 1660–1730* (Cambridge, 1992).

11. V. Barrie-Curien, *Clergé et Pastorale en Angleterre au XVIIIe Siècle: le Diocese de Londres* (Paris, 1992); J.R. Guy (ed.), *The Diocese of Llandaff in 1763, The Primary Visitation of Bishop Ewer* (Cardiff, 1991); L. Butler (ed.), *The Archdeaconry of Richmond in the Eighteenth Century* (Leeds, 1990).
12. D. Hempton and M. Hill, *Evangelical Protestantism in Ulster Society 1740–1890* (1992).
13. N. Yates, R. Hume and P. Hastings, *Religion and Society in Kent, 1640–1914* (Woodbridge, 1994).
14. A. Armstrong, *The Church of England, the Methodists and Society 1700–1850* (1973).
15. Wesley to Matthew Ridley, 26 Oct. 1745, Northumberland CRO. ZRI 27/5.
16. C. Annesley and P. Hoskin (eds.), *Archbishop Drummond's Visitation Returns 1764* (2 vols, York, 1997–8).
17. A.D. Gilbert, *Religion and Society in Industrial England* (1976), pp. 37–8; H.S. Skeats, *A History of the Free Churches of England 1688–1851* (1869), pp. 448–9.
18. M. Watts, *The Dissenters: From the Reformation to the French Revolution* (Oxford, 1978); E. Welch, 'The origins of the New Connexion of General Baptists in Leicestershire', *Transactions of the Leicestershire Archaeological and Historical Society*, 69 (1995), pp. 59–70.
19. C. Podmore, *The Moravian Church in England, 1728–1760* (Oxford, 1998).
20. C. Haydon, *Anti-Catholicism in Eighteenth-Century England, c. 1714–80: A Political and Social Study* (Manchester, 1993).
21. C. Haydon, 'The Gordon Riots in the English Provinces', *Historical Research*, 63 (1990), pp. 354–9.
22. P. Gauci, *Politics and Society in Great Yarmouth, 1660–1722* (Oxford, 1996).
23. Richard Browne to his father, 24 Aug. 1765, BL. RP. 3284.

9

Enlightenment and science

The pre-Revolutionary eighteenth century in Europe is often referred to as the Enlightenment or the Age of Enlightenment, but the relationship of the British Isles to this movement is far from clear. It is generally agreed that there was a Scottish Enlightenment, but many writers do not discern or discuss an English one. This is mistaken, arising from the traditional concentration in Enlightenment studies on the writings of a small number of French thinkers, reflects the difficulty of defining the term, and also underrates the extent to which prominent Continental commentators, such as Leibniz and Voltaire, saw Britain, by which they tended to mean England, more specifically London, as a cradle of enlightenment. Thinkers such as Locke, Newton and Toland were heroes to many Continental intellectuals.

Rather than seeing the Enlightenment as a French-dominated movement, it could better be described as a tendency towards critical enquiry and the application of reason in which British intellectuals played a major role. Reason was a goal as well as a method of Enlightenment thinkers. They believed it necessary to use reason in order to appreciate man, society and the universe, and thus to improve human circumstances, an objective in which utilitarianism, religious faith, and the search for human happiness could combine. Certain thinkers, especially in France, believed that existing authorities were an active restraint on the quest of, and for, reason and accordingly adopted critical, even radical, views, but such a clash was untypical. Reason was believed to be the distinguishing mark of man, and the insane were commonly regarded as monstrous. Reason was seen not only as the characteristic of the human species, but also of human development and social organisation. In contrast, the savage mind was held to be wild as well as heathen, and as obsessed by a world of terror, in which monstrous anxieties were projected into nature.

Contemporaries claimed that reason freed men from unnecessary fears and could continue to do so. Thus, the great astronomer Sir Isaac Newton (1642–1727) had demonstrated that comets were integral to nature, not portents (although in religion he was sympathetic to mysticism). God was believed to act through the normal laws of physics; not to break them. Reason was seen as aiding human development by helping man to explore, understand and shape his environment, and it was argued that this was facilitated by a reliance on empirical method and a questioning of received wisdom.

Reason led very few in Britain to attack Christianity. Instead, Reason was believed to support the established procedures of Christianity, not least in opposition to the claims of religious enthusiasts. Reason could be used to confirm revelation. If the Scottish philosopher David Hume (1711–76), in his *Essay on Miracles* (1748), challenged their existence, Thomas Sherlock, an influential Anglican bishop, was able in his *Trial of the Witnesses of the Resurrection* (1729) to come to an opposite conclusion. Sherlock's *Trial* was a counterblast to Thomas Woolston's *Discourses on Miracles* (1727–9), in which Woolston stated the Deists' opposition to miracles. Sherlock tried to use reason and strongly empirical methods – the book was written as a trial with witnesses cross-examined – to argue the rational case for revealed religion. The Deist Thomas Chubb attacked Sherlock's *Trial*, but a response by Charles Moss, Sherlock's chaplain, re-asserted the *Trial*'s view that the laws of reason did not mean that miracles were 'incredible'. The controversy reflected widespread interest in the subject, and also the extent to which heterodox opinions could be expressed. An Established Church did not preclude debate.

In 1749, Conyers Middleton, a Church of England cleric, sought to reconcile history and religion with his *Free Enquiry into the Miraculous Powers which are supposed to have subsisted in the Christian Church*, which denied the credibility of the stories of miracles in periods subsequent to the first age of the Church. This was rejected by Wesley who, in his *Letter to Conyers Middleton*, stated that divine intervention had occurred all through history. Wesley himself was interested in science as evidence of divine mysteries.

The limited impact of scepticism was indicated in 1751 when widespread anxieties arising from English earthquakes led Hume's publisher to delay the second edition of his *Philosophical Essays*. The Port Royal and London earthquakes of 1692 had been seen as a warning of God's anger. In 1758, writing to his sister from London with a long account of comets, John Rolls struck a common note,

> Let not however any specious part of reason prevent our concern at such phenomena, but rather put us in mind of the end and final conclusion of all things ... induce us to pay a more than common homage at the foot stool of the throne of our good Almighty God, who with a nod or touch or breath can hurl us with fury and terrible destruction to all eternity, or gather us up like a scroll in a moment.[1]

The major Lisbon earthquake of 1755 led to calls for compassion as well as repentance. There was great controversy in London in 1762 about the veracity of a ghost which appeared in Cock-Lane. In fact, this was the product of a commercial and litigious society, as the ghost was thought up by James Parsons in order to make a creditor who had sued him appear a murderer.

Most intellectuals and churchmen shared John Locke's view that a rational appreciation of man's situation would lead people to be Christians. By treating reason as a divine gift and the universe as a divine creation, they established a framework in which observation need not be viewed as hostile to faith. Far from being compromises with tradition and religion, these views reflected the attempts of pious men in a religious society to comprehend the achievements and possibilities of scientific discoveries. In his unpublished *Essay towards an Abridgement of the English History* (1757–60), Edmund Burke ascribed the development of human society to Providence's role in providing suitable conditions. The hymnwriter Isaac Watts wrote *The Knowledge of the Heavens and the Earth Made Easy* (1726) in order to introduce beginners to astronomy. He believed that it would reinforce religious knowledge. Edmund Gibson and William Warburton, two of the most influential Anglican bishops, both defended John Locke from the charge of deism. They clearly felt that Locke's strongly rationalist stance was not inconsistent with Anglicanism. In university curricula, natural knowledge was seen as a potent weapon against atheism and deism, and a preoccupation with morals and religion led to a greater stress on the natural sciences.[2]

There was a powerful trend among Anglican clergy away from the mystical and 'spiritualistic' and towards strongly rational sermons. In his sermon on 'The use of Reason in Religion', George Smalridge, Tory Bishop of Bristol 1714–19, used reason to support the doctrine of the Trinity. Sermons became analytical examinations of the meanings of biblical texts, sometimes quite explicitly championing the cause of reason. John Wynne, Bishop of St Asaph 1715–27 and of Bath and Wells 1727–43, published an *Abridgement of John Locke's Essay on the Human Understanding* (1696), which was praised by Locke, and, in his *Sermon before the Society for the Reformation of Manners, January 1726*, claimed that men and women needed to call on their reason and intelligence to overcome any sense of shame or embarrassment for their faith: reason had to conquer irrational feelings for the benefit of religion. This, more generally, was the theme of the Societies for the Reformation of Manners: reason harnessed to religion in order to overcome moral 'incontinence' and immorality. Knowledge was also seen as a potent weapon against atheism and deism.

Yet, whatever their personal faith, the work of many scientists made little reference to God. His intervention in the world He had created, allowed for by Newton, was increasingly restricted by the explanation of supposed anomalies between observation and scientific laws. Geological discoveries and theories threw doubt on the biblical creation story, the universal flood and Old Testament chronology, while astronomical work challenged received notions of the universe, and the idea that it was static. Much medical experimentation and psychological speculation placed little weight on the idea of the soul.

The thought of the period was far from uniform. There were pessimistic and optimistic strains, and also humanitarian, liberal, moral and authoritarian dimensions. This diversity makes it doubtful whether the search for the origins or chronology of Enlightenment is particularly helpful. The origins have been found in a reaction against Louis XIV among English, Dutch and French writers, in a reaction against the baroque, in the scientific revolution of the seventeenth century, and in a crisis of conscience at the end of that period.

Theoretical ideas were advanced from general principles in a number of fields. [There was also a concern with the social context and with the relationship between theory and practice.] Abstract thought was important, most obviously with the work of Hume. He argued, in his *Treatise of Human Nature* (1738), that only impressions definitely existed, and that it was impossible to prove the existence of the mind and the nature of causality.

Thinkers were as much concerned with discovery, whether through exploration, observation or historical study,[3] as with speculation; and rationalistic and critical methods of scholarship developed to classify, integrate and exploit what was discovered. Captain Cook charted the Pacific. Hogarth's *Analysis of Beauty* (1753) was based on empirical observation, not Classical authority. Edward Gibbon based his masterly account of the *Decline and Fall of the Roman Empire* (1776–88) on massive scholarship. Experimental verification played a major role in the controversy over how best to determine longitude at sea. The 1714 Longitude Act offered a reward for a successful solution and John Harrison received the prize in 1773 for experiments which went back to the 1730s: he had devised a marine chronometer that erred by only eighteen miles in measurement of a distance of a return journey to Jamaica in 1761–2. Though the nature and closeness of the relationship between discovery and speculation varied by individual and subject, it was crucial to the development and application of thought in this period. Methodism can, in part, be understood as a consequence of Wesley's stress on an individual's ability to understand and know salvation.

Publications were the main channel through which new ideas were diffused, and its strongly-developed culture of print was an important dimension of the British Enlightenment. The press played a major role in spreading knowledge. The *Leeds Mercury* of 26 December 1775 began an article, 'The present appearance of the grand planet, Jupiter, upon the meridian, at midnight, excites the curiosity of astronomers; we insert the following for the perusal of those less conversant in that science'. The book trade and the network of correspondents that lay behind scholarly journals provided the channels for ideas. The extent of the culture of print varied greatly. It was strongest in major urban centres and weakest in distant rural areas. Thus, whereas, during most of the second half of the century, Derby usually had four booksellers, no newspaper was printed in Wales and, aside from abortive secret Catholic enterprises, there were no printing presses there until 1718. Only towards the close of the century did literacy and prosperity combine to increase book purchases and allow a development of Welsh printing.

The culture of print was both public and spread knowledge rapidly, although it is important not to take an unproblematic approach to this knowledge. Much that was printed would not strike modern readers as enlightened. For example, the 'Observations on March' 1706 in *Riders British Merlin*, a popular work of astrology, followed advice on the harvest with

Now advise with the honest and able astrological physician. It is good to purge and let blood, for in this month the humours and blood increase, and gross

feelings breeds gross blood and humours; therefore use meats of good diges-
tion, and such as afford good juice and nutriment to the body. Forbear all
things salt, purge the blood by potions and blood-letting. Sweetmeats and
drinks are commendable. Be sure to eat in the morning before you drink.

Two months later, 'Green whey excellent against cholar [sic]', and in August 'red
wine and claret are excellent remedies for children against the worms'.

At the same time, such works were evidence of the entrepreneurship that print
facilitated. Thus, the September item included an advertisement for 'Buckworth's
loxings [sic], famous for the cure of coughs, colds, catarrhs and hoarseness etc.,
being also a great cordial and sovereign preservative against all contagious dis-
tempers, malignant air, and unwholsm weather'.[4]

Riders British Merlin ensured that this London-made and authenticated product
could be advertised around the country. Print brought publicity and authentication.
Although the protective value of cowpox against smallpox was not unknown before
Edward Jenner experimented with, and in 1798 published on the value of, vaccination, his publication turned folk wisdom into readily accessible knowledge.

The corollary of the publications were the societies, ranging from the infor-
mality of coffee-houses to organised academies, that discussed ideas. Clubs and
institutions, ranging from the subscription concert to the Masonic lodge, were
a popular feature of cultural and intellectual life, the corporatist spirit being central
in many spheres of eighteenth-century society.

The spread of new ideas was not simply a matter of the existence of the necessary channels of communications. In part, it reflected a conscious reaction
against the past, as with the Scottish Enlightenment, but in England there was
a less marked sense of discontinuity. The Scottish Enlightenment had many distinctive features, one of which was the application of reason to knowledge as
a general principle. Important developments included the foundation of econom-
ics by Sir James Steuart (1712–80), whose *Inquiry into the Principles of Political
Economy* (1767) was the first systematic treatment of the subject in English,
and Adam Smith (1723–90), Professor of Moral Philosophy in Glasgow. Smith
advised the government on economic matters in 1773–6 and in 1776 published
The Wealth of Nations, a work emphasising the value of an absence of government regulation in ensuring economic growth.

Adam Ferguson (1723–1816), Professor of Pneumatics and Moral Philosophy
at Edinburgh, helped to found sociology with his *Essay on the History of Civil
Society* (1767). There were also important developments in psychology and history, and in geology with James Hutton's *Theory of the Earth* (1785). In episte-
mological and theological terms, geology was one of the most significant
branches of eighteenth-century science and, unintentionally, the most subversive
as it challenged biblical creation teaching, although for most of the period earth
science did not clash with scripture. Thus, Thomas Burnet's *Sacred Theory of the
Earth* (1689) explained the Earth's development in large part with reference to
Noah's Flood. In 1692 Burnet published an attempt to reconcile his theory with
Genesis. The jurist James, Lord Monboddo (1714–99) played a major role in the

development of anthropology. His *Of the Origin and Progress of Language* (1773–92) treated the development of man in a social state as a natural process.

There was a renaissance in literature with the works of Scots such as Burns, Fergusson, Hogg, Mackenzie, Scott, Smollett and Thomson. The first professorship in English anywhere was founded at Edinburgh in 1762 and occupied by Hugh Blair (1718–1800), an Edinburgh cleric who was a prominent member of the Edinburgh Enlightenment. There was also a renaissance in painting in Scotland, with works by Ramsay, Raeburn, Nasmyth and Wilkie. A university curriculum focusing on philosophy was created. Legal codification proceeded with Stair's *Institutions* and Erskine's *Institute of the Law of Scotland* (1773). In England, the preservation of an Anglican imperium over higher education helped ensure that the curriculum was slower to incorporate recent scholarly and scientific developments, although mathematics became fundamental to Cambridge courses during the eighteenth century.

Science was a major field of innovation, both north and south of the border. The so-called Scientific Revolution of the late seventeenth century had seen major advances in discovering the operations of natural laws, particularly the developments in astronomy, mathematics and physics associated with Newton, such as his laws of motion, which offered a coherent system of the universe at once mechanical and mathematically consistent. In place of the idea that man was only intended to know the mind of God as interpreted by the Church or as found in scriptures, Francis Bacon (1561–1626) had popularized the concept that God intended man to recover that mastery over nature which he had lost at the fall: it was (along with the Protestant Reformation) part of the preparation for the second coming of Christ.

Thus, scientific enquiry not only became legitimate, but almost a religious duty to the devout Protestant. This idea became immensely influential among the English and Dutch intelligentsia of the mid- and late-seventeenth century, and had a major long-term impact in preparing the way for the Scientific Revolution. Furthermore, however tenuously, a link can be drawn between increased interest in taking an active role in first understanding the world and then seeking to profit from this understanding, and a willingness to conceive of new political structures and governmental arrangements.

For many people, nevertheless, the ideas associated with Newton and the standards of proof implied were little understood. The new science was ignored by much of the population, and the Copernican cosmology was not accepted by all; although traditional ideas had only a limited resonance in the culture of print. In 1728, the mathematician Joseph Morgan published *The Immobility of the Earth Demonstrated Proving the Earth to be the Center of the Universe*, a translation of a French work by Etienne Lécuyer de la Jonchère, but this work had little impact. About nine years later, appeared a work that indicated interest in Newtonian physics outside 'polite' circles. Benjamin Parker, a Derby stocking-maker turned author, and sometime vendor of Restorative Jelly, published his *A Journal Thro' the World ... An Explanation into the Beginning of our Existence*, which argued for the 'non-eternity of matter' and 'that the soul is immortal'. Although the book carried a London imprint, it was probably printed in Birmingham.

It was still widely believed that astrological anatomies and zodiacs were keys to character and guides to the future, that extra-terrestrial forces intervened in the affairs of the world, particularly human and animal health and the state of the crops and weather, and that each constellation in the zodiac presided over a particular part of man, with guidance to this process being provided by almanacs. Ptolemaic geocentricism continued important in this literature, while many almanac writers boasted of being anti-Newtonian. Astrology flourished at the popular level in rural areas and provincial towns.[5]

Popular conservatism was not the sole factor inhibiting the diffusion of new scientific ideas and methods. More generally, there was no simple 'correct' line of scientific development which led smoothly to modern conceptions of science. Indeed, unsound theories, such as the phlogiston explanation of combustion, could lead to greater clarification of the issues involved, and were not simply worthless. A form of history of science and medicine was emerging which identified a mainstream tradition stressing observation, experiment and careful deduction of laws, within which contemporary work and 'discoveries' could be located, but the very looseness of the processes involved made this difficult to apply to separate 'sound' from 'unsound' science.

The sense of a great tradition, correct approach and recent important breakthroughs in light and gravitation gave a rough framework for what was and what was not scientific. There was confidence that knowledge was increasing and better understood. Newton's work contributed powerfully to a developing ideology of scientific advance. In his *History of the Present State of Electricity* (1767), Joseph Priestley claimed that recent discoveries of electrical phenomena would extend 'the bounds of natural science ... New worlds may open to our view, and the glory of the great Sir Isaac Newton himself, and all his contemporaries, be eclipsed by a new set of philosophers.' The notion of an age of progress became well established.

However, the creative tension in eighteenth-century science, of experimentation and speculative systematisation, did not foster simply one approach to any particular problem. Instead, a wide range of approaches was adopted and conclusions drawn. It was difficult to establish any individual interpretation in an age where standards of scientific proof were not always rigorous and the facilities for the necessary experimentation often absent. The amateur and commercial nature of much scientific activity possibly exacerbated the problem, although the world of scholarship, too, was not free from serious error. The belief that man could come to understand much about himself and the world through his own reason and through empirical investigation had played a major role in the Scientific Revolution. However, science was a process, rather than a set of answers, and this belief encouraged not only the activities and acceptance of charlatans, but also the continued intertwining of metaphysics, theology, human interest, and scientific thought and experimentation that had been so important in the previous century.

There was no shortage of charlatans, but, in putting scientific interest and methods to personal profit, they also revealed the varied relationship of both of these to the widespread desire, at the individual and the social level, to understand and control the environment. This desire was only imperfectly catered for by existing formal institutions. Quack-doctors won fame and fortune with their remedies. Joshua Ward (1685–1761), for example, gained tremendous popularity and a considerable fortune from 1734, and was patronised by George II, despite the fact that his remedies killed as many as they cured. There was a tar-water mania in which it was regarded as a remedy for all ills. One wild claim was that tar water could heal amputees in three days. In addition, alchemy continued to be important. Giuseppe Balsamo, 'Count Cagliostro' (1743–95), began his career as an alchemist by seeking to transmute excrement, hair, herbs, minerals, urine and wood into gold in London in 1776–7. Some scientists were interested in alchemy. The eminent chemist Peter Woulfe (*c.*1727–1803), who developed an apparatus for passing gases through liquids, also pursued alchemical investigations, fixing prayers to his apparatus.

The idea of direct divine intervention was not only held by the populace. Newton himself argued that God acted in order to keep heavenly bodies in their place. The idea that personal moral faults or the malevolent intentions of others were responsible for mishaps, such as accidents, proved difficult to dispel, whatever the current teaching on cosmology, physics and medicine. Medicine was a particular field of misapprehension because much about both body and mind was not understood. It was widely believed, for example that masturbation was the specific cause of mental and physical diseases, and there was much ignorance about menstruation. Mary Toft, the 'rabbit-woman of Godalming', who claimed to have given birth to rabbits, was believed by many, including several prominent physicians, in 1726.

Much scientific work advanced inaccurate theses that were contested, but, as such work often used principles of hypothesis and experimentation similar to those employed by its critics, it was difficult to disprove. Thus scientific activity and experimentation did not necessarily advance knowledge. John Needham (1713–81), the first Catholic cleric elected a fellow of the Royal Society of London (1747), published in 1749 his experimental proof of the theory of spontaneous generation, the idea that inanimate matter could come alive, and thus that mutations and new creations of species were possible. The fallacy of his experiment was not demonstrated until 1760. A polymath in the manner of a period where modern distinctions between branches of knowledge had little meaning, Needham also published on ants, the Alps, electricity – one of the great interests of the period, his correspondence with Voltaire on miracles, and in 1761 a widely discussed, but speedily refuted, book that sought, by the use of Chinese characters, to interpret an Egyptian inscription. On his circumnavigation of the world in 1764–6, John Byron inaccurately reported the existence of Patagonian giants.

Experimentation, even if designed to sustain established views, reflected a determination to expand on received information, while, through taxonomy, scholars sought to classify and organise knowledge, in part so that it could be better applied. Exploration played an important role, especially in cartography, botany, astronomy and geology. The botanist Joseph Banks (1743–1820) sailed round the world with Cook and also collected plants on expeditions to Newfoundland and Iceland. Succeeding George III's favourite, John, 3rd Earl of Bute, as Director of the new Royal Botanic gardens at Kew (founded 1759), Banks helped to make them a centre for botanical research based on holdings from around the world.[6]

Nevil Maskelyne (1732–1811), Astronomer Royal from 1765, was sent by the Royal Society to observe the transit of Venus of 1761 from the island of St Helena. While on his way, he experimented in taking longitudes by lunar distances and, while there, kept tidal records. In 1766, he began the annual production and publication of the *Nautical Almanac and Astronomical Ephemeris*, a book of tables of the predicted positions of celestial bodies at a series of times, that was of great value to navigators and at once sold 10,000 copies. Maskelyne also improved the accuracy of astronomical instruments.

There was also a process of cultural exploration. In 1734, George Sale published a translation of the Koran, arguing that, 'to be acquainted with the various laws and constitutions of civilised nations, especially of those who flourish in our own time, is, perhaps, the most useful part of knowledge'. This was not, however, intended by Sale to suggest any equivalence. Indeed, he was certain that Providence had reserved the glory of the overthrow of Islam to the Protestants.[7] Sir William Jones, who made his reputation translating Persian works in the 1770s, issuing a *Grammar of the Persian Language* in 1771, mastered Sanskrit in the following decade, and translated several Hindu classics, helping to interpret Indian culture for a British audience.

The British played a major role in exploration, especially in the South Seas. In 1767, a naval officer, Samuel Wallis, 'discovered' many islands in the Pacific, including King George the Third's Island, better known as Tahiti. The collaborative international observation of Venus' transit across the sun in 1769, took another naval officer, James Cook (1728–79), in HMS *Endeavour*, to Tahiti, whence he conducted the first circuit and charting of New Zealand and the charting of the east coast of Australia. Here, in 1770, Cook landed in Botany Bay and claimed the territory for George III. In 1772–5, Cook's repeated efforts to find a great southern continent, including the first passage of the Antarctic circle, failed. Cook, however, 'discovered' New Caledonia and Hawaii, and in 1778 he proved that pack ice blocked any possible North West passage from the Atlantic to the Pacific. Exploration helped to fire a view of Britain as a global maritime power. The projection of British power in the southern hemisphere in the 1780s, including the establishment of a settlement in Australia in 1788, was to be easier as a result of the information gathered in the 1770s.

Land exploration received less government support and faced an often hostile environment. Much of the interior of North America was explored by the British. In 1771–2, Samuel Hearne reached the Great Slave Lake. In Africa, James Bruce 'discovered' the Abyssinian source of the Blue Nile in 1770.

Alongside structural trends and 'enablers' in intellectual life, such as greater religious tolerance, individuals played a prominent role. The Reverend John Walker (1731–1804) was typical of many clergymen in his interest in botany and geology. A friend of Kames, and from 1779 Professor of Natural History in Edinburgh, he met Rousseau and Franklin and corresponded with Linnaeus. He won medals from the Edinburgh Society in the 1750s for his collections of natural manures and in 1761–4 his mineralogical researches led to the discovery of Strontianite. Walker helped organise the Royal Society of Edinburgh and its Natural History (1782) and Agricultural (1792) Societies. Walker was not only a pillar of the Edinburgh enlightenment, but also an avid collector of geological and botanical specimens. As professor, Walker emphasised laboratory work and he and his pupils established Scottish geological studies.

Individual scholars not only responded to (and helped frame) institutional developments, but also to the intellectual patterning created by systems of classification. Major works of classification included Edward Lhuyd's comparative ethnology in his *Archaeologica Britannica* (1707), Thomas Pennant's *British Zoology* (1766–8) and John Lightfoot's *Flora Scotica* (1778). Lightfoot, the Oxford-educated son of a Gloucestershire yeoman who became librarian and chaplain of the Dowager-Duchess of Portland, arranged his work on the Linnean system. He also first described the reed-warbler. The naturalist Pennant (1726–98) also visited Scotland, publishing a *Tour in Scotland* (1771, 5th ed. 1790) that increased English awareness of its customs and natural history. William Withering (1741–99), an Edinburgh-educated doctor, who was physician to the Staffordshire County Infirmary (1767–75) and subsequently Chief Physician to the Birmingham General Hospital, published *A Botanical Arrangement of all the Vegetables naturally growing in Great Britain... with an easy Introduction to the Study of Botany* (1776), and subjected digitalis to scientific study, writing *An Account of the Foxglove and some of its Medical Uses* (1785).

Though measurement played a major role in the experimentation of the period, there were major problems. It was difficult to make standard instruments and replicate laboratory results, and research in chemistry was hindered by the difficulty of quantifying chemical reactions. Vulcanised tubing did not appear until the mid-1840s. The astronomer William Herschel (1738–1822), who, from Bath, found Uranus in 1781, the first planet discovered since antiquity, encountered numerous failures in 1773–4 in the construction of his first telescope. Yet, in 1706, Francis Hauksbee was able to construct the first machine to generate electricity. The mapping of the reverse side of the earth was one of the great European achievements of the century.

The virtues of experimentation were widely praised in scientific circles and it led to a number of major advances, such as those in chemistry and medicine. Stephen Hales (1677–1761), a clergyman like many of the scientists of the period, was typical in his wide-ranging interests. Besides inventing artificial ventilators, and quantifying various aspects of plant physiology, Hales opened the way for a correct appreciation of blood pressure thanks to his conception of the living organism as a self-regulating machine and his experiments.

Typical of the interrelationship between experimentation and application was the work of Chester Hall (1703–71), a lawyer whose study of the human eye convinced him that achromatic lenses were possible. His success in about 1733 in making them laid the basis for an improvement in the performance of almost all optical instruments. In 1750, the optician James Ayscough published an account of the nature of spectacles, in which he recommended a tinted glass to reduce glare, and in 1755 an *Account of the Eye and the Nature of Vision.*

Medical research became more important. The appointment of physicians to the London charity hospitals turned them into centres of research and in Edinburgh the modernisation of the curriculum strengthened the role of hospital-based research.[8] The surgeon John Hunter, who rebelled against the predominant European method of medical training, with its emphasis on the study of classical texts, and refused to 'stuff Latin and Greek at the university', was typical of many leading surgeons in his willingness to try new methods, even when the theoretical explanation was unclear. In England, the training of surgeons was increasingly conducted in hospital schools rather than through apprenticeships.

There were major advances in chemistry. William Brownrigg (1711–1800) formulated the concept of a multiplicity of chemically distinctive gases. Joseph Black (1728–99), professor of chemistry at Glasgow and later Edinburgh, discovered latent heat and first fixed the compound carbon dioxide. Henry Cavendish (1731–1810), a master of quantitative analysis, was, in 1766, the first to define hydrogen as a distinct substance and, in 1781, the first to determine the composition of water by exploding a mixture of hydrogen and oxygen in a sealed vessel. Priestley (1733–1804) discovered a number of gases and oxides and carried out experimental work on astronomy, electricity, optics and respiration. He also made considerable advances in the equipment for studying gases.

Much chemical research was directly intended for practical purposes. The Edinburgh doctor Francis Home (1719–1813), who first called attention to croup as a distinct disease in 1765, tested water for bleaching and in 1756 published *Experiments on Bleaching.* In 1746, the English doctor John Roebuck (1718–94) revolutionised the manufacture of sulphuric acid, reducing it to a quarter of its former cost, by substituting leaden chambers for glass globes for the purpose of condensation. In 1779, Bryan Higgins, an Irish-born doctor, who in 1774 had opened a school of practical chemistry in London, patented a cheap and durable cement.

However, the chemistry of such operations as brewing and iron-making was far from understood. The chemistry of industrial processes was still largely traditional, and arrived at by a long process of local trial and error. In brewing, the processes varied from region to region, with top- or bottom-fermentation and the evolution of local yeast strains. Some of these methods were doubtless better than others at excluding the contaminated air, but all were vulnerable as the biochemistry was not yet understood. Pasteur's work on yeasts was not done until the 1850s, and enzymes were not discovered until the end of the nineteenth century. Consequently, when large-scale brewing began later in the eighteenth century, the hazards of sudden losses of huge and costly batches of porter were great. The big London brewers only used their fermentation vats in the winter.

Leather tanning was in the same state. Processes were technically developed, but not capable of easy change and experimentation, since no distinction existed between the truly important and the accidental elements in the process. Iron-making also was largely unscientific, at least at the level of ordinary practice; when to add the handful of sand to the furnace, when to tap the ore, and how much blast to permit tended to be skilled judgements resting in the person of the workman. Dyeing was mainly with vegetable products and often focused on local specialisms and processes, again with little possibility of improvement because of uncertainty about the active principles.

Similarly, bleaching of cottons and linens was a long-drawn-out process which occupied much space and time, with comparatively little change. Sulphuric acid was used only for vegetable fibres. Woollens were quicker to bleach with a mixture of washing in stale urine, and then 'storing' which was effectively giving them a mild sulphuric acid bath by burning sulphur in a large closed chamber and letting the products condense over the cloth. There was little pressure to develop a complete understanding of the process, or to apply new methods. The introduction of chlorine for rag bleaching in the paper industry began only in the 1790s.

The nature of naval conflict also reflected the limitations of eighteenth-century technology. The optimal conditions for combat were to come from windward in a force 4–6 wind across a sea that was relatively flat; it was more difficult to range guns in a swell. Limitations on manoeuvrability ensured that ships were deployed in line in order to maximise their firepower. The skill in handling ships entailed getting wind behind the topsails. Limitations in communications and surveillance ensured that battles arose from chance encounters.

In many fields, experimentation was designed to try to overcome technological limitations. However, the growing prestige of science reflected the sense not only that it could have practical value, but also that, by increasing man's knowledge, it was worthy of praise and was both a civilising influence and a cultural resource. Dissenting Academies introduced the teaching of experimental science as a means of understanding the wisdom of God. George III patronised astronomy, although he did not understand the complex mathematics that played an increasing role in it. Earlier, as Princess of Wales, Queen Caroline had visited John Flamsteed (1646–1719), the first Astronomer Royal, at Greenwich. As Prince of Wales, George III visited the house of William Watson (1715–87) in order to see his electrical experiments.

Scientific and rational approaches to the world became the fashion. Public awareness of science increased. A big market developed for scientific textbooks and works of popularisation, including books for women and children. Francesco Algarotti's *Il Newtonianismo per le Dame* (1739), which explained the theories of light and gravitation in a series of dialogues, was translated into English in 1739. James Ferguson's *Astronomy explained on Sir Isaac Newton's Principles* (1750) achieved great success because he used familiar language. 'Tom Telescope's' *The Newtonian System of Philosophy, adapted to the capacities of young gentlemen and ladies* went through many editions. Magazines devoted much space to scientific advances and related speculation.

Experimentation became a theme in art, most powerfully in Joseph Wright of Derby's *A Philosopher giving that Lecture on the Orrery, in which a lamp is put in place of the Sun* (1766) and in his *An Experiment on a Bird in the Air Pump* (1768). This was a culture in which Enlightenment values permeated perhaps more deeply than anywhere else in Europe.

Museums of natural history were created, public scientific lectures developed, with lecturers such as J.T. Desaguliers, John Harris, John Horsley and William Whiston, and societies of enthusiastic amateurs were founded. Knowledge and science became genteel and a focus for sociability. In Norwich, a Natural History Society was founded in 1746, a Norwich Botanical Society in the 1760s, and two general scientific societies in the 1750s and 1780s. The Manchester Literary and Philosophical Society was founded in 1779. Lecturers were not restricted to the major towns. In 1775, John Banks published at Kendal *An Epitome of a Course of Lectures on Natural and Experimental Philosophy*, a manual to a series of scientific lectures, with sections on hydraulics, hydrostatics, pneumatics, optics and electricity.

Accounts of exploration, for example of the voyages of Anson and Cook or Dalrymple's *Collection of Voyages to the South Seas* (1770–1), were very popular. The theme of an expanding world was captured in Edward Wells's *New Set of Maps Both of Antient and Present Geography* (Oxford, 1700), dedicated to the Duke of Gloucester, which revealed contemporary knowledge as being far more extensive. An entire hemisphere was 'unknown to the Antients', unless North America was their Atlantis. Even so, the Ancients could not map it, whereas the Moderns could. California, however, was still believed to be an island.

Britain's maritime role and ambitions also led to a greater interest in charting the wider world. Between 1698 and 1700 Edmund Halley and HMS *Paramour* had discovered the extent of magnetic variation and the precise longitude and latitude of the American colonies.

More generally, cartography was a vital aspect of the ability to synthesise, disseminate, utilise and reproduce information that was crucial to British hegemony. The movement of ships could be planned and predicted, facilitating not only trade but also amphibious operations. Maps served to record and replicate information about areas in which Britain had an interest and to organise, indeed centre, this world on themes of European concern and power. The sprinkling of much of the world with British placenames reflected not only British explorers and power, but also its registration through surveying, charting and cartography.

Knowledge of the British Isles was also increased by the growing availability of more accurate maps. Hitherto, Elizabethan maps had been reprinted with scant alteration, due to the absence of new field work. In the eighteenth century, new surveys of entire counties were undertaken and maps were produced on detailed scales: one or more inches to the mile. The work from 1759 was in part encouraged by prizes awarded by the Royal Society of Arts, one of the major 'improving' bodies of the period. The first of the county maps – that of Cornwall by Joel Gascoyne, appeared in 1699. By 1750, only eight counties had been mapped at one-inch to a mile or larger, but, by 1775, nearly half of the English counties had been thus surveyed. Essex, for example, was surveyed by John Chapman in 1772–4 and the resulting maps published in 1777.

Enclosure maps reflected the use of cartography as an aid to control. There could be a hostile response to surveying. Opposition to the enclosure of the former Malvern Chase in 1776 led local people to prevent the surveyor from marking out the enclosure boundaries.

The government survey of Scotland between 1747 and 1755 in order to produce a map that would, it was hoped, enable the army to respond better to any repetition of the Jacobite rising of 1745, was another aspect of mapping as an aid to control. Six surveying parties were employed in a move that was to parallel the road and fortress-building of the same years. Fortresses anchored the government position and maps provided guidance in the planning and use of force, offering the prospect of a strategic, Scotland-wide, response to any future uprising.

CONCLUSION

If science became public, fashionable and a matter of cultural status in some areas, the level of scientific knowledge was rarely profound and much of the interest was dilettante and restricted to display rather than theory. The mathematisation of science possibly made theories harder to grasp. Instead, as can be seen in Wright's paintings, it was the phenomena themselves that attracted attention because they appealed to the imagination as well as or rather than to the intellect. This was true of star-gazing, mesmerism and electricity.

Interest in phenomena and the environment reflected in part the belief that man was actively shaped by outside forces. Locke's *Essay Concerning Human Understanding* (1690) argued that all knowledge consisted of ideas which originated in sensation. Psychological theories suggested that man, both as an individual and as a social being, could be improved by education and a better environment, bringing and reflecting progress. Activity, rather than the passive acceptance of divine will and an unchanging universe, was stressed. Locke's theory of personal identity challenged traditional Christian notions of the soul, although this was not seen as so at the time.

Few, however, were led towards the idea of evolution. Most writers clung to the notions of the fixity of individual species and of a static natural environment. Knowledge concerning human conception and the origin of man's characteristics, both as individuals and as a species, was still too limited to help to clarify theoretical speculation. Among scientists, there was a reluctance to abandon the notion of a ladder of nature with species occupying fixed positions, and to probe the world of plant and animal breeders and their attempts to enhance particular characteristics, for example by hybridisation. The relationship between experimentation and theorisation was not always close or productive, and theoretical advances were not always easy to apply. Possibly more important was the establishment of the idea that man could understand and influence his environment, even altering the calendar by switching from Old to New Style in 1752. The ideology of scientific advance was well developed by the end of the century, even if most people knew nothing of it and understood their lives, jobs and environment through the teaching of their predecessors.

NOTES

1. Exeter, Devon CRO. 64/12/29/1/26.
2. P.B. Wood, *The Aberdeen Enlightenment: The Arts Curriculum in the Eighteenth Century* (Aberdeen, 1993).
3. L. Okie, *Augustan Historical Writing. Histories of England in the English Enlightenment* (Lanham, Maryland, 1991).
4. *Riders British Merlin* (1706), BL. Add. 74642 fols 18, 26, 39, 43.
5. P. Curry, *Prophecy and Power: Astrology in Early Modern England* (1989).
6. J. Gascoigne, *Joseph Banks and the English Enlightenment: Useful Knowledge and Polite Culture* (Cambridge, 1994); R. Drayton, *Nature's Government: Science, Imperial Britain, and the 'Improvement' of the World* (New Haven, 2000).
7. G. Sale (ed.), *The Koran* (1734), dedication, iv.
8. A. Doig, J.P.S. Ferguson, I.A. Milne, R. Passmore (eds), *William Cullen and the Eighteenth Century Medical World* (Edinburgh, 1993).

10

Culture and the arts

There is no single approach to the culture of eighteenth-century Britain. One method is to focus on developments in style and artistic movements, from Baroque to Romanticism. It is also possible to focus on spheres of patronage, more particularly the nature of the so-called consumer society which has become a much studied theme of late. Much recent scholarship has associated the cultural patterns of the century with the various forces of social and economic change. Above all this branch of scholarship has tended to link cultural development with the new forms of leisure and recreation in the period. It has been suggested that cultural diffusion can be seen as one way of accounting for the so-called stability of eighteenth-century England, the growth of leisure and refinement helping to defuse the political tensions of the previous century.

Yet caution is needed in seeing society as consumer-led, with culture as just a response to market forces. A more complex relationship existed between producers, suppliers and the market. Far from being primarily an off-shoot of middle-class leisure activity, cultural activity had a wider social context and was also often closely bound up with the worlds of local politics and religion. The spread and diffusion of culture could have more to do with political and religious crises than with consumption. Those who agreed on an ethics of politeness and a morality of moderation, which are seen as the criteria of middle-class culture, might disagree on much else. Culture could become an expression of conflict rather than a panacea for strife.

One area of potential conflict was that between popular and elite culture. The late Edward Thompson focused attention on the world of 'plebian', as opposed to 'patrician', culture. His work has been crucial in alerting historians to the social and political messages of ritual within society, showing the unwritten cultural and political assumptions behind what he valuably termed the 'moral economy' of the crowd.[1] It is, however, also possible to modify this analysis of a bi-focal cultural world by seeing, instead, cultural gradations and/or a world that encompassed populace and elite. Furthermore, it is probable that the oft-cited dichotomy between written and oral culture, the former progressive and the latter conservative, should be replaced by an emphasis on gradations within a cultural world that encompassed both written and oral forms.

Aside from problems in analysing causes and patterns of cultural diffusion and patronage, there are also problems in describing changes in style, particularly since these developments can be perceived fully only through an appreciation of specific texts, objects and performances. Rather than thinking in terms of competing styles and influences, it is more appropriate to emphasise their co-existence, even though public criticisms of existing styles were part of the establishment of an identity for newer styles.

The appropriateness of the accepted stylistic vocabulary is also open to question: a vocabulary or chronology that might suit portraiture is not necessarily appropriate for opera. Movements such as the English Baroque, associated in particular with Sir Christopher Wren and Sir John Vanbrugh, are open to very different definitions. If common themes can be discerned in some fields, it is more appropriate to write in terms of stylistic tendencies, rather than to suggest that distinct uniformities can be discerned.

In addition, it is possible to discern several important sources of patronage and different artistic market-places, although it would be inappropriate to suggest that they were necessarily distinct and unrelated. The situation varied not only by artistic form, the churches featuring as patrons of music but not of novels, but also by place: towns were a different cultural world to heavily rural areas.

By European standards, the British monarchs were not great patrons. Their courts were settings of elegance and sometimes splendour, but not to compare with their Continental counterparts, and they were not centres of high culture. William III demolished earlier work and built essentially new palaces at Hampton Court and Kensington, both carefully integrated with their gardens. Sir Christopher Wren remodelled Hampton Court with scant concern for the Tudor fabric. Anne, however, was not a great builder, and the palace that dates from her reign is that of the Duke of Marlborough at Blenheim. The accession of the Hanoverian dynasty in 1714 did not have a dramatic cultural effect, because of the relatively small scale of their royal patronage and the absence of a strong indigenous Hanoverian culture. George I had Kensington Palace expanded, but he, George II and George III did not compare in their building with George IV or such Continental monarchs as Elizabeth I and Catherine II of Russia. Indeed, George III chose rather to purchase than to build, a new London residence – Buckingham House. Though keen on the music of Handel, and a patron of the architect Sir William Chambers (1726–96), who had taught him architectural drawing, George III was more interested in astronomy and farming than most of the arts. His grandfather, George II, was also not a noted sponsor of culture, certainly far less so than George III's father, Frederick, Prince of Wales, who was a significant supporter of music, gardens and literature, and an important patron of Rococo art in England. Frederick's widow, Augusta, employed Chambers to adorn the gardens of her house at Kew and in 1757–62 he erected a number of buildings there in oriental or classical styles that had a great impact. As Prince of Wales, the future George IV reached his majority in 1783 and within a year had expensively remodelled Carlton House.

Handel produced and conducted the coronation anthems for George II's coronation and had been awarded £200 annually for life by Queen Anne as a reward for his birthday ode of 1713 and his thanksgiving for the Peace of Utrecht; but his livelihood depended on the commercial success of his works on the London stage. More generally, the history of theatre during the century revealed the declining significance of royal patronage. George II preferred hunting and drilling soldiers, although the established routine of court festivities and the embellishment of palaces helped in general to ensure that portraits were painted and furniture and porcelain purchased. This was an important ingredient in the shift from 'grand' culture to 'domestic' culture, which was more accessible to the middling orders.

In Britain, the landed elite played a greater role in artistic patronage than the monarchy. 'Taste' came from outside the royal court. This was particularly the case with architecture and portraiture. The stately homes of the period were a testimony to wealth, confidence, the profits of agricultural improvement, the greater social stability that followed the Restoration of Charles II in 1660, and the increased political stability of the eighteenth century. At the time of the '45, a loyal Scottish peer, Lord Glenorchy, wrote to his daughter regretting that, like so many landowners, he had weakened his house in modernising it: 'I have often repented taking out the iron bars from the windows and sashing them, and taking away a great iron door, and weakening the house as to resistance by adding modern wings to it. If it had remained in the old castle way as it was before, I might have slept very sound in it, for their whole army could not have taken it without cannon.'[2]

In some cases, social stability was more directly linked with elite culture: portraiture and architecture promoted stability by emphasising the power and immutability of the elite leadership of society. Ralph, 1st Duke of Montagu had his coat of arms and family tree carved on his staircase at Boughton House to promote the idea of an unchanging family succession. Stately homes such as Wentworth Woodhouse were monuments of ostentation that dominated the countryside. They were also new. Although stately homes proclaimed hierarchy and status, they also reflected a concern to be up-to-date. The latter indeed was an affirmation of status.

This rejection of the past was dramatised when older mansions were rebuilt, as classical ideas and designs came to inform British architecture, aspects of a redefinition of taste and style that reordered fashion and acceptability. In the 1690s, William Blathwayt totally transformed the Tudor house at Dyrham Park. In the 1720s, the Tudor Lyme Park was transformed by the Venetian architect Giacomo Leone; he also built Clandon Park to replace an earlier Elizabethan house. The Tudor Dunham Massey was rebuilt in 1758 for George, 2nd Earl of Warrington, and in 1761 the Tudor Osterley Park was remodelled by Robert Adam. Other Tudor houses, such as Killerton and Wallington, were also rebuilt. Thus, while landed estates might suggest continuity, their stately homes, like their enclosures, reflected change.

There were differences between Whig and Tory cultural preferences, seen very clearly by visitors to the grounds of Viscount Cobham's seat at Stowe, with its sculptural lessons about the need for true Whiggery. However, shared values were of greater importance, and can be seen in elite lifestyle and culture.

Lesser houses reflected the motifs and styles of greater works. Sir John Vanbrugh (1664–1726), a leading exponent of the English Baroque and a playwright of note, displayed at the Duke of Marlborough's seat at Blenheim, the Earl of Carlisle's at Castle Howard and Admiral Delaval's at Seaton Delaval, a degree of spatial enterprise similar to the architects of princely palaces on the Continent. He also pioneered informally laid out gardens and parks.[3]

In contrast to the heaviness of Vanbrugh's architecture, the Scottish architect Colen Campbell (d. 1729) was influenced by Andrea Palladio and Inigo Jones, as was his principal patron Lord Burlington, who was responsible for Chiswick House. Both sought to encourage what they saw as a distinctly British style in contrast to the Baroque of Christopher Wren, Vanbrugh and Nicholas Hawksmoor. Campbell's works included Wanstead House, Mereworth, and Stourhead, and he also designed Houghton for Sir Robert Walpole. There was also a vogue for Palladianism in Ireland until about 1760. Sir Edward Lovett Pearce was responsible for the Parliament House in Dublin and for Castletown, while Francis Bindon worked on Russborough House.

Palladianism also influenced the extension of Bath, with John Wood the Elder's Queen's Square (1728–34) and Circus (1754–64), his son's Royal Crescent (1767–74), and Assembly Rooms (1769–71), and the Palladian Bridge created in the nearby gardens of Prior Park. More generally, Classical ideas were transferred to houses, churches and public buildings. This was not easy as the prototypes were mostly temples, baths etc. and it proved necessary to design a new architectural grammar for design and ornamentation. This encouraged recourse to books of designs.[4]

Major figures proclaimed their prominence with new or greatly rebuilt mansions, such as the Duke of Chandos' at Canons, the Earl of Hardwicke's at Wimpole, Sir George Lyttelton's at Hagley Hall, the Ansons' at Shugborough, and William Duff, 1st Earl of Fife's, at Duff House. The last was designed by the Scot William Adam, whose brother Robert (1728–92) rebuilt or redesigned many stately homes, including Culzean, Kedleston, Luton Hoo, Osterley, Mellerstain, Syon House for the Duke of Northumberland, and Kenwood for the Earl of Mansfield. There was no regional pattern; this was a national style. Competition was important. Ralph, 2nd Lord Verney, rebuilt much of Claydon House in order to rival Earl Temple's work at nearby Stowe. Houghton rivalled Viscount Townshend's Raynham.

Alongside Palladianism, there was also a continuing interest in the Gothic style, which influenced both domestic and ecclesiastical architecture. Thus, Henrietta Howard, Countess of Oxford, rebuilt Welbeck Abbey in the Gothic style from 1752. Alnwick Castle was remodelled in a Gothic fashion from 1750. In 1742, the first English book on Gothic architecture appeared, Batty Langley's *Ancient Architecture Restored and Improved by a Great Variety of Grand and Usefull Designs, entirely new in the Gothick Mode for ornamenting of Buildings and Gardens*. However, the Gothic was not used for new seats, only for rebuilding, and Horace Walpole's Gothic suburban villa at Twickenham, Strawberry Hill, was unusual in being a new house. Gothic was not seen as a style equal to Classicism until the work of architects such as James Wyatt at the close of the century.

Landscape gardening, closely linked to wealthy landed patronage, flourished and was influential on the Continent where a vogue developed for the 'English Garden'. Landscape gardening represented an Anglicisation of classical notions of rural harmony, retreat and beauty, as well as nature tamed by reason, and both Tories and Whigs embraced these trends. New developments in horticulture, especially imports, mainly from North America, greatly extended the range of possible trees, shrubs and flowers, while classical texts provided inspiration. Newly-introduced plants included the rhododendron (1736), magnolia grandi-flora (1737), camellia (1739), buddleia (1774), and strelitzia (1780s).

British gardens in the early decades of the period, for example Pitmedden in Scotland, were created in the formal geometric patterns that characterised Continental designs. They were an opportunity for ostentation and display. Those at Hampton Court have recently been returned to their original form.

The separation of garden and park (grounds) ended under the influence of the architect William Kent (1684–1748) who developed and decorated parks at, for example, Stowe, Chiswick, Claremont and Rousham, in order to provide an appropriate setting for buildings. He used the 'ha-ha' (a term first used in 1712), a ditch, sunk from view, to create a boundary between garden and park that did not interrupt the prospect. Sunken fences were employed to conceal the limits of the property. Influential as Kent was to be, it is important not to exaggerate the extent to which new ideas were adopted. At Stowe, although Kent's work had an impact from the 1730s, Charles Bridgeman's formal central axis with its geometric pond remained until the second half of the century.

Trained under Kent, Lancelot 'Capability' Brown (1716–83) rejected the rigid formality associated with geometric Continental models, contriving a setting that appeared natural, but was, nevertheless, carefully designed for effect. His landscapes of serpentine lakes, gentle hills, copses on the brow of hitherto bare hills, and scattered groups of newly planted trees swiftly established a fashion. Brown laid out or remodelled the grounds at about 180 houses, including Audley End, Blenheim, Chatsworth, Eywood, Ingestre, Kew, Kirtlington, Nuneham Courtenay, Petworth and Trentham, and Burton Pynsent for Pitt the Elder. His work brought him substantial wealth and, having begun work as a kitchen gardener, he became High Sheriff of Huntingdonshire.

Brown and Kent's system was criticised for formalism by Sir Uvedale Price, who argued in favour of a wilder, more natural and 'picturesque' beauty that would accord with 'all the principles of landscape-painting'. This influenced Humphry Repton (1752–1818), who transformed about 220 gardens, and developed Brown's ideas in accordance with the concept of the 'picturesque', which stressed the individual character of each landscape and the need to retain it, while making improvements to remove what were judged blemishes and obstructions and to open up vistas.

Many landowners displayed a close personal interest in the landscaping of their own and friends' parks. Prominent examples included Burlington, Lord Cobham at Stowe, George Bowes at Gibside, the 5th Lord Byron at Newstead, William Pitt the Elder, and Thomas Jones at Hafod, which was landscaped in the 'picturesque' style by 'Warwick' Smith. The 3rd Duke of Bridgewater, famous as the 'Canal Duke', also, in 1759–68, employed Henry Holland to work on his seat at Ashridge and Brown to landscape the park.

Though park landscape was not without economic value, sheep serving as more than natural lawnmowers, the labour required to excavate basins for artificial lakes or to create hills was considerable. In short, considerable expense was incurred. Landscape gardening reflected and created a new aesthetic that was interested in nature, albeit an altered nature. In her poetic account of an English country house, *Crumble Hall*, Mary Leapor, a kitchen-maid, wrote of climbing up to the roof to view the 'beauteous Order' of a landscaped park. The new fashion entailed stylistic conventions and derived from artistic models, for example the presentation of the landscapes of Roman Italy in the paintings of Claude Lorraine, which influenced the banker Henry Hoare when he laid out the gardens at Stourhead which he inherited in 1741. The imitation Temple of Theseus (or Pephaestus) designed for the grounds of Hagley Hall by James 'Athenian' Stuart in 1758 was the first copy of a Greek Doric-style temple. Parks were embellished with grottoes, follies, shell houses, columns and classical statues, for example the column and statue of liberty at Gibside, a Roman Doric column topped by a statue of liberty dressed in classical drapery and carrying the cap of liberty.

The new fashion in landscaping was less rigid and formal than its predecessor, and this permitted a more personal response by visitors to the tamed natural environment that was presented, a direction that led towards the more personal response to nature that was to be such a major theme in Romanticism. In 1762, Lord Lyttelton revealed a sense of confident cultural competitiveness at Stourhead, the grounds of which had been enhanced with classical features:

> The Pantheon [by Flitcroft] is finished, and is an abode worthy of all the deities in Olympius ... I think I never saw the Graces of Sculpture and all the power of that divine art, before I saw them there. I would have every Frenchman that comes to England be brought to this place, not only that he may see the perfection of our taste, but to show him that we have citizens who have a truer politeness in their manners, and a nobler elegance in their minds, than any Count or Duke in France.[5]

A receptiveness to the 'picturesque' from the 1760s and, more particularly, the 1770s, led to a new responsiveness to landscape and thus to the parts of the British Isles which were 'constructed' in light of the aesthetic preferences of the pre-Romantic movement. This affected attitudes to the Lake and Peak Districts, the Scottish Highlands and Wales, for example the Wye Valley. These new portrayals were popularised in print, for example in Thomas Pennant's *Twelve Views in Aquatint from Drawings taken on the Spot, in South Wales* (1775–7) and in his *Tours of Wales* (1778–83).

The stately homes that were built had to be decorated and furnished. This led to a massive amount of patronage ranging from frescoes to furniture. Styles varied. At Houghton, the decoration was a riot in gilt and stucco, with an ample use of expensive woods, including much mahogany, for extensive and ornate wood-carving. Pillars, pilasters, capitals, friezes, marble overmantles, dramatic chimneypieces, brackets, impressive staircases, and lavish tapestries contributed to a heady sense of opulence that contrasted with the more restrained taste that tended to prevail with a more general shift of sensibility away from baroque and rococo themes, and towards a quieter neo-classicism. Setting a less ornate tone, Thomas Chippendale (1718–79) from Yorkshire, who became one of the leading furniture makers in mid-century London, dedicated his book of designs for furniture, *The Gentleman and Cabinet Maker's Director* (1754), to Hugh, Earl of Northumberland. Publication brought his work to the attention of an elite readership, and new editions appeared in 1759 and 1762.

Patronage was also a means to establish, in the public mind, the unassailability of the 'taste' and position of the Earl, who was concerned about his social position: he was only an in-law of the Percys, obtained the title by a curious creation, and much of his behaviour was aimed at striking the pose of a 'real' nobleman – he employed more flambards to light the route of his carriage than royalty. The Earl, Duke of Northumberland from 1766, had Alnwick Castle extensively decorated with coats of arms of the Percys and related families.

A lighter, less ornamented and simpler style than that of Chippendale was developed subsequently by Hepplewhite and Sheraton. Thomas Sheraton (1751–1806) from Stockton, established himself in London in about 1790 and began publication of a series of manuals of furniture design. Thanks to such books of designs, fixtures, fittings and furniture became more standardised.

Aside from furniture, the new houses required large numbers of books for the libraries which became an established feature, and of portraits for the large spaces created in their public rooms, particularly the grand, often two-storied entrance-halls, as at Seaton Delaval and Beningbrough. Many members of the elite were keen collectors of paintings. An important theme was aristocratic recreations, particularly horses and hunting, as in the works of George Stubbs (1724–1806). The classical interests of patrons and artists combined in the depiction of classical landscapes and stories, the heroes of ancient Rome being suitable companions for the portraits of modern aristocrats. At Petworth, the Duke of Somerset invited artists and craftsmen to 'design' pieces for particular places and spaces in the house. The Lowthers patronised Mathias Read (1669–1747), a Londoner who in 1690 settled in Whitehaven, which the Lowthers were developing. Read painted many of the Cumbrian country houses for their owners and was one of the first native painters of English landscape, painting Cumbrian mountains and skies. Read was the only notable pre-picturesque painter of the Lake District.[6]

In Ireland, Scotland and Wales the landed elite responded to and shaped the same cultural impulses as their English counterparts. Their patronage of distinctive cultural traditions, such as bardic poetry, declined, and these traditions suffered. Roderick Morison (*c.* 1656–*c.* 1714) was the last famous bard/harper of Gaelic Scotland. However, Highland dancing was being renewed by 1780.

The Welsh gentry increasingly intermarried with their English counterparts, while a greater number of heirs were educated in England. British cultural norms had a growing appeal, for example in architecture and landscape gardening. In Wales, new building, such as Nanteos for the Powells, and enhancements, such as the stately rooms at Chirk Castle for the Myddletons and the ballroom at Powis Castle for the Herberts, were produced in what were established British aristo-cratic styles. This was also true of the gardens. William Emes advised Philip Yorke at Erddig between 1767 and 1789, creating hanging gardens and 'natural' clumps of trees. He was also responsible for the landscaping at Chirk Castle and Powis Castle, and for work at Wimpole in England. Thomas Jones (1743–1803), one of the leading Welsh painters of the period, and a painter of Welsh scenery, studied at Oxford and from 1762 lived for many years in London, following the style of his teacher Richard Wilson.

The role of wealthy landowners as patrons and leaders of fashion ensured that they played a crucial role in the artistic world. Display was a major part of the nature of patronage, and the conspicuous consumption and display of culture emphasised social status. Major stately homes, such as Houghton, Castle Howard and Stourhead, were open to respectable looking visitors, and acted as display models for architectural, artistic and landscape styles. Guidebooks for the most notable were published from mid-century. Kedleston was always open to the public and was perhaps the most admired. The period saw literal and metaphoric distance grow between landowners and the rest of society, but this socio-cultural distance did not equate with an impassable gulf between the culture of the elite and that of other ranks.[7]

If less affluent gentry could neither emulate the patronage of the elite nor share in their role, they were nevertheless of considerable importance in rural regions. Their influence has received insufficient scholarly attention, not least because they could not afford to patronise major artists. However, they were arguably a central means by which new styles, whether in clothes or portraits, buildings or gardens, were disseminated. At the same time, contrasts can be drawn between the 'alien architectural intrusions' favoured by the elite and the more accessible works of the gentry.[8]

The churches were also important patrons, while religion continued to be a major theme of the arts. What was judged immoral or sacrilegious in lay culture could be condemned. There was a strong criticism of the alleged profanity and immorality of the stage, for example by the non-juror cleric Jeremy Collier in his pamphlet *A Short View of the Immorality and Profaneness of the English Stage* (1698), and this led in February 1699 to government pressure on London play-houses, and to Congreve and Vanbrugh making some alterations in their plays. In 1712, the Society for Promoting Christian Knowledge asked Collier to write a pamphlet discouraging the teaching of lewd songs and the composing of music to profane ballads. Thomas Herring, later Archbishop of first York and then Canterbury, condemned John Gay's *Beggar's Opera* (1728) for immorality, as did Hogarth. The Methodists were strong critics of theatres. In 1766, Wesley, who in 1764 had praised the conversion of Birmingham's first theatre into a Methodist chapel, criticised the building of the new theatre in Bristol.

The churches, however, regarded the arts, especially music, as important means for the glorification of God; although fear of accusations of crypto-Catholicism led the Bishop of London in 1773 to block attempts by the Dean of St Paul's to commission religious paintings for the interior of the cathedral, and, in general, church patronage of art was less fulsome than that for music and popular prayer books. The enjoyment of religious art was suspicious to most divines. Nevertheless, much depended on the subject matter and there were some important private clerical collections.

The construction and decoration of churches and chapels involved much activity, although far less than in the next century. Although the population rose, the episcopal and parochial organisation of England did not alter, so there was relatively little call for new construction. When the Commission for Building Fifty New Churches in London and Westminster, established in 1711, was abolished in 1758, owing to the inadequacy of its principal source of funds, the coal duty, it had authorised the construction of only twelve churches. Yet there was important building, and the careers of several architects reflected this. Nicholas Hawksmoor (1661–1736) was responsible for several of the London churches and for the west towers of Westminster Abbey. James Gibbs (1682–1754), an Aberdonian who studied in Rome and settled in London, was responsible for important work in Cambridge and Oxford, including the Radcliffe Library in Oxford, but also for St Mary-le-Strand, St Peter's Vere Street and St Martin-in-the-Fields (1721–6) in London, All Saints, Derby and St Nicholas, Aberdeen. Henry Flitcroft (1697–1769), a protégé of Burlington who became Comptroller of the Works and worked on Wentworth House for the Marquis of Rockingham and Woburn Abbey for the Duke of Bedford, was also responsible for the new church of St Giles-in-the-Fields in London which cost over £10,000, the church of St Olave in Southwark, that of St John at Hampstead and for rebuilding the church at Wimpole. The decoration of churches was also important. In 1741, William Kent designed a pulpit and choir furniture in York Minster and a choir screen in Gloucester Cathedral. Much effort was put into funerary monuments. John Flaxman (1755–1826), for example, decorated grand tombs and monuments for Chichester and Winchester cathedrals.

Religion also provided patronage and themes for music, while the churches provided training and employment for many musicians. It was a great age of hymns and psalms by masters such as William Cowper, John Newton, Christopher Smart, Isaac Watts, Charles Wesley and William Williams.[9] They offered clear and attractive expressions of religious tenets and messages. The greatest English musician of the period, Henry Purcell, was employed as organist of Westminster Abbey in 1680–95 and composed a large number of anthems, hymns and services. He had a vast influence on the next generation. John Weldon (1676–1736), another successful composer of much sacred and secular music, was organist of New College Oxford and later in the Chapel Royal, St Bride's Fleet Street and St Martin's-in-the-Fields. Religious art and music were determined by the elite but also enjoyed by the congregations. They were at once elite and 'mass' culture.[10]

Religious literature was also of importance, and popular religious works sold incredibly well, although the percentage of works published in London on religious and theological topics declined. Nevertheless, devotional verse and religious poetry were of importance, sermons were a major branch of literature, translations of and commentaries on the Psalms abounded, and some novels, such as those of the firm Anglican Samuel Richardson, can be seen in part as Christian fables.

The patronage of the middling orders was of growing importance. Unable individually to provide sustained patronage, they participated through public performances of works and public markets for the arts, and these expanded considerably during the century. The patronage of the anonymous public was crucial to the performers chosen: singers at the concerts at Vauxhall gardens in the second half of the eighteenth century knew that their future engagements depended on the number of encores the audience demanded. The 'No Dedication' for the 'Apology for Painters' that Hogarth was working on at the end of his life was dedicated not to 'any man of quality', but 'to every body'.[11]

However, the nature and role of the commercial market could lead to concern, which was generally related to perceptions of the domestic political and social situation. Thus in the 1730s, a time of particularly marked and partisan cultural discontent,[12] both James Thomson and Aaron Hill felt that the arts were in decline and sacrificed to the commercial market-place, that it was necessary to revitalise national culture, and that this would both further and benefit from a wider national regeneration. The art market was criticised as fraudulent in Hogarth's *The Battle of the Pictures* (1745). In the second half of the century, the theme of the enervating threat of luxury to taste and, more seriously, civilisation was also a weighty motif of socio-cultural anxiety. It contributed to caricatures of fashion in prints and prose and was reflected in much of the literature of the period.[13] The need to satisfy prevailing tastes affected not only the content of new works, but also of their predecessors. Shakespeare's plays were 'improved', with a happy ending added to *King Lear*.

There was an increasing dissemination of new works. Most of the means of diffusion, such as engravings, newspapers and books, were far from new, but there was a definite expansion in the scale and variety of the culture of print. The lapse of the Licensing Act in 1695 was followed by the spread of provincial printing; hitherto in England and Wales limited to London, Cambridge and Oxford. The first press in Exeter was founded in 1698 and the first long-lasting one in Cornwall in 1753. The reproduction of paintings for wealthy collectors had commonly taken the form of having individual copies painted, but there was now a considerable increase in their mass reproduction in the form of engravings, for example of the works of William Hogarth (1697–1764). This created copyright problems. Print shops displayed such works in windows for public entertainment and 'consumption'. About 15,000 satirical prints were published in 1740–1800.

'Pictures' became an important element in print culture in the eighteenth century and, whilst mezzotinting was invented in the 1640s, it was very much improved after Wren worked on it. By early eighteenth century, it had speeded up the process of producing large numbers of inexpensive copies from engraved plates. In place of wood prints there were now fine copper plate prints and cheap mezzotints.

The public sale of paintings, and production for such sales, rather than in response to a specific commission, were far from novel, but there was a considerable expansion of the art market in London. The expansion of art dealership and of middlemen, such as the dealer Robert Bragge and the auctioneer Christopher Cock, led to an enormous market for fakes. Economic expansion helped to fuel this market, as did widespread interest in artistic issues, which extended to a development of printed art criticism.[14] Jonathan Richardson's *Essay on the Theory of Painting* (1715) both developed art criticism in England and argued that English painters could equal Italian old masters.

The ethics of 'politeness' affected ideological justifications for art. Painting increasingly addressed public audiences, at the same time that economic and commercial progress enabled the creation of public spaces and places for the enjoyment of art, such as Vauxhall and Ranelagh Gardens in London; as well as the foundation of clubs and societies. There were also new points of connection between artists and patrons, such as the London Foundling Hospital where both artists and aristocrats were governors. Art was seen as a public media that could improve society, rather than a private luxury.

Paintings were also used as furniture. There was a tendency to hang particular kinds of paintings in certain rooms, for example still lifes in the dining room to remind people of food, and hunting scenes in the main entrance hall of country houses such as Althorp. Greater wealth and more material goods also offered new subjects for depiction.[15]

Though many musical productions were still private, the musical world was becoming more public. The opera houses were centres of fashion, and public concerts became more frequent. In Dublin, foreign composers such as Francesco Geminiani and Handel, as well as Irish counterparts such as Garret Wesley (1735–81), father of the Duke of Wellington, enjoyed great success. In Edinburgh, weekly concerts were held for most of the year by the Musical Society, established in 1728. In 1736, the composer Charles Avison started winter subscription concerts in Newcastle; the Assembly Rooms, also opened in 1736, were a popular venue. In Hertford, there were subscription concerts in a specially built concert room from 1753 to 1767, and in the 1770s concerts in the new Shire Hall, completed in 1771, which had assembly rooms built for such functions. In Francis Lynch's play *The Independent Patriot* (1737) a character complained, 'Music has engrossed the attention of the whole people. The Duchess and her woman, the Duke and his postilion, are equally infected.' Mozart visited London in 1764 and Haydn came there in 1791 and 1794 to give very successful public concerts for which he wrote his London symphonies. Such concerts encouraged and reflected the more frequent performance of popular works.

It was easy for amateurs to participate in instrumental music: William Felton (1715–69), a cleric attached to Hereford Cathedral, wrote 32 keyboard concertos, more than anybody else in Britain, as well as popular practice pieces. Chamber and solo works intended for amateurs enjoyed considerable popularity, and instruments, music and manuals were produced accordingly. An idea of the scale of activity can be grasped from the accounts of Thomas Green (1719–91), a Hertfordshire organist, tuner of musical instruments and teacher of music. In 1755–65, he tuned about 180 different harpsichords, 115 spinets and 40 pianofortes, nearly all within eight miles of Hertford.[16] In 1785, a French visitor commented that music was cultivated 'universally, in London as it is throughout the kingdom'.[17] Music teachers came to play a major role.

Instruments were displayed and played in the fine rooms constructed in so many houses during the major re-housing of much of the better-off in both town and countryside.[18] New houses also had more furniture, especially chairs, tables, dressers, clocks and looking-glasses, as well as plastered ceilings, curtains and fireplaces. All provided opportunities and employment for craftsmen.

Musical journalism developed in response to the increase in public interest in music, and provided a forum for a stylistic debate that opposed new operatic forms to the dominant *opera seria*, a world of classical mythology, serious heroism and solemn music brought to life in London by Italian singers. The ballad opera, exemplified by John Gay's popular *Beggar's Opera* (1728), which was significantly influenced by Allan Ramsay's *Gentle Shepherd* (1725), offered popular tunes and songs and scenes from low life, in a deliberate attack on the Italianate operas patronised by the cosmopolitan court and composed by, among others, Handel. These operas were driven out of fashion. Handel produced his last in 1741, but he went on to enjoy a great success with his *Messiah*, an oratorio that revealed the commercial possibilities of sacred music.

Middle-class patronage was also crucial in the theatre, which developed both in London and elsewhere: purpose-built theatres opened in Bath in 1705, Bristol in 1729, and York in 1734. The Orchard Street Theatre at Bath opened in 1750, the New Street Theatre in Birmingham in 1774, the fourth in the city but the first to be a longstanding institution, and the first permanent theatre building in Lancaster was constructed in 1781. The Theatre Royal in Bristol built in 1766 had a capacity of about 1,600. Regional circuits developed out of the routes of strolling players, and they increasingly acted in purpose-built playhouses. When, in 1786, the leading theatrical company in East Anglia, the Norwich Comedians or the Duke of Grafton's Servants, ceased to tour smaller towns, it was still able to concentrate its attentions on Norwich, King's Lynn, Great Yarmouth, Barnwell (Cambridge), Bury St Edmunds, Colchester and Ipswich.

However, the operations of theatres were regulated by the Licensing Act of 1737 which gave the Lord Chamberlain power to censor plays. This was a response to attacks on the Walpole government on the stage. The Act confirmed the position of the two London theatres with royal patents to stage spoken drama – Covent Garden and Drury Lane – and closed down competing playhouses. The consequences were less severe in practice outside London, as other theatres could obtain permission – existing ones being licensed under the Act while new ones could receive special approval – although doing so made them vulnerable to their opponents. The net result was similar to that of much eighteenth-century legislation and regulation: a situation of considerable variety.[19] There was also expansion in theatres in Ireland. In Scotland, where a theatre was founded by Ramsay in Edinburgh in 1736, the Kirk authorities, who used the 1737 Act to shut him down, held up theatre expansion until after 1750, and until after 1770 in some areas.

The amorality and bawdy of much late-seventeenth-century comedy was moderated by the religious critiques of commentators such as Jeremy Collier and by the rise of sentimentality. Many plays encouraged a bourgeois consciousness equally opposed to indulgence, whether decadent 'aristocratic' mores or popular ignorance and vice. In Sir Richard Steele's *The Conscious Lovers* (1722) virtue and sensitivity are rewarded. Virtue was similarly identified with the middling orders in George Lillo's *The London Merchant* (1731) in which a weak apprentice commits murder and then undergoes an exemplary repentance. This popular work represented a major change in tragedy in that it was written in a prose idiom and given a bourgeois setting and values. Such a work can be seen as a moral counterpart to Hogarth's satires and Richardson's novels. It is indicative of the cultural importance of the London stage that Lillo's play made his name, while the court masque he wrote in 1733 for the marriage of the Princess Royal was unperformed because of the postponement of the marriage, and made no impact. As Henry Fielding noted in the prologue to Lillo's tragedy *Fatal Curiosity* (1736),

> No fustian Hero rages here to Night
> No Armies fall, to fix a Tyrant's Right:
> From lower Life we draw our Scene's Distress:
> Let not your Equals move your Pity less.

In the 1740s, the leading actor and theatrical entrepreneur David Garrick (1717–79) sought to raise the moral tone of the theatre, as others, such as Dennis, Hill and Thomson, had earlier sought to do. The sentimental comedy that resulted generally lacked bite, and British theatre did not greatly flourish in the second half of the century, but its morality reflected audience wishes.

If morality was increasingly prescribed and indulgence proscribed this represented not a bourgeois reaction against noble culture, but a shift in sensibility common to both. For every decadent aristocrat depicted on the stage in the second half of the century, there were several royal or aristocratic heroes. Hogarth similarly criticised aristocratic mores, but most painters depicted aristocrats in an exemplary light. Thus, instead of seeing the commercialisation of leisure as a triumph of bourgeois culture, the role of the middling orders was largely one of patronising both new and traditional artistic forms, rather than developing or demanding distinct styles.

The rise of the novel can best be seen as an important instance of the embourgeoisement of culture if that is regarded as a matter of patronage rather than content. Novels created and responded to a large readership, and were not dependent on a distinguished list of subscribers, or on political patronage. Fielding's *Joseph Andrews* sold 6,500 copies in 1742. In contrast, epics were not compatible with the commercial literary climate.

The growth of circulation, proprietary and subscription libraries, as well as the serial publication of books, permitted those who could not afford to purchase them to read them. A new public library opened in Bristol in 1740 and the first in Lancaster in 1768. Manchester gained its first circulating library in 1757. The first of the many proprietary libraries whose members owned shares was the Liverpool Library, formed in 1758. Membership was already 140 in 1758, 300 by 1770 and over 400 by 1799. Between 1758 and 1800, the Library acquired an average of almost 200 books annually. Smaller towns also gained libraries: St Asaph in 1711 thanks to the Dean and Chapter. There were about 1,000 circulating libraries by the end of the century.

Far from conforming to a common tone, form or intention, novels varied greatly in content and approach,[20] a trend encouraged by the size and diversity of the reading public. Thus, Richardson's first novel, *Pamela* (1740), a very popular book on the prudence of virtue and the virtue of prudence, was countered by Fielding's satirical *Apology for the Life of Mrs Shamela Andrews* and his *Joseph Andrews*. John Cleland employed the epistolary style of *Pamela* in his pornographic novel *Memoirs of a Woman of Pleasure*, otherwise known as *Fanny Hill* (1749). By the end of the century, about 150 novels, 90 of them new, were being published annually.

Publishing expanded greatly. As there were few technical innovations, profitability depended on increased sales, and publishers such as William Strahan in London, producing sizeable editions, had to be sensitive to the market. The Edinburgh-born Strahan (1715–85) was publisher to Blackstone, Blair, Cook, Gibbon, Hume, Johnson, Robertson and Smith, made a lot of money and became a MP. The growth of the reading public affected literature. In the field of history, authors such as Gibbon, Hume and William Robertson, and hack writers, such as Richard Rolt, were able to write for a large and immediate readership, producing a clearly commercial product, in contrast to the classical model of history for the benefit of friends and a posthumous public. Gibbon and Robertson both made substantial sums.

Works were produced to supply new and developing specialisations. For the popular world of horticulture, Peter Miller's *The Gardener's Dictionary* (1724), Robert Furber's *Short Introduction to Gardening* (1733), James Lee's *Introduction to Botany* (1760), William Hanbury's *A Complete Body of Planting and Gardening* (1770), John Kennedy's *Treatise upon Planting* (1776) and Loddiges's *The Botanical Cabinet* (1777) were followed in 1786 by *The Botanical Magazine*.

Authors sought to make their writings as comprehensible as possible to the anonymous, expanding literate population, and modern concepts of authorship development. Books, magazines, newspapers and dictionaries assisted the spread of new ideas, transmitting the grand themes of artistic and intellectual life. Treatises on taste (aesthetics), were designed to guide appreciation and patronage. Thus, Gerard Langbaine's *Account of the English Dramatik Poets* (1691) offered a tabular ranking that sought to establish a national dramatic heritage free of borrowings from French romances.[21] The designs for his St Martin-in-the-Fields in James Gibbs's *Book of Architecture* (1728), influenced designs elsewhere. The second edition of Batty Langley's *Ancient Architecture Restored* was entitled *Gothic Architecture, improved by Rules and Proportions* (1747); he had already published *New Principles of Gardening* (1728). James Granger's *Biographical History of England...adapted to a Methodical Catalogue of Engraved British Heads. Intended as an Essay towards reducing our Biography to System, and a help to the knowledge of Portraits* (1769) was intended to assist portrait collectors, and indeed led to a rapid rise in the price of portraits.

Ephraim Chambers' *Cyclopaedia, or an Universal Dictionary of Arts and Sciences* (1728) attempted a classification of all knowledge, and was successful, with new editions printed in 1738, 1739, 1741 and 1746. This was followed by the *Encyclopaedia Britannica* in 1768–71. Published by a consortium of Edinburgh printers, this was a reply to the French *Encyclopédie* and a reflection of the market opportunities provided by public interest in the expanding world of knowledge.

Samuel Johnson's massive *Dictionary of the English Language* (1755) sought to clarify meanings and included an English grammar. The plan of 1747 declared 'The chief intent...to preserve the purity and ascertain the meaning of our English idiom'. Johnson's citations reflected his sense of the role of a national canon of literature: half of all the quotations in the *Dictionary* came from only seven sources: Shakespeare, Dryden, Milton, Addison, Pope and the Authorised Version of the Bible, all works produced over the previous 170 years, many over the previous 80, and thus an affirmation of the value of recent literature. Johnson also published a ten-volume *Lives of the Most Eminent English Poets*, creating a national heritage of literature. John Walter published an English – Welsh dictionary in parts in 1770–94.

The culture of print accustomed part of the population to experience information and news through print. This lessened the role and sway of foci of oral culture. 2,000 copies of the folio edition of Johnson's *Dictionary* were printed and the price was £4 10s (£4.50). It was soon followed by a second edition published in 165 weekly sections at sixpence each.

The spread of new ideas was easiest in an urban setting, and, together, towns were the principal context of cultural patronage by the middling orders. The London pleasure gardens were showpieces for all kinds of art and music, and they, and the walks and assembly rooms of London, were emulated in other cities and towns. The ethos of polite society helped to blur culture and leisure, spectator and performer. Many cultural institutions, learned societies, periodicals and theatres helped to create a cultural climate more sensitive to new ideas. Reviews, such as *The Critical Review* and the *British Magazine*, guided book purchasers, and thus helped to define the market and interpret and shape taste.[22] There was a willingness to accept frequent revisions of taste. In Norwich, for example, where there was a very active musical life, both public and performers were ready to accept quite rapid change, and at the end of the century, concert-goers were able to hear the latest British and German works. Exposure to novelty was not a process restricted to the major towns. The first theatre in Lincolnshire was built in Stamford soon after 1718. Others followed in Lincoln (*c.* 1731), Spalding (*c.* 1760), Gainsborough (1775), Boston (1777) and Grantham (1777). Wordsworth's Preface to his *Lyrical Ballads* (1798) asserted the pernicious consequences of the move to the cities, but, in practice, this social phenomenon helped to produce an appetite for recreational literature.

Although the century saw a major increase in public cultural activity outside London, in England it was very much dominated by the metropolis. The Belfast printer John Tisdal published in 1782 *Flora's Banquet*, a collection of Irish poems he had edited. Tisdal stated, 'it does not follow, that works of merit can *only* originate in the metropolis of England; and that, unless a new book is distinguished by a *London* title page, and character in the review, it is beneath the notice of the curious. There have been some instances to the contrary in *this* kingdom.' The promised second volume did not appear.

There was, however, a strong and distinctive Scottish public culture. This included the self-conscious creation of the Edinburgh New Town as a northern metropolis, the integration of folk airs in musical culture, the spread of 'Highland' dancing and piping, and the cult of Ossian. There was also a strong Scottish publishing base by late century.

High and popular culture are frequently sharply differentiated and then presented in terms of a 'battle of cultures'. Popular culture is often presented as being under assault from the moral didacticism of the secular and ecclesiastical authorities and the middling orders. It is not only in the artistic sphere that this tension has been discerned and that the analysis of relationships has been coloured by the use of words and phrases such as oppressive, control, and protective mechanisms. Indeed, the discernment of artistic duality is but part of a wider sense, or allegation, of cultural control, of different *mentalités*, of worlds in collision, which has also influenced the assessment of popular religiosity. New intellectual and artistic fashions and codes of behaviour are held to have corroded the loyalty of the upper and middling orders to traditional beliefs and pastimes, and it is claimed that religious activity, the Scientific Revolution, the Enlightenment, and the cult of sensibility marginalised the common culture and pushed it down the social scale. Given such an analysis, it is unsurprising that attention has been devoted to the contrast between popular and elite culture and that this is held to have inspired initiatives to 'reform' popular practices. Newspapers of the period attacked such popular practices as wife-selling, gambling, the shooting of street lamps for fun, boxing, swearing and cruelty to animals, although all bar wife-selling were also popular with the aristocracy.

However, it could be argued that the idea of a sharp distinction between the culture of the élites and that of the bulk of the population is misleading, not least because the use of the vernacular allowed a degree of democratisation and inclusion in religion, culture, society and government. Whereas cosmopolitan languages – French, German and Italian – were the languages of the European élites, or, at least, of much of their culture, in Britain the elite and imperialising language was English. Whereas in the United Provinces the major newspapers were published in French, in Britain French-language periodicals were few and short-lived.

The notion of a common culture, albeit one with different styles, is appropri-ate: that there were not contrasting *mentalités*, but, rather, a shared currency of interests, notions and idioms, and a mutual interchange of ideas. Performers and the public sought to investigate and express common problems and emotions, to make sense of a common world in a number of different styles and formats. There was noticeable overlap between the amusements of the 'best people' and the rest at the theatre, and at such entertainments as public executions, horse racing, cricket, bear baiting, cock fighting and boxing. Far from 'art' and 'folk' music being distinct and antithetical, the folk music being conservative and transmitted almost solely in oral tradition, there is considerable evidence of interrelationship and change, both thematic and stylistic. If for the bulk of the population, music meant ballads, hymns and primitive instruments, that does not mean that popular music was necessarily unsophisticated or unchanging.

In part, the relationship between sections of élite and popular culture derived from the greater interest in popular culture displayed by artists and intellectuals. By the 1770s, there was more interest in the supposed lifestyle of the peasantry, a process that matched growing fascination with landscape. However, the routine grind and miseries of rural life were generally ignored and, instead, an idealised view was presented, as with the stylised charm of Gainsborough's cottages.

The folk tales of the peasantry were also of less interest than those of ancient times. Much attention was devoted to the latter in what is termed the Pre-Romantic period, which stretched from the 1760s and 1770s to whenever the Romantic period is held to begin. To the antiquarian tradition of interest in ancient literature, such as the Anglo-Saxon studies of the English clergyman Edward Lye (1694–1767), and Sean Ó Neachtain's preservation of old Irish manuscripts, and the invention of much Welsh folk law, was added a fascination with ancient 'folk' literature which was presented as offering an imaginative perspective capable of reviving culture. James Macpherson (1736–96) published poems which he claimed to have translated from the Gaelic of a third-century Highland bard called Ossian. His *Fragments of Ancient Poetry collected in the Highlands* (1760), brought him fame, and were followed by *Fingal* (1761), dedicated to George III's favourite, the Earl of Bute, the preface of which proclaimed the superiority of Celtic to Greek heroic poetry, and by *Temora* (1763). These works, in part his own creation, in part based on genuine Gaelic poems and ballads, enjoyed a phenome-nal success and made primitivism popular, although they were bitterly criticised by evangelical Highland Church of Scotland ministers and by Johnson.

Impressed by Macpherson, Thomas Percy (1729–1811), a grocer's son who sought to show his descent from the medieval Dukes of Northumberland, pub-lished *Reliques of Ancient English Poetry* (1765, 4 edns by 1794), an edition of old ballads which promoted a revival of interest in the subject. An interest in traditional Scots tunes led to the publication of a series of works beginning with *Orpheus Caledonius* (1725). Evan Evans edited *Some Specimens of the Poetry of the Antient Welsh Bards* (1764), and Phys Jones *Gorchestion Beirdd Cymru* [*The Masterpieces of the Welsh Poets*] (1773). 'Medievalism' also led to the success of Thomas Chatterton (1752–70), who invented and wrote the works of a fifteenth-century poet Thomas Rowley. William Stukeley (1687–1765) developed enthusiasm for medieval antiquities. He also played a major role in the growing interest in pre-Roman antiquities. This was both academic in flavour and capable of serving the cause of cultural nationalism.

If the peasantry appeared less interesting and uplifting as an artistic topic than ancient Celts and medieval Britons, it was also the case that very few peasants became artists enjoying élite patronage. George Crabbe observed in *The Village* 'Save honest Duck, what son of verse could share// The poet's rapture and the peasant's care?' Stephen Duck (1705–56), the 'Thresher Poet', was an agricultural labourer who taught himself to read and write, and, thanks to the support of the local clergy, won fame and, in 1730, Queen Caroline's patronage. John Bancks (1709–51), the 'Weaver Poet', failed to emulate his success. Female plebeian poets included Mary Leapor, Ann Yearsley and Mary Collier, the last a Hampshire washerwoman who became a housekeeper on a farm. Collier's *The Woman's Labour* (1739) covered the burdens of working women: childcare, housework and employment. Gaelic poets included Robb Donn Mackay (1714–78), a Highland cattle drover, and Duncan Ban MacIntyre (1724–1812), a gamekeeper. For Irish Gaelic and, to a lesser extent, Scottish Gaelic writers, it was typical to have humble occupations.

While popular culture is a subject that is still largely uncharted, and in which generalisations about peasant conservatism and cultural borrowing from the élite are still too common, there are also problems in assessing the relationship between cultural cosmopolitanism and xenophobia, the history of which is still largely unwritten. Cosmopolitanism was aided by travel, patronage, the role of cultural intermediaries and the process of emulation. Travel helped to spread knowledge of present, as well as past, artistic developments among patrons. As the Grand Tour became fashionable, increasing numbers travelled for pleasure and, at a formative period in their life, were exposed to foreign culture. Artists, such as the painters Allan Ramsay, Joshua Reynolds and Richard Wilson, and the architects Matthew Brettingham and William Kent, also travelled in order to acquire training, employment and inspiration. Ramsay spent a total of eight years in Italy.

Patronage was inspired by, and sustained, an élite cosmopolitan culture. The role of cultural intermediaries was facilitated by the appreciable number of foreigners in London, especially, in the first half of the century, by the number of Huguenots (French Protestant refugees), who had close links with both France and the United Provinces.

Emulation and fashion were significant. At the level of élite culture, particularly in the early decades of the century, there was a strong sense of inferiority to the cultural life and products of France and Italy. This sense of inferiority took a number of forms and had a variety of consequences, including the attempt to implant foreign fashions and the patronage of foreign artists. France was a major leader in fashion, including women's clothes, and behaviour. The morning levée and the umbrella were introduced into Britain from France. France's position in fashion encouraged the demand for French clothes, hairdressers, cooks, food and wine in elite circles in London.

Britain's was part of a European culture. All the major stylistic and thematic changes occurred on a continent-wide scale, though there were significant national variations and differences in chronology. Just as the Baroque and Rococo styles struck resonances while Chinese and Turkish motifs were repeated across Europe, so the discussion of the arts in different countries tended to be similar, and critical tendencies, towards sentimentality at mid-century or Romantic from the 1770s, were generally international in their scope. Cosmopolitanism implied neither similar circumstances nor identical developments, but it did encourage eclecticism.

British influence abroad was strongest in intellectual life, literature and gardening. The Adam style of interior decoration was paralleled in Paris in the 1780s, a period in which significant numbers of the French élite were affected by an anglomania, the effects of which included an interest in horse-racing and a male fashion for English clothes. While some aspects of British culture became more influential abroad, there was also a shift in attitude towards Britain's cultural relations with the rest of Europe. Thanks to a burgeoning economy, an apparently successful political system and a great and powerful world empire there was less of a sense of inferiority than there had been in the seventeenth century; at that time, to its own people, Britain had seemed superior in little besides its Protestantism.

By the eighteenth century, in spite of the popularity of Batoni, Mengs, Piranesi and other Rome-based artists, it appeared that the country of Newton and Sloane, Reynolds and Watt, had little to learn from modern Italy, and, if it did, a process of Anglicisation occurred, as with the Palladian style of architecture which was presented through works such as Colen Campbell's *Vitruvius Britannicus* (1725). In 1720, James Thornhill became the first English artist to be knighted. Prior to that, the great names in British portraiture had been foreign, Van Dyck, Lely and John de Medina becoming knights and Kneller a baronet. Thornhill's masterpiece was his painted Hall in Wren's Royal Hospital at Greenwich (1708–12), an explicitly British grand state painting, and a depiction of naval power. Thornhill also worked in Chatsworth, Hampton Court, and St Paul's Cathedral. His son-in-law, Hogarth, another product of the metropolitan forcing-house of artistic activity and cultural values, advocated a specifically English style.

In mid-century, Canaletto, with his splendid canvases, used talents developed to depict Venice in order to show the glories of modern London. A neo-imperial, modern pride of London was expressed in his views, with new buildings such as Greenwich Observatory, Somerset House, Westminster Bridge and the rebuilt towers of Westminster Abbey playing a prominent role. In contrast, Italy was increasingly seen as a decayed civilisation, and there was greater interest in Classical, not contemporary, Italy. Admiration for republican Rome helped to unite the elite.[23] British commentators claimed Rome's mantle of civilisation, and the spectre of the fallen Roman empire emphasised, in contrast, Britain's present potency. Modern Britain was held to define civilisation, an assessment that owed much to the Whig myth.

This approach was more successful and lasting in creating standards by which Britain appeared superior to foreign countries than in sustaining a coherent and united viewpoint on domestic politics. It was no coincidence that 'God Save the King' and 'Rule Britannia' (1740) both emerged in mid-century. 'God Save the King' had originated as a song in honour of Louis XIV and had been sung by Jacobites, but it became an indication of loyalty and a popular song. Whig confidence had broadened into the cultural moulding of the notion and (to a considerable degree after 1746) reality of a united and powerful country. British self-regard and condescension towards foreign countries was not dependent on contemporary foreign praise for Britain as a country of liberty and progress,[24] although, in so far as British commentators were aware of it, such praise could not but have contributed.

Similarly, there was a greater interest in aspects of England's cultural past, part of the process by which a more self-confident nation focused on native values and models. An English canon was defined in the middle decades of the century. In this process, critical discussion interacted with the demands of the book trade and the shaping of the market.[25] Shakespeare was praised as the National Poet with his monument in Westminster Abbey. Shakespeare was the most frequently cited authority in Johnson's *Dictionary*, and there were no less than six major editions of his complete works in the century: by Rowe (1709), Pope (1725), Theobald (1733), Warburton (1747), Johnson (1765) and Malone (1790). Garrick was responsible for his plays being staged more frequently and actively promoted the Shakespeare Jubilee in 1769, the year of the publication of Elizabeth Montagu's *An Essay on the Writings and Genius of Shakespeare*. Interest in Stratford-upon-Avon as a cultural shrine developed. Even a Shakespeare forgery industry developed.[26]

Similar views lay behind the interest in earlier English music, particularly Purcell and Handel, that led to cathedral festivals of music, the Academy of Ancient Music, the fashionable Concert of Ancient Music established in 1776 by aristocrats led by John, 4th Earl of Sandwich, and, finally, the mighty Handel Commemoration celebrations in 1784. The last were so successful that they were repeated in 1785–7, 1790, and in 1791 with over 1,000 performers and in the presence of George III.[27]

In literature, there was a movement away from classical and towards British values and models. This entailed the searching and utilisation of a polyglot cultural inheritance in order to serve the needs of a distinctive British culture. A quest for what could be presented as Britishness and a celebration of the modern entailed an anglicisation of classical and Hebraic forms, techniques and preoccupations. John Dryden anglicised the epic and Abraham Cowley the ode,[28] while the novel presented a new and accessible (to the literate) form.

In 1731, English replaced 'law French' as the language of authority in the common law courts. English law became a subject of study. In 1713, Matthew Hale published the *History of the Common Law of England*, which linked the Common Law, Parliament and national identity. William Blackstone, appointed, in 1758, the first Vinerian Professor of English Law at Oxford, published the *Commentaries on the Laws of England* (1765–9), in part to acclaim English common law against Roman law. In contrast, Stair's *Institutes* helped define Scots law as Roman-leaning.

The domestic cultural tradition became stronger in the second half of the century, in part thanks to the institutionalisation of art, not least through the Royal Academy, established in 1768, and to greater national wealth. Artists and craftsmen developed products of excellence in areas formerly dominated by foreign work: English silverware gained in importance, and ceramics produced in London and Staffordshire were admired for their beauty. For design, Wedgwood called on the artistic skills of Flaxman and Stubbs. In painting, a modernized classical style was popularised by Reynolds and taught at the Royal Academy. Garrick developed a naturalistic school of acting believed to be superior to Continental acting methods. The painters who accompanied Cook on his voyages, such as William Hodges and John Webber, provided a powerful visual image of the South Seas.

In 1777–83, James Barry produced a set of paintings to decorate the Great Hall of the Society for the Encouragement of Arts, Commerce and Manufactures, a body, founded in 1754, that produced decorative medals and premiums which rewarded innovations in various fields including the arts.[29] The array of philosophers, scientists and others displayed by Barry reached back to the ancient world, and culminated with modern British talent, for example poets from Homer to Goldsmith. To Barry and to his patrons, the British could be seen as the new Olympians, equal to the greatness of the past.

NOTES

1. E.P. Thompson, *Customs in Common* (1993).
2. Glenorchy to Marchioness Grey, 15 Ap. 1746, Bedford CRO. L30/9/17/3.
3. C. Ridgway, *Sir John Vanburgh, a Biography* (1987).
4. A. White, *The Buildings of Georgian Lancaster* (Lancaster, 1992), p. 10.
5. Lyttelton to Elizabeth Montagu, 21 July 1762, BL. RP. 2377i.
6. J. Sellars (ed.), *The Art of Thomas Chippendale Master Furniture Maker* (Harewood, 2000); M.E. Burkett and D. Sloss, *Read's Point of View. Paintings of the Cumbrian Countryside* (Bowness, 1995).
7. J. Rosenheim, *The Emergence of a Ruling Order. English Landed Society, 1650–1750* (1998).
8. T. Williamson, 'Estate Management and Landscape Design', in C. Ridgway and R. Williams (eds), *Sir John Vanbrugh and Landscape Architecture in Baroque England 1690–1730* (Stroud, 2000), p. 28.
9. D. Davie, *The Eighteenth-Century Hymn in England* (Cambridge, 1993).
10. W. Shaw, *The Three Choirs Festival: The Official History of the Meetings of the Three Choirs of Gloucester, Hereford and Worcester, c. 1713–1953* (Worcester, 1954).
11. BL. Add. 39672 fol. 88.
12. C. Gerrard, *The Patriot Opposition to Walpole. Politics, Poetry, and National Myth, 1725–1742* (Oxford, 1994).
13. J. Raven, *Judging New Wealth. Popular Publishing and Responses to Commerce in England 1750–1800* (Oxford, 1992).
14. L. Lippincott, *Selling Art in Georgian London: The Rise of Arthur Pond* (New Haven, 1983); I. Pears, *The Discovery of Painting: The Growth of Interest in the Arts in England, 1680–1768* (New Haven, 1988).
15. D.H. Solkin, *Painting for Money. The Visual Arts and the Public Sphere in Eighteenth-Century England* (New Haven, 1993).

16. G. Sheldrick (ed.), *The Accounts of Thomas Green 1741–1790* (Hertford, 1992).
17. N. Scarfe, *Innocent Espionage. The La Rochefoucauld Brothers' Tour of England in 1785* (Woodbridge, 1995), p. 208.
18. R. Leppert, *Music and Image: Domesticity, Ideology and Socio-Cultural Formation in Eighteenth-Century England* (1988).
19. V.J. Liesenfeld, *The Licensing Act of 1737* (Madison, 1984).
20. T. Keymer, *Richardson's 'Clarissa' and the Eighteenth-Century Reader* (Cambridge, 1992).
21. P. Kewes, *Authorship and Appropriation: Writing for the Stage in England, 1660–1710* (Oxford, 1998).
22. F. Donoghue, *The Fame Machine* (Stanford, 1996).
23. P. Ayres, *Classical Culture and the Idea of Rome in Eighteenth-Century England* (1997).
24. More generally, see P. Langford, *Englishness Identified. Manners and Character 1650–1850* (Oxford, 2000).
25. J.B. Kramnick, *Making the English Canon: Print, Capitalism and the Cultural Past, 1700–1770* (Cambridge, 1999).
26. J. Bate, *Shakespearean Constitutions: Politics, Theatre, Criticism 1730–1830* (Oxford, 1989); M. Dobron, *The Making of the National Poet: Shakespeare, Adaptation, and Authorship, 1660–1769* (Oxford, 1992).
27. W. Weber, *The Rise of Musical Classics in Eighteenth-Century England: A Study in Canon, Ritual and Ideology* (Oxford, 1992).
28. H.D. Weinbrot, *Britannia's Issue. The Rise of British Literature from Dryden to Ossian* (Cambridge, 1993).
29. D.G.C. Allan and J.L. Abbot (eds), *The Virtuoso Tribe of Arts and Sciences: Studies in the Eighteenth-Century Work and Membership of the London Society of Arts* (Athens, Georgia, 1992).

Authority, the state and administration

Societies are structured by patterns of authority. For most individuals this is primarily a matter of relations within the family, at the workplace, and in the local community, but the context framing these relations is commonly provided by the state and in some spheres, particularly law and order, individuals are brought into direct contact with the state. The state itself, however, should not be seen as an abstract force outside society and rarely impacting upon it. Rather the state, though possessing its own autonomous institutions and conventions, is also an expression of social and economic structures and values which it helps to shape and is, in turn, shaped by.

The essential nature of a political system can be revealed under pressure: the role of force was readily apparent in the crises of the period, while, in addition, the implicit threat of force was important. It was through force that James II and VII had been driven from Britain and that Jacobite plans were subsequently thwarted. However, as overseas with the role of North American colonists and chartered companies, especially the East India Company, the military system depended on active and extensive co-operation. In the '45 the army was supplemented by allowing trusted loyal aristocrats to raise regiments, and selected Lord Lieutenants were empowered to raise their own units. More generally, militia and other volunteer service in periods of crisis was offered on terms. Crown requirements were balanced by other interests. For example, militia colonels treated their regiments as patronage fiefs, valuable to them as county magnates and public men. The conditional nature of such service reflected existing authority patterns, not the demands of a centralising, impersonal state.[1]

Authority took many forms in eighteenth-century Britain, some of which are discussed in other chapters. Within the family there was the authority of age and the power of patriarchy. In the local community, there was the power of landowners and employers, the authority of Justices of the Peace (JPs) and, in Scotland, sheriffs, generally the same people, and the pressure of neighbours and colleagues. In the wider polity, governmental power and authority were not concentrated, but, instead, widely distributed among a large number of individuals and bodies.[2]

However, this distribution was primarily in accord with the structure of the social system. This was an inegalitarian system of authority in which the representative dimension was slight. It is unclear whether non-governmental aspects of authority weakened in this period, possibly leading to an increase in law-breaking. Patriarchy, religion (and ecclesiastical discipline and courts), and the 'moral economy' of the community were all under stress from socio-economic developments, while the Act of Toleration of 1689 encouraged a ecclesiastical pluralism that challenged religious authority. Possibly these shifts led to a crumbling both in important external pressures, particularly that of the established Church, and in the internalisation of authority, so that the agencies and pretensions of the state were increasingly left to resist criminality and to establish social norms.

The nature of government, however, was such that any concentration on the administration and its officials can be misleading. Government was the function and privilege of a large number of individuals and institutions who were guided by their own conventions and ideas. This posed a political problem for central government in the event of non-co-operation, but it also vastly extended its range. The relationship involved a persisting pattern of definition and compromise, rather than antagonism and conflict. By modern standards, many government functions were 'privatised', including most of social welfare, education and health. Prisons, for example, were private businesses whose keepers bid for leases and expected to make a profit from the fees that prisoners paid for accommodation and food. The 'private' nature of authority limited the applicability of modern notions of corruption, for the distinction between private and public funds was less clear than today, and can be seen in key areas.

The production and distribution of gunpowder was a matter jointly for private manufacturers and for the Ordnance Office. Whether in government or in opposition, politicians were unwilling to extend the powers of government in this crucial field, even though they were aware of their inadequacy. At the outset of the Seven Years' War the makers failed to provide the required and agreed amount, so that the war effort in 1756–8 depended partly on substantial imports from the United Provinces. In the winter of 1761–2 some warships had to sail from Portsmouth and Plymouth without their full complement of powder. In addition, much of the powder submitted to the Ordnance Office did not meet its high standards of quality. The government did not own any mills until 1759 when it purchased those at Faversham, but their performance was never distinguished.

The press-gang was a harsh way to raise sailors for the largest navy in the world. The formation of a reserve of seamen proved ineffective: the Register Act of 1696, which provided for a voluntary register of seamen, proved unworkable and was repealed in 1710. The press-gang was not only arbitrary (although by law it applied only to professional seamen), but also only partially successful. Possibly, there was no better option, in the absence of any training system for the navy, and given the difficulty of making recruitment attractive when length of service was until the end of the war. The government never seriously considered paying sailors more, and in light of contemporary concern about naval expenditure this is not surprising. However, on numerous occasions naval preparations and operations were handicapped by a lack of sailors. A deep reluctance to embark on fundamental change characterised government policy both in this field and more generally.

Clear hostility to the idea of despotism, and conventions of acceptable governmental behaviour, limited the possibilities for state action by setting restrictive parameters of consent, although the constitutional and political expression of the latter varied. Government was expected to operate against a background of legality and tradition, and this made new initiatives politically hazardous and administratively difficult. When, in 1762, the Commissioners for lighting Westminster claimed the right to standardise lamp-irons and remove non-standard ones, this was bitterly attacked in a periodical, the *Contrast*, of 2 November:

> The security of property in this happy kingdom is held so sacred, that the Parliament cannot divest an innocent subject of any part of his effects, without giving him a valuable consideration, and that not to be determined by a state tool, but by a jury; and even this has never been done by compulsory laws, except in cases of the greatest necessity, such as the making new or enlarging old avenues, road-acts, and the acts for building Westminster and Blackfriars bridges etc. Though road-acts give a liberty to cut new roads through any person's lands, it is never without paying them to the utmost, and repairing all kind of damages.

Aside from the ideology of limited government that arose from the defeats that royal authority had suffered in the seventeenth century, there were also practical problems in exerting control. The number of trained officials was limited, communications were poor, the government was short of money and, in a generally pre-statistical age, it was difficult to obtain adequate and accurate information. Thus the most effective way to govern was in co-operation with those who wielded social power and with the institutions which had local authority. The crucial figures were the JPs, about 8,000 in number in 1760. They were the linchpins of local administration, the central figures in the law and order of the localities.[3] They were responsible for the implementation of social policy (a field in which the central government played little role), but, in doing so, had to respond to local factors. JPs were appointed by the government and could be removed, but their effectiveness was seen in part to rest on the degree to which the locally prominent were appointed. They were unpaid (except from fees) and untrained: their role was seen to come from the responsibility of high-ranking social position.

The gentry JPs who controlled the localities were complemented in those towns that were incorporated (had gained a charter of incorporation). These gave the towns powers to hold courts where local matters, such as debts and town business, were regulated. Such towns also had rights of criminal jurisdiction. Town corporations also administered charities.

The weak nature of the rather small government bureaucracy, and the widespread reliance of the ministry on outside bodies for advice, and even for assistance in the drafting of legislation, helped to increase the impact of lobbying groups. A stress on the problems facing government and on its co-operative nature provides the best basis from which the initiatives of the period can be assessed. The extent to which initiatives, such as changes in taxation or the calendar, should be seen as reforms is questionable. Though the opponents of reform could be stigmatised as selfish protectors of particular interests, such an analysis ignored the ambiguity of reform. Instead of reform being the cutting edge of the modern state, most administrative agencies were not particularly effective, but instead represented fresh and unpopular fiscal demands and novel interventions in proven existing practices that were frequently more responsive to local interests and needs.

Government was expected to protect people and their property, provide justice and suppress disorder. Crime was regarded as a major problem and casual violence was indeed endemic. There was much brutality and cruelty in everyday life. It is very difficult to establish crime rates, in part for reasons that still pertain, such as victims being too frightened to report crimes, or not sufficiently bothered, or preferring to seek redress by direct action. Crime was likely to run in families, was committed by the middling orders as well as the working classes, and worsened as transportation links improved: the criminal's ability to evade justice grew in direct proportion. In his speech opening Parliament on 15 November 1753, George II declared that he was appalled by the rise in murders and robberies.

The repression of crime was often brutal, especially in England and Wales. Deterrence through execution or transportation, rather than incarceration, was generally favoured, imprisonment being seen as an expensive method commonly used principally for those who were suffering civil action, in particular, debtors. In 1776, 60 per cent of the prison population were debtors and many were awaiting transportation. Conditions in many gaols were also very poor: food was meagre, sanitary arrangements primitive, and water supplies limited. In 1729–30, the House of Commons Gaols Committee revealed shocking conditions in the Fleet Prison. Nevertheless, there were also new gaols, for example in Coventry in 1772. However, some eighteenth-century gaols were not built until the close of the century: for example, new county gaols in Exeter (1787), Norwich (1792–3) and Hereford (1793).

Concern about rising crime after the War of the Spanish Succession (1702–13) led to the Transportation Act (1718) which, for the first time, allowed for transportation not only as part of the pardoning process in the case of capital offences (thus enabling a strong discretionary element in the system of capital punishment), but also as a penalty for a wide range of non-capital crimes, including grand larceny – the theft of property between a shilling (5 new pence) and £2. Parliament went on to pass another 16 acts between 1720 and 1763 that established transportation as a penalty for crimes from perjury to poaching. Returning from transportation was a capital offence. As many as 50,000 convicts were transported from England to America and the West Indies in 1718–75,[4] but, after the War of American Independence, transportation came temporarily to an end and a substantial number of major offenders were released back into the community, leading to a crime wave. After considering transportation to Africa, Australia was founded as a penal colony in 1788. At least 10 per cent of those transported to America were expected to die on the convict ships, a British counterpart to the cruel treatment of Africans sent to the New World as slaves. Reliance upon transportation ensured that there was less need for a system of penalties focused on the executions of the 'bloody code'. The Penitentiary Act of 1779 led to a further diminution by encouraging a tendency to imprisonment.

The extent of crime is difficult to evaluate, not least because of uncertainty as to how the percentage reported varied. Bad harvests could take misery to the point of desperation. The severe winter of 1740–1 led to a doubling of theft figures in Lindsey in Lincolnshire,[5] and, more generally, crime rates, at least in part, seem to have been related to economic circumstances. Transported felons were mostly poor young men, typically who had found it difficult to gain employment in the major cities. Towns provided criminals with opportunities for recruitment, activity and concealment.

Crime seems to have risen after wars were ended, because men accustomed to fight were demobilised without adequate provision in a labour market in which un- and under-employment were chronic.[6] After the War of the Austrian Succession, there was believed to be a crime wave in the early 1750s. The long-serving Austrian agent, Zamboni, reported that due to the rise in thefts and murders it was unsafe in London, both in houses and on the streets at night. He also claimed it was dangerous to go into the provinces, and that policing was negligent.[7] Post-war demobilisation led to another reported crime wave in 1783–4. Conversely, the outbreak of a war acted as a damper on crime because many desperate individuals enlisted. On the other hand, the statistical basis for such observations is not strong enough for comfort, and it is possible that the lack of war news led the newspapers to devote more attention to crime.

More generally, reporting and discussing crime and criminality was part of a wider concern about change. Most commentators blamed crime not on poverty but on luxury, specifically a search for exalted status that signified a refusal to accept social position and thus social disorder. This was seen to lead to attempts to acquire a social presence, reflected in clothes, watches and other goods that were believed to inspire crime. Vagrancy was seen as the mobility of the idle poor, and thus as dangerous, rather than as the result of the character of the labour market. The press was dominated by reports of urban, particularly London, crime. Street robbery was the main issue in the discussion of crime for much of the period, for example for the early 1750s when the Fieldings were particularly prominent.

The Scottish criminal justice system, from which there was no appeal to London, differed from the English system not only in punishments, but also in other respects, including fifteen-strong juries, more limited use of jury trials, and the not proven verdict. The poet Robert Southey thought crime was less rife in Scotland because the disparity in wealth was less and there was less envy.

Policing was weak, and there was no national police force. Landowners could rely on their own 'police' of estate workers and employees, who could surround a household in some degree of security. In Ireland, under an Act of 1715, only Protestants could be constables, but, in many districts, it was difficult to find them to fill this unpaid office. The weakness of formal policing mechanisms in the British Isles ensured that informally raised forces were used on an *ad hoc* basis. There was no centralised policing system. However, that did not mean that policing was absent. Instead, local initiatives led to the adoption of Watching Acts and other initiatives. Most London parishes had obtained such Acts by the 1780s, largely in response to concern about property crime. Rising levels of household theft in Lancaster in the 1780s led the Corporation to open a subscription for a town watch and in 1790 a private watchman was hired by individual subscribers to patrol the main streets.

Local initiatives also owed much to entrepreneurship, as prominent and dynamic individuals saw opportunities and needs. For example in West Ham, watchmen and constables earned reasonable sums from the reward system.[8] The use of thief-takers was rife with abuse, as in London in 1745–54 where they fabricated crimes in order to collect rewards.

The most famous thief-taker, Jonathan Wild (1683–1725), exemplified the possibilities of developments in the relationship between capitalism and crime.[9] Born in Wolverhampton and originally a buckle-maker, Wild gravitated to the vortex of opportunities in London. Once in the world of crime, he moved from the established techniques of extortion and protection rackets to develop the trade of receiving stolen goods. Sidelining the fences by paying thieves a higher price for stolen goods, Wild used newspaper advertisements and other methods to resell them to their original owners. He also profited from the rewards for turning in criminals, including members of his own gang. In the early 1720s, Wild destroyed rival gangs including the Spiggott, Hawkins and Currick gangs. Hanged for receiving stolen goods, Wild achieved continuing fame as a character type. He was the model for 'Rachum' in Gay's *The Beggar's Opera* and his career was compared to that of Walpole.[10]

The role of thief-takers was a response to the deficiencies of locally controlled urban police forces. They generally contained part-time and poorly armed watchmen who were unable to deal with major outbreaks of crime. Policing agencies responded to what was urgent or particularly violent, and a certain equilibrium that offered a reasonable amount of peace tended to reign, but this did not free the population from fear and the need to consider their own defence, while the agencies ignored the non-observance of much of the law. Fear of policing areas where criminals congregated was an important problem. As a result, criminals could easily evade arrest.

Serious breakdowns of law and order could only be dealt with by calling on the army, a method that was generally unpopular and was fraught with complications and legal hazards. Troops were deployed against the Cornish tinners in 1757 and again, when they seized grain, in 1773. The effectiveness of the military in dealing with domestic challenges was necessarily reactive and limited to those that were seen as major threats requiring a military response. The army was handicapped by the lack of clarity over its position under the Riot Act of 1715, by its limited numbers, mobility and training, and by the absence of any equipment other than firearms. The last led to fatalities that could outrage local opinion, as when the Edinburgh town guard under Captain John Porteous responded to disturbances, after Andrew Wilson, a popular smuggler, was executed in 1736; they fired on the crowd, causing fatalities. Porteous was subsequently lynched. The disturbances were politicised because smuggling was in part a political crime linked in Scotland to opposition to excise and (more generally) 'English' taxes. The use of troops led to fatalities in Glasgow in the malt tax riots in 1725, in London in the St George's Fields Massacre in 1768 and the Gordon Riots in 1780, and also in the Boston (Massachusetts) Massacre of 1770.

A sense of precariousness was captured in the response of Charles Cathcart, a member of the Scottish nobility and of the circle of the Prince of Wales, to the Glasgow riots of 1725: 'If the disturbers of the public peace there are not soon brought to condign punishment I am much afraid a thorough disregard and contempt to all laws will obtain over the whole country.' He also feared that the social sway of the gentry was at risk: 'If any wrong step is taken at Edinburgh, it will hardly be in the power of our gentry to keep our folk from following any bad example that may be set to them.'[11]

Most of the army's domestic responsibilities did not involve fighting, although the threat of force was important to its effectiveness. Guard functions were widespread. Troops escorted valuable loads, especially of bullion and coin, guarded prisoners going to trial, jail and execution, and theatres. They thus acted to overawe and contain potentially troublesome public gatherings. Tax collectors and revenue officers were given escorts, and the army built roads in Scotland in order to improve its responsiveness to any Jacobite action.

Nevertheless, the militarised remedies of the past seemed increasingly inappropriate. Walls no longer appeared either necessary or an appropriate symbol of town or state. Old gates and walls were demolished and not replaced. In 1694, the Irish castle of Kells was converted into a market-house and court-house. The walls of many Irish towns, for example Carrick, Cashel and Clonmel, were breached.

Instead, new initiatives to maintain law and order were launched. John Fielding, an active JP and a half-brother of the novelist, organised mounted police patrols in and around London in the 1750s. Efforts were also made to deal with the problem of prosecution. Instead of, as today, having a system of public prosecution, it was up to the victims to decide to prosecute, but they often did not do so for reasons of expense. This encouraged the formation of societies in which subscribers agreed to fund prosecutions. A prosecution society was established in London in the late 1750s, and *Drewry's Derby Mercury* reported on 8 October 1773, 'The frequency of all kinds of felonies is complained of by all degrees of people, and some counties have (in order to lighten the burden from an individual) laudably formed associations for apprehending and prosecuting all offenders.' The paper urged that the same be done in Derbyshire. Aside from Associations for the Prosecution of Felons, there were also Watch and Ward Societies. In the early 1780s, Yorkshire magistrates led moves for the increased regulation and policing of the bulk of the population, part of the process in which control moved from being a parish issue. Asylums and prisons were administered and funded at a county level.

An unsympathetic sense of the poor as a problem, and a linkage of policing with social control, were clearly presented in the discussion of many reforming proposals, as in a report from a Dublin official in 1774:

> Our police has undergone a great improvement lately by the establishment of a receptacle for the miserable vagrants who infested the streets of this metropolis. The great work of cleansing Madrid was not more necessary, nor in appearance more difficult to be effected; but by some humane and resolute people applying themselves seriously to the task, the streets of Dublin are now as exempt from that shocking nuisance as those of London and a man may get back to his home with the same quantity of silver in his pocket as he carries out of it.[12]

In 1785, a bill was introduced in Parliament to create a single centrally controlled police force for London, in place of the existing local ward and vestry constables and watchmen. Though it was defeated, due to fears about the consequences for liberty and opposition from local interests, similar legislation was passed for Dublin by the Irish Parliament in 1786. The Corporation opposed the new force without success and a local rate was introduced to pay for it, while the force, unlike the parochial watchmen, was given arms. It had to battle a crime wave which included well-organised violence by journeymen committees out to win industrial disputes in the face of a hostile legislative framework.[13]

Punishment for crime and disorder could be harsh. The judicial system has sometimes been presented by modern scholars as an aspect of social control by the élite and/or political control by the state. The Riot Act of 1715, passed in order to deal with Jacobite disturbances, made rioting and riotous assembly felonies. The number of capital offences increased greatly in England, and the method of hanging was fairly primitive, so that a quick death was not always obtained. When the famous pirate, Captain Kidd, was executed in 1701 the rope broke. Pressing to death for refusal to plead to an indictment was only abolished in England in 1772. Branding and nailing by the ear to the pillory were penalties both still in use in Scotland. Punishment worked on what was referred to as the terror of the example. People were not so much hanged for stealing a horse, but in order that horses should not be stolen. The large increase in sheep stealing in 1740 as a result of the dearth of that year led to it being made a capital offence in 1741.

By modern standards, the accused were harshly treated, not least because they only were infrequently permitted to employ a lawyer or to mount a defence.

> Hurried trials, overawed prisoners, ambivalent judges, convictions on flimsy evidence, reward-hungry entrepreneurial police, and many other more structural aspects of the judicial system, such as the gender- and property-based qualifications that had to be met by jurors and magistrates, discourage any idealization of the quality of justice in this period.[14]

If the mob strongly disapproved of a felon, the pillory could be *de facto* a death sentence, as people were stoned to death, a form of punishment by popular will.

However, the number of those hanged in London was far lower in the late eighteenth than in the early seventeenth century. In the 1730s and 1740s, almost half of those condemned to die in England received a royal pardon. The percentage of those sentenced to death in London and Middlesex who were actually executed fell from 72 in 1753 to 43 in 1756, and in the 1780s to less than a third. In part this reflected concern about the efficacy of hanging for theft. Many criminals were sent to America to be indentured servants. Local juries frequently acquitted minor offenders. In Ireland, a high proportion of criminal trials ended in acquittal, and there was a relatively low number of capital sentences and executions. The same was also true of murder cases in England, for example in Berkshire.

There is also evidence that the law served all social groups, albeit without equal access and favour. 'Middling men were the main decision-makers, the main group that made things happen',[15] but the labouring poor also made extensive use of the law, although that does not mean that it necessarily enjoyed widespread acceptance among them. In Surrey an appreciable percentage of prosecutions were initiated by labourers or servants, although there, as in London, they initiated proportionately few prosecutions. The use of legal redress in civil disputes was widespread. Courts of Requests were founded in England to get people to pay their debts at a time when the central common law courts were pricing themselves out of business. They were, in effect, small debts courts. Birmingham's was founded in 1752.

There was considerable flexibility in dealing with petty crimes. Many JPs sought to resolve disputes by informal mediation and sanctions, rather than the penalties of the law, although in this, as in other respects, the attitudes and styles of JPs varied greatly. Flexibility in the use of legal procedures was restricted, however, for the poor, the socially unconnected and women. Among Londoners, it was the unemployed, the unconnected, the newly-arrived migrant, and young single women who were generally the most badly treated by the judicial system; they were most likely to be suspected of crimes and brought before JPs. The notebook of Henry Norris, a Hackney JP, reveals that he was honest but had little sympathy with the plight of the poor and was rarely lenient. He readily imprisoned those found pilfering crops, even when they were obviously in want. Over two-thirds of the offences brought before him involved some form of assault, while allegations of theft or damage to property formed the second largest category. Justice was swift but rough. Without legal representation and the right to present their case to a jury, defendants were at the mercy of the JP.[16] More generally, people of all social classes appear to have used the law as only one of several possible methods of confronting people with their misdeeds, and not as the sole arbiter of criminal accusations.[17]

There was considerable variety in popular attitudes, not least in response to the variety of crimes and courts. Although there was much criticism of the cost and processes of the civil law, especially in the 1690s, 1720s and 1790s,[18] the common law faced less hostility, particularly before mid-century and outside London, possibly because, prior to a trial, the criminal law was essentially a local process run by constables and JPs. Concern about reputations on the part of women led to a dramatic growth in actions for defamation in archdeacons and consistory courts. Church courts played a major role in sexual regulation.[19]

It would be misleading to suggest that the norms and practices of institutional justice were accepted by all. It is possible that much of the population settled their own problems without recourse to judicial agencies. Feuds, attempts to enforce particular norms of behaviour, generally eluded control by the authorities and were common. In addition, gangs of poachers became more active and more violent from mid-century, but were already prominent in southern England in the 1720s, leading to the 'Black Act' of 1723 which created about fifty new capital offences, including maiming cattle, killing game, breaking down fences, arson, blackmail, trespass and going in disguise. In part, this Act reflected concern about Jacobite activity, and there was fear of co-operation between the 'Blacks' (who used the disguise of a blackened face) and Jacobites. In other words, the massive expansion of the capital legislation was largely designed to deal with a specific conjuncture. Furthermore, the 'Blacks' were not operating throughout the country but rather in particular areas, especially in Surrey and Berkshire. Indeed, as they concentrated on deer poaching, they were really a problem in woodlands, especially Windsor Forest and the Bishop of Winchester's deer park at Farnham. However, the national character of judicial policy and legislation was shown by the national scope of the 'Black Act', or, to give its full title, 'An Act for the More Effectual Punishing Wicked and Evil-Disposed Persons Going Armed in Disguise, and Doing Injuries and Violences to the Persons and Properties of his Majesty's Subjects, and for the More Speedy Bringing the Offenders to Justice'.[20]

A conviction that lawlessness was related to disloyalty was expressed in 1750 by Captain James Molesworth, then serving in Fort William:

> the thievish and the rebellious spirit are so intimately connected, that those measures which crush the thief, cannot fail to disconcert the rebel; let vigilance and force make the Highlanders honest, reason and interest will make them loyal ... that natural hatred of the English so industriously ... fomented among these people.[21]

It is difficult to assess popular attitudes towards the law and its enforcement. Crime literature presented prominent criminals, particularly highwaymen such as Dick Turpin, in a heroic light. On the other hand, the participation of ordinary citizens through jury service led to a widespread sense that the system provided justice. This justice was not just that of the rich, but also of what was termed the 'better sort' of the parish. As a result, it was not surprising that those punished were disproportionately not from the 'better sort'. Outsiders, such as vagrants, and those seen as morally loose, were especially prone to suffer. This also reflected the important role of the perceived moral worth of accused and accuser and of character witnesses. Thus, among the poor who were punished, those who lacked masters to speak up for them were at a disadvantage.

Authority was defied both at the centres of power and on the margins. City crowds rioted against unpopular policies, and smugglers and other criminal gangs operated in cities and towns. In his diary, George Sloper noted on 12 December 1783, 'Smugglers to the number of 40 or more came to Devizes Friday night between 11 and 12 and retook a large quantity of tea from Mr Woods the Supervisor.'[22]

In more distant regions, the law was regularly openly defied. When, in 1703, Maurice Donnellan, the Catholic Bishop of Clonfert in Ireland, was arrested under the Banishment Act of 1697, he was rescued by an armed crowd of nearly 300. The government was unable to discover and punish his rescuers, and Donnellan remained at liberty until his death in 1706. In Scotland, although not England, armed gangs of beggars were not uncommon and they could terrorise rural areas. One such was led by James MacPherson who was hanged at Banff in 1700. It was difficult to enforce laws against smuggling, poaching and illicit distilling, especially in areas remote from centres of authority. Cattle rustling was a major problem in Highland Scotland as late as the 1720s. Illicit distilling was significant both there and in Ireland. 'Wrecking', looting the cargoes of wrecked ships, and in some cases luring them to their destruction, was a problem in many coastal areas, including Cornwall, the Wirral, and the Welsh and Irish coasts. Distant Cardiganshire was notorious for gangs of brigands in the Ystwyth valley and also for polygamy, a sign of weak Church government.

Smuggling increased appreciably in scale and organisation from the 1690s, despite the Smuggling Acts of 1698, 1717, 1721 and 1745. The very passage of so many Acts reflected the severity of the situation. Smugglers began to organise large land-smuggling gangs from the 1720s. In 1720, about 200 members of the Mayfield gang fought revenue officers in Sussex, and hostilities in Sussex in the 1740s were large-scale. On 4 February 1734, a petition of those dealing in tea complaining about the impact of smuggling was presented to Parliament. Henry Pelham, then Paymaster General, told the Commons he was conscious 'of the great enormities committed by the smugglers, especially in those counties which are in the neighbourhood of this city. The open and the outrageous manner in which they carry on their frauds, is well known, I believe, to most gentlemen in this house.'[23] By mid-century smuggling accounted for a major portion of trade with France and the United Provinces and had a major effect on prices and distribution. Smuggling was helped by the sympathy of some landowners.

Yet smuggling was not the same as a breakdown of government. The Jacobite rising in Northumberland in 1715 was the last in northern England, and the reach of government was more effective than a century earlier. Furthermore, there was no programme of fortification against domestic opponents outside Highland Scotland. Elsewhere, city walls and fortified positions fell into disrepair or were demolished, rather than being improved. Castles decayed because they were uncomfortable to live in. In 1739, the castle at Tonbridge began to be used as a quarry.

If lawlessness was primarily a problem for individuals, government was more concerned about financial issues, although smuggling represented a fusion of the two. Britain relied upon taxes on property, principally the Land Tax, introduced in 1692, and taxes on articles of general consumption: excise duty. Taxes on individuals and households did not play a role in the finances of central government in Britain. From 1698, the Land Tax was a fixed tax with a quota of assessment applied to each county, the administration of which was responsible for dividing it between parishes and townships. The Tax was not an effective tax on income. Due to the largely unsupervised role of landowners in the process, there were serious problems of assessment, with assessment practices varying greatly within and between counties; whereas excise duty was easier to assess and collect.[24] A critical re-evaluation of the Land Tax has argued that the significance of the 1692 legislation has been exaggerated, that the Tax 'was little more than an extension of earlier levies, albeit at a higher rate of poundage', that it was retained because successive governments were unable or unwilling to assess income and property realistically, and that there was no genuine innovation in taxation until William Pitt the Younger's income tax reforms of the 1790s.[25]

Despite rumoured plans in 1727, there was no 'new survey of the lands in order to increase the revenue from the land tax'.[26] In 1747, Henry Rooke, the London agent of the Bishop of Carlisle, warned the bishop that attempts to evade the window tax were foolish as they might draw attention to the limited amount of Land Tax paid by the region:

> The stopping up of windows, which your Lordship mentioned in a former letter, as a thing which people in the North parts were busy in doing; is not well judged ... as they are favourably dealt with in regard to the Land Tax ... especially in a time of war, when money must be raised.[27]

A study of the Land Tax in East Sussex in 1785 reveals there is no evidence of any general reassessment of the value of land there after 1692, but also that the surviving commissioners' minutes make no reference to even local reassessments except in terms of alterations on individual appeal.[28]

Instead of trying to tax income and property effectively, there was an emphasis on indirect taxes. Excise duties on alcohol rose after William III came to the throne and Britain began a lengthy period of expensive warfare. Salt was taxed from 1694, seaborne coal from 1695, malt and leather from 1697. There were also new taxes on spices, wine, spirits, tea, coffee, cocoa, and tobacco; but no general excise, because this was seen as politically unacceptable. Hackney coaches in London were taxed from 1694 and the window tax was introduced two years later (and lasted until 1798).

The willingness of governments to try to change the tax system reflected more than wartime needs. In 1723, following Walpole's comprehensive customs reforms in 1721–2, most of the existing British customs duties on coffee, tea, chocolate and coconuts were replaced by an excise duty on their domestic consumption. All dealers and retailers had to register with the excise officials, who enjoyed powers of inspection and summary justice, and whose responsibility for the excise on beer and malt ensured a nationwide presence. The legislation of 1723 led to a major increase in revenue, but Walpole's proposals to extend these arrangements to wine and tobacco in 1733 provoked a furious political row, and the ministry had to abandon the scheme.

Walpole saw it as a technical financial measure designed to make revenue raising more efficient, not least by cutting smuggling, but the opposition exploited fears that the government was going on to tax other commodities and that it would deploy an army of excise officers to raid homes and control elections.[29] Both were crucial issues. The threat of excise duties on food seemed to move Britain closer to the image of a heavily taxed and regulated Continental state. The nature of excise powers challenged suppositions about the constitution and the character of British liberties. Excise officers and commissioners were seen as arbitrary figures unconstrained by jury trials. Contemporaries could not believe that Walpole would not use the right to search by excise officers in elections as he used customs officers, for example in Liverpool.

After the Seven Years' War (1756–63) the government again sought to extend excise duties. George Grenville, First Lord of the Treasury from 1763 until 1765, was concerned about 'the exhausted state of the public revenues'.[30] Considerable opposition to the cider excise of 1763 led, however, to its repeal in 1766, and the imposition of duties in North America, including those on stamped paper (Stamp Act, 1765) and on glass, paper, lead and tea imported into the colonies (Townshend Acts, 1767), had similar results. Despite this, excise duties remained very important to the British state, and their collection was a major demonstration of the potential strength and sophistication of central government. By 1770, the Excise had a staff of 4,075 in England and Wales.

The burdens produced by the War of American Independence led to fresh extensions in taxation, with general excise duties raised in 1779, 1781 and 1782, and specific rises of duties on beer, spirits, wine and salt (1780), and tobacco and soap (1782). These rises ensured that tax income rose – from £10.5 million in 1770 to £11.8 million in 1780 – while taxation's share of national income, which had fallen after the Seven Years' War, not least thanks to rapid economic growth, rose, so that the rate in 1780 (11.7 per cent) was higher than that in 1760 (11.5 per cent).[31] In 1777, Charles Mellish MP wrote from Nottinghamshire to his patron, the 2nd Duke of Newcastle, 'this county is weeping over the tax upon bricks'.[32]

The extension in excises ensured that as a percentage of total government revenues they rose from 27 in 1698–1701 to 43 in 1786–9, while Land Tax fell from 31 to 18 and customs from 32 to 24, but the general fiscal policy was conservative. Income tax was not introduced until 1798, when wartime needs called for far more than traditional expedients. The Irish Parliament also preferred to tax commerce and did not introduce a land tax. The regressive character of excises was captured by the *Manufacturer* of 25 April 1720, when it complained that for 'the Poor ... not a pound of candles, or a bushel of coals they burn; not a peck of salt they eat, or a pot of beer they drink' was not taxed.

Rising taxation was made necessary by the increased cost of government, especially the military, and by the cost of war. Wars, in 1689–97 and 1702–13, were financed by parliamentary support and authority, albeit with considerable difficulty, in contrast to the debacle of the last Stuart war, the Third Anglo-Dutch War (1672–4) for which there had been no sound financial base. Much of the cost of war was met by borrowing. Over 30 per cent of the total government expenditure during the Nine Years' War and the War of the Spanish Succession was financed by public borrowing. In 1747, during the War of Austrian Succession, Charles Wyndham MP wrote, 'Mr Pelham has opened his budget as we call it in the House of Commons. The services of the current year will not come under the monstrous sum of eleven millions … He moved for the raising six millions by subscription, which they say they are sure of having filled immediately'.[33] The national debt rose from £46.9 million in 1739 to £76.1 million in 1748.

The government borrowed about 37 per cent of the £83 million it spent in the Seven Years' War, and the national debt rose from £74.6 million in 1756 to £132.6 million in 1763. In the War of American Independence almost half the cost was covered by borrowing. Annual public expenditure rose from £10.4 million in 1775 to £29.3 million by 1782, £114.6 million was spent in 1776–82, and the national debt rose from £127.3 million (1775) to £232 million (1783). Owing to debt servicing, peacetime expenditure after each conflict was higher than the pre-war level.

Vast sums were raised, far more easily than elsewhere in Europe. A confidence in the soundness of financial institutions and structures, and in the fiscal role and responsibility of parliamentary government, enabled the mobilisation of national financial resources in the service of the state. The funded national debt, guaranteed by Parliament and based on the Bank of England, which had been founded in 1694, enabled the borrowing of hitherto unprecedented sums and at low rates of interest. Whereas, in the early 1690s, the government was paying up to 14 per cent for long-term loans, the rate of interest fell to 6–7 per cent in 1702–14, also a period of war, 4 per cent in the late 1720s, at or below 3 per cent in the late 1730s, and, after a wartime rise, 3.5 per cent in 1750.[34]

In 1741, Corbyn Morris observed that 'the Public Credit is in some measure the pulse of the Nation'.[35] In 1757, the 1st Duke of Newcastle, then First Lord of the Treasury, noted that there appeared to be no difficulty in meeting the new commitment to provide greater military support to Prussia: 'towards that I have already been offered near six millions … and all this money will be borrowed (if necessary) something under $3\frac{1}{2}$ per cent; when France gives 11 per cent and cannot fill the subscriptions.'[36] However, by 1762 he feared that the burden of the war might lead to a collapse of public credit.[37]

Parliamentary financial arrangements and taxation were accepted as legal even if they could produce criticism. Many continental states, not least France, found it difficult to devise politically-acceptable methods to raise taxation, largely because the politically and socially powerful were unwilling to increase their commitments. In contrast, parliamentary taxation and a parliamentary-funded national debt raised the substantial sums that funded Britain's wars, and without creating incapacitating political, regional and social divides. More generally, the ability of the British state to provide subsidies to other powers was an indication of the fundamental strength provided by the combination of parliamentary government and burgeoning commerce.

The general benefit to the economy of low rates of interest on government debt and to the political system of a funded national debt were considerable. Possibly, however, the funds invested in the national debt might have played a more beneficial economic role if invested elsewhere, in the productive economy.

The attitudes and actions of government servants were another problem, interacting with administrative systems that were often weak and archaic. For example, much of the work of the Exchequer was still conducted according to medieval forms, and the efficiency of the Treasury and revenue departments was found wanting during the War of American Independence, leading to reform in the postwar period. In 1758, the Duke of Newcastle noted about money for Hanover, 'His Majesty wanted this money to be sent away in 24 hours. I told him this holiday time nobody was in town, no office open, that caused very severe reflections.'[38]

Corruption was a widespread problem, reflecting the importance of tax revenues as a form of ready wealth, proprietary attitudes towards posts, and the general practice of paying officials by allowing them to retain part of the proceeds of their positions. Officials saw themselves as office-holders rather than employees. Office was seen as a form of property. It was common for positions to be inherited. The 26-year-old Vicesimus Knox was a good appointment as Headmaster of Tonbridge School in 1778; he was also the son of his predecessor. At Oakham the vicarage passed from father to son in three generations from 1736 to 1806.

This could lead to abuses. Coventry Corporation was self-perpetuating and corrupt, a closed corporation in which councillors chose all officials except the town clerk. Leases were granted to councillors at low rents, the funds of charities in their care disappeared, and the creation of freemen was manipulated for electoral advantage. In the Armagh district of Ireland, the Cust family used the local collectorship of taxes so as to end up as substantial rentiers in the area. The unacceptable level of Henry Cust's corruption led to his losing his post in 1761, but he suffered no social or financial penalty and in 1769 was appointed High Sheriff of Armagh.

There was also corruption in national government, although it was so well-established and part of the fabric and culture of activity that it is not always clear that the term corruption is helpful. Instead, that commonly related to what was judged to be an unaccustomed level of abuse. A London item in the *Newcastle Journal* of 19 January 1754 noted:

> It is believed by many persons of great experience, and who have a due regard for the honour of public offices, that it would contribute very much to the dispatch of business, and prevent a multitude of inconveniences, if no persons employed in small offices within their respective departments were permitted on any pretence to receive fees, presents or gratifications for expediting or soliciting affairs depending before their principals.

Corruption was but one aspect of an administrative ethos and practice for which the connotations of the term bureaucracy are inappropriate. Administrative organisations reflected the values and methods of the social system. Appointment and promotion often resulted from social rank, patronage and inheritance, rather than from educational qualifications or what might later be seen as objectively assessed merit. Merit in this period meant connection, wealth and rank, and much of the concern about the role of 'corruption' in appointments was a nineteenth-century invention. It is anachronistic to talk of meritocratic standards before they were invented. The universities did not serve to train an administrative élite; instead, particularly in England, they produced numerous clerics and acted as finishing schools for the social elite. 'Unreformed' or pre-Victorian government, both national and local, looked very poor by later studies, but, within the parameters of the time, it was generally effective. In 1763, George Grenville, the First Lord of the Treasury, was told

> that Mr Pelham has allowed Lord Galloway to recommend all the little custom house offices in the shire of Wigtown and the district of burghs within it whilst the members who served for them were chosen by him and supported the measures of the government.[39]

Indeed the MP for Wigtownshire was then James Murray of Broughton, nephew and son-in-law of the Earl of Galloway.

Patronage was ubiquitous; as George Bubb Doddington pointed out, 'service is obligation, obligation implies return'.[40] Patronage networks were a feature of the society of the period, often controlled by private citizens for socio-economic as well as political purposes, and not merely the aberrant creation of Crown and ministers. Apart from the clientage systems of landed magnates and borough-mongers, patronage relationships of one kind or another were also involved in the gentry's control of parochial appointments in the Church; their bestowing land tenures based on favourable leases, or with the suspension of onerous terms; the commercial relationships between wealthier members of the community and the merchants and artisans whose products and services they consumed; the distribution of commissions and contracts to architects, builders and civil engineers by town corporations as well as by aristocratic patrons; the control exercised by bishops, deans and chapters over both property and benefices; and also the appointment of parish pump officials (constables, church wardens, overseers of the poor) by the influence of social superiors. Patronage gave currency to personal relations and family connections,[41] and helped make them central to government.

Social assumptions, the role played by patronage, the political importance of administrative posts and the opportunities for gain, both legal and illegal, helped to ensure that senior posts were occupied by men of rank. As a result, those who wielded authority and controlled the power for change were often gentlemen amateurs, frequently without vocation or aptitude, rather than professional experts. The expert assistants were generally too humble in status to be able to push through changes, particularly in a society and within an administrative ethos where precedent commanded both respect and legal authority.

The dominance of patronage and the vulnerable position of many ministers encouraged them to favour clients and relatives, which further encouraged factionalism, but could also ensure loyal and possibly effective employees. In 1739,

Sir James Lowther, MP for Cumberland, wrote of John Hill MP, a Commissioner of Customs,

> Mr Hill is a great operator for Sir Robert [Walpole]... as he finds Sir Robert looks upon me as a hearty friend he would have me to dispose of things in Cumberland both in Customs and Excise. At this rate are things managed in every part of the revenue. It is suffered to go on very often to the prejudice of the public ... to gratify the friends of great men.

Two years earlier, Lowther had informed the Bishop of Carlisle that in order to get his nephew a post in the Customs at Whitehaven, the bishop 'should write directly to Sir Robert Walpole, for it is he alone that disposes of all these places, and expects application for them to be made to himself'.[42] In 1748, the Duke of Newcastle explained to the Duke of Cumberland the choice of 'Mr Elliot, son of Lord Minto for [Sheriff-deputy for] the Shire of Roxburgh ... Lord Minto is reputed to be zealously attached to His Majesty's government, and to have great influence in the county.'[43]

The government's ability to use secret service funds and other aspects of ministerial patronage ensured that there was great pressure to do so. There was also a dark side to the manipulation of power. Legal and extra-legal pressures could be used ruthlessly against opponents such as opposition publishers. Under Walpole, the Secret Office of the Post Office systematically opened the post of opposition politicians, including non-Jacobites, encouraging a sense of persecution that was in large part justified.

Factionalism was also encouraged by the weakness, and sometimes absence, of agreed administrative procedures, and the limited authority of government institutions, which ensured that posts became influential often because of the individuals who filled them. Similar problems of amateurishness and factionalism affected the armed forces. Absenteeism, cronyism and the pursuit of the financial benefits of command occupied the time of most officers, a reflection both of the extent to which the army shared in the values of society and of its institutional character. Many of the offices of the Minorca garrison, which fell to the French in 1756, were absent when the attack came. Appointments to senior positions reflected family influence and royal favour. Thus, Sir Charles Hotham received his first commission in 1706 when only 13 and was promoted to Lieutenant-Colonel in 1720, Colonel in 1731, and Colonel in the fashionable First Troop of Horse Grenadier Guards in 1735, thanks to his friendship with George II. More generally, thanks to hostility on the part of the opposition and to governmental wishes to cut expenditure, little was spent on the army, and dedication and morale, among both officers and soldiers, were not high. Far from training for battle, the army was divided into small units and its command positions were generally deployed for political purposes.

Both George I and George II promoted the principle of long service as the main way to advancement, and did their best to counter the purchase of commissions. George II used his formidable memory for names to good effect in keeping oversight of the leading members of the officer class. Although the desire of both monarchs to end corrupt financial practices and, in particular, officers' pecuniary perquisites was only partially successful, the traditional character of proprietary soldiering at troop and company level was fundamentally changed, to the significant detriment of the incidental income of captains. Regimental entrepreneurship, however, largely escaped, and colonels maintained their private financial position until the reign of Victoria. Until the 1750s, regiments were known by the names of their colonels. When George II asked General Churchill what had become of his hautboys, the General struck his hand on his breeches pocket, so as to make the money rattle, and answered, 'Here they are, please your Majesty, don't you hear them.'

This was not the best basis for an effective response to the French army. The British army was not at the cutting edge in tactical practice, let alone debate or innovation. Nor was it improved as a campaigning force. Administration remained under a number of discrete and often clashing departments and officials, including the Board of Ordnance, the Paymaster General, the Secretary at War, and the Secretaries of State. The artillery had begun to improve with the creation of a regimental structure and the Woolwich Arsenal in 1716, but such changes did not amount to a major programme of raised capability for the army as a whole.[44]

The problems of government were not restricted to the maintenance of law, order, and effective armed forces, financial difficulties, unreliable officials, factional politics, unresponsive local communities, and the absence of reliable information. Changes in government and political disorder could also create many problems. These difficulties were not peculiar to the national government. Major institutions and landlords faced similar problems, as they strove to reconcile traditional practices and assumptions with the desire to achieve specific goals. The Glengarry estate in the Scottish Highlands, in which timber was illegally cut by tenants in 1769, was not the only estate that found it difficult to control the activities of dependants, although it was more remote than most and its Chief particularly unpleasant. Supervision was made difficult for all institutions by the relatively small size of their staff.

As a result of the limitations of administrative procedures, consent and co-operation played a major role in successful government, at both the national and the local level. A crucial aspect of this was the importance of parliamentary support in the establishment and maintenance of the funded national debt. This was both the source of the government's financial strength and the product of the co-operation between crown and political society after 1688, and more clearly after the Act of Settlement of 1701, that was expressed in the constitutional position of Parliament and the policies of successive ministries. Parliament's business was dominated by local issues, such as turnpikes, canals, enclosures and bridges. Its views were a reflection of continual pressure from outside Westminster, through personal contacts, the press and pressure groups.

Despite the problems of government, it would be mistaken to argue that ministries were opposed to considering change. 'Let sleeping dogs lie', Walpole's maxim, does not describe the typical late-eighteenth-century administration, for officials and politicians were often willing to act in accordance with the principles of state-directed action. The structure of colonial administration and commercial regulation received much attention, and there was considerable administrative reform and government activity, for example with the navy. If much action was in response to crises, that is more generally true of the history of government. Just as the administrative and judicial system in Scotland, especially the Highlands, was remodelled after the '45, so the size of the national debt at the end of the Seven Years' War led to an attempt at financial retrenchment and reorganisation. Similarly, the crisis of the American War led to a powerful impetus behind post-war reform initiatives which were particularly important in colonial, commercial and financial matters.

In addition, work on eighteenth-century administration at the local level, on JPs, law-enforcement, urban communities and prison administration, has stressed the significance of planning and policy, showing change as well as continuity. For example, a study of quarter sessions records for Lindsey in Lincolnshire, points to a more systematised practice of justice, with petty sessions introduced and the quarter sessions reorganised in 1749, and a major change in the sessions documents from the late 1760s, as the rolls became thicker and better organised, and the minutes longer and full of new regulations and procedures.[45]

The local and the national were linked, especially through the legislative role of Parliament. The devastating fire in Warwick in 1694 led to a concerted attempt to rebuild the town. The Commissioners, whose authority rested on Act of Parliament, itself a sign of the changing political world, distributed charity money to encourage the builders and compensation for land taken to widen streets, and dictated the style of prominent houses. The powers of the Commissioners ceased in 1704, but they had showed the potential effectiveness of administrative agencies at the local level and the ability of Parliament to play an enabling role.[46]

More generally, the role of Parliament was seen in Improvement Acts which empowered individuals, as commissioners, to fund and implement schemes for improving the paving, lighting and cleaning of towns. Commissioners were permitted to levy rates and were separate from the municipal corporation. Salisbury obtained such a commission for paving, lighting and watching the city in 1736, but the major surge in such commissions was begun by Liverpool in 1748 and became especially strong after the peace of 1763. Southampton obtained one in 1770.

The process of urban improvement was continual in the second half of the century and was much encouraged by emulation, Southampton following Portsmouth's example. An Act of 1750 for enlarging the streets and market-places of Gloucester led to the removal of old market-places, as well as the pillory and the stocks. A Streets Improvement Act for Bristol was passed in 1766. Acts for Worcester of 1770, 1771 and 1780 permitted a new bridge, a better water supply and the first street lights. Under a Lamp Act for Hereford of 1774, town commissioners were appointed to improve street paving, lighting and cleaning. The open, rubbish-filled brooks which ran through streets were covered over.

Such activity reflected a concern with the urban environment, a confidence that it could be improved, and a determination to act. Towns appeared to be one of the principal products of human activity, the section of the environment most amenable to action, and where society was open to regulation. Interest in public hygiene, open spaces, air and light led to an emphasis on wide streets and squares, and the introduction of pavements, attention to drains and street cleaning, as in Birmingham after Street Commissioners were appointed in 1769.

These priorities reflected common themes. The creation of a regulated environment was not simply functional in its rationality; it also reflected a moral vision that was in some respects as traditional in aspiration as it was progressive. The specific manifestations of this concept ranged from new drains to police forces, but the need for conscious improvement to the urban environment was accepted.

Action derived in part from the scale of the problems of regulation and control facing urban communities. Poverty and crime were concentrated in towns, as were problems of sanitation and health. The nature of urban life, with a relatively large number of people living in marginal circumstances, often in disrupted family situations and outside established patterns of hierarchical authority, all aspects exacerbated by the very growth of towns and by immigration, posed major problems.[47]

CONCLUSIONS

Unlike on much of the Continent in the second half of the eighteenth century, 'reform' impulses in Britain, both then and earlier in the century, reflected co-operation between centre and localities. 'Enlightened Despotism' in Britain was, parliamentary, not despotic, in character. This is important, because a potential challenge to the practice, personnel and ideology of landed power in eighteenth-century Europe came from royal initiatives; indeed, until the French Revolution, they were the sole serious threat to those who possessed landed power. Thus, potentially at least, notions such as Peter the Great's Table of Ranks (1722), which made it clear that social and political privilege derived from monarchical approval on a continuing basis, were subversive.

In England, there was no comparable attempt to create a 'service nobility'. Furthermore, in contrast with Ireland in the 1690s and the Scottish Highlands after 1746, there was no attempt to alter the politico-social complexion of power. As in many other respects, it is a fundamental conservatism that is most striking, certainly in comparison with say the Austria of Joseph II, a state where Enlightened Despotism was pushed hard despite élite and popular hostility. This conservatism accorded with the ideal of moderation, which was the backbone of a society wary of enthusiasm and excess; indeed, moderation was advocated for aesthetic, ethical and political reasons.

Yet this conservatism was both sensitive to political expectations and options and able to accommodate, and at times assist, commercial, industrial and imperial growth. There is no reason to suppose that a 'conservative' political system is necessarily incompatible with change. Any emphasis on confrontation, challenge and tension between conservatism and change is problematic, because it presupposes a rigidity on the part of the established order, an inability to accommodate change, and a necessity for transformation through struggle, that reflects modern ideological presuppositions, rather than the complex and nuanced reality of the period. As also specifically with electoral 'management' (see Chapter 12), so more generally both with the role of the landed order in the political system and with the very nature of that system, it is necessary to offer a more sensitive account and one that would stress co-operation. It is also important not to read the ideological idioms and clash of the French Revolutionary era back into the previous decades.

The discussion in this chapter differs therefore from John Brewer's *The Sinews of Power: War, Money and the English State, 1688–1783* (1989) which suggests that a strong British state, made necessary by war, developed in accordance with the dynamic forces within an essentially commercial society. Furthermore, in terms of comparative state development, the British state is presented as more effective and powerful than its continental counterparts. Although British public finances and naval administration were stronger, this approach can be questioned both by reference to deficiencies and lacunae in the governmental structure (both central government and the local government that Brewer is apt to neglect), and also by drawing attention to a political culture that emphasised the desirability of a weak state and the un-British, particularly un-English, character of strong government. In political language 'there was a persistent current of individualism and that seems to have militated against any tendency to treat the collectivity with either reverence or theoretical profundity'.[48] At another level, the legislative process revealed not only a major role for private legislation and a widespread interaction of public and private activity, but also an absence of state-directed codification comparable to that in Continental states such as Austria.

NOTES

1. J. Cookson, *The British Armed Nation, 1793–1815* (Oxford, 1997).
2. P. Langford, *Public Life and the Propertied Englishman, 1689–1798* (Oxford, 1991).
3. N. Landau, *The Justices of the Peace, 1679–1760* (Berkeley, 1984); D. Eastwood, *Government and Community in the English Provinces, 1700–1870* (1997).
4. J. Beattie, 'London crime and the making of the "Bloody Code", 1689–1718', in L. Davison, T. Hitchcock, T. Keirn, and R.B. Shoemaker (eds), *Stilling the Grumbling Hive: The Response to Social and Economic Problems in England, 1689–1750* (Stroud, 1992), pp. 49–76; A.R. Ekirch, *Bound for America: The Transportation of British Convicts to the Colonies, 1718–1775* (Oxford, 1987).
5. B.J. Davey, *Rural Crime in the Eighteenth Century* (Hull, 1994).
6. D. Hay, 'War, dearth and theft in the eighteenth century: the record of the English courts', *Past and Present*, no. 95 (1982), pp. 117–60.
7. Zamboni to Kaunitz, 6 Mar. 1752, Vienna, Haus-, Hof-, und Staatsarchiv, England, Varia 10 f. 104.
8. E.A. Reynolds, *The Night Watch and Police Reform in Metropolitan London, 1720–1830* (Stanford, 1998).

9. G. Howson, *Thief-Taker General: The Rise and Fall of Jonathan Wild* (1970).
10. For example, in Henry Fielding's fictional *The Life of Jonathan Wild the Great* (1743).
11. Cathcart to Earl of Loudoun, 4, 29 July 1725, HL. LO 7897, 7943.
12. Jephson to Viscount Townshend, 21 Jan. 1774, Manchester, John Rylands Library Eng. MSS 940.
13. B. Henry, *Dublin Hanged. Crime, Law Enforcement and Punishment in late Eighteenth-Century Britain* (Dublin, 1994).
14. P. King, *Crime, Justice, and Discretion in England 1740–1820* (Oxford, 2000), p. 371.
15. P. King, *Crime, Justice, and Discretion*, pp. 359 (quote), 365.
16. R. Paley (ed.), *Justice in Eighteenth-Century Hackney. The Justicing Notebook of Henry Norris and the Hackney Pettey Sessions Book* (1991).
17. R.B. Shoemaker, *Prosecution and Punishment: Petty Crime and the Law in London and Rural Middlesex, c. 1660–1725* (Cambridge, 1991).
18. C.W. Brooks, 'Interpersonal conflict and social tension: civil litigation in England, 1640–1830', in A.L. Beier, D. Cannadine, and J.M. Rosenheim (eds.), *The First Modern Society: Essays in English History in Honour of Lawrence Stone* (Cambridge, 1989), pp. 357–99.
19. T. Hitchcock, *English Sexualities 1700–1800* (1997), p. 97.
20. E.P. Thompson, *Whigs and Hunters: The Origin of the Black Act* (1975); J. Broad, 'Whigs and deer-stealers in other guises: a return to the origins of the Black Act', *Past and Present*, no. 119 (1988), pp. 56–72.
21. Molesworth's memorial, 20 Nov. 1750, BL. Add. 51378 fols 87, 89.
22. P. Colman, *The Baker's Diary. Life in Georgian England from the Book of George Sloper, a Wiltshire baker, 1753–1810* (Trowbridge, 1991), p. 31.
23. *A Collection of the Parliamentary Debates in England*, XI (1740), p. 337.
24. D. Ginter, *A Measure of Wealth. The English Land Tax in Historical Analysis* (1992) is substantially based on Yorkshire.
25. J.V. Beckett, 'Land tax or excise: the levying of taxation in seventeenth- and eighteenth-century England', *English Historical Review* (1985), pp. 285–308.
26. Andrew Ramsay to Hay, Jacobite Secretary of State, 23 Feb. 1727, Windsor Castle, Royal Archives, Stuart Papers 104/21.
27. 12 May 1747, Carlisle, Cumbria CRO. D/Sen/Fleming/17.
28. R. Davey, *East Sussex Land Tax, 1785* (Lewes, 1991).
29. J. Price, 'The Excise Affair revisited: the administrative and colonial dimensions of a parliamentary crisis', in S. Baxter (ed.), *England's Rise to Greatness* (Berkeley, 1983), pp. 257–321.
30. Grenville to Robert Waller, 29 Sept. 1763, HL. ST7 vol. 1.
31. P.K. O'Brien, 'The political economy of British taxation, 1660–1815', *Economic History Review*, 41 (1988), pp. 1–32.
32. 5 May 1777, Nottingham, University Library, NeC 2815.
33. Wyndham to Duke of Somerset, 8 Dec. 1747, Exeter, Devon CRO. 1392 M/L 18 47/7.
34. P.G.M. Dickson, *The Financial Revolution in England: A Study in the Development of Public Credit 1688–1756* (1967).
35. C. Morris, *A Letter from a By-Stander* (1741), p. 9.
36. Newcastle to Andrew Mitchell, 8 Dec. 1757, BL. Add. 6832 f. 31.
37. Newcastle to Hardwicke, 25 Feb. 1762, BL. Add. 35421 fols 200–1.
38. Newcastle to Hardwicke, 3 Jan. 1758, BL. Add. 35417 f. 171.
39. Grenville to Duke of Bedford, 27 Dec. 1763, HL. ST7 vol. 1.
40. J. Carswell and L.A. Drake (eds), *The Political Journal of George Bubb Doddington* (Oxford, 1965), p. 281.
41. R.L. Emerson, *Professors, Patronage and Politics. The Aberdeen Universities in the Eighteenth Century* (Aberdeen, 1992).
42. Lowther to John Spedding, 8 Dec. 1739, Lowther to Bishop Fleming, 30 Oct. 1737, Carlisle, Cumbria RO. D/Lons/W, D/Sen/Fleming/14.

43. Newcastle to Cumberland, 18 Mar. 1748, Windsor Castle, Royal Archives, Cumberland Papers 32/339.
44. A. Guy, *Oeconomy and Discipline. Officership and Administration in the British Army 1714–63* (Manchester, 1985).
45. B.J. Davey, *Rural Crime in the Eighteenth Century* (Hull, 1994).
46. M. Farr (ed.), *The Great Fire of Warwick, 1694* (Stratford-upon-Avon, 1992).
47. L. Davison *et al.*, *Stilling the Grumbling Hive*.
48. J.A.W. Gunn, 'Eighteenth-century Britain. In search of the state and finding the Quarter Sessions', in J. Brewer and E. Hellmuth (eds), *Rethinking Leviathan. The Eighteenth-Century State in Britain and Germany* (Oxford, 1999), p. 124.

12

Political worlds

The political structure of Britain in this period can be presented using several approaches. It can be anatomised in formal terms, by means of a description of constitutional conventions, parliamentary rights and electoral arrangements, as well as in the informal terms of the patronage networks which linked politicians and peers capable of exerting influence at the centres of power. It is also possible to put diversity first, not by turning to a descending system of government, one that focuses on and traces the impacts, influences and networks of national institutions and politicians, but rather by beginning in the localities. This approach builds on that of the earlier chapters with their stress on the diversity of society.

The localities should not be ignored. Alongside the aspects of a national economy, suggested most obviously by the absence of internal tariffs within Britain, was the continued medley of local economies, the worlds of clay and chalk, arable and pastoral, dairying and sheep-and-corn, with all their varied social consequences, in terms of settlement patterns, social practices and discipline, and the complex relationships between local worlds and the regions with distinct identities they formed part of, both counties and sub-county regions, such as Hallamshire, the region round Sheffield.[1] This diversity was related to political and religious variations, although much of the detailed work necessary to chart and understand this situation has not been done. For example, the relationship between areas of rural industry and pressures for political and religious change has been argued for some regions, such as Gloucestershire,[2] but not studied across the country.

Nor has there been any systematic study of the relationship between this diversity of localities and the electoral process. Diversity was certainly a characteristic of the electoral system, and it is instructive to consider this as it says a lot about the willingness to accept established practices and the eventual timing and character of demands for change. After the parliamentary Union of England and Scotland in 1707, the House of Commons contained 558 MPs elected by 314 constituencies: forty English counties (each of which elected two MPs), 203 English boroughs, two English universities, twelve Welsh counties (excluding Monmouthshire), twelve Welsh boroughs and forty-five Scottish constituencies.

These categories were themselves far from uniform. The 203 English boroughs returned 405 MPs, the overwhelming majority of the House of Commons. Two boroughs, the City of London and the united boroughs of Weymouth and Melcombe Regis, returned four MPs each, 196 returned two each, and five returned one each. Bar for the last, voters were permitted to cast two votes, although they could choose to use only one. All the Welsh constituencies (bar Monmouthshire if that is to be included as Welsh) returned one MP each, but seven of the seats were groups of boroughs united for electoral purposes, one, Cardiff, containing eight boroughs. Twenty-seven of the thirty-three Scottish counties each sent one MP to the Commons, but the other six were grouped in pairs, one of each alternating with the other in electing MPs. Bar Edinburgh, the Scottish burghs were combined in groups in order to elect MPs.

The size of the electorate varied greatly within and between categories. Yorkshire had the largest electorate with 20,000 voters, and its electoral results were regarded as particularly significant, while the Scottish county of Sutherland had only about ten voters in 1754. Even when the franchise (right of voting) was nominally the same, there could be significant variations in the size of the electorate. In the first half of the eighteenth century, Kent had about 7,000 voters, but Huntingdonshire, a smaller, less populous and poorer county, only about 1,500.

The franchise, however, was far from uniform. Under a statute of 1429, the English counties theoretically all had a franchise based on the 40-shilling freehold: the possession (not necessarily ownership) of freehold property valued at 40 shillings per year. In practice, both freehold and the 40-shilling value were open to various definitions, aspects of the diversity and long-standing local conventions of English politics, that can be seen to parallel the different weights and measures referred to in Chapter 5. For example, in early-eighteenth century Cheshire, the term 'freehold' had to be mediated through a manorial structure with a complex lease and rental system, and 40 shillings could refer to a property valuation for the land tax, to rent paid, or to annual yield. However, in accordance with the general tendency towards systematisation, the situation was clarified by legislation in 1745 and 1780.

The English borough franchise was consciously varied, with different categories of boroughs: householder, freeman, scot and lot, corporation, burgage, and freeholder boroughs. In the twelve householder or 'potwalloper' boroughs, the right of voting was enjoyed by all male inhabitants not receiving poor relief or charity. The qualifications for becoming freemen in the ninety-two freeman boroughs varied greatly, although generally the influence of the corporation over the creation of freemen ensured that its views had to be considered. The thirty-seven scot and lot constituencies gave the vote to inhabitant householders, so that occupation of property was crucial. In some of these constituencies, it was necessary also to pay the poor rate; in others the franchise was enjoyed by inhabitant householders receiving neither alms nor poor relief. This group included Westminster, the borough constituency with the largest electorate: about 8,000 voters in the first half of the century.

In the twenty-seven corporation boroughs, the right of voting was limited to the corporation; in the twenty-nine burgage boroughs to specific pieces of property; and in the six freeholder boroughs to those who owned freeholds. These constituencies had smaller electorates than the householder, freeman, and scot and lot boroughs. Although the boroughs with smaller electorates did not all provide a picture of oligarchic control and corrupt practices, they were generally more stable in their politics and more amenable to outside influence than those with larger electorates. The seats with small electorates tended to have MPs who supported the government, increasingly so in the period of Old Corps Whiggery (1714–60), while, in that period, those with larger electorates were more likely to vote for opposition candidates, as was seen in Westminster.

Some settlements with very small populations were parliamentary boroughs. Cornwall was particularly over-represented with reference to the size of its towns, as, more generally, was the south-west of England. Conversely, some major towns, including Birmingham, Chatham, Falmouth, Leeds, Manchester, Sheffield and Whitehaven, were not parliamentary boroughs. However, it would be wrong to claim that they were unrepresented as their voters could play a major role in county contests. Shifts in population did not lead to any redistribution of representation, nor to any powerful call to do so from within the political system. Thus, the growing population of northern and Midland towns was noted only in so far as the size of the county electorate increased.

In Scotland, there was also considerable variety in the franchise. In the county seats, the right to vote belonged to freeholders possessing land valued at 40 shillings 'of old [medieval] extent', and to owners of land held of the Crown rated at £400 Scots. This restricted the electorate to men of landed substance, and in no county did the electorate exceed 200. These were very much 'known' electorates, where candidates or their agents tended to know all of the electorate and to be able to make accurate predictions about their voting intentions. In the Orkney and Shetland constituency, there were no Shetland voters, as none of the Shetland landowners had applied for Scottish charters or a valuation of their holdings. Sutherland had a distinctive franchise, as the right to vote extended to those who were vassals of the Earl of Sutherland, a stark reminder of the power of some of the Scottish landowners. The councils of Scottish burghs each elected a delegate, and the delegates of each group of burghs then jointly elected an MP.

Although Scottish constituencies required careful management, they tended to be a reliable source of support for the government. In Scottish counties with hereditary sheriffs, the latter could return whomever they liked without consulting the freeholders, until such sheriffdoms were abolished after the '45 as part of the process by which the central government tried to regulate Highland society. The Welsh boroughs mirrored the English franchises, with corporation, freemen, and scot and lot electorates.

Aside from differences in parliamentary representation, there were variations in local political cultures. These variations had been accentuated as a consequence of the acute and often traumatic political and religious divisions of the 1620s to 1680s. The legacy of the Civil Wars, the Interregnum governments, and the royalist reactions of the early 1660s and of 1681–5 were particularly potent in defining and exacerbating local differences.

The role of local political divisions helps to explain the vitality of the local response to national issues. Far from their being a trickle-down system, in which the crucial debates and disputes occurred at the national level, and those in the localities were simply a reflection of these, there was a far more dynamic relationship. This was unsurprising given the major role of independence from outside interests in many electoral contests.

Instead of politics being a case of national and local, it was rather one of metropolitan and local, the former comprising Whitehall and Westminster but not the City of London which was a separate local political sphere. The metropolitan and local combined constituted national politics and gave it its special character and energy. Because the government tended to dominate Parliament, it was frequently in the localities and in the means by which they were linked to the centres, that the principal political battles occurred, and, in part, it was in this sphere the character of the British state was defined.[3]

Locality is an ambiguous term, but one that captures a range of interrelated and important political worlds stretching from particular communities to shires.[4] However, localities were very varied. The politics of Dublin were not the same as those of Norwich. The extent to which the term region is also appropriate is less clear, not least because the political history of English and Scottish regionalism in this period has not been written.[5] There was certainly no institutional format between country and county, nor any practice of co-operation between what has been termed county communities. Part of the strength of the state as a political system was indeed that patterns of identity and action above the local/county level were national, not regional in character, although the extent to which this was true of Britain, as opposed to England and, separately, Scotland, is unclear. The militia issue of 1756–63 was a national Scottish issue which mobilised opinion on Scottish, not regional, lines.

Any stress on national issues is not intended to deny the major role of patronage, interests and corruption, which, themselves, cannot always be readily separated from an approach to politics based on issues. Many parliamentary seats were not contested at elections, and there were a large number that were 'pocket boroughs': controlled or heavily influenced by patrons. Thus, William Pitt the Elder came into Parliament in 1735 when he was elected unopposed for Old Sarum, a quintessential rotten borough that returned two MPs despite being depopulated. Pitt's grandfather, Thomas 'Diamond' Pitt, who had made a fortune trading to India, had purchased the property that carried the right of election in 1691, and, at the general election of 1734, William's elder brother, Thomas, was returned unopposed. As he was also returned unopposed for Okehampton, where he owned much property, Thomas brought in his brother for Old Sarum. William was re-elected in 1742, but in 1747 transferred to Seaford, a pocket borough of the Duke of Newcastle, who was electorally powerful in Sussex and Yorkshire. In 1756, Pitt, who was no longer an ally of the Duke of Newcastle, was elected for Okehampton, and also for the pocket borough of his Grenville in-laws at Buckingham, and in 1757 he transferred to Bath, which he had been invited to represent by the corporation, which enjoyed a monopoly of the franchise. Only one of his elections, Seaford in 1747, was contested.

Aside from private patronage, there were also boroughs in which government influence was sufficient to get nominees elected. This was true, for example, of ports, such as Harwich, where the navy or the Post Office had a major presence. Ministers, such as the Duke of Newcastle, took great pains to use such influence in order to elect government supporters. State employees such as customs and excise officers were expected to support ministerial candidates. The absence of secret ballots enabled the monitoring of voters, and poll books recorded their votes.

Complaints about electoral corruption were frequently voiced by opposition spokesmen, who tended to lack the resources of the ministry, but not only by them. In 1702, John Evelyn referred to the 'infamous borough of Mitchell, a paultry [Cornish] village consisting of about 20 poor thatched cottages ... the chief support of the place is election for burgesses, at which time they make no scruple of selling their votes to the highest bidder, and afterwards inform against their benefactors if the adverse party will bribe them to it.'[6]

Contested elections were expensive for most candidates, as electors expected to be entertained, and often to be given financial inducements. The expense encouraged uncontested returns, which was totally different to the modern situation. Henry Ibbetson and William Thornton offered to stand for York in 1747 against the Tory MPs, but only provided the Whig gentry in the county agreed to subscribe to their expenses. Ibbetson also asked the ministry for £2,000. There was little response from the county Whigs, possibly because the decision had been taken to accept a compromise over the county representation, and because they harboured bitter memories of the expensive subscription campaign that had failed to reverse the opposition victory in the 1734 county election by a parliamentary petition. Fearing the financial troubles that the ministerial victor in 1741 had suffered, Ibbetson withdrew from the contest. One of the Tories did likewise and thus there was an uncontested election. Similarly, a series of expensive elections for Northumberland was followed by electoral truces in 1741, 1747, 1754, 1761 and 1768.

Several contested elections, including Oxfordshire in 1754 and Northampton in 1768, were notoriously expensive. After 1754 there was no Oxfordshire contest until 1826. The Northampton contest, which arose from an attempt by Earl Spencer to break the influence of two other county peers, the Earls of Northampton and Halifax, helped to bankrupt the two latter.

Financial resources, and detailed calculations about how best to appeal to the personal interests of constituents, thus seem to have been crucial in many elections. This could lead to a situation in which consultation and representation, let alone any element of democracy, might seem absent. The ability of estate stewards to organise the votes of tenants and the success of electoral agents can both be emphasised. Many elections were unopposed. There was no contest for the Nottinghamshire county seats between 1722 and 1832, or for those in Shropshire between 1722 and 1831, Dorset (1727–1806), Cheshire (1734–1832), Lancashire (1747–1820) and Staffordshire (1747–1832).

This matched the social politics of the country. Landed continuity on the part of the élite had political, social and cultural consequences, and contributed greatly to the exclusion by social status that was so important in politics, government and society. This was a hierarchical society, and there were few challenges to the social assumptions that reflected and sustained this situation. The distribution of governmental power and authority fundamentally accorded with the structure of the social system, not with democratic representation. There were shifts, not least an ecclesiastical pluralism that challenged religious authority following the Act of Toleration of 1689. Nevertheless, the ethos and practice of politics showed far more continuity than had been the case in the seventeenth century.

It was possible to encompass political and religious divisions, bar Jacobitism, within the system. Although much commentary naturally related to political tension and disagreements, and there was consistent criticism of opposition termed factious, the structure of politics and government, far from precluding debate and discussion, expected them. In politics, aside from the institutional framework of contention – elections and Parliament, the court and ministerial context of élite politics was not one of uniform opinions and an absence of debate. Indeed, it would be wrong to suggest that the English *ancien régime* was stable if that is intended to imply an absence of debate and of new ideas and initiatives. Moreover, lacking both a substantial bureaucracy and a well-developed bureaucratic ethos, government relied on co-operation.

After the defeat of Jacobitism at Culloden in 1746, the British state became more stable, and this stability was not maintained at the cost of any permanent struggle with the world of extra-parliamentary politics. There was no such struggle, nor any rigid divide. Indeed, the measure of the conservatism of the period was that stability was a case not of radicalism overcome or resisted, as in the early 1660s, when monarchy, episcopacy and the traditional rulers of the localities had sought to eradicate the legacy of the Interregnum, but, instead, of a society with few radical options, certainly until the last quarter of the eighteenth century.

The political system was dominated by the socially prominent. Oxfordshire, for example, might have a large electorate of about 4,000 voters, the forty-shilling freeholders, but those elected were scarcely ordinary freeholders. From 1740 to 1790 the county was represented by Sir James Dashwood, George, Viscount Quarendon, Norreys Bertie, Thomas, Viscount Parker, Sir Edward Turner, Lord Charles Spencer, and Philip, 4th Viscount Wenman. The sole apparent non-aristocrat, Norreys Bertie, was in fact the grandson and great-grandson of MPs, and the grand-nephew of the 1st Earl of Abingdon. The politics of the great houses were important in the county, as they were elsewhere.[7]

In addition, quite populous boroughs were under the electoral control of particular, often non-resident, families. Such control commonly reflected local property, although it was generally a relationship that had to be kept alive by careful management, as much as by expenditure. Indeed, the electors could exert considerable leverage. The Ryders controlled one of the Tiverton seats from 1734 to the Great Reform Act of 1832, although their interest had to be managed with care, as did that of the Dukes of Bedford in Bedford.[8]

Irrespective of any urban property, local aristocrats and gentry could be of considerable consequence in controlling or influencing borough representation, for example the Dukes of Bolton and Chandos at Winchester, where, in the thirty-five years after the Winchester by-election of 1751, none of the six general and three by-elections was contested. Similar influence could also be seen with the Dukes of Beaufort at Monmouth, the Dukes of Bedford at Tavistock, the Earls of Bristol and the Dukes of Grafton at Bury St Edmunds, the Earls Gower at Newcastle under Lyme, the Bruces at Marlborough, the Robartes of Lanhydrock at Bodmin, the Luttrells of Dunster Castle at Minehead, and with many other constituencies.

This influence was not always uncontentious. In 1722 and 1748, Derby successfully resisted the usually dominant interests of the Dukes of Devonshire and the Earls of Chesterfield, and in 1747 the Ansons of Shugborough and Gowers of Trentham were only just able to overthrow the sitting Tory MPs in Lichfield, becoming very unpopular locally in the process. Yet, in general, particularly in smaller boroughs, the influence of the rural elite was strong. Many boroughs, such as Exeter, that, in the seventeenth century, had chosen townsmen as MPs, chose country gentlemen the following century. This was true whether or not the franchise was wide. In West Wales, the Cardigan Boroughs seat was chosen by the freemen of the four boroughs. Yet the county grandees dominated the 'election' of burgesses at their court leets, and there was something of a race to enrol large numbers of freemen. The electorate there was dramatically widened, but it was done so to choose only gentry candidates, the Pryses of Gogerddan and the Lloyds of Peterwell. Granting honorary freedoms of the borough to aristocrats, knights, baronets, clergy and gentry, compromised the freedom of the borough of Ipswich. Freedoms were also sold. By 1710, honorary and non-resident freemen were beginning to swamp elections. This affected not only parliamentary elections, but also those for borough offices, and helped to accentuate party politicisation in Ipswich.[9] As a consequence of such processes, despite the preponderance of borough seats in Britain, the county élite dominated Parliament.

In central, as well as local, government, and in the Church of England, as well as in the army, landed power and influence were supreme. The practices of patronage sustained it, as did dominant social assumptions. Landed power prevailed: it represented the leading members of a society that was fundamentally inegalitarian and hierarchical. The strength of these assumptions, the basic premises that helped to sustain landed power and to ensure its wider social resonance, require noting, alongside any focus on radical critics.

In Oxfordshire, élite influence can be seen at opposite ends of the parliamentary spectrum, with both the two county seats, and also the single member constituency of Banbury, where the right to vote rested with the 18 members of the corporation. The county seats of Oxfordshire were uncontested between 1710 and 1754 and were securely held by the Tories. Although an opposition party, they scarcely came from the ranks of the socially excluded. Sir Robert Jenkinson, MP 1710–17, was a baronet and the son of an MP, and had seats in Walcot, Oxfordshire and Hawkesbury, Gloucestershire. His brother, Robert Bankes Jenkinson, MP 1717–27, succeeded to the baronetcy, the country seats and the seat in Parliament. Both men were educated at Trinity, Oxford and Lincoln's Inn.

The father of Henry Perrot, MP 1721–40, was nicknamed 'Golden Perrot' thanks to his wealth. Sir William Stapleton, MP 1727–40, was a baronet, was educated at Christ Church, and married the granddaughter of an Earl. Sir James Dashwood, MP 1740–54 and 1761–8, had estates that were so extensive that allegedly he could ride direct from Kirtlington to Banbury on his own lands. Educated at Eton, he built a house at Kirtlington second only in size in Oxfordshire to the Whig stronghold of Blenheim. George Lee, Viscount Quarendon, MP 1740–3, was the heir to the 2nd Earl of Lichfield. Philip, 3rd Viscount Wenman, MP for Oxford in 1749–54, who stood for the county in 1754, had large estates around his seat at Thame Park.

In 1754, in possibly the most controversial county election of the century, the Oxfordshire Tory interest was challenged by the Whig or new interest. Sir Edward Turner and Lord Parker stood for the Whigs, and were supported by the Duke of Marlborough, Earl Harcourt, and the Earl of Macclesfield. Parker was the heir to George, 2nd Earl of Macclesfield, and Turner, a baronet with a seat at Ambrosden. Yet, as the defeated candidates were Dashwood and Wenman, it is a little difficult to present this as a case of social oppression. The Tories spent over £20,000 on the election, a double return was made, and the election was decided in favour of the Whigs by the partisan House of Commons which they dominated.

Banbury was also influenced greatly by the landed elite. The major interests at first were two landed families, the Copes of Hanwell, two miles away, and the Norths of Croxton, a mile further. Sir Jonathan Cope was MP 1713–22, and his relative Monoux Cope MP in 1722–7, but from 1740 the choice rested with the Norths. Frederick, Lord North, the Oxford-educated head of the government that lost America, was uncontested MP from 1754 until he succeeded his father as 2nd Earl of Guilford in 1790.

Of the other seats in Oxfordshire, Oxford was a freeman borough with 1,200 voters in 1722. Most elections were uncontested, and the corporation had the strongest interest. From 1715 to 1784 there were contests only in 1722, 1768 and 1780. In addition, the city was not a source of resistance to the rural hinterland. Such a clash existed in parts of England, especially where towns dominated by Nonconformist Whigs clashed with hinterlands whose political culture was predominantly Tory and Church of England, but not across much of the country. In the case of Oxford, a common Toryism lessened tensions, as did the social, economic, and cultural role of the borough as a county capital and market centre, rather than, for example, an 'enclave' port and/or an industrial town, such as Whitehaven, with few links to the hinterland.

Oxford MPs did not all have country seats. Thomas Rowney, MP 1695–1722, lived in St Giles's in Oxford. Matthew Skinner, another lawyer, MP 1734–8, and Recorder of Oxford, also lived in the city. Yet other Oxford MPs were country gentlemen, while the landed order itself had much influence in the city. This was especially true of the Tory Earls of Abingdon. Montagu Bertie, 2nd Earl, was High Steward of Oxford until 1743, and a supporter of Matthew Skinner. His steward's son, George Nares, was Town Clerk 1746–56, Recorder 1766–71, and MP 1768–71, although, by 1768, he was on the Marlborough interest. Despite the corporation's criticism of the Earl of Abingdon in 1768, it is difficult to see the election of that year as a rejection of aristocratic influence. The other MP returned for Oxford in 1768 was the Honourable William Harcourt, son of the First Earl, a local aristocrat, and himself a Lieutenant-Colonel in the Dragoons.

Electoral corruption and coercion in the constituencies might seem to be linked to corruption at the political centre; as part of a world in which ideas were subordinated to self-interest. Yet, it is also necessary to note the role of issues and of political independence, and the extent to which corrupt practices can, in part, be seen as means by which politics continued in a world in which ideology and conviction played a major role.

This was true at both the national and the local level. Patronage and political management alone were insufficient to keep governments in power. Just as there were limits to the deference of voters towards their social superiors, not least landlords, so also the effectiveness and consequences of parliamentary management should not be exaggerated. Policies were important. Sir Robert Walpole, leading minister from 1721 to 1742, for example, devised a programme of peace, low taxation, no further legislative favours for the Dissenters, and no extension of governmental power into the localities, that was also followed by his protégé Henry Pelham, First Lord of the Treasury from 1743 to 1754, and that helped to produce parliamentary and ministerial stability for much of the period 1721–38 and 1747–54. Conversely, the patronage resources at the disposal of long-established ministries could not prevent serious political crises when they took initiatives that failed to carry political opinion: for example, over the Excise Bill in 1733 and the Jewish Naturalisation Act in 1753.

At the local level, the independence of the electorate and the role of issues emerge clearly. The two were sometimes combined in a preference for electing local men. Independence from interests deemed outside was seen as a crucial issue in what was often an intensely local political world. This world was more open, especially through the press, to outside views, than ever before, but still saw them through a local prism. Elected for the populous and politically-aware seat of Bristol in 1774, Edmund Burke argued to his constituents that an MP should be guided by 'the general good', but his neglect of 'local prejudices', in the shape of Bristol's negative views on proposals of freer trade for his native Ireland, helped him to come bottom of the poll in 1780.

Election propaganda could stress the local dimension, not least the role of MPs in forwarding local legislation at Westminster. In the bitterly contested Preston election of 1768, Lord Strange, son of the Earl of Derby, a prominent local landowner, won, defeating the Corporation's interest. The election propaganda on behalf of the latter made much of a sense of urban autonomy, combining it with an assault on the social character of Strange's supporters. Indeed Strange's candidates won by being able to have a poll of all (adult male) inhabitants rather than the freemen constituency pressed by the Corporation. A flysheet declared: 'nor shall this borough ever be annexed to any family ... Reflect one moment of your Candidate – his being your townsman ... and the respectable body of tradesmen of the borough who support his cause.'[10]

Whatever the strength of their position, MPs were expected to take note of the interests of their constituents. These were not confined to matters of patronage, or, rather, patronage should not be interpreted in a narrow sense. National issues were translated to the local scale, and vice versa. In Weymouth, opposition to Walpole was bound up in disputes over the town's charter. John Tucker, one of the MPs, took great care to keep his constituents informed.[11]

Such activities were part of what was, simultaneously, the maintenance of political links between centre and locality, and a process of politicisation or the deepening of a national political consciousness. Major controversies led people to stress their perception of a fundamental unity between local and national political structures and alignments.

If, for example, the elections for the Oxfordshire borough seats suggest social cohesion between élite and electorate, rather than social chasms, Oxford University and its parliamentary representation were redolent of ideological division. The University was a Jacobite stronghold, and was proud of its strong Toryism. After its Jacobite Chancellor, the 2nd Duke of Ormonde, was attainted in 1715, he was succeeded by another Jacobite, his brother, Lord Arran, who held the post until his death in 1758. George, 3rd Earl of Lichfield, formerly MP for Oxfordshire and another Jacobite, was High Steward of the University in 1760–2 and Chancellor from 1762 until 1792. The University MPs were all Tory.

The University of Oxford acted as a centre of Tory intellectual activity, and this was serious given the role of the two English universities in training the clergy of the Church of England. The government did not press plans for extending regulation that were considered in 1719 and 1749. Such a step would have been contentious and a reminder of James II's unpopular attack on the rights of the fellows of Magdalen College, and did not accord with Whig caution about infringing the rights of the propertied. Shorn of its early radicalism, Whig government very much located itself within the context of maintaining established rights.

Ideological division over the succession and the rights and consequences of the exclusion of James II helped divide the elite from the 'Glorious Revolution' of 1688 until George III ended the proscription of the Tories after his accession in 1760. This division provided much of the dynamic for local politics, providing real bite to personal and family rivalries. In 1698, Sir Henry Hobart of Blickling Hall, a firm Whig, was killed in a duel with his Tory neighbour, Oliver Le Neve, that arose from election-time allegations. Le Neve fled the country. After they came to power in 1714, the Whigs carried out a purge of many of the Tory JPs. This purge had achieved its aim by 1719, ensuring that the Tories had only minority status in the Commissions of the Peace, and Walpole made no effort to complete it. It sufficed that the Tories were not strong enough to dominate the Commissions; there was no attempt to remove them completely from positions of authority.

Yet, the purge of other local offices (Lord Lieutenancy, Deputy Lieutenancies, Custos Rotulorum, Duchy offices in Cornwall and Lancaster) was more complete than that of the JPs. Furthermore, many of the new Whig JPs were not of gentry origins, and this was greeted with outrage in what was still a hierarchical society that assumed office should equate with social status. The Tories pressed for higher landed qualifications for JPs, as they had done successfully for MPs.

Walpole's policy was to avoid provoking the Tories, but this did not mean that they were satisfied, understandably so as they were excluded from office and were dissatisfied with Whig toleration of Dissenters. Tory opposition to the Old Corps Whigs was contained, not conciliated, and, in some respects, their exclusion repeated that of the Catholics. Yet hostility was not generally pushed as far as actual conflict. Anglican neighbours were willing to hold Catholic property in trust for Catholic friends after 1715 in northern England. Most of England, including all of the south, was not directly affected by the Jacobite risings in 1715 or 1745. Thus there was no immediate issue to provoke clear signs of allegiance or acts of disloyalty. As a consequence, it is possible to emphasise the general success of the eighteenth-century English political system in preventing civil conflict, rather than to stress the divisions within it; although the situation looks different in Scotland and Ireland where divisions were more apparent and their consequences harsher.

It would be a mistake to see a development of national political connections and consciousness in linear terms. The religious changes of 1530–1665 had led to repeated centrally-directed local changes, and no eighteenth-century government acted, or sought to act, in as intrusive a fashion as Henry VIII had done with the dissolution of the monasteries in the 1530s or Oliver Cromwell with the rule of the Major-Generals in the 1650s. Yet, agencies for articulating a national political debate and for representing local views at the centre had been weak in the sixteenth and seventeenth centuries, not least because, for long periods, Parliament did not meet.

The shift, as a result of the working through of the 'Glorious Revolution', to annual sessions of a Parliament elected at least at regular intervals (though not in Ireland until 1768), and with defined powers, therefore made possible a major change in the political culture. Parliament was important not so much as a forum where government could be defeated, a relatively rare occurrence, but as one that encouraged a change in the nature of political debate, by creating a regular agency for publicly representing political views.

The Westminster Parliament was a great success in this period. It passed a growing quantity of legislation, which was a testimony to its importance in the political system. Thanks to the Act of Union with Scotland, the scope of the Westminster Parliament increased. Only in Sweden, Poland and the United Provinces (Netherlands) were there national representative institutions, but none was comparable and none was so successful: the Swedish Age of Liberty came to an end in 1772, while the Dutch Estates General and the Polish Diet were proverbial for delay and disagreement. The British system, in contrast, was presented by many contemporaries as excellent, at least in theory, and it attracted considerable foreign interest. This excellence supposedly reflected the balanced nature of the constitution and was demonstrated by the success in avoiding autocracy at home and by victory in the imperial struggle with France in the Seven Years' War (fighting, 1754–63, war declared 1756).

Parliament played an important role in the political system and in the political culture of the age, but its role was complex and, in addition, it is necessary not to exaggerate its impact. Parliament's executive and regulatory functions were both limited. For example, parliamentary inquiries into accounts lapsed after 1714, estimates of annual military expenditure were generally passed without detailed scrutiny, and successive ministries ignored appropriation clauses. In 1733, the French envoy, who had close links with the opposition, reported that it planned to establish a permanent committee of the two houses of Parliament to administer the national finances.[12] This never happened, although the war of American Independence made Parliament more watchful of government. In addition, the ability of Parliament to overthrow ministries was limited.

Furthermore Parliament was a sphere of political activity and a means for other agencies to pursue their interests and views, as much as an autonomous force. More generally, the tendency to stress public spheres of discussion can be misleading. They were less commonly spheres of decision-making, or sources of the decisions that were taken, than is usually appreciated. There is a reluctance to accept this and to consider the consequences. Instead, there is a powerful sense that the public sphere – Parliament, the culture of print, and the world of campaigns, agitation, propaganda and public opinion – must somehow have been, not solely important, but, instead, central to the processes of decision-making. At times, however, this is an act of faith rather than an assessment based on an understanding of the steps by which political and governmental decisions were usually taken.

More particularly, by concentrating on crises in which public manifestations of opposition to the government were notable, it is possible to present a misleading view of the difficulties that ministries encountered, one that concentrates on the relationship between policy and public, especially popular, opposition. As the crises are automatically defined by the strength of the latter, an impression is created that the central political problem was that of defending policy in such contexts, and that the political chronology of the period can readily be traced from crisis to crisis. A structure of politics, based on urban institutions, sociability, clubs, petitions, newspapers, instructions and addresses, has been advanced for this public opposition; as well as an ideology involving patriotism, nationalism and commercial expansion.

To consider government policy without paying attention to the range, intensity and impact of public debate would be foolish. An ability to profit from, or manipulate, extra-parliamentary public pressures could indeed be crucial politically, but their impact has been exaggerated, not least in terms of their role in defining a chronology of crisis and an agenda of study. Thus, the period 1730–70 apparently becomes the Excise Crisis of 1733, followed by the Jenkins's Ear agitation of 1738–9, the support for Admiral Vernon in 1739–41, the anti-Hanoverian upsurge of 1742–4, the agitation against Jewish naturalisation in 1753, the Pittite onslaught on the Duke of Newcastle in 1754–6, the controversy over peace in 1762–3, the agitation against the cider excise in 1763–6, and, from 1763, the Wilkesite controversy. Comparisons and links between crisis can be discerned, and it is possible to point to elements of consistency and coherence in the public debate. However, the direct political consequence of such controversies was far more episodic. Furthermore, a concentration on them creates a misleading impression of the principal political problems facing ministries in the field of policy, not least one that minimises the impact of dissension within governments.

This approach leads to a misunderstanding of the role of Parliament, and to its presentation largely in terms of a forum for the advancement or rejection of public aspirations, a sphere in short for the conduct of public politics. Such an approach limits its role unduly. By focusing on the debate between government and opposition, and then largely in terms of this as an aspect of a wider struggle between antithetical values and 'consciousnesses', the importance of Parliament in three fields is minimised.

First, it is important to note the passage of private and local Acts, which took up much parliamentary time and reflected the often very specific importance of parliamentary legislation, for example enclosure and turnpike Acts. Sixty-eight private bills were passed by the Commons in 1760 alone.

Secondly, there was general legislation that was not controversial in party political terms. This was true, for example, of proposals concerned with social policy, such as the reform of the Poor Law, the financing of workhouses, the punishment of crime, bills against blasphemy and duelling, and the treatment of debtors. Such legislation reflected the 'reactive' nature of much government, for much was undertaken not by ministerial initiative, but as the result of back-bench moves or pressure from lobby groups, such as the Society for the Promotion of Christian Knowledge. Thus, the importance of public opinion for Parliament was not restricted to elections. Parliamentary views were, in part, a reflection of continual pressure from outside Westminster, through personal contacts, pressure groups and the press.

Thirdly, the importance of Parliament to discussion and contention within government has been underrated, or, more commonly, neglected. And yet, its role in this field was of major significance. Prior to the death of George II in 1760, the struggle over foreign policy and related matters, such as the size of the armed forces, were the crucial political issues in 1700, 1712, 1717–18, and for most of the 1740s and 1750s. These issues did not lay between government and people, however defined and represented, with Parliament managed by the former but open to the arguments of the latter, but rather within the government. In 1714–60, these disputes centred on the apparent need created by the interests of George I and George II as Elector of Hanover.

The situation altered when George III (1760–1820) became king. Hanover was displaced, but not due to any triumph by extra-parliamentary forces or by widely-held 'Patriot' attitudes. Instead, the change reflected a marked shift in the dynastic dynamic, away from the Anglo-Hanoverian monarchy of George I[13] and George II, and towards a more clearly British conception on the part of the new king.

Parliamentary attitudes and the real, or alleged, problems of managing the Commons played a major role in discussions over policy within the government. In whatever way party alignments were defined, ministerial majorities were uncertain. Victory in elections, and the subsequent opening of the bazaar of patronage to parliamentarians, did not necessarily entail either quiescent sessions or stable majorities. Far from Parliament being part of a corrupt but stable *ancien régime*, which could only be swayed, and, eventually, overthrown, by outside pressure and mass politicisation, Parliament, instead, was an integral part of a political system that was open to debate and far from inflexible over policy. The management of Parliament was seen as a central task of government, and bore directly on differences over policy and place within ministries. An awareness of the likely response of Parliament to particular proposals was as important as patronage in retaining control of the legislature. This helped to make Britain a functioning parliamentary monarchy, one in which, despite problems, Parliament and Crown sought to operate in harmony. Monarchs chose ministers, and Lord North told the Commons on 27 February 1782:

> the King had a right to admit and dismiss from his councils whomever he pleased: and he might, without assigning any cause, or without fixing any guilt upon the person, recall that confidence which he had been graciously pleased to bestow upon any one of his servants.[14]

However, monarchs needed to create a ministry that could get government business through Parliament. An emphasis on the need to manage Parliament could also be advanced for tactical political reasons, rather than as an objective assessment of the views of parliamentarians or the exigencies of parliamentary management. This was the case with the rise of William Pitt the Elder. In late 1745, George II argued that the defeat of opposition motions indicated that Pitt's support for the ministry was unnecessary, and the same appeared true in late 1754 and again in the winter of 1755–6. This, however, did not prevent Pitt's entry into office, nor his subsequent return as Secretary of State.

Aside from the fact that political and parliamentary confidence were not measurable by objective criteria, not simply a matter of the size of majorities, and that this was especially the case in periods of crisis, the resort to the issue of parliamentary management in order to advance particular political goals was tactically valuable in political discussion as it was difficult to contradict. Parliament did need to be managed and appointing Pitt to office seemed likely to make this easier; as indeed proved to be the case.

Understanding of the political role of the Westminster Parliament can be enhanced by considering its Dublin counterpart. There also, developments in the reigns of William III and Anne were crucial, not least growing government expenditure as a result of war, and Parliament's refusal to vote any more hereditary revenues. As a consequence, in a context of political strife as well as compromise and negotiation, new constitutional and political conventions developed. A new process of revenue supply was linked to the advent of regular parliaments:

> By 1714 there was a clear understanding of what the various principles were. Parliamentary provision of money was based on a two-year duration of taxation, thereby dictating that Irish parliaments would meet every second year. The ways and means of raising taxation in Ireland was the preserve of the Commons, which in itself gave control of the purse-strings to parliament. The

government was accountable to parliament in relation to public income and expenditure, given that the Commons, and the committee of public accounts in particular, could wreck the supply should they so choose.[15]

Conventions and assumptions played a major role in politics on both sides of the Irish Sea.

It was not simply deceit in convoluted political manoeuvres that explains the central enigma of Hanoverian politics: the apparent need of ministers, in secure control of Parliament, and confident that this control would not be overthrown by the electoral process, to consider the attitudes and activities of the opposition, both within and without Parliament. The process culminated in the collapse of the Newcastle ministry in 1756. Unlike that of Walpole in 1742, after the 1741 general election, the Newcastle ministry was not affected by electoral defeat, for the 1754 general election had been a triumph for the government. Nevertheless, the ministry apparently fell as a result of the popular agitation over the humiliating loss of Minorca to the French.

The situation was in fact more complex. The likely parliamentary storm over Minorca also brought to a head relations between Newcastle and Henry Fox, the manager of the Commons, and thus created a crisis of parliamentary management irrespective of the activities of the opposition. Thus, the crisis of 1756 echoed others, such as those of 1717, 1742, 1744 and 1746, in which the government was divided. Under these circumstances, it was important for politicians to consider how best to create a new, stable ministerial alignment, and it was felt necessary to consider the views of parliamentarians and to take note of the public debate over policy.

Many parliamentarians had opinions on policy; they were not simply manoeuvring to their own personal or factional advantage. For example, the papers of William Hay reveal him as a committed ministerial Whig MP who disapproved of the opposition Whig 'Patriots', but could also be critical of the government. He exercised independent judgement as an MP, and, to gain his support, the ministry had to rely on principle and policy, not bribery or intimidation.[16]

As Parliament was the public forum in which the ministry formally presented and defended its policy and was criticised in a fashion that obliged it to reply, it was Parliament where the public debate over policy can be seen as most intense and effective. There was an obligation to respond that was lacking in the world of print, and an immediate linkage between the debates and the taking of decisions, the debates themselves being occasioned by the discussion of these very decisions. In addition, the financial power of Parliament, the need for government to turn to it in order to obtain the finance necessary for operating and for initiatives, gave it a role in the field of policy, especially foreign policy, that it otherwise lacked.

Uncertainty concerning likely developments emerges clearly from political correspondence, both government and opposition. This uncertainty indicates the danger of placing too much weight on the public, especially printed, debate over policy. The debate suggested a false clarity over policy, in which, for example, diplomatic and military strategies were predetermined by partisan political traditions, the weight of history interacting with specific and clashing partisan viewpoints. Thus, particular views could be regarded as Tory, Whig, Country or Patriot, and they could be associated with distinct policies.

Such an approach was employed to serve partisan points, commonly in terms of arguments about consistency or, more commonly, inconsistency. However, it was frequently by no means clear to parliamentarians what policy would be followed, or how issues and events were related to existing political groups. This was most apparent at points of discontinuity, whether domestic (changes in monarch or ministry), or international (the outbreak of war and the negotiation of peace). These could combine to create a serious discontinuity, as in 1741–2 with the outbreak of war on the Continent and the fall of the Walpole ministry. Correspondence then reveals not simply the hesitation of MPs faced by a change of ministry, but also the uncertainty provoked by a volatile situation in which the views of most politicians were unclear and their alignments were changing.

Indeed, the very stress on consistency that characterised much of the public debate reflected the difficulty of defining and maintaining a coherent position and of persuading others that this had been done in a rapidly changing world. Thus, for example, although the Tories were in opposition under George I and George II, and able to offer consistent denunciation of the political system as corrupt, they also had to adapt to circumstances in deciding how best to further their aims of opposition. Effective opposition required co-operation with dissident Whigs, but the ideology and polemic of co-operation in what was termed a 'Country' opposition did not describe the reality of clashing Tory and Whig traditions and views and the stubborn maintenance of differing legacies.

Historians have disagreed substantially over the nature of party in the period. Earlier views of a world of national parties were challenged in 1929 with the publication of Lewis Namier's *The Structure of Politics at the Accession of George III*. In place of party and ideology, Namier emphasised patronage, corruption and (self-) interest. He found the structure of politics in the personal and factional connections of a small number of politicians, those who dominated, indeed constituted, a world of élite politics. Crucial to Namier's analysis was his determination to present the view that ideological considerations played little role in the composition of élite factional groups, or in their political activities. Politics was the pursuit of place for profit and power; and power was a matter of patronage rather than policy. Namier discussed the extent of political influence, the number of placemen and the secret service accounts, through which support was apparently purchased by the government.

Namier's work was very influential in studies of the period, but, from the 1960s, it became more common to stress ideology and issues as causes of political configurations. This led to a re-evaluation of the role of party, and the concept now plays a major role, especially in writing on the reigns of Anne, George I and George II. It is also now easier to appreciate eighteenth-century parties on their own terms, rather than as unsatisfactory anticipations of modern equivalents.

However, there were important changes in the place of parties during the period. Furthermore, parties played very different roles, first in the formation of ministries, secondly, in the maintenance or weakening of parliamentary majorities, and, thirdly, in elections and in the country at large. Parties were generally more important in political battles in the Commons than in the world of Court and Cabinet; while, in the country at large, the intensity of the party struggle, and, to a certain extent, political alignments, varied considerably.

Though firm control over a disciplined parliamentary party was absent, ministries that had won an election were likely to be longer-lasting than those that had not had an opportunity to do so. An absence or loss of royal favour could, however, be fatal, as Godolphin discovered in 1710, Newcastle in 1762, Grenville in 1765, Rockingham in 1766, and the Fox–North ministry in 1783. Failure in war could also play a major role in the fall of ministries, as with Newcastle in 1756 and North in 1782.

In the first half of the eighteenth century, there was a fundamentally two-party Whig-Tory alignment, albeit one in which the role of opposition Whigs was often crucial. From the 1760s, and particularly in that decade, the situation was more loose and shifting. George III was keen to rule without party factionalism and determined to end the exclusion of the Tories. In addition, the leaders of the Old Corps Whigs, particularly Newcastle, were ageing. A new generation of ministers was required, but George neither waited for his grandfather's ministers to die or retire, nor took their advice on their successors. Responding to the admission of Tories to court office, Elizabeth Montagu thought that ministerial posts should and would be different:

> The admission of Lord Bruce etc. into the King's Bedchamber it seems was done without the participation of either of our great ministers nor do I blame the King that he gives places himself instead of suffering as his grandfather [George II] did. It is right that those who by their favour in administration are as it were accountable to the people for the execution of great and important offices should choose the men whose conduct they are to answer for, but as to a place in which nothing but court attendance is required, I see not why a king may not choose the person as one well powdered lord will suffice for it as well as another well powdered lord.[17]

However, George III's policies destroyed the coherence and undermined the assumptions of the Old Corps Whigs. Instead, in the 1760s, support in the House of Commons for the government rested on an uneasy combination of MPs whose primary loyalty was to the monarch, groups of active politicians after power, and independent MPs. The role of competing personal groups, operating without the semi-imperatives of fear and loyalty created by the Jacobite challenge and the response to it, helped to produce ministerial and parliamentary insecurity in the 1760s.

The existence and role of independent MPs reflected the limited nature of the party configuration in Parliament. Independents rarely took the initiative in matters of national politics, and generally gave their support to the Crown and the ministers who enjoyed the confidence of the monarch. They were, however, willing to withdraw support over particular issues, and this represented an important, but unpredictable, constraint on government policy. When ministerial defeats occurred in Parliament, they reflected not the strength of the opposition, but the loss, on specific issues, of the influential and numerous independents.

In the Lords, there had been considerable problems of management during Anne's reign (1702–14). Thereafter, the 'Party of the Crown', composed of archbishops, bishops, royal household officers, Scottish representative peers, and newly-created or promoted peers, provided a consistent basis for the ministerial majority. Patronage was applied in a consistent fashion, and the absence of issues as controversial as those of the succession, the Church and foreign policy had been during Anne's reign reduced tension. The smaller House of Lords was a less volatile body than the Commons and peers did not have constituents to consider. As a result, the government could have contentious legislation thrown out in the Lords, for example the Pension Bill in 1731. A decade later, the Place Bill was flung out there as the Walpole government thought opposition to it in the Commons unwise on the eve of an election.

'Management' of the world outside Westminster was more diffuse and less consistent than that of Parliament, or, looked at differently, was fundamentally a matter of responding to the parameters, which included a considerable amount of self-government by the localities. Conversely, extra-parliamentary political action was an aspect of a multi-faceted political world. In this, established institutions, such as town councils, could play a role, but new or developing aspects of politics were also important. These aspects included the greatly expanded role of the press, as well as the rising importance of lobby and interest groups. These groups reflected, though they were not limited by, urbanisation, professionalisation, and the broadening strata of the middling orders in society. Care was taken to keep these groups informed of political developments and to win their support. Petitions, meetings and print were all aspects of an interactive political world in which widespread interest and commitment were necessary and present.

This world was not equally open to all interests, let alone all social groups. For example, the interests of agriculture tended to lack the vocal advocates of trade. Thus, Walpole never received the political credit that he deserved for his pro-agrarian policies of the mid-1730s: both the attempt to shift the burden of taxation away from the land tax, and British neutrality in the War of the Polish Succession (1733–5), which permitted a boom in grain exports to Iberia and Italy. This was of major benefit to the economy, in terms of specie gained, as well as for the grain-producing areas, especially of East Anglia, which were depressed as a result of slack domestic demand caused by the stagnant demographic situation and of the low prices caused by good harvests. In contrast, the losses suffered when a few merchants, some of whom were smuggling, were seized by the Spaniards in the West Indies were minor, and yet it was these that received attention and became a political issue.

The impact of certain politicians on opinion outside the heart of politics played a major role not only in eliciting and channelling popular political views, but also, though more episodically, on the course of high politics. Thus, Pitt the Elder owed his importance in the political manoeuvres of 1765–6 in large part to the sense that he was crucial to governmental stability and popularity, although, in practice, he was, in many respects, inadequate to the new demands, in both politics and policy, of the 1760s.

The growth of the press was central to the development of public politics, and thus to the definition and expression of concepts of politics that owed nothing to individual and familial links or to deference. This discourse could be used by those excluded from a stake in conventional politics to claim a stake in national affairs. These ideas could also be used by politicians seeking to win public support or its appearance, and trying to derive benefits as a consequence.[18]

However, in arguing for the existence of an 'open society', it is not necessary to advance dubious suggestions that public opinion, however defined, explained policy. The press, and the amorphous pressures, interests and opinions understood by the term public opinion, were part of the political process. Propaganda was not simply the recourse of opposition groups, as governments adopted the medium of print to serve their purposes and used, to that end, the particular forms that were available, including the sponsored press. If the direct political influence of the press on decision making was limited, it was, nevertheless, of significance from the point of view of the creation of an 'open society' because it offered the possibility of a pluralism of opinion and of public debates that modern assessments of ideological coherence and homogeneity in this period leaves little room for.

Following the lapsing of the Licensing Act (requiring approval for publication) in 1695, the eighteenth century witnessed a massive expansion in total sales and in the number of titles, as well as the first daily, Sunday and provincial papers. The appearance of London dailies from 1702 marked the creation of a regular and responsive world of printed news, interacting with political events far more closely than was possible with pamphlets, books or even weekly newspapers. From the early 1770s, parliamentary reporting also came to play an accepted and regular role in the press, as the attempt to prevent it collapsed in the face of serious controversy. During the session, such reporting took up much of the non-advertising space in the press. Parliamentary reporting was a major aspect of the growing national focus of political culture. The press provided an increasingly national forum for the expression of political views.

The early provincial press was very important in distributing metropolitan news and news of foreign affairs. Most local newspapers consisted largely of material pirated from the London press. Thus, this 'provincial press' in its first flush was actually spreading metropolitan opinion, rather than reflecting local views. This played a major role in the development of national political campaigns, such as the Wilkesite movement, the county petitioning movements of the early 1780s for economical and parliamentary reform, and Lord George Gordon's Protestant Association. Newspaper reporting came to be seen as important in contested elections. Thus, in 1768, the leading Edinburgh paper, the *Caledonian Mercury*, carried a report about the Cromartyshire election that criticised the process by which William Pulteney had beaten Sir John Gordon. Pulteney felt obliged to reply, and the next issue carried his letter accordingly. It is significant that politicians competing for the support of a tiny electorate of fewer than twenty should have felt it important to create a favourable impression in the world of print.

The press was central to the process of politicisation, the strengthening, sustaining and widening, if not of a specific political consciousness, then at least of national political awareness. Politically, the crucial fact was that the Licensing Act was not reintroduced after it had lapsed in 1695. This created a context in which, rather than seeking to suppress opinion, political groups sought to foster favourable reporting. This was only within certain parameters that excluded Jacobitism, just as book publishing excluded blasphemy. Nevertheless, the marked level of criticism that was voiced, and that became more pronounced during the century, was such that opposition to government policy could be freely encouraged, a position that differed from most Continental states. The political controversies of 1695–1701 were largely conducted in pamphlets, but, from the early 1710s, newspapers played the leading role, although pamphlets remained crucial in ecclesiastical disputes. The regularity of newspapers made them different to pamphlets and other printed works, although the popularity of newspapers depended, in part, on the remainder of the culture of print: it familiarised the public with the idea that print was both attractive and authoritative.[19]

The culture of print also provided talking points. This was true of newspaper wars and also of caricatures. In February 1741, John Campbell MP sent his son from London 'the political print I mentioned', and another the following month. In 1762, Thomas, 1st Duke of Newcastle wrote to Hardwicke, 'I own I don't understand any of these prints and burlesques ... I detest the whole thing but they have their real consequences, and there is an amazing tameness in not daring to take any notice of them.'[20] Rising newspaper sales and advertisement revenues encouraged the launching of new titles. In 1775, 12.6 million newspaper stamps (showing that duty had been paid) were issued. This was far more than earlier in the century, but not the scale understood by 'mass' or 'popular' when applied to mid-Victorian politics. For the eighteenth century, it is more appropriate to employ the term 'public' politics, as that does not imply the massive numbers and politicisation of the bulk of the population implied by the terms mass and popular. A smaller scale of activity is not, however, the same as a lack of consequence.

When, in 1763, George Villiers, 4th Earl of Jersey wrote that 'political confusions have so engrossed the conversations of every living creature both in town and country',[21] he was referring to the impact of the Wilkesite controversy, but also asserting a central role for political consciousness that was questionable. Nevertheless, such assertions were frequent. In Delarivier Manley's novel *Secret History of Queen Zarah and the Zarazians* (1705), an attack on the 1st Duke and, in particular, Sarah, Duchess of Marlborough, there is no sense of government as a mystery:

> The youth of that country, encouraged by their parents' examples, aspire to be Privy Counsellors before they get rid of the rod of their schoolmasters; and apprentice boys assume the air of statesmen before they have learned the mystery of trade.

Mechanics of the meanest rank plead for a liberty to abuse their betters, and turn out ministers of state with the same freedom that they smoke tobacco. Carmen and cobblers over coffee draw up Articles of Peace and War, and make Partition Treaties at their will and pleasure; in a word, from the Prince to the peasant every one here enjoys his natural liberty.[22]

The press played a major role, as part of the world of print, in fostering and sustaining a political world very different to that of the calculations of borough patronage. For example, the press played a major role in the rise of petitioning. In part, as a result of the rise of extra-parliamentary associations, the presentation of petitions on national issues to Parliament rose considerably in the last quarter of the eighteenth century. In the boroughs, the number of signatories was greater than that of electors, a clear indication of the extent to which the 'political nation' was not limited to the electorate.[23] Instead, politics encompassed a considerable amount of activity by the more humble members of the community (although mostly men), and thus, to an extent, directed, expressed and contained their views.

Though the rising importance of the press deserves emphasis, it would be misleading to suggest that it was a precondition for public awareness of parliamentary, or other, politics. In addition, the notion of representation by MPs, and their responsiveness to constituents, was not dependent on this agency of public politics, though the growth of the press fostered it.

These notions had an electoral impact. It is possible, in many constituencies, to discern a return in the second half of the eighteenth century to levels of politicisation after a measure of mid-century hiatus. After a fall in the number of contested elections in England, from an average of 110 for 1722–34 and 55.4 in 1741–54 to 46 in 1761, the average for 1768–80 rose to 75.7.[24] Politicisation in England as a whole in the 1760s owed much to the Wilkesite controversy (see Chapter 13), which was especially important for the London region. This controversy can be seen as significant of a wider failure of the political system to incorporate new movements, although such a process was far from easy, and the most dynamic popular political world, London, had for long been volatile.

If such a failure of incorporation can be seen, and it would be wise not to exaggerate the severity of the situation, then it was bound up with a crisis in Whig identity and development. Whiggery had a number of strands. It was originally an opposition movement with new ideas, and that provided much of its vitality. However, its potency rested on royal favour – the replacement of James II by William III and, more securely, the accession of the Hanoverians. Office led to a reconfiguration of Whiggery that marginalised those unwilling to accept the disciplines of party and government. This was symbolised by the career of Thomas, 1st Duke of Newcastle, who was very much an establishment figure, and whose political career took place during long years of unbroken (although not unchallenged) Whig hegemony. He was never an MP and had little knowledge or understanding of the populist, let alone radical, dimensions to Whiggery. That cannot be presented as a simple measure of failure: such dimensions were neither expected of him, nor were they crucial to his falls, in 1756 and 1762. Yet, if most of his limitations derived from his personality, it can also be suggested that his problems reflected, in part, the narrowing of the Whig tradition during a period of growing change in British society and political culture.

In the 1770s and early 1780s, there were calls for substantial changes in the political system. The Society of the Supporters of the Bill of Rights, established in 1769 by a group of London radicals, including John Horne Tooke and John Sawbridge, supported not only Wilkes but also political reform, specifically shorter parliaments and a redistribution of seats. This programme was continued by the Constitutional Society established in London in 1771.

Fresh demands for reform led in 1779–80 to the establishment of the Yorkshire Association and the Society for Constitutional Information. The first served in 1780 as a model for the establishment of reforming associations elsewhere. Christopher Wyvill, a Yorkshire landowner, sought to create a co-ordinated movement. This led in 1780–1 to nationwide petitioning (60,000 signatures in 1780) and national conventions, but the divided movement achieved little.

The Society for Constitutional Information, established in London in April 1780 by a group of Rational Dissenters, including John Cartwright and Thomas Brand Hollis, printed a mass of material, much of it free, in favour of parliamentary reform; at least 88,000 copies of thirty-three different publications in 1780–3. The Society substantially supported the 1780 programme of the committee of the Westminster Association, including universal manhood suffrage, annual elections, the secret ballot and equal constituencies. Although without effect, this agenda was very different in content to the far more abbreviated public debate that had surrounded the 'Glorious Revolution'. The polarised and polarising nature of radical calls can be gauged from such titles as Cartwright's *The Legislative Rights of the Commonality Vindicated; or Take Your Choice! Representation and Respect/Imposition and Contempt. Annual Parliaments and Liberty/Long Parliaments and Slavery* (1776). The American and French Revolutions impacted on a society and political culture that was far from static.

NOTES

1. D. Hey, *The Fiery Blades of Hallamshire: Sheffield and Its Neighbourhood, 1660–1740* (Leicester, 1991).
2. D. Rollison, *The Local Origins of Modern Society, Gloucestershire 1500–1800* (1992).
3. V.L. Stater, *Noble Government: The Stuart Lord Lieutenancy and the Transformation of English Politics* (Athens, Georgia, 1994); J.R. Kent, 'The Centre and the Localities: State Formation and Parish Government in England circa 1640–1740', *Historical Journal*, 38 (1995), pp. 363–404.
4. See, for example, P. Gauci, *Politics and Society in Great Yarmouth 1660–1722* (Oxford, 1996).
5. For regions see C. Phythian-Adams (ed.), *Societies, Cultures and Kinship, 1580–1850. Cultural Provinces and English Local History* (Leicester, 1992); S. King, *Poverty and Welfare in England, 1700–1850. A Regional Perspective* (Manchester, 2000).
6. BL. Evelyn vol. 49 fols 25–6.

7. P.D.G. Thomas, 'The Monmouthshire Election of 1771', *Historical Research*, 72 (1999), pp. 44–57.
8. H. Wellenreuther, 'Activities of an estate agent in mid-eighteenth century England: Robert Butcher and the town of Bedford', *Bedfordshire Historical Miscellany: Essays in Honour of Patricia Bell* (Bedford, 1993), p. 170.
9. F. Grace, 'The Governance of Ipswich *c*.1550–1835', in D. Allen, *Ipswich Borough Archives 1255–1835. A Catalogue* (Woodbridge, 2000), xxxx–xl.
10. 'To the worthy and independent Freemen...', Preston, Lancashire Record Office DDPr 131/7.
11. B. Harris and J. Black, 'John Tucker, MP, and mid-eighteenth-century British politics', *Albion*, 29 (1997), pp. 15–38.
12. Chavigny to Chauvelin, French foreign minister, 17 July 1733, AE. CP. Angleterre 381 fol. 121.
13. R.M. Hatton, *George I. Elector and King* (1978).
14. *The Parliamentary Register*, vol. 6 (1782), p. 324.
15. C.I. McGrath, *The Making of the Eighteenth-Century Irish Constitution. Government, Parliament and the Revenue, 1692–1714* (Dublin, 2000), p. 288.
16. S. Taylor and C. Jones (eds), *Tory and Whig: the Parliamentary Papers of Edward Harley, Third Earl of Oxford, and William Hay, MP for Seaford, 1716–1753* (Woodbridge, 1998).
17. Elizabeth to Edward Montagu, 20 Nov. 1760, HL. MO. 2404.
18. K. Wilson, *The Sense of the People: Politics, Culture and Imperialism in England, 1715–1785* (Cambridge, 1995).
19. B. Harris, *Politics and the Rise of the Press. Britain and France, 1620–1800* (1996); J. Black, *The English Press 1621–1861* (Stroud 2001).
20. John to Pryse Campbell, 21 Feb., 28 Mar. 1741, Carmarthen CRO., Cawdor Muniments Box 138; Newcastle to Hardwicke, 30 Sept. 1762, BL. Add. 32942 fol. 429. On prints more generally, M. Duffy (ed.), *The English Satirical Print, 1600–1832* (7 vols., Cambridge, 1986) and D. Donald, *The Age of Caricature: Satirical Prints in the Reign of George III* (New Haven, 1996).
21. Jersey to Lady Spencer, 4 Sept. 1763, BL. Althorp mss. F 101.
22. D. Manley, *Secret History of Queen Zarah and the Zarazians* (1705), pp. 2–3.
23. J.E. Bradley, *Popular Politics and the American Revolution in England: Petitions, the Crown, and Public Opinion* (Macon, Georgia, 1986).
24. W.A. Speck, 'Northumberland elections in the eighteenth century', *Northern History*, 28 (1992), p. 164.

13

Politics

The creation of the modern political system, first parliamentary government and then democratisation, has for long seemed to be the major theme in British history. Due to the Whig myth of history, and the concept of political Darwinism (that the most appropriate wins out), this process was automatically associated with progress. The period 1688–1783 could be readily understood in such a schema. It was the period between the establishment of parliamentary government thanks to the 'Glorious Revolution' and the nineteenth-century moves towards (male) democratisation, beginning with the First Reform Act of 1832.

This analysis was linked with a shift in sympathies: the aristocrats who acquired praise by defying James II were replaced by descendants who could be stigmatised for benefiting from stagnation, if not corruption, and for resisting reform. The place of opinion 'out of doors', outside the world of Court and Parliament, was apparently similarly clear. Its development indicated the limits of the representative system, and, in turn, helped eventually to secure its failure.

Such an analysis was an aspect of the important role of history as public myth, but has grave limitations. It is mistaken to treat a struggle for change in the political system as the central political issue. Those active in politics, both in and outside the élite, chose generally to work within the system. There was no revolutionary consciousness in a modern sense. Indeed, in 1685–1746, radicalism could be found almost exclusively not with proto-democrats, but with those who sought to change the monarch: the Duke of Monmouth in 1685, William III in 1688–9, and the Jacobites thereafter.

All turning points invite qualification and the search for continuities. Nevertheless, eighteenth-century Britain really began in 1688. The 'Glorious Revolution' of that year led to constitutional change, set a new political agenda, and transformed the relationship between the parts of the British Isles. It was to be the central point of reference in subsequent discussion of the political system, and played a crucial role in the public ideology of the state for over a century.

The events of 1688–9 have to be understood not only in terms of their future significance, but also as a consequence of the divisions, tensions and fears of seventeenth-century British politics, especially those of the 1670s and 1680s.[1] In 1688, the last male Stuart ruler of Britain, James II of England, Wales and Ireland and VII of Scotland (1685–8), was driven from power by his son-in-law and nephew William III of Orange. This, the last successful political coup d'état or revolution in British history until the Irish revolution of 1916–21, reflected hostility to the policies and Catholic faith of James. There was a long-standing suspicion that the Catholics would try to seize power by conspiratorial means and this had led to a protracted crisis in 1678–81 – the Popish Plot followed by the Exclusion Crisis – during the reign of James' elder and more cautious brother, Charles II (1660–85). This polarised politics, but, from 1681, Charles regained control helped by a measure of public support,[2] and James was able to succeed to the throne without difficulty. His position was then challenged by James, Duke of Monmouth, an illegitimate son of Charles II, but his rebellion was swiftly defeated.

Victory gave James conviction of divine approval, and the rebellion led him to increase his army. Parliament was unhappy with this, especially with the appointment of Catholic officers. James prorogued Parliament in November 1685 and moved towards the catholicising of the government. The changes necessary to establish full religious and civil equality for Catholics entailed a destruction of the privileges of the Church of England and a challenge to assumptions about the place of the Church. The changes also entailed a policy of appointing Catholics, the insistent use of royal prerogative action, and preparations for a packed Parliament.

Unlike with James's father, Charles I, in 1638–42, there was no violent response. The Stuart monarchy was now strong enough to survive domestic challenges. James's basis of support was narrow. The political culture of the period assumed deference in return for good kingship, expectations of political behaviour that involved a measure of implicit contractualism, although a theory of that type was anathema to royalists and, even, most whigs. James spurned these boundaries, but there was no clear and prudent political course for those who were disenchanted, and no institutional expression of national discontent that could instigate a change in policy and recreate the consensus between crown and social elite that was the hallmark of early-modern government.[3]

The birth of a Prince of Wales on 10 June 1688 to James's second and Catholic wife, Mary of Modena, changed the situation. Hitherto, his heirs had been Mary and Anne, Protestant daughters from his first marriage. Mary, the elder, was married to William III of Orange, the leading Dutch political figure, a Protestant, and the most active opponent of Louis XIV of France, the most dynamic and threatening Catholic ruler. A Catholic son threatened to make James's changes permanent. Seven politicians invited William to intervene in order to protect Protestantism and traditional liberties. Motivated by a desire to keep Britain out of Louis' camp, William had already decided to invade.[4]

William's first invasion attempt – in mid-October 1688 – was defeated by storms at sea, but, on his second attempt, he faced an unopposed passage. Landing at Brixham in Devon on 5 November 1688, William benefited from a collapse of will on the part of James, who had the larger army. James was hit by indecision, ill-health, and dissension and conspiracy among his officers. His position was also affected by a number of provincial uprisings, although, alongside towns seized for William, such as Derby, Durham, Hull, Nottingham and York, were others, such as Carlisle, Chester and Newcastle, that successfully resisted. The Lord Lieutenants had largely abandoned James.

As James's resolve failed, the morale of his army disintegrated, and a vacuum of power developed. William refused to stop his advance to permit negotiations. Most people did not want any breach in the hereditary succession, and William had initially pretended that he had no designs on the Crown. On 28 December 1688, he accepted the government of the kingdom from an irregular assembly of peers and former MPs summoned by him on the 26th. However, as the situation developed favourably, especially when James had been driven into exile, William made it clear that he sought the throne. His seizure of power was accepted, by the Convention he called, in the Bill of Rights of 12 February 1689 which declared the throne vacant and invited William and Mary to occupy it as joint monarchs; William was not willing to concede that his wife should rule alone. It was possible to minimise the element of innovation by claiming that it was only a vacancy that was being filled; rather than endorsing the more radical notion that James had been deposed. However, all Catholics were debarred from the succession, ending the rights of James's infant son. The Bill of Rights dealt the divine right theory of monarchy a fatal blow by obliging rulers to adhere to their subjects' religion.[5] Anne's rights in the succession were subordinated to those of William.

There were also restrictions on royal power. The financial settlement left William with an ordinary revenue that was too small for his peacetime needs, obliging him to turn to Parliament for support. A standing army was prohibited unless permitted by Parliament. The Revolution Settlement was to be seen subsequently as a decisive break with autocratic practices. In a speech of 1710 supporting the impeachment of the Tory High-Churchman Henry Sacheverell, Robert Walpole declared

> The doctrine of unlimited, unconditional passive obedience [to a monarch] was first invented to support arbitrary and despotic power ... What then can be the designs of preaching this doctrine now, unasked, unsought for, in Her Majesty's reign, where the law is the only rule and measure of the power of the Crown, and of the obedience of the people.[6]

In Scotland, James's position collapsed in December 1688. The Convention of the Estates which met in Edinburgh the following March was dominated by supporters of William, and on 4 April 1689 the Crown of Scotland was declared forfeit, William and Mary being proclaimed joint sovereigns a week later. Catholics were excluded from the Scottish throne and from public office. The contractual nature of the Revolution Settlement, the extent to which the Crown had been obtained by William and Mary on conditions, was far more apparent in Scotland than in England. The offer of the crown to William and Mary was made conditional on their acceptance of the Claim of Right issued by the Scottish Convention which stated that James VII had forfeited the crown by his policies and that no Catholic could become ruler of Scotland or hold public office. The degree of radicalism in the Scottish constitutional settlement reflected different political circumstances to those in England. These included the far greater impact of William III's wishes in England.

James II and VII was determined to regain his thrones and the 'Glorious Revolution' launched Jacobitism, as the cause of the exiled Stuarts came to be known from the Latin for James, Jacobus. Initially, James controlled most of Ireland and had support in Scotland. This situation looked back to the last period of Stuart dispossession, the English Civil Wars and Interregnum (1642–60), although that had ended with the 'Restoration' of Stuart monarchy in the shape of Charles II.

James's standard was raised in Scotland in April 1689 by John Graham of Claverhouse, who was backed by the Episcopalians, the supporters of a Scottish Church controlled, like that of England, by bishops. At the battle of Killiecrankie on 27 July, Claverhouse's Highlanders routed their opponents, but their leader was killed and the cause collapsed under his mediocre successors. Most of the Highland chiefs swore allegiance to William in late 1691.

James's supporters dominated most of Ireland in 1689, though Derry, fearing Catholic massacre, resisted a siege and was relieved by the English fleet. In 1690–1, Ireland was conquered, the crucial battle being William's victory at the Boyne on 1 July 1690, which was followed by the capture of Dublin. After victory at Aughrim on 12 July 1691, Galway fell on 21 July and Sligo on 14 September and Limerick was besieged. The Jacobites surrendered with the Treaty of Limerick on 3 October, many, known as the 'Wild Geese', going to serve James in France.

Ireland was then subjected to an Anglican ascendancy. The Catholics held 22 per cent of the land in 1688 but only 14 per cent of the land in 1703 and 5 in 1778. Catholics were prevented from freely acquiring or bequeathing land or property and were disfranchised and debarred from all political, military and legal offices, and from Parliament. The culture of power in Ireland became thoroughly and often aggressively Protestant, so that, even when in 1749 the Dublin election was contested by Protestant zealots, the charges of popery and Jacobitism appeared the most effective that could be used against rivals.

The 'Glorious Revolution' led to English domination of the British Isles, albeit domination that was helped by and shared with important sections of the Irish and Scottish population, Irish Anglicans and, more significantly, Scottish Presbyterians. The alternative had been glimpsed in 1689 when James II's Parliament in Dublin had rejected much of the authority of the Westminster Parliament. This path, however, had been blocked.

Jacobitism, and the strategic threat to England posed by an autonomous or independent Scotland and Ireland, pushed together those politicians in the three kingdoms who were in favour of the Revolution Settlement. Indeed the Union of 1707 between England and Scotland arose essentially from English concern about the possible hazards posed by an autonomous, if not independent, Scotland when Anne eventually died. There was some support for the measure in Scotland, though its passage through the Scottish Parliament in 1706 ultimately depended on successful political management, corruption, self-interest, and determination not to be shut out from the English and colonial market. The Scottish economy was in a poor state, and this had been emphasised by the failure of the Darien Scheme to establish a Scottish commercial entrepot near Panama. Conversely, the strengthening pull of the London market had a growing effect on the Scottish economy. The civil war of 1689–91 had underlined the divisions in Scottish society and indicated the difficulty of independence from England. The powerful leadership of the Presbyterian Church accepted the union as a political necessity. There was no good Protestant alternative: the refusal of the exiled Stuarts to convert to Protestantism lessened Scottish options.[7]

This was to be an incorporating, not a confederal, union. In 1708, the new Parliament of Great Britain abolished the Scottish Privy Council, the principal executive agency for Scotland, and thus ensured that there would be one British Privy Council sitting in London. The governmental implications for England were less important, because it was the more populous and wealthier of the two states and dominated the new British political system. However, Union was crucial to the political geography of Britain over the following century. An independent or autonomous Scotland would have provided the French with opportunities for intervention. The prospect of Franco-Scottish alliance had been a threat for centuries and its removal was crucial to the geopolitics of the British state. Furthermore, Scotland now contributed powerfully to the resources of this state. Without Scottish troops, the British army would have been less successful. Thus, the Union had a compound effect on the growth of British power.

There was also some support in Ireland for Union with England. Union had been considered by English ministers in 1697 and the Irish Parliament petitioned for it in 1703. Union, however, had little to offer to English politicians, and Ireland was treated with scant consideration. The Westminster Parliament's Declaratory Act of 1720 stated its supremacy over that of Dublin. Protectionist legislation in Westminster hindered Irish exports, while the granting of Irish lands and pensions to favoured courtiers accentuated the problem of absentee landowners and revenue-holders, with a consequent loss of money to the country.

A sense of exploitation was exacerbated by particular steps. In 1722, a Wolverhampton ironmaster, William Wood, purchased a patent to mint copper coins for Ireland, a step that led to bitter complaints; constitutional and political weakness were seen as leading to economic problems. As a result of the agitation, Walpole's government was obliged to cancel the patent in 1725. Walpole was lacerated for his treatment of Ireland by Jonathan Swift in his *Drapier's Letters*.

Thereafter, greater care was taken of Irish sensitivities, but the relationship with England was still far from equal. The Irish Parliament had to pay the cost of quartering a large part of the army in Ireland to support the Anglo-Irish establishment and hide the size of the army from English public opinion. Long-standing politico-religious grievances were to help exacerbate Irish disaffection in the 1790s. England might dominate the British Isles from 1691, but a sense of separate identity and national privileges continued to be important in Ireland and Scotland, though not Wales. This sense of separation was accentuated at the ecclesiastical level, as in 1689 the Scottish Parliament abolished Episcopacy and in 1690 a Presbyterian Church was established there. As a result, the Union of 1707 led to the creation of a multi-confessional state. Scotland also had a distinctive legal system.

Ireland retained its Parliament until the Act of Union of 1800, and the need to manage this Parliament obliged London politicians to devise strategies including winning over Irish 'undertakers', the key politicians in the Dublin Parliament. Issues as much as patronage were at stake. The preservation of a Parliament in Dublin enabled Ireland's Protestant politicians to retain a measure of importance and independence.[8] However, when in 1755, William, Marquess of Hartington, the Lord Lieutenant of Ireland, wrote 'This country is divided into two parties both party near equal, each struggling for the superiority,'[9] he was referring to factionalism within the political elite rather than to any really widespread political alignments.

Although possibly over 80, or even 90 per cent of its population used Welsh as the medium of communication, Wales lacked centralising institutions, or distinctive social, ecclesiastical and legal arrangements. In part because resistance to the 'Glorious Revolution' was perfunctory (unlike in Ireland or Scotland), there was no attempt to transform Welsh politics and society. The Catholic William, 1st Marquess of Powis fled into exile with James, and his estates were granted to Dutch followers of William who were made Duke of Portland and Earl of Rochford, but the estates were restored to the 2nd Marquess in 1722. The suppression of the Council of Wales and the Marches in 1689 was scarcely comparable to developments in Scotland and Ireland, and did not lead to any sense of loss. This was important to the stability of Wales over the following century, a stability that was only to be disrupted subsequently by the pressures of industrialisation and social change.

Welsh, Irish and Scots sought to benefit from links with England. Scots came to play a major role in the expansion of empire, not least through service in war. This process had begun in the seventeenth century, especially under William III. On the eve of the parliamentary union, Scots held 10 per cent of the regimental colonelcies in the British army, and between 1714 and 1763 this increased to 20 per cent.

Protestantism, war with France and the benefits of empire, it has been argued,[10] helped to create a British nationhood, which developed alongside the still strong senses of English, Scottish and Irish identity. It is, however, difficult to determine the extent of the sense of British nationhood: it is not easy to demonstrate the everyday attitudes of the majority of the population. While this is always true, it is of particular importance when a new development is under consideration. Although 'Britain' preceded 1707, not least as a result of the Union of the English and Scottish Crowns in 1603, British nationhood was imposed by legislation and it is unclear what it meant, and how important it was, for many.

The principal political threats to the Protestant succession and the Whig system was seen as coming from Jacobitism until mid-century, and from France. James II was succeeded in 1701 by 'James III', and, although his attempt to invade Scotland with French support in 1708 failed, his claim was a threat to the Hanoverian succession. Mary became joint monarch with William and acted as regent in his absence, although he wielded real power. She died, childless, of smallpox, and William did not remarry. The childless William III (1689–1702) was succeeded by his sister-in-law Anne (1702–14), but none of her many children succeeded to adulthood. Under the Act of Settlement of 1701, she was to be succeeded by the German house of Hanover, Protestant (Lutheran not Anglican) descendants of Elizabeth, daughter of James I of England and VI of Scotland.

The succession played a major role in the complex politics of the reigns of William III and Anne. It was related to such divisive issues as church government, religious toleration, foreign policy and military strategy. Political groupings had developed during the Exclusion Crisis, although they remained in a state of flux in which circumstances played a major role. The opponents of Charles II were known as Whigs, an abusive term referring to Scottish Presbyterian rebels, originally used by their opponents, the Tories, initially another abusive term referring to Irish Catholic brigands. In fact, Tory perceptions of the nature of authority drew on Anglican tradition, especially with reference to support for legally constituted authority.

In William's reign, a Tory–Whig polarity was confused by a Country–Court opposition. However, in the late 1690s the Country Whigs were largely absorbed by the Tories, so that a Whig-Tory division was central to Anne's reign. Toryism found it difficult to cope with the consequences of the Revolution Settlement. Some Tories were prepared to accept that the legally constituted authority was now that of William III, but others sought his overthrow. This tension in Toryism remained strong until the collapse of Jacobitism in 1746, but did not prevent the development of a Tory parliamentary politics opposed to the Whigs.

The 1690s saw increased party organisation in part because of more elections and of parliamentary sessions becoming more frequent, and in part because royal attempts to govern without relying on an individual party were abandoned. William tried to do so, but from late 1693 he came to rely increasingly on the Whigs, and, by the following summer, a largely Whig government was in power. By the late 1690s, the leading Whig ministers, the so-called Junto, held frequent meetings in order to maintain party consistency in government. This was a limitation on the king's freedom of manoeuvre.

The extent to which William was able to impose his views indicated his political importance as the arbitrator of court factionalism and the ministerial struggle for influence.[11] This role was not really compromised by the emergence of political parties, because they lacked the structure and ethos necessary to provide clear leadership and agreed policy. The continued role of the monarch as arbitrator was demonstrated by Anne's importance in the struggle for primacy within the Tory ministry between Bolingbroke and Harley in 1714.

In hindsight, the 'Glorious Revolution' was frequently seen as essentially conservative, especially in comparison with the social disruption of the Civil Wars, and because it eventually led to a government by the Old Corps Whigs who were to be criticised by radical politicians. However, it really was a revolution, especially to Tories and High Churchmen. Parallels between Cromwell and William III were made, and the breach in the succession and the strains of the Nine Years' War with France (1689–97) provided occasion and cause for bitter debate about the role of Providence.[12] The 'Glorious Revolution' led to a crisis over the nature of authority in Church and State.

Furthermore, William lacked the freedom given James by peace. Between 1691 and 1697, the army and the navy each cost an annual average of £2.5 million. War also hit trade, making it more difficult to finance huge external remittances. This led to expedients, such as the clipping of the coinage, and to financial crises,[13] particularly in 1694 and 1696. William was a poor communicator and an indifferent manager of domestic politics, whose conduct of the war led to serious criticism, which escalated in response to his post-war diplomacy. The costs of the war forced a parliamentary monarchy on William. Elections became more frequent. The Triennial Act of 1694 ensured regular meetings of the Westminster Parliament and, by limiting their life-span to a maximum of three years, required regular elections. There were ten elections between 1695 and 1715, and this helped to encourage a sense of volatility.[14] The Triennial Act limited the royal power to dissolve Parliament.

The war also led to a reorganisation of public finances that introduced principles of openness and parliamentary responsibility. The funded national debt, based on the Bank of England, which was founded in 1694, was guaranteed by Parliament. In a political situation in which conventions of behaviour were slowly adapting to the consequences of annual parliamentary sessions, and thus to an enhanced role for parliamentary leadership and management, William, however, continued not only to follow his own views, but also to underrate the importance of political management. The consequent political crisis was encapsulated in the title of the Act of Settlement, 'an Act for further limitation of the Crown and for better securing the rights and liberties of the subject' (1701).

William's lack of interest in Parliament's views had led to bitter political divisions that weakened his international position. This was especially true of the size of the army, an issue that had been politically charged for decades. Critics were concerned not so much about foreign policy as about the possible consequences of a large army for domestic politics. On 2 December 1697, at the opening of the session, William told Parliament that the maintenance of a standing force was essential. Nine days later, the Commons decided to disband all land forces that had been raised since 1680. As a result, the English establishment was cut to 10,000 men. A year later, the Commons decided to reduce the English establishment to 7,000 and its Irish counterpart to 12,000, and to restrict it to native troops, thus ensuring that Dutch regiments would have to return to the United Provinces, a blow to William which he tried without success to reverse. In contrast, the Dutch army was kept at 45,500. There was little doubt where William's views

were more influential. Furthermore, in another sign of parliamentary assertiveness, in 1701 the leading Whig ministers were impeached for their alleged
responsibility in signing the Partition Treaties with France.

These attacks produced a greater degree of accommodation on the part of the
Crown, as relations with France deteriorated in 1701–2. On 18 March 1701,
William sent Parliament a report on the negotiations at The Hague, giving as his
reason his 'gracious intention to acquaint you, from time to time, with the state
and progress of those negotiations'. He knew he needed parliamentary support,
not least for the expansion of the army. In 1702, the declaration of war was made
by royal authority, but in response to the addresses and resolutions of both
Houses of Parliament, a pattern in some respects matching that of the constitutional settlement of the Crown in 1689.

There had been and continued to be the working out of a process of consultation and review whereby the monarch retained the initiative over foreign and
military policy. Parliament could debate and fund proposals and investigate
outcomes, but it did not make policy. The somewhat uncertain use of royal authority under William III gave way to a more managed approach under Anne and
George I. The role of the monarch had also become more defined. For example,
whereas in 1689 the independence of the judiciary was in practice established,
under the Act of Settlement judges became only removable after Parliament had
played a role.

Anne (1702–14) has been re-evaluated as an able and independent monarch,
less dependent on her courtiers than has been hitherto believed.[15] As she had no
domestic programme of change, she was a relatively uncontroversial figure, and
indeed political criticism in her reign was centred on ministers, not monarch. Anne
followed William III in sustaining the Grand Alliance created to fight Louis.
Amidst an atmosphere of distrust caused by Louis XIV's acceptance in 1700 of
the will of the last Habsburg king of Spain, which left his dominions to Louis' second grandson, attempts to settle Anglo-French differences, which included in 1701
Louis' recognition of James II's son as King of England, broke down.

In the War of the Spanish Succession, in which Britain was involved between
1702 and 1713, troops under John Churchill, from 1704 1st Duke of Marlborough,
drove the French from Germany and the Low Countries, but other forces were
less successful in Spain. Marlborough won major victories at Blenheim (1704),
Ramillies (1706) and Oudenaarde (1708), but was less successful at Malplaquet
(1709). Under Marlborough, the British army reached a peak of success that it
was not to repeat in Europe for another century. He handled his artillery well,
made his cavalry act like a shock force, and was particularly successful in coor-
dinating the deployment and use of infantry, cavalry and artillery on the battlefield, and in integrating operations across an extended front. Marlborough was
also skilful in holding the anti-French coalition together. He and his close ally
Sidney Godolphin, the Lord Treasurer, were moderate Tories who were disenchanted with much of the Tory party and allied with the Whigs to dominate politics, although Marlborough and Godolphin found it increasingly difficult to
restrain Whig efforts to increase their power.

Like William at the end of the Nine Years' War, Anne realised that a compromise peace would have to be negotiated. Her sense in 1709–10 that the war was unpopular and that the vital war goals had already been obtained played a major role in weakening the Whig ministry, which wanted to fight on. In addition, at court the Marlborough interest was under challenge, not least because Anne had wearied of her favourite, Sarah, Duchess of Marlborough. Now without the support of the Crown, the Whigs did badly in the 1710 election.

Conversely, Anne supported their Tory successors – Robert Harley, soon to be Earl of Oxford, and Henry St John, soon to be Viscount Bolingbroke – in their contentious task of negotiating peace and was willing to create Tory peers in order to ensure that the peace preliminaries passed the Lords. The Peace of Utrecht of 1713 brought French recognition of a failure to dominate Europe and of the Protestant Succession in Britain. Wartime gains – Gibraltar, Minorca and Nova Scotia – were formally ceded to Britain, and she also gained the right to a (controlled) trade with the Spanish New World.

In office, the Tories had turned on the Whigs and their supporters, legislating against the Dissenters, with the Occasional Conformity Act of 1711 and the Schism Act of 1714. There was also a general attack on the financial administration of the Godolphin ministry in the 1700s. The Tory Commission of Public Accounts was partisan, but their findings were not necessarily untrue. What they said about Marlborough's corruption was accurate. One of the most active younger Whigs, Robert Walpole, a Norfolk gentleman landowner, was accused of receiving bribes whilst making forage contracts for the army in Scotland in 1709–10, and in 1712 was expelled from the Commons and committed to the Tower, a sign of the acute partisanship of politics.

The peaceful accession of George I in 1714 was a major disappointment for 'James III'. The threat of a Jacobite rebellion had been taken seriously, but, largely as a result of inadequate Jacobite preparations and a refusal of several possible backers to provide support, this potential danger was avoided in 1714. The consequences were not totally unhelpful for the Jacobites, for George's support for the Whigs, who did well in the 1715 general election, alienated the Tories and helped to revive Jacobitism. George distrusted the Tories, whom he regarded as sympathetic to Jacobitism, although he saw the danger of being a prisoner of a Whig ministry. However, it was difficult to operate a mixed Whig-Tory ministry. George's replacement of Anne's Tory ministers by a Whig ascendancy left the Tories no option in government service. George I had told his first Privy Council that he wished for the repeal of the Occasional Conformity and Schism Acts. In 1715, Walpole was appointed chairman of the Committee of Secrecy established to punish those who had plotted to restore 'James III'. Walpole drew up the resulting report and was responsible for the impeachment of Bolingbroke and other leading Tories.

Party politics and ministerial instability since 1688 had revealed the grave limitations of the 'Glorious Revolution'. A parliamentary monarchy could not simply be legislated into existence. It required the development of conventions and patterns of political behaviour that would permit a constructive resolution of contrary opinions within a system where there was no single source of dominant power. The slowness of the development of these patterns was particularly serious as Britain was at war for much of the period and Jacobitism was a significant force. The Revolution Settlement had created the constitutional basis for an effective parliamentary monarchy, with parliamentary control over the finances of the state – the aim of many of the critics of Charles II – but the instability of the ministries of the period suggests that the political environment within which such a monarchy could be effective had not been created.

Jacobite plans led to the '15: risings in Scotland and northern England in the autumn of 1715 that were defeated. This lent fresh energy to the purge of Tories. They were excluded from senior posts in government, the armed forces, the judiciary and the Church. In 1719, there was an unsuccessful pro-Jacobite Spanish invasion of Scotland. Three years later, the Atterbury Plot, a plan to seize London, was blocked by prompt government action, including the creation of a large army camp in Hyde Park.

Having defeated the Tories, the Whigs divided. Hanover's close involvement in the Great Northern War of 1700–21, at this stage a struggle to partition Charles XII of Sweden's Baltic empire, meant that George I expected commitment to Hanoverian interests from his British ministers and treated differences of opinion over foreign policy as tests of loyalty. Matters were made worse by tensions between George I and his son, George, Prince of Wales, later George II, and among the Whig elite and by the relationship between the two. Whig unity had ebbed as soon as the dangers posed by Toryism and Jacobitism had receded.

The ministry split openly in the spring of 1717 with Walpole, then First Lord of the Treasury, and his brother-in-law Charles, Viscount Townshend opposing George's anti-Swedish policy which was supported by Charles, 3rd Earl of Sunderland and James Stanhope, the two Secretaries of State. This helped drive George further into the arms of Stanhope and Sunderland. Townshend was dismissed, Walpole resigned and the two men tried co-operating with the Tories in order to thwart the ministry. This helped block ministerial plans to introduce legislation favourable to the Dissenters in the 1718 session. Walpole's co-operation with the Tories helped shape the contours of the subsequent decades. At the same time, it raised the always fluid and uncertain confluence of principled stands with the political tactics of the moment and threw light on the difficulties confronting opposition. Indeed, the political crisis of 1718 foreshadowed the developments of the subsequent quarter-century, the 'Age of Walpole'. A lasting alliance between the Tories and opposition Whigs was impossible due to differences over foreign policy and ecclesiastical issues. In foreign policy, most Whigs sought to limit the personal role and Hanoverian aspirations of George I and George II. However, they were more willing than the Tories to comply with the monarch's wishes than the Tories. The latter, who harped incessantly on the theme of British resources being used to help Hanover, specifically to make territorial gains, were distrusted by the monarch. Walpole's failure to use the Tories to force himself back into office in 1718 prefigured the later failure against him as first minister of the more famous 'Patriot' platform of Viscount Bolingbroke and William Pulteney, which was as unoriginal as it was unsuccessful. Forced to oppose foreign policy, and thus to anger the king, the opposition Whigs of the late 1720s and 1730s reaped only failure from their Tory alliance.

Walpole's success in influencing governmental legislative policy in 1718 did not take him into office, but it did challenge the cohesion and confidence of the ministry. Walpole made it clear that a Whig government could not necessarily expect, still less command, the support of Whig parliamentarians, a lesson that his own years in office were to show that he had learned well. His years in opposition showed that Walpole's political skills were not simply dependent on his deployment of the fruits of patronage. He was also an effective parliamentarian – as speaker, leader, organiser and tactician.

In 1720, Walpole returned to office. He benefited from tension between George I's German confidants, and Stanhope and Sunderland, and from a reconciliation between George I and the Prince of Wales, which he helped broker. Breaking with the Tories, Walpole began to steer government business through the Commons.

He was helped by the bursting of the South Sea Bubble and the subsequent political fall-out. The rise in the shares of this finance company had been seen as a way to private wealth and public stability: it was presented as a way to help pay off the national debt. The collapse of the Company's stock in September 1720 ruined the finances and hopes of many, and led to accusations of fraud against the directors and the ministers close to them. Some of the latter had indeed been rewarded with large amounts of stock, and several had been implicated in the very dubious financial practices of the directors. As Bank of England and East India Company stock also fell heavily, there was a danger of a widespread financial collapse.

Walpole played a central role in producing a plan involving the rescheduling of the inflated debts of the Company and a writing down of its capital. There were many losers, but fewer and far less than had seemed likely prior to Walpole's restructuring. He helped restore confidence both in the financial system, and in the government's financial activity, probity and prospects.

Although criticised for defending ministerial colleagues implicated in the Company, Walpole benefited from their problems. In April 1721, he became First Lord of the Treasury, while Townshend became a Secretary of State. Walpole faced problems aplenty, not least Sunderland's continued role at Court, but was now as clearly the dominant figure in the ministry as he had been in the Commons since his return to office in 1720.

The 1720s and 1730s were bleak years for the Stuart cause. The venal, but able, Walpole followed policies that were less aggressive and objectionable to the Tories than the Stanhope–Sunderland ministry of 1717–20. He was also more adroit. Walpole resisted opponents outside government and supplanted rivals within until his fall and retirement in 1742. Once in office, Walpole swiftly rose to dominate politics. The parliamentary opposition had negotiated with Sunderland in 1721 as he sought to outmanoeuvre Walpole. The failure of these negotiations led in the autumn of 1721 to a regrouping by the opposition which produced an alliance between the Tories and a group of dissident Whigs led by Earl Cowper and the Duke of Wharton. In November 1721, this group began a bitter parliamentary assault on the ministry. There was little hope that the government could be defeated in Parliament, but the opposition hoped to discredit it in the eyes of the electorate. Thanks largely to Walpole's skill in presenting the ministerial case in the Commons and in managing government patronage, the opposition failed.

Within government, a struggle between Walpole and Sunderland for dominance that involved ministerial patronage ended when Sunderland suddenly died of pleurisy on 19 April 1722; Stanhope had suddenly died the previous year. Their former adherents were removed from office, although the process took several years. Walpole was invaluable to George I (1714–27) and George II (1727–60) as government manager and principal spokesman in the House of Commons and as a skilful manager of the state's finances. He also played a key role in the successful elections of 1722, 1727 and 1734. Aside from his policies, Walpole was adept in parliamentary management and in his control of government patronage. He helped to provide valuable continuity and experience to the combination of limited monarchy with parliamentary sovereignty. In the first session after the 1722 general election, Walpole displayed his mastery of the Commons. On 26 October 1722, there was a majority of 71 on a motion to increase the size of the army. The following August, Walpole congratulated himself on the flourishing condition of public credit and of having accurately predicted to George I the price of stocks, adding, 'I think it is plain we shall have the whole supply of next year at 3 per cent ... and I flatter myself that the next session of Parliament will bring no discredit to those that have the honour to serve the king in his revenue'.[16]

The failure to appoint William Pulteney Secretary of State led him to go into opposition in 1725, creating an articulate and active opposition Whig group. Walpole, however, still enjoyed substantial majorities in Commons divisions: 262 to 89 against an opposition motion of 9 February 1726 for an inquiry into the national debt, and 251 to 85 on the Address on 17 January 1727.

Aware of opposition within the ministry, Walpole was conscious of the need to maintain royal support. His relations with George, Prince of Wales was not particularly good, and it was expected that the Prince's Treasurer, Spencer Compton, Speaker of the Commons, would replace Walpole. However the accession of a new monarch meant that Parliament had to be summoned, the Civil List (annual grant paid to the Crown by Parliament) settled, and elections held for a new Parliament. With his proven track record as a parliamentary manager, Walpole was needed for these purposes, and he also benefited from the support of Queen Caroline. Walpole secured an enlarged Civil List from Parliament, and made full use of government interests to increase the government majority in the Commons.

Opposition attacks on the consequences of the French alliance cut government majorities in 1729 and 1730, with a degree of Tory-opposition Whig co-operation that posed a real threat in the session of 1730. The same year, poor relations between Walpole and Townshend, again mostly over foreign policy, were resolved when Townshend resigned. The crisis ended with Walpole's position strengthened in the ministry. He was given an opportunity to dominate policy. The settlement of differences with Austria in 1731 helped lead to a fall in taxes. The land tax fell to one shilling in the pound in 1732 and 1733. Parliamentary majorities varied in 1731 and 1732, but were generally comfortable. Ironically, the situation deteriorated sharply in 1733 over what Walpole had not seen as likely to cause a major political storm, a proposal to extend the excise (see Chapter 11). The critical Master of the Rolls, Sir Joseph Jekyll, 'said he was sorry a Whig ministry would bring in a Bill, a Tory ministry never durst attempt'.[17] Walpole had not learned the lesson of the malt tax disturbances in Scotland in 1725. On 10 April 1733, the government majority fell to 17. This was against an opposition motion to hear by counsel a petition from the City of London critical of the Excise Scheme. The petition was a testimony to the Scheme's unpopularity and to the opposition's skill in orchestrating a public campaign of criticism. The belief that the unpopularity of the Bill affected the views of MPs is an interesting comment on contemporary assumptions about how the political system worked. On 6 February 1733, Henry Goodricke wrote from London: 'The rising tempest of an excise makes a furious roar in this town ... people have taken a general and violent prejudice to Sir Robert's proposal even before they know what it is; and elections being so near at hand many members will be cautious how they vote full against the bent of their electors'.[18] By withdrawing the Bill on 11 April, Walpole survived the crisis. His majority rose at once.

More immediately, Walpole was protected by his supporters from the brawling crowd in the lobby which tried to attack him. George II's backing was crucial to ending the crisis. A number of prominent Whig peers, the Dukes of Bolton and Montrose, the Earls of Marchmont and Stair, and Viscount Cobham, were dismissed for voting with the opposition in the Lords. The dismissals were a public show of royal support, but they helped lose Walpole the backing of the clients and allies of the dismissed who sat in the Commons. Walpole's majority fell significantly in the 1734 general election, but the majority was still sufficient to enable him to govern easily.

The Walpolean system had its defeats, but it lasted until 1742, the longest period of stable one-party rule in a system of regular parliamentary scrutiny in Britain. By keeping Britain at peace for most of the period, Walpole denied the Jacobites foreign support. Walpole was corrupt and his ministry was a Whig monopoly of power, but he caused offence principally to those who took a close interest in politics, rather than to the wider political nation, whose position was eased by his generally successful determination to reduce taxation. Walpole actively promoted the relaxation of tension, and his ministry did witness a gradual lessening of political and religious tension that is readily apparent in comparison with the situation over the previous century.

The Walpolean system broke down in his last years as minister. Anglo-Spanish relations collapsed over vigorous Spanish policing of what they claimed was illegal British trade with their Caribbean possessions, symbolised by the display to a committee of the House of Commons of the allegedly severed ear of a merchant captain, Robert Jenkins. A peace deal, the Convention of the Pardo, was with difficulty negotiated in 1738, but it unravelled the following year, causing a war that Walpole had sought to avoid.

Initially, the war united the country, but a lack of success, combined with poor relations between George II and his eldest son, Frederick, Prince of Wales, gravely weakened Walpole politically. In addition, the ministry was divided and there was a sense that Walpole was losing his grip. He did very badly in the general election of 1741 and his inability to continue to command majorities in the Commons led to his fall in February 1742.[19]

Instead of Walpole being replaced by a united opposition ministry, most of the opposition Whig leaders abandoned their Tory allies and joined the bulk of the Walpolean Whigs in a new government. Ministries remained Whig, and the Tories continued in opposition. Under the dynamic leadership of John, Lord Carteret, the ministry abandoned Walpole's policy of peace with France. This led to French support for Jacobitism, but their invasion attempt in 1744 was blocked by a storm in the Channel.

The following year, 'James III and VIII's' eldest son, Charles Edward (Bonnie Prince Charlie), evaded British warships and landed in the Western Isles. He quickly overran most of Scotland, despite the reluctance of some Jacobite clans to rise for a prince who had brought no soldiers, and the hostility of many Scots who were not Jacobites. The British force in Scotland was outmanoeuvred and then fell victim to a Highland charge at Prestonpans outside Edinburgh on 21 September. The Jacobites, however, did not only want a Stuart Scotland, not least because a Hanoverian England would not allow its existence. Crossing into England on 8 November 1745, Charles Edward took Carlisle after a brief siege and then, without any resistance, Lancaster, Preston, Manchester and Derby, which was entered on 4 December. The British armies had been outmanoeuvred, and, although this was an invasion and few English Jacobites had risen to help Charles, his opponents were hit by panic. The Jacobite council, however, decided on 5 December to retreat, despite Charles's wish to press on to London. The lack of English support (as well as the absence of a promised French landing in southern England) weighed most heavily with the Highland chiefs. There had been a crucial breakdown of confidence in the prince among his supporters, arising from the failure of his promises over support. The Scots considered themselves as having been tricked into a risky situation.

Had the Jacobites pressed on, they might have won, capturing weakly-defended London and thus destroying the logistical and financial infrastructure of their opponents. By retreating, they made defeat almost certain, not least because, in combination with bad weather and the British navy, the retreat led the French to abandon a planned supporting invasion of southern England. Charles evaded pursuit, retreated to Scotland successfully, and on 17 January 1746 beat a British army at Falkirk. However, soon after, Charles abandoned the Central Lowlands for the Highlands. The dynamic of Jacobite success had been lost. George II's inexorable younger son, William, Duke of Cumberland, brought up a formidable army and on Culloden Moor near Inverness on 16 April 1746 his superior firepower smashed the outnumbered, underfed and poorly-led Jacobite army. Cumberland had secured the Protestant Succession established by William III.

The aftermath was harsh. The Hanoverian regime had been temporarily over-thrown in Scotland, and the army humiliated. The government was determined to ensure that there was no repetition of the '45. The 'pacification' of the Highlands was to be characterised first by killings, rapes and systematic devastation, and, secondly, by a determined attempt to alter the political, social and strategic culture of the Highlands. The clans were disarmed and the clan system broken up, while roads to open up the Highlands and forts to awe them were constructed. Heritable jurisdictions were abolished and the wearing of Highland clothes prohibited. The rebellion and its suppression thus gave cause and opportunity for the sort of radi-cal state-directed action against traditional 'liberties' and inherited privilege, espe-cially regional 'liberties' and aristocratic privilege, that was so rare in Britain.

More long-term political changes were also important. In effect Scotland, like many dependent parts of multiple kingdoms or federal states, was losing its capacity for important independent political initiatives. This affected both the Highlands, and the country as a whole. However, it was not a case of English pressure on an unwilling people, for political changes profited, and were in part shaped by, local politicians. Many Scots were firm opponents of the Stuarts and supporters of the Protestant Succession. London relied on Scottish politicians, not Englishmen sent to govern Scotland.

After Culloden, Jacobite conspiracies continued, and contemporaries were still concerned about the situation. Nevertheless, the strategic situation had altered greatly as a result of the crushing of Scottish Jacobitism, and support for 'James III' in England appeared increasingly marginal and inconsequential. Charles Edward successfully fled into exile in 1746, but his idiosyncratic and undisci-plined behaviour in the following years greatly reduced foreign support. His con-version to the Church of England on a secret visit to London in 1750 did not lead to any rallying to the Jacobite cause, and the Elibank Plot of 1751–3, a scheme for a *coup d'état* in London involving the kidnapping of George II, was betrayed.

The combination of the Jacobite threat and of French success in the War of the Austrian Succession (1740–8) had constituted what was truly a mid-eighteenth-century crisis, and underlines the extent to which issues were impor-tant in the politics of the period. Issues of competence and of policy played a major role in the manoeuvres of politicians for office. The crisis led in 1744–6 to the consolidation of a ministry led by Henry Pelham, First Lord of the Treasury from 1743, that was based on widespread Whig support. Followed by the defeat of the Jacobites, the government's sweeping success in the 1747 general election, and the negotiation of acceptable peace terms with France and Spain in 1748 after a less than successful war, all helped to lower the political temperature. A protégé of Walpole (who died in 1745), Pelham was in a position to pursue Walpolean policies: fiscal restraint, unenterprising legislation, preserving a Whig monopoly of power, and the status quo in the Church, and trying to preserve peace.

It is arguably more appropriate to write of a duumvirate than a prime minister. Pelham was the manager of the Commons and a crucial minister, but his brother

Newcastle, as effective Foreign Minister, most influential politician in the Lords, and wielder of much government and church patronage, was definitely not subordinate. Their correspondence survives, and it is clear that each was frustrated by the difficulty of managing the other: Pelham thought Newcastle's diplomatic commitments too expensive and sought to limit them.

Parliamentary attendance slackened as the political situation eased in the late 1740s. There was a strong sense that existing policies and personnel would last until the ministerial revolution that was expected to follow the eventual accession of Frederick, Prince of Wales. The attention of foreign diplomats, an important gauge of the perception of the location of political power, was concentrated on Court and ministry, not Parliament.

The anticipated discontinuity did not occur for, far from the elderly George II dying, Frederick predeceased him in 1751. Indeed, George II, born in 1683, was to live longer than any previous monarch. Instead, it was the unexpected death of Pelham in 1754, touching off a lengthy struggle for power within the government, and the coming of war with France in 1754, the early stages of which were not successful, that produced a serious discontinuity.

Serious political problems were exacerbated by Newcastle's insecure, frenetic and over-anxious personality. Newcastle lacked both the personality and the position to sustain the political structure that his paranoia dictated: a concentration of decision-making and power on his own person. He could not be a second Walpole. His personality was not strong enough to take and, more crucially, bear responsibility for decisions, and his anxiety led to indecisiveness. Newcastle wanted strong colleagues able to take such responsibility, and for that reason operated best with Walpole, Pelham and Pitt. Yet he wanted his colleagues subordinate and could not psychologically accept his own dependence on them; he was weak, but did not wish to acknowledge this weakness.

Aside from lacking the character for the successful retention of high office, Newcastle did not hold an office that would free him from, or at least lessen, his anxieties. For all his frenetic activity, and the time and personal wealth he devoted to patronage, Newcastle was only the most important member of the ministry. The King was the head of the government and played a crucial role in the complex political negotiations of 1754–7. George II was not close to Newcastle, and this was a major source of the Duke's anxiety.

Newcastle was similarly unsure of Parliament. Despite devoting so much of his time to electoral patronage and parliamentary management, Newcastle knew that it was difficult to maintain the impression of governmental control of the Commons. This, as well as his difficulty in accepting criticism, led Newcastle to devote so much time to patronage and management.

His was a personal example of a more general weakness. The Old Corps Whig political system could not cope with failure. The absence of a reliable party unity on which government could rest left politicians feeling vulnerable to attack. Thus, Pitt in opposition was an obvious threat for, although enjoying a measure of Tory support, he was a Whig able to exploit adverse developments in the war, and it was difficult to feel confident of political success against such a figure. This exacerbated

Newcastle's anxiety. Controlling neither Crown nor Commons, Newcastle sought to be a crucial intermediary but this was an unstable basis for political control.

When Pelham died in 1754, Newcastle sought to entrust the management of the Commons to Henry Fox, but he refused to accept the task when he discovered that the Duke intended to retain full control of all government patronage and to manage the forthcoming general election: that would have left him without the power to give substance to his management. Newcastle turned to Sir Thomas Robinson, a pliable ex-diplomat with no independent political base. Robinson was not strong enough to deal with the political problems of 1754–5 as Britain, moving closer to full-scale war with France, found her allies unwilling to support her. In November 1755, Newcastle agreed to make Fox Secretary of State and Commons leader, but this distrustful relationship collapsed the following year.

Newcastle tried to deal with the crisis by winning over opposition, neutering hostility by accommodating it in terms of government position. After Fox resigned in October 1756, Newcastle persuaded George III to permit him to offer Pitt a Secretaryship of State in return for his support. Pitt, however, sought not a reconstitution of the ministry, but a rejection of the government and its policies. He demanded the resignation of Newcastle, an inquiry into recent setbacks, and the dismissal of foreign troops in British pay. Pitt was determined that he should not simply defend government policy, which was what Newcastle sought. He insisted that a scheme of measures be adopted that he could approve and defend.

George II rejected Pitt's terms, but Newcastle, unsuccessful in his attempt to find a Commons leader other than Fox or Pitt, told the king that he could not engage to conduct business in the Commons and resigned.

This was followed by a shortlived ministry of Pitt and an unenthusiastic William, 4th Duke of Devonshire, and in July 1757 Newcastle returned to office. It proved necessary for both Newcastle and Pitt to compromise. His apparent indispensability in the Commons had allowed Pitt to set Newcastle and Fox at defiance in October 1756, and, despite Pitt's unpopularity with George II, neither Newcastle nor Fox seemed to have a good chance of forming a government that could survive in the Commons without Pitt; in large measure because it would be vulnerable to devastating oratory from Pitt if anything went wrong with the handling of the war. Fox did not have the stomach for the fight, and Newcastle had no one of sufficient stature or courage to take Pitt on. Pitt's position might have looked weak, but it was stronger than anyone else's, although not strong enough for him to run a government all by himself.

The different positions in which Newcastle found himself during the wartime political crises of 1744–6 and 1756–7 throw much light on the politics of the period. In the former, it was the Pelhams who could offer Commons management while Carteret, weakened by his inability to do so, fell in 1744 and could not sustain a return to office in 1746. In 1756–7, Newcastle could not promise a pliant Commons. Without his brother, he was in a far weaker position, but this also owed much to Pitt's ability to strike a popular political resonance, accessible to Whigs and Tories within and outside Parliament; a skill Carteret lacked both for personal reasons and because of the policies he actively advanced.

The Newcastle-Pitt ministry of 1757–61 was really a duumvirate. Pitt did not wield the degree of power that is sometimes attributed to him. Newcastle was concerned about more than patronage, George II still exercised considerable power, and Pitt's role in the formulation of policy was not unchallenged. The crucial importance of the financing of the war ensured that Newcastle's post as First Lord of the Treasury was a key one. Nevertheless, Pitt played a central role in maintaining parliamentary and public support for the war. To Pitt, the link between government policy and parliamentary control was not as it seemed to Newcastle. Pitt put an emphasis on parliamentary leadership, rather than management. When, on 2 September 1755, Newcastle sought to win him over to manage the Commons, he found 'such a firm resolution, so solemnly declared, both as to persons and things that, if complied with, must produce a total change of the present system, both as to measures and men'. Pitt said:

> that I did not know the state of the House of Commons; which he might say without vanity, he did, better than anybody ... that the business of the House of Commons could not go on, without there was a minister (a subordinate one, perhaps) which should go directly between the King and them ... that he could not, and would not, take an *active part* in the House of Commons, without he had an *office of advice*, as well as of *execution*; – and that was the distinction he made throughout the whole conversation – that he would support the measures which he himself had advised; but would not, like a lawyer, talk from a *brief* '.[20]

Once the political crisis had been resolved, in the shape of the stable Newcastle-Pitt ministry, then Parliament became of less political consequence, although it remained significant as a key component in the system of assured public finance that enabled the government to fight the war with such persistence. Parliament might have been the scene for more serious attacks on the ministry, had the limited military success of 1755–7 not been transformed into glorious victory, but, as a consequence of both repeated military triumphs and ministerial stability, Parliament was quiescent, certainly compared to the situation during the Nine Years' War and the War of the Spanish Succession.

The '45 had both revealed the vulnerability of, and led to the firm establishment of, the Hanoverian regime. It thus closed a long period of instability and, instead, provided the basis for a fundamental recasting of British politics in which Toryism lost its Jacobite aspect. This facilitated the dissolution of the Whig–Tory divide in the two decades after Culloden. Attempts to conciliate and comprehend opponents within ministerial ranks, and expectations concerning the future behaviour of the heir to the throne, Frederick, Prince of Wales and, after his death in 1751, the future George III, compromised the cohesion and identity of the Tories. This was taken much further after George III came to the throne in 1760 and sought to reign without party. In addition, co-operation in the localities between Whigs and Tories increased after 1746; while the relationship between England and Scotland became essentially one of the willing co-option of the powerful Scots through patronage, with no alternative Jacobite or nationalist focus of loyalty and with a diminishing emphasis on coercion. This unification of Britain helped her in the Seven Years' War with France (1756–63).

The Whig–Tory two-party system, or at least concept, was replaced in the 1760s by a number of essentially personal political groups, with the rivalries of factional leaders and the changing preferences of George III fostering instability. Aside from a new king, there was also a new generation of political leaders, as well as new issues. In combination, these ensured a very different political situation.

This is a matter of controversy. It can be argued that 1720–60 was really dominated by the personal factionalism of Walpole and the Pelhams, which looked like a party because of their longevity in office. This would suggest that there was less a change to the politics of personal factions from 1760 than a case of factions swapping places frequently. However, the crucial division between Tories and opposition Whigs, and the role of issues, on which there were recognisable party positions in the politics of the first half of the century, suggests that it is appropriate to adopt a party approach to the politics of the period. In the early 1760s, the Tories atomised, joining a variety of political groups, including the government establishment in the Commons.

As much as any Continental ruler who did not have to face a powerful representative institution, George III was determined to reject what he saw as the politics of faction, and, in particular, to thwart the efforts of unacceptable politicians to force their way into office. He thought that much about the political system was corrupt, and, in part, ascribed this to the size of the national debt. As a consequence, George's moral reformism was specifically aimed against faction and luxury. In addition, like other rulers, George found it most difficult to create acceptable relationships with senior politicians at his accession, when he had to persuade both those who had had a good working relationship with his predecessor, and those who had looked for a dramatic change, to adjust to his wishes. George broke with Pitt in 1761 and Newcastle in 1762, and made his favourite, John, 3rd Earl of Bute, First Lord of the Treasury in 1762. This was not simply a matter of the politics of office. Issues were at stake. Pitt was a determined advocate of continued war with the Bourbons until they were crushed, and was unwilling to heed financial arguments for peace. In May 1762, he told the Commons:

> When I give my advice in the House I consider myself as giving my advice to the crown … I am convinced this country can raise 12, 13, 14 or even 15 million the next year: I know it without seeking information from bundles of papers and accounts. The only question is whether grievous and permanent as that tax must be, it is not to be preferred to the perpetual dishonour of the nation, the aggrandisement of the enemy, and the desertion of your allies, all which tend to an inglorious and precarious peace'.[21]

However, the general desire for peace, the initial popularity of the new king, and the government's success in both war and peace blunted the force of parliamentary and political criticism. The Peace of Paris (1763) encountered more parliamentary attacks than that of Aix-la-Chapelle (1748) had done, a measure of the stronger sense that Britain had had a bad deal, but the ministry carried the

Address of Thanks on 9 December 1762 by 319 to 65, and there was no division in the Lords. As so often in Hanoverian Britain, it was the parliamentary strength of the government, rather than the vigour of its critics, that was most strikingly apparent to observers, both domestic and foreign, and their view of ministerial power owed much to this strength.

Nevertheless, ministerial stability proved elusive and the weak-willed Bute resigned in 1763 in the face of bitter domestic opposition. The ambiguity of a number of constitutional points, such as the collective responsibility of the Cabinet and the degree to which the monarch had to choose his ministers from those who had the confidence of Parliament, exacerbated the situation. Not until 1770 did George find a satisfactory minister who could control Parliament, lead a ministry and run the government, Frederick, Lord North (who sat in the Commons). What Bute called 'the violence of party'[22] owed much to the king's conscious abandonment of party government. The ending of Old Corps Whig cohesion was an important aspect of the instability of the 1760s. It is difficult to imagine Walpole and Pelham losing power as their successors in the 1760s were to do. The dearth of Commons leadership was also important. Before the time of Lord Liverpool (1812–27) there was not to be a single Lords-led Hanoverian ministry that endured any time. On the other hand, the sole ministry led by some-one sitting in the Commons not to have a substantial period in office was that of George Grenville (1763–5). Circumstances varied, but it seems clear that divid-ing the key functions of the Treasury and the leadership of the Commons made for weak and unstable government.

The volatile political atmosphere in London also contributed to a sense of crisis in the 1760s. Dissatisfaction there was exploited by a squinting anti-hero, John Wilkes, an entrepreneur of faction and libertine MP, who fell foul of George III as a result of bitter attacks on the government in his newspaper, the *North Briton*. Wilkes's denunciation in number 45 (23 April 1763) of the Peace of Paris with its implication that George had lied in his speech from the throne led to a charge of seditious libel. The government took a number of contentious steps, issuing a general warrant for the arrest of all those involved in the publication of the issue and seeking to arrest Wilkes despite his parliamentary privilege. Though released, Wilkes, later in 1763, was accused of blasphemy because he attributed his indecent *Essay on Woman* to a cleric. The Commons resolved that seditious libel was not covered by parliamentary privilege and in 1764 Wilkes was expelled and eventually outlawed. His expulsion was exploited by opposition politicians keen to throw doubts on the legality of ministerial actions. In 1768, he returned to England and was elected for the populous and populist constituency of Middlesex. However, he was imprisoned for blasphemy and libel and expelled from the Commons. Three times re-elected for Middlesex in 1769, Wilkes was declared incapable of being re-elected by Parliament and his opponent was declared elected, a thwarting of the views of the electors that aroused anger.[23]

Wilkes was the focus of more widespread popular opposition to the govern-ment, of fears of royal tyranny or aristocratic oligarchy, and of a measure of rad-icalism, owing something to economic problems, that led in 1768 to a series of riots in London. Five years earlier, there had been resistance to the burning of No. 45: 'Mr Harley, the Sheriff, no sooner appeared with the paper to give it up to the all devouring flames, than the mob arming themselves immediately with the faggots already laid for the conflagration, drove Mr Harley back into his chariot with the loss of some blood on his part'.[24]

Public discontents interacted with ministerial divisions. Although his ministry enjoyed solid majorities in both Houses of Parliament, Bute found the stress of politics unbearable. He was replaced as First Lord of the Treasury in 1763 by George Grenville, whom George III soon found arrogant and overbearing. The King himself was acutely irritable, possibly as a result of poor health.

In 1765, George III was able to dispense with Grenville, though his replacement, Charles Watson-Wentworth, 2nd Marquess of Rockingham, a former protégé of the Duke of Newcastle, was not much to his liking. The new government inherited a difficult political situation. Britain after 1763 was a much wealthier and more self-confident nation than hitherto, but faced serious problems in imperial government and finance. The role of the British state in the affairs of the East India Company and the protection of British India increased appreciably, and this proved a source of considerable controversy. American affairs proved more politically charged, not least because of the large number of British emigrants in North America, the close links with the British economy, and the controversial issues raised by the determination to make colonies unrepresented in Parliament pay a portion of their defence burden in accordance with the views of Parliament.

The strains of paying for the Seven Years' War, never appreciated sufficiently by the bellicose Pitt and his supporters, had forced the ministers of the early 1760s to think of retrenchment and new taxation. The unpopular cider tax of 1763, repealed in 1766, created a furore, but nothing to compare with Grenville's Stamp Act of 1765 which imposed a series of duties in the North American colonies and raised the issue of parliamentary authority there. The Rockingham ministry sought to defuse the crisis. Concerned about the violent response in America and influenced by pressure from British merchants, worried about an American commercial blockade, the Rockinghamites repealed the Stamp Act in 1766, despite the reluctance of George III. Nevertheless, when the Act was repealed, a Declaratory Act was passed, stating that Parliament 'had, hath and of right ought to have full power and authority to make laws and statutes of sufficient form and validity to bind the colonies and people of America in all cases whatsoever'.

The Rockingham ministry suffered not only from royal disfavour, but also from division. Hoping 'to extricate this country out of faction', in July 1766 George III sent for Pitt. His divided ministry was not a success, in part because Pitt's acceptance of a peerage as Earl of Chatham weakened his control of the Commons. The sickly Pitt became an invalid in the spring of 1767, in part probably as a consequence of stress and depression, but the ministry of Augustus, 3rd Duke of Grafton which followed that of Pitt was also weak and divided.

Nevertheless, there was no fundamental political crisis, and, instead, the reintegration of the Tories into the political mainstream helped heal a long-standing divide dating from the mid-seventeenth century. Once George III had found an effective parliamentary manager in Lord North in 1770, the political situation within Britain, and Parliament's role within it, became far more quiescent. North was also able to manage government business and maintain a united government. He was helped by the disunited nature of the opposition, especially the rivalry between Chatham and the Rockinghamites, and by a rallying of support to the Crown, the natural focus of most politicians' loyalty, in response to the extremism of some of the Wilkesites. North had little difficulty in winning the general elections of 1774 and 1780 or in keeping the Rockinghamite opposition at bay. The latter was convinced that there was a royal conspiracy against liberty, and provided a paranoid tone to politics. Few, however, in, or outside, the political nation believed that they were suffering under executive tyranny.

Nevertheless, the war with the American colonies that broke out in 1775 created strains and divisions as well as problems of political management. For example, opposition to the war impeded recruitment, and the latter further fuelled the protests against the war. North's reliance on Highland Scots and Irish Catholic regiments added to parliamentary disquiet.

The situation did not change until Cornwallis's surrender at Yorktown in October 1781 led to a collapse of confidence in the war in America and the North ministry as many independent MPs shifted their support. On 27 February 1782, the government lost a Commons' motion relating to the further prosecution of the war in America. On 20 March, North announced his resignation. George III was forced to turn to the Rockinghamites, a group he distrusted, who were pledged to independence for America. After Rockingham died, William, 2nd Earl of Shelburne was appointed to head the ministry in July 1782. A protégé of Pitt the Elder, who had served as a Secretary of State in 1766–8 and 1782, Shelburne was an opponent of party, or, in his words, faction, a view he took from Pitt. This was an important theme in eighteenth-century political thought that looked back to the 'Country' opposition to Walpole and that greatly affected George III. Shelburne's views on the matter helped to ensure that although his interest in parliamentary reform and his somewhat radical views were unwelcome to George, nevertheless, he was acceptable as a first minister, certainly more so than any Rockinghamite.

George's failure to choose the new leader of the Rockinghamites, the Duke of Portland, led to a resignation of prominent Rockinghamites, especially Charles James Fox, but the King's determination to defend his prerogative of choosing his own ministers was generally accepted. Shelburne defended the King's right to choose his ministers and his rejection of Foxite ideas regarding the choice of prime minister and collective responsibility within the Cabinet.[25]

Widely distrusted, and disliked for arrogance, Shelburne's brief period as first minister revealed how a personally unpopular prime minister who lacked the support of a party and had to win parliamentary support for contentious measures could not prevail. In February 1783, Shelburne had to persuade Parliament to accept peace preliminaries that were genuinely unpopular, especially the lack of any guarantees for the Loyalists and for British debts. Defeated twice, he resigned.

The largest groupings in the Commons, led by Fox and North, were aiming to secure office, and were prepared to do so regardless of any claim by the King to choose his ministers. Former enemies, they formed a coalition ministry, headed by the Duke of Portland in April 1783, despite the bitter disapproval of George III.

These changes, and more specifically the formation of the Fox–North ministry, helped to contribute to a sense of political failure, even collapse. This suggests that contemporary expectations of the political system were not of frequent changes of government in response to shifts in parliamentary and electoral opinion, but, rather, of a stable ministry responsive to, and thus, if necessary, limited by responsible parliamentary and popular opinion. This assumption was shared abroad. Rulers such as Catherine II (the Great) of Russia, Frederick II (the Great) of Prussia and Joseph II of Austria argued in the early 1780s that Britain was weak, that this was due to her politics, which would probably lead to the dissolution of her empire, and that her weakness made her an undesirable ally.

The resolution of the crisis in the shape of a stable ministry under William Pitt the Younger was far from inevitable. It was not certain that Pitt would secure a Commons majority simply because George III had appointed him to office in December 1783, after helping defeat the East India Bill, a crucial item of government business, in the Lords. George's action brought out the lack of agreement about the constitution and the fluidity of constitutional conventions that tend all too often to be forgotten. George's actions, which were regarded by some as unconstitutional, were countered by a collective resignation of office holders. George saw himself as 'on the edge of a precipice'.[26] Commons defeats in January 1784 led Pitt to think of resigning and George III to reiterate his willingness to abdicate.

An unsuccessful attempt by independent MPs to create a broad-based government of national unity, a frequently-expressed aspiration during the century that reflected widespread suspicion of what was seen as the factious nature of party politics, gave Pitt breathing space. His position was improved further by a swelling tide of favourable public opinion, shown in a large number of addresses from counties and boroughs, with over 50,000 signatures in total, in favour of the free exercise of the royal prerogative in choosing ministers. The formation of the Pitt government had brought monarch and government on to the same side. The public nature of the crisis led to an upsurge in popular interest which focused on support for George, itself a testimony to the potential popularity of the monarchy, and thus for his new ministers. Parliament was dissolved when Pitt felt able to face a general election, and the elections, many of which were contested on national political grounds, were very favourable for the ministry.

On the other hand, a sense of the precariousness of the Anglo-Irish link was captured by Shelburne in 1786 when he stressed the need for major change in Ireland, particularly the commutation of tithe payments to the clergy of the (Anglican) Church of England and the ending of abuses by the latter:

> the Church of England runs the risk of falling in Ireland and if great care is not taken all property and government will be endangered at the same time ... Force never has effected good on either side, and on which ever side it is exerted, carries with it something abhorrent to our manners and government. Preventive

wisdom is certainly the greatest qualification which government can have ... the circumstances of Ireland and England are so very different, in regard to religion, that they must necessarily require a different system in that respect.[27]

At the close of the period, as at its start, different assumptions about the nature and stability of the political stability can be stressed, especially if the circumstances of particular years are considered: conclusions based on 1688 or 1783 would be challenged if the year for consideration was 1687 or 1784. This is an important reminder of the volatility of the politics of the period.

NOTES

1. T. Harris, *Politics under the Later Stuarts 1660–1715* (Harlow, 1993).
2. T. Harris, 'Was the Tory reaction popular? Attitudes of Londoners towards the Prosecution of Dissent, 1681–86', *London Journal*, 13 (1988), pp. 106–20.
3. J. Miller, *James II* (2nd edn, New Haven, 2000).
4. W.A. Speck, *Reluctant Revolutionaries: England and the Revolution of 1688* (Oxford, 1988); G.H. Jones, *Convergent Forces: Immediate Causes of the Revolution of 1688 in England* (Ames, Iowa, 1990).
5. D. Hoak and M. Feingold (eds), *The World of William and Mary: Anglo-Dutch Perspectives on the Revolution of 1688–89* (Stanford, 1996), p. 7.
6. BL. Add. 9131 fol. 8; J. Israel (ed.), *The Anglo-Dutch Moment: Essays on the Glorious Revolution and its World Impact* (Cambridge, 1991).
7. C.A. Whatley, *'Bought and sold for English gold'. Explaining the Union of 1707* (Edinburgh, 1994); J. Robertson (ed.), *A Union for Empire: Political Thought and the British Union of 1707* (Cambridge, 1995).
8. R.E. Burns, *Irish Parliamentary Politics in the Eighteenth Century, II: 1730–1760* (Washington, 1990).
9. Hartington to Newcastle, 30 July 1755, BL. Add. 32857 fol. 462.
10. L. Colley, *Britons: Forging the Nation 1707–1837* (New Haven, 1992).
11. A. Marshall, *The Age of Faction: Court Politics, 1660–1702* (Manchester, 1999), pp. 154–83.
12. C. Rose, *England in the 1690s: Revolution, Religion and War* (Oxford, 1999).
13. D.W. Jones, *War and Economy in the Age of William III and Marlborough* (Oxford, 1988).
14. W.A. Speck, *Tory and Whig: the Struggle in the Constituencies 1701–15* (1970); G. Holmes, *British Politics in the Age of Anne* (2nd edn, 1987).
15. E. Gregg, *Queen Anne* (1980).
16. Walpole to Townshend, 30 Aug. 1723, PRO. SP. 43/4 fol. 292.
17. BL. Add. 64929 fol. 77.
18. Goodricke to Edward Hopkins, 6 Feb. 1733, BL. Add. 64939 fol. 81.
19. Black, *Walpole in Power* (Stroud, 2001).
20. Newcastle to Hardwicke, 3 Sept. 1755, BL. Add. 32858 fols 408–10.
21. James West MP, report on parliamentary proceedings, 12 May 1762, BL. Add. 32938 fols 186–7.
22. Bute to Shelburne, 4 Sept. 1763, Bowood, papers of 2nd Earl of Shelburne, Box 37.
23. P.D.G. Thomas, *John Wilkes: A Friend to Liberty* (Oxford, 1996).
24. George Villiers to Lady Spencer, 6 Dec. 1763, BL. Althorp F 101.
25. Cobbett, XXIII, 191.
26. George III to Pitt, 23 Dec. 1783, PRO. 30/8/103 fol. 14.
27. Shelburne to Silver Oliver MP, 26 July 1786, Bowood, Shelburne papers, Box 59.

14

Continental comparisons and links

From 1688, Britain might seem to have diverged from a common European course, not only because of a more 'liberal' constitutional regime in the 'Glorious Revolution', but also as a result of the breach in the succession and the consequent instability and civil violence much of which had religious and 'regional' aspects. This thus represented a repetition, albeit with considerable differences, of the situation arising from the Henrician Reformation, at a time when domestic political and religious order had been restored in most European states. Such disorder was not, however, restricted to Britain in the early eighteenth century. The continued problems that the Habsburgs faced in Hungary with a substantially Protestant nobility keen on its privileges and on limiting the powers of the Habsburg sovereign, in the late seventeenth and early eighteenth century, culminating in the Rákóczi rebellion of 1703–11, indicated the difficulties that a nobility with a sense of distinct political and religious privileges could create in the absence of harmony with the Crown. Royal power in Hungary was not to increase appreciably until the reigns of Charles VI (1711–40) and, more particularly, Maria Theresa (1740–80) brought a measure of such co-operation. In Spain, the long and bitter war of succession following the death of Charles II in 1700 did not have a religious aspect, but was related to the struggle for primacy between Castile and the lands of the Crown of Aragon, particularly Catalonia.

Britain cannot therefore be seen as unique in the challenge to governmental authority. In addition, albeit with the delays consequent upon the disruption of and from the 1680s, Britain took part in the more general movement towards a reconciliation between crowns and elites that was so characteristic of Europe in the late-seventeenth century. In England and Wales there was far less resistance than in Scotland and Ireland, to William III and, after 1714, to the new Hanoverian dynasty, although the extent of enthusiasm for them was limited. Nevertheless, Parliament and the government, both central and local, secular and ecclesiastical, were dominated by the nobility and their relatives and dependents and this brought a measure of unity. In England, the religious settlement of 1688–9, in which the exclusion of the Catholic James was central, ended several decades of uncertainty over the position of the Church of England. This served as a basis for the development of new constitutional relationships between crown and Parliament, and, eventually, for a less volatile political situation. Politics were contentious, and the fundamental stability of the system was challenged by the evidence of a Stuart claim to the throne, but, compared to the political world of 1678–88, that after 1689, and especially after the consolidation of Whig hegemony in 1716–21, was more settled. The situation was less benign if Scotland and Ireland are included. The new order was enforced in both at the cost of the exclusion of important sections of both the general population and the élite.

The 'Glorious Revolution' led to a stronger contemporary emphasis on exceptionalism (the notion that the country was distinctive) that has been of considerable importance since. The Whig tradition made much of the redefinition of parliamentary monarchy in which Parliament met every year, of regular elections (as a result of the Triennal Act of 1694), the freedom of the press (as a consequence of the lapsing of the Licensing Act in 1695), and the establishment in 1694 of a funded national debt. The Revolution Settlement was seen by most commentators as clearly separating Britain from the general pattern of Continental development. Indeed, to use a modern term, it was as if history had ended, for if history was an account of the process by which the constitution was established and defended, then the Revolution Settlement could be presented as a definitive constitutional settlement, and it could be argued that the 'Glorious Revolution' had saved Britain from the general European move towards absolutism and, to a certain extent, Catholicism. In Strasbourg in 1753, Voltaire told William Lee, a well-connected English tourist, that he, i.e. Lee, came from 'the only nation where the least shadow of liberty remains in Europe'. The following year Stanislaw Poniatowski, later king of Poland, visited England. His friendship with Charles Yorke, the lawyer, would inspire his reforming constitutionalism as king.[1]

EIGHTEENTH-CENTURY ENGLAND AS THE MODEL OF A PROGRESSIVE SOCIETY

For fashionable intellectuals on the Continent, Britain offered a model of a progressive society, one that replaced the Dutch model that had been so attractive the previous century, though there was also criticism of aspects of British society. The perception by Continental intellectuals was crucial to the presentation of Britain as a progressive society. Many eighteenth- and nineteenth-century French and German historians and lawyers looked to Britain as culturally and constitutionally superior, and thus as a model to be copied. They talked however about 'England' not 'Britain'. For Georg Christoph Lichtenberg (1742–99), the London of the 1770s was an exciting centre of civilisation where he could meet Priestley or Banks and see Garrick on the stage. British institutions were widely admired, and the most influential thinkers of the century included British philosophers and political economists.

Britain was not only praised by intellectuals from nearby states. Its impact was wider ranging. Swedes who hoped to improve their political system looked to British constitutional practice, to trial by jury, primogeniture, and independent local government and other features of British society, although, as later with the French Revolutionaries, their analysis of the situation in Britain was sometimes overly simplistic if not misleading and there were aspects that they did not seek to emulate.

English literature was more widely read abroad than ever before, and, for the first time, Britain had a school of native painters, whose work merited comparison with the best in Europe. The young Johann Winckelmann, later an influential writer on cultural history, was influenced by *Cato's Letters*, a British opposition periodical that he read in the library of a Saxon aristocrat. Montesquieu, Voltaire and Rousseau, the leading French writers of the century, all visited England and were well acquainted with the leading figures of British intellectual life. More minor French figures also visited Britain, corresponded with British intellectuals and read British books. Alary, the founder of the Club de l'Entresol, an influential intellectual Parisian club of the 1720s that included the British ambassador Horatio Walpole among its members, spoke English and greatly enjoyed his trip to England in 1725. On it, he met Newton and attended a meeting of the Royal Society, a popular venue for many French tourists. The British constitution was praised in the *Encyclopédie* (1751–65), initially a project to translate Ephraim Chambers' *Cyclopaedia or an Universal Dictionary of Arts and Sciences* (1728), although swiftly transformed into a vehicle for propaganda for the ideas of the *philosophes*, French thinkers who presented themselves as progressive and enlightened.

With time, Britain became more important as an economic model and a source of technological and entrepreneurial innovation. Duke Karl of Brunswick received details of a planned English lottery in 1740.[2] British machinery, especially textile machinery, was smuggled abroad, and skilled British workers recruited by foreign manufacturers. Crucial Continental manufacturing plants owed their origin to British skills.

The Society of Arts in London had connections with most of the major economic societies in the Continent, and disseminated knowledge of British innovations. Forty-nine per cent of the Fellows of the Royal Society in 1740 were foreigners.[3] Britain was also attractive as a financial proposition. Foreign, particularly Dutch, holdings in the British national debt were significant, but one aspect of the important financial and business links that bound Britain and the Continent, more especially London and Amsterdam together. The Huguenot diaspora played a major role in this relationship, as did its Jewish counterpart, which was also important in Anglo-Portuguese financial relations. Similarly, British families had members or connections abroad: Catholic Irish merchants had close links with Iberia and France, while English and Scottish merchants had many connections in the Low Countries. William III found titles for Dutch favourites – Bentinck becoming Duke of Portland; while under Anne, the Duke of Marlborough was made a Prince of the Holy Roman Empire.

Continental intellectuals often neglected to note the fundamental controversies that were such an obvious feature of the Hanoverian period, or offered a simple account that found virtue only on one side, although there was criticism, in part a product of the influence of British opposition writers, especially Bolingbroke.

Lesage condemned the brutality and grossness of British manners. British political instability, partisanship and turbulence was criticised by some authors. Muralt attacked the role of corruption; the *Encyclopédie* was not free from criticism; and Holbach, in his 'Réflexions sur le gouvernement britannique', castigated the corruption of British public life, for which he cited a British political pamphlet, the instability of British politics, and the venality, viciousness, arrogance and injustice of the British nation; although he also noted that in the eyes of many the British constitution was a major achievement of the human spirit.[4]

In practice, within Britain, politics, religion, culture and morality, none of them really separable, were occasions and sources of strife and polemic, and the same was true not only of views of recent history, most obviously the Revolution Settlement, but also of the very question of the relationship between Britain and the Continent. Alongside the notion of uniqueness as derived from and encapsulated in that Settlement, there was also a habit, especially marked in opposition circles, of seeking parallels abroad. These were designed to make polemical points, but their use also reflected a sense that parallels could be drawn. Thus, the long ministry of Sweden's Count Horn could be compared with that of Walpole, while the opposition press could suggest in 1732–3 that the Parlement of Paris was readier to display independence than the Westminster Parliament.[5]

This habit was accentuated from 1714 by the Hanoverian connection, for, under both George I and George II, the contentiousness of that connection led to a sustained political discourse about the extent to which Britain was both being ruled in accordance with the foreign interests of her monarchs and was being affected in other ways, especially cultural. A London item in the *Bristol Gazette and Public Advertiser* of 12 September 1771 argued the case for similarities between British and French developments:

> There is a striking similitude between the present situation of the people of England and the people of France. In both the people are alike oppressed; in both the finances of the public are in a wretched condition; in both the reins of government are guided by a woman; in both their Parliaments have been essentially suppressed, the one by force, the other by fraud; in both their Princes do not rely on the affections of their subjects, but on large standing armies; in both the King's will and pleasure is the only law; in both the just and constitutional rights and liberties of the people have been infringed and trampled upon; in both there have been frequent remonstrances to their kings, which have been totally disregarded; and in both there is such a general ferment and discontent, they may probably bring on a confusion, and end in a change of their present forms of conduct.

If the view of France as a menacing despotism heavily influenced British public debate, it did not preclude praise for specific aspects of French society and government. On 25 June 1737, the prohibition of slaughtering meat in Paris was held up for emulation in *Wye's Letter*, and French regulatory practices were frequently applauded. Indeed, citing French examples in a hostile fashion could lead to disputes. When a ministerial speaker claimed in the Commons in 1717 that French taxes were as heavy as those in Britain, and their collecting methods more grievous, an opposition MP retorted that French manufacturing and commerce were increasing. On 17 February 1722, *Applebee's Original Weekly Journal* challenged one of the fundamental premises of British political thought when it cited France as an example for attacking the claim in the *London Journal* that trade required liberty. In 1736, in a debate in the Lords on a bill to prevent smuggling it was claimed that, despite punitive legal powers in France, smuggling there was nearly as bad as in Britain. Walpole observed in the Commons in 1739 that

> gentlemen, in their opposition to the administration, make it their business to collect precedents and examples from our neighbours, and if they can find anything parallel to them practised by the government, let it be never so reasonable, then it is always the universal clamour that the government immediately designs to reduce the whole constitution to the French form, that they make themselves arbitrary. But if some gentlemen have a favourite measure in view which corresponds with anything practised by the French government, that agreement is so far from being a reproach to it, and a reason why it ought not to be pursued that it is recommended solely on that account.[6]

Walpole was more correct in his first point, but this range of reference indicates the problems with modern judgements that simplify attitudes, and also throws light on the difficulties in assessing the degree of similarity or contrast between Britain and continental states in this period.

Eighteenth-century British, particularly English, political debates looked back to the controversies of the previous century over Gothicism and the Norman Yoke. These centred on the notion that post-Roman Europe was originally unified by sharing Germanic freedoms, but that this liberty of the forest had been lost in England as a consequence of William I's victory in 1066 and the imposition of the Norman Yoke, an argument that had been pushed by opponents of the Stuarts and was inherited by the Whigs. Thus, England needed to restore its original freedom, a freedom that it had shared with the Continent, but which had been lost, in England by invasion, and, across much of Europe, by political developments and, in particular, by the corrupting tendencies of the medieval Church, itself a corruption of the primitive Church. The 'Glorious Revolution' could be presented as a recovery of original freedoms, a process that separated Britain from most of Continental Europe.

A shared heritage could, nevertheless, reflect differences in literary and political culture as different elements in that heritage were highlighted. This was true for example of the very important classical heritage. Thus, in England the French were seen as fawning followers of Horace, civilised, urbane, sophisticated, fashionable servants or slaves; the English as rugged, no-nonsense, plain-speaking followers of Juvenal, hence free. The glory of Augustan Rome encompassed both Horace and Juvenal, but in England and Scotland there was an important theme of classical republican virtue that looked back to republican Rome. This has been termed the 'Catonic perspective', a reference to an image of Cato that was powerful in the early-eighteenth century.[7]

While the modern political notion of British specificity and uniqueness dates from the 'Glorious Revolution', its economic counterpart is dated later and less specifically, from the later eighteenth century, although the Industrial Revolution can in part be linked to the earlier political changes by arguing that they were a crucial prerequisite (for example by offering security against the fiscal policies of an arbitrary government), an argument that by its very nature is difficult to prove or disprove. As with the 'Glorious Revolution', the very nature and consequences of the Industrial Revolution are matters of serious historical dispute. The Hanoverian age has been returned to the context of fundamental controversy that was such an obvious feature of the period.

The 'Glorious Revolution' was crucial to the Whig myth, or interpretation of British history, and central to the notion of British uniqueness. Celebrating the centenary, the *Leeds Mercury* of 11 November 1788 declared that 'It was from that glorious period, [that] the animating breath of Liberty has diffused peace and increased commerce among the subjects of Britain'. Political and religious liberty were seen as mutually supportive. In the dedication of 1760 for the fourteenth edition of his *A New History of England*, the prolific writer John Lockman (1698–1771) 'endeavoured to set the whole in such a light, as may inspire the readers with an ardent love for our pure religion, and its darling attendant, liberty; and, on the other hand, with a just abhorrence of popery, and its companion, slavery.'[8] Lockman was one of the large number of lesser writers on numerous topics who helped to reiterate public ideology, but who tend to be overlooked. In 1760, he published *A History of the Cruel Sufferings of the Protestants and others by Popish Persecutions in various Countries*. As secretary to the British Herring Fishery, Lockman sought to develop the industry in the Shetlands. He also wrote a number of literary works.

A sense of being outside Europe characterised most British political debate. It strengthened and intertwined with other senses of uniqueness or specificity that were not without cause. The Common Law was seen as a particularly English creation, was contrasted with legal precepts and practice in, above all, France, and enjoyed marked attention in the age of the jurist Sir William Blackstone (1723–80). Indeed, Blackstonian notions of the constitution as an appropriately regulated system of checks and balances played a major role in the ideology of the late-eighteenth-century British state.

It has been argued that because English law emphasised absolute ownership in right, the right to dispose of property as thought appropriate at death, and the landowner's right to minerals and coal under his property, it promoted enterprise and ensured that landlords were better placed to mobilise capital. This has been seen as important in a recent comparative study of the role of transportation in English and French industrial development. Legal rights have been presented as important to English success in creating a transportation system that facilitated the emergence of new industries, regional specialisation, an increase in the scale and standardisation of production, and wider markets. In addition, the political institutions and culture of England were more conducive for the local initiatives and control required for the creation of new transportation links – canals and turnpikes; whereas in France control was more in the hands of a small bureaucracy that was less responsive to local needs, although in France the right to charge tolls, such as those on British turnpikes, was usually presented by reformers as an obstacle to wealth creation. The situation in England was eased by the possibility of establishing trusts by private Acts of Parliament, while in France the insistence on central government control precluded necessary private investment and led to a concentration on a small number of prestige projects.[9]

The British social system was praised for its degree of social mobility and for the presence, in both town and countryside, of groups that enjoyed a measure of prosperity and position. Thus, in 1792, John Trevor, the long-serving Envoy Extraordinary in Turin, reported,

the misfortune is that in this country [Kingdom of Sardinia, more particularly Piedmont] the whole society is divided into two classes, the *Court* and *Nobility*, and the *Bourgeoisie*, and the line drawn between them is so rude and marked that the two Parties have long been jealous and might too easily become *hostile*; there are none of those intermediate shades which blend the whole together into one harmonious mass as in our happy country.[10]

Aspects of the British situation conducive to social cohesion, such as social mobility, have been cited as a major reason why Britain avoided revolution in the 1790s; although so did other European states, such as Russia, whose social circumstances were somewhat different.

Views of foreign countries were an important means by which attitudes to British government and society were advanced and debated. France dominated Britain's conceptions of the outside world, and negative themes prevailed. France was generally presented as an autocracy, and a society run by a corrupt and effete court, that, simultaneously, used violence to maintain its position – the Bastille, lettres de cachet and torture – and yet did not need to do so because the populace were happy: their faculties ensnared by Catholicism, and their past liberties surrendered thanks to corruption. Historical arguments were based on the view that national character, far from being immutable, could alter as a result of social and political changes, a warning to Britain. In 1740, George Lyttelton, an opposition Whig MP, declared in the Commons: 'It is not Spanish or French arms, but Spanish and French maxims of government that we should have most to fear.'[11]

The public myth of uniqueness that played such a major role in the Whig inheritance (by the 1760s most politicians could see themselves as Whigs), from 1688 on was qualified by domestic critics who charged, with reason, that the Whigs had abandoned their late-seventeenth-century radical ideas, and who also sometimes denied that the British system was better than those across the Channel. Particular attention was focused on the way in which the 'executive' had allegedly subverted the freedom of Parliment by corruption. In short, the Revolution Settlement could be subverted from within, by moral and political corruption, the two aspects of the same threat, continually challenging the achievement of liberty, so that the price of liberty was eternal vigilance. This was a view particularly associated, in the first

half of the eighteenth century, with the Opposition Whigs, critical of the governing Old Corps Whigs and with Hanoverian Tories, willing to work with George I
and George II, but unhappy about government policy. Though different in their
analysis and political prescription, those who held these views could still agree
that the Revolution Settlement was distinctive and worth preserving, and this was
the assessment picked up and propagated by foreign communicators. Critics of
this assessment of the Revolution Settlement existed, but both the Jacobites and
the radical Whigs, who criticised all or many aspects of the post-1688 world, had
been marginalised by military and political developments.

CULTURAL LINKS

Aside from close political links, there were important cultural relations between
Britain and the Continent. The royal court was less important as a source and
sphere of cultural patronage than was the case in most Continental states,
although it did serve, under William III and Georges I and II, as a means for the
dissemination of Continental artistic developments. George I was an active patron
of the German-born composer Georg Friedrich Handel, who was naturalised in
1726, George II of the German enamellist C.F. Zincke. The Huguenot diaspora
helped to consolidate and broaden intellectual and cultural relations, not least in
furthering the important Holland–London news axis of the early British press.

The sea proved no barrier to foreign influences. William III's arrival from
Holland in 1688, and the coming of George I from Hanover in 1714, imposed
Calvinist and Lutheran monarchs, and opened the way to Dutch and Germans
who followed in their wake. In the same decades, persecutions on the Continent
introduced other adherents of foreign churches. Refugees from France and
the Catholic parts of the Holy Roman Empire – Huguenots, Palatines and
Moravians – sought sanctuary in London, but resisted integration into the English
establishment and worshipped separately from their new hosts, although by the
mid-eighteenth-century the Huguenots conformed, largely through Secker's
influence. He encouraged the French congregations in London and Southampton
to conform to Anglican liturgy translated into French.

In addition, the international republic of letters had important British branches.
A network of correspondence and lobbyists introduced forms of foreign spiritual-
ity into the country. A prime example was the fascination for the Pietist experiment at Halle. The educational and social work undertaken by these German
Protestants became the inspiration for many British initiatives, gaining particular
converts among enthusiasts for workhouses, charity schools and the SPCK.

Furthermore, the already strong appeal of Continental Catholic culture to part
of the British élite, which had been such an obvious feature of the courts of Charles
I and Charles II, became more marked in the early-eighteenth-century, not least as
a result of the vogue for the Grand Tour and the consequent personal influence on
prominent individuals. Cultural, stylistic, intellectual and religious fashions and
impulses crossed the Channel and had a major impact on the British élite, as well
as an influence on other groups. They included Italian opera, Palladianism, French
cooking, card games and pornography, the Rococo, Neoclassicism, Protestant

evangelicalism, and, in the 1780s, ballooning. The morning levée and toilet was introduced into Britain from France, as was the umbrella.

A large number of French artists practised in Britain, particularly from the 1710s to 1760s. Alexandre Desportes painted many hunting scenes on his visit in 1712–13. Maurice Quentin La Tour, a portrait painter admired by Hogarth, had a successful visit to London in 1723. Andien de Clermont spent from the mid-1710s to the mid-1750s in England, carrying out decorative painting at Kew, Strawberry Hill and Wilton. The portrait painter Jean Van Loo arrived in London in 1737 and spent a lucrative five years taking commissions from resentful English rivals. The draughtsman Hubert Gravelot arrived in London in 1733 and stayed until the '45 led him and his compatriot, the artist Philip Mercier, to leave for France. As a teacher at the St Martin's Lane Academy, he trained a whole generation of British artists, including Gainsborough. The painter Charles Clerisseau was invited to London in 1771 by Robert Adam and exhibited with much sucesss at the Royal Academy. Italian, Swiss and German artists were also important: Canaletto, Zuccarelli, Cipriani, Kauffmann and Zoffany.

British porcelain was influenced by French models, as were other crafts. The role of French society as a model for genteel behaviour was significant in the importance of French dancing masters, hairdressers and clothes-makers. The ready availability of translations played a significant role in cultural interchange. Translations ranged from Pope to Shakespeare to Robert Chasles' amorous scandalous fiction which appeared in its first English edition in 1727 (a second following twelve years later) as *The Illustrious French Lovers; being the histories of the amours of several French persons of quality*. More utility might have been derived from the 1757 first French edition of John Bartlet's veterinary work or from *A Treatise upon the Culture of Peach Trees* (1768), a translation of Combles' 1745 book.

The works of some leading Continental intellectuals were influential in Britain. This was particularly true of Montesquieu and the Italian legal writer Beccaria. Montesquieu's major work *L'Esprit des Loix* (1748) was published in a translation by Thomas Nugent (*c*. 1700–72) two years later. Born in Ireland, Nugent spent most of his life in London and his work as a translator indicated the close interest shown in Britain in intellectual developments on the Continent. His translations included Jean Baptiste Dubos' *Critical Reflections on Poetry, Painting, and Music* (1748), Burlamaqui's *Principles of Natural Law* (1748), and his *Principles of Politic Law* (1752), Voltaire's *Essay on Universal History* (1759) and Rousseau's *Emilius* (1763). Nugent also published accounts of his travels on the Continent, a history of Mecklenburg, whence George III's wife, Queen Charlotte, had come, and an English–French pocket dictionary.

The popularity of such dictionaries was a testimony to the strength of foreign cultural links, as well as a product of the rise in book-ownership. More direct influences can be seen in the works of some writers. Stephen Payne Adye, the Deputy Judge Advocate, acknowledged his debt to Montesquieu and Beccaria, in his *Essay on Military Punishments and Rewards* (1769) which called for the enlightened reform of the British system of military justice. The willingness of some commentators to look at Continental ideas and models is notable given the distinctive character of the English legal system. A laudatory tone characterised the well-travelled William Mildmay's *The Police of France: or, an Account of the Laws and Regulations Established in the Kingdom for the Preservation of Police and the Preventing of Robberies* (1763).

The direction of influence was not all one way: English landscaping had a major impact abroad. It was adopted more readily, because it was partly modelled on a truly cosmopolitan source, the classics. Freemasonry spread from Britain into fashionable Continental circles in the eighteenth century. British influence abroad was strong in intellectual life and literature. Modern authors, such as the novelists Fielding and Sterne and the philosopher Shaftesbury, and earlier writers, in particular Shakespeare, had a considerable impact in the Low Countries and Germany. Ossian, the Scottish Homer, swept Europe, and, translated into several European languages, including German (1768), French (1777), Russian (1792), Dutch (1805), Danish (1807–9) and Czech (1827), influenced Goethe, Napoleon and Schiller. The appearance of a translation of Ossian played a crucial role in the plot of Goethe's *Werther* (1774). Other British works were not self-consciously primitive. In Russia, in 1741–1800, 245 books were published that can be traced back to original English language works by British authors, many via a French translation. The Russian dramatist Aleksandr Sumarokov first produced his adaptation of *Hamlet* in 1750, although the anguish of the original was replaced by clear moral purpose.

Despite these cultural links, the British view of the Continent became more distant in the 1760s, 1770s and 1780s as imperial issues and an oceanic identity came to the fore. The view also became less hostile. This can be seen in the move away from an often automatically hostile Whiggish approach to foreign countries on the part of travellers, to a more varied response. Among the élite, hostility to Catholicism diminished. Popular hostility, however, remained strong, a reminder of the need to avoid any simplistic account of national attitudes.

COMPARISONS

Cultural links stemmed from an interest in foreign countries that encouraged comparison. Continental views of Britain are instructive, although most foreigners visited only southern England, particularly London: stereotypes of Englishness hardened and the distinctiveness of the English and their national triumphs were associated with a marked degree of self-discipline and self-dedication.[12]

It is also instructive to look for comparisons in more modern terms. These can be anachronistic, but also fruitful. In employing criteria, there is often a search for functional, rather than ideological, structures, i.e. on how systems worked, rather than on the values they affirmed. One such structure was that of multiple statehood, a characteristic Britain shared with, for example, Austria, Prussia, Spain and Denmark. In other words, it was an amalgamation of formerly disparate units that at least in part retained a separate governmental identity. At the same time, such states had a centre of activity.

The crushing of the '45 at Culloden in 1746 ensured that the new British state created by the parliamentary union of 1707 would continue to be one whose political tone and agenda were set in London and southern England. This was the basis of British consciousness, a development that did not so much alter the views of the English political élite for whom Britain was essentially an extension of England, but, rather, that reflected the determination of the Scottish and, to a lesser extent, Welsh and Irish Protestant elites to link their fate with that of the British state; indeed the Anglican élite in Ireland persisted in defining itself as English (although this was changing fast from the 1760s).

Such a development did not, however, prevent the coincident still vigorous senses of local, provincial and national identities. This situation repeated the earlier combination of the 'English national myth' with the linguistic, cultural and ethnic diversity of an England that stretched from Cornwall, whose distinctive language only disappeared in about 1780, to the Scottish borders. As so often, such combinations were in part expressed through hostility to outsiders. This process of nationalism was not unique to Britain but was shared by Continental societies, albeit also within the context of multiple identities and with a cultural rather than a political focus.

Yet, the continued, indeed greater from 1694 and 1707, role of the Westminster Parliament was a major difference to the situation in most of Europe. In Parliament, Britain had a more effective 'hinge' or means of achieving, eliciting, sustaining and legitimating co-operation between the Crown and a widespread political nation for the achievement of common action than existed in other European states of comparable size. After 1688 institutions and, more importantly, a political culture embodying genuine modes of representation had developed in Britain. This helped give a distinctive character to British politics and led foreign visitors to show particular interest in attending both parliamentary debates and elections. The sight of a first minister having to defend policy was not a familiar one.

The scrutiny of differences between Britain and the Continent has to make allowance for variations within the latter and must not be blind to those who suffered hardship within the British system, but instructive contrasts can still be found. Although the Royal Navy continued to be dependent in wartime on forcible impressment by press gangs, there was no national system of conscription for land or sea service. Widespread conscription for the army on the model of Austria, Prussia, Sweden or Russia was unacceptable. Indeed, the very fact that Continental states resorted to such methods established them as unacceptable, although there was impressment of the unemployed during some periods of acute manpower shortage, for example during the War of the Spanish Succession. In 1756, a Press Act made possible the compulsory enlistment of 'such able-bodied men as do not follow any lawful calling or employment, or have not some other lawful and sufficient support and maintenance'. The Act, however, disappointed expectations. It proved difficult for officials to raise sufficient men, their quality was low, and desertion was a major problem. The system fell into disuse in 1758. Britain lacked a regulatory regime and social system akin to that of Prussia or Russia, and, without them, it was difficult to make a success of conscription or to limit desertion. The army remained a volunteer force, and Britain remained unusual as a great power in that it lacked a large army. Including the Irish establishment, the peacetime army was only about 30,000 strong in the first half of the century, and 45,000 strong in the 1760s.

Furthermore, Britain's economic expansion, which was impressive by Continental standards, had an impact: job opportunities affected army recruitment, and that for the navy was hit by the higher rates of pay provided by the merchant marine. The impact of commerce can also be seen in the use of subsidised foreign forces, for example Hessians and Dutch. It has been suggested that the availability of such troops enabled Britain to have a freer use of its own labour and to preserve better its own liberties, but that this was achieved at the cost of an opposite process occurring in Hesse-Cassel.[13]

This thesis, a variation on the core-periphery model of early-modern economic developments, with the periphery serving the needs of the core, offers an approach to the distinctive spatial and dynamic character of British power, as well as a way both to integrate Britain and the wider world, and to look at relations within Britain. It can for example be extended to include the extensive recruitment of sepoys for the East India Company and also Scottish Highlanders for the British army from the mid-eighteenth-century, and, in the economic sphere, helps to explain the use of slaves.

CONCLUSION

Britain emerges as distinctive because it was better able to develop and use such dynamic relationships. Trade, finance and force helped to structure relationships within the expanding Western world to Britain's benefit. For example, the Royal Navy protected trade revenues that could finance subsidy forces. It would be misleading to contrast Britain and the Continent too starkly in this respect. Other Atlantic states sought to do the same, but the British system was supported by a more flexible system of state regulation and was more open to entrepreneurial activity than those of the other two leading naval powers, France and Spain. Yet, as the next chapter will show, British successes had to be fought for and then defended. For most of the period, Britain was at war with other European states (1689–97, 1702–13, 1718–20, 1739–48, 1754–63, 1778–83) or close to war (1725–9, 1733–5, 1770–1, 1776–7).

NOTES

1. J. Black, 'Meeting Voltaire', *Yale University Library Gazette*, 66 (1992), pp. 168–9; R. Butterwick, *Poland's Last King and English Culture. Stanislaw August Poniatowski 1732–1798* (Oxford, 1998).
2. Weichman, Brunswick representative at Hamburg, to Karl, 23 Nov. 1740, Wolfenbüttel, Staatsarchiv 1 Alt 22, 749 fol. 89.
3. H. Lyons, *The Royal Society 1660–1940* (Cambridge, 1944), pp. 126, 344.
4. G. Lesage, *Remarques sur l'Angleterre* (Amsterdam, 1715); Holbach, *Le Système Social* (3 vols, 1774), II, 66–76; J. Lough, *The Encyclopédie* (1971), pp. 297, 318–19.
5. *Craftsman*, 22 July 1732; *Fog's Weekly Journal*, 24 Mar., 21 Apr. 1733.
6. BL. Add. 12130 fols 53–5; Cobbett, IX, 1239, XI, 207.

7. R. Browning, *Political and Constitutional Ideas of the Court Whigs* (Baton Rouge, Louisiana, 1982).
8. J. Lockman, *A New History of England* (1794 edn), ix–x.
9. R. Szostak, *The Role of Transportation in the Industrial Revolution: A Comparison of England and France* (Montreal, 1991).
10. Trevor to Lord Grenville, Foreign Secretary, 8 Oct. 1792, PRO. Foreign Office 67/10.
11. Cobbett, XI, 338.
12. P. Langford, *Englishness Identified: Manners and Character 1650–1850* (Oxford, 2000).
13. P. Taylor, *Indentured to Liberty: Peasant Life and the Hessian Military State, 1688–1815* (Ithaca, New York, 1994).

15

The rise of a world power

The medieval polities of western Europe were pale shadows of the governmental power, range and sophistication of imperial Rome and, especially once the crusading states had been driven from the Middle East, there was little to suggest that western Europe would signify greatly in global history. Its population, wealth, civilisation and governmental structure did not compare favourably with those of other major settled civilisations, especially those of China, northern India, Persia and the Middle East. Furthermore, the Europeans lacked the capacity to project their power great distance, displayed for example on land by the Mongols and at sea by Arabs, Indians and Chinese traders in the Indian Ocean and nearby seas. For complex reasons, this situation changed dramatically towards the close of the fifteenth and in the early decades of the sixteenth century. The Portuguese sailed round what was for them the Cape of Good Hope and established themselves as the foremost naval power in the Indian Ocean. The Spaniards overthrew the Aztecs and Incas in the New World. The Europeans were able to project their power as no other society had done. Philip II of Spain (1556–98) was the first ruler of whom it was true to say that the sun never set on his dominions.

Britain's role in this expansion of European contacts and power was limited. Scotland, Ireland and Wales made scant impact, and English maritime activity was at the margins, both in terms of the legality of their infringement of the hastily asserted territorial rights of other European powers and with regard to its profitability. Whereas Spain gained rich gold and silver mines, English sailors got fish off Newfoundland. Attempts to establish colonies in what is now the USA in the sixteenth century were few and unsuccessful. Despite the fame gained by Francis Drake, English 'sea dogs' found it difficult to make any lasting impact on Spain's position in the West Indies. In the first half of the seventeenth century, it was to be another northern-European, Protestant power, the United Provinces (Dutch), that was to be far more successful in establishing itself as a maritime and colonial challenger to Spain and Portugal. The English East India Company made less of an impact in Asia than its Dutch counterpart.

Yet the situation increasingly changed in England's favour in the second half of the century and this was not to be hindered by the Dutch invasion of 1688 and the subsequent accession of the leading Dutch politician, William III of Orange, as William III of England. Thus the period of imperial, colonial, commercial and maritime growth, aggrandisement and activity in the eighteenth century had earlier roots.

Any explanation of success in these spheres is complex, but it is misleading to look first at the domestic situation. British actions and achievements have to be set in a comparative context, both with reference to other trans-oceanic European states and with regard to native opponents. In the former case, Britain, which in 1650 was less consequential as an imperial power than Spain, the Dutch, Portugal and France, had by 1763 become clearly the most successful trans-oceanic European power. In the latter, the British developed strategies to deal with a wide range of eco-systems and a variety of opponents, including the frozen shores of Hudson Bay, and the temperate forests of the middle American colonies, the heat, humidity and diseases of the southern colonies, the West Indies and India. In India, British interests had to be advanced in the context of major states with numerous forces, whereas in North America the British were faced with less numerous native tribes with only a limited capacity for co-operation. If on land there was a great range in real or potential opponents, one that was to be enlarged when a colony was established in Australia in 1788, at sea the British essentially had only to consider European rivals operating in a familiar context, for it was only in Indian waters that they confronted other naval forces and these were of limited strength and technological sophistication.

Britain was successful in her maritime struggle with her European rivals, and it was this that allowed her to develop and sustain her colonial and commercial position. It is attractive to present this success in terms of 'structural' factors or aspects of Britain's position, for example her system of public finance, but it is important to note the extent to which this success appeared far from inevitable to contemporaries. In 1690, and again in 1779, a French fleet dominated the Channel and, in 1744 and, again, in 1759 the French navy attempted to cover an invasion of England.

To move from the sure facts of victory in battle or size of fleet to the reasons thereof is to enter the sphere of controversy. Again, the comparative dimension is arresting. It reveals that Britain was already one of the two leading naval powers before the period began.

The sailing-ship navies: relative size in percentages of total size

	Britain	**France**	**Netherlands**	**Spain**
1680	29.3	29.9	14.5	3.4
1690	25.1	28.5	13.7	6.0
1700	25.8	25.7	14.9	2.6
1710	26.4	22.4	15.6	1.3
1720	28.3	7.8	12.9	3.6
1730	28.1	10.8	1.2	10.8
1740	29.5	13.8	9.8	13.8
1750	36.5	15.2	8.2	5.4
1760	37.6	15.6	6.2	13.7

	Britain	**France**	**Netherlands**	**Spain**
1770	32.3	20.2	7.3	15.2
1780	28.8	21.7	5.6	15.7
1785	30.5	18.4	8.5	14.5

Source: Jan Glete, *Navies and Nations* (Stockholm, 1993), I, 242, 312.

Thus, the major build-up of British naval strength under the Rump Parliament, the Protectorate of Oliver Cromwell, and the restored monarchy of Charles II had combined to produce a great naval power. Particular domestic constitutional arrangements were less important than a governmental determination to use money in order to exploit the maritime resources of the country. These resources, especially shipbuilding skill and facilities, and sailors experienced in long-distance voyages, were a product of England's commercial expansion in the seventeenth century, and this relationship was to be sustained during the following century.

This combination was not only of practical value to Britain as a power. It also served to generate a set of political and ideological assumptions and preferences that played a major role in shaping British public consciousness in the eighteenth century. To say that the British saw themselves as a maritime nation would be to ignore the large numbers who expressed no such preference, but, insofar as a preference was expressed, it was this one that was central.

The British world changed considerably in the period 1688–1783. This was true not only politically, but also demographically, economically and imaginatively. Whichever is placed first appears most important, and it is conventional to begin with shifts in colonial control. These were indeed significant, but they were the sum of other changes as well as their cause. Furthermore, a stress on political control can lead to a misleading emphasis on central direction.

In the case of the British empire, such direction was limited. Instead, it was the ability of the British system to benefit from the initiatives of individuals, families, and companies that was crucial; just as, later, the failure to respond led to the sundering of the empire with the loss of the Thirteen Colonies that were to be the basis of the United States of America. In contrast to French North America, the British colonies had seen a tremendous population growth. The population quintupled to over a million between 1675 and 1740, and its growth continued thereafter. Settlement spread geographically – westward away from the Atlantic coast onto the Piedmont – and also in the gaps between the coastal enclaves. Numerous towns were founded, including Baltimore (1729), Richmond (1733) and Charlottesville (1744). There was also a significant expansion of settlement to the south, whence, first, rice and, then, cotton were exported to Europe. Slaves were sent to Carolina in order to develop rice growing. Carolina was divided into North and South in 1713, Georgetown being founded in 1735 and Charlotte in 1750. Georgia was established in 1732, Savannah being founded the following year.

The British North American colonies were settlement colonies, inhabited by large numbers of Europeans, although appreciable numbers of Africans were forcibly brought in as slaves, largely to work the plantations. By 1740, two-thirds of the population of South Carolina were slaves, a figure that made it more like the British West Indian colonies than those of northern British America. By 1740, five out of six people living in the British West Indies were slaves, and the contrast subsequently became more pronounced. In contrast, the colony of New York was five-sixths white in 1738. Unlike the French, the British were happy to allow other Europeans to settle in their colonies, although rights for Catholics were limited. Driven by economic difficulties or religious persecution, and lured by hopes of opportunity and freedom, many Germans migrated to the British colonies.

The English Atlantic 'shrank' between 1675 and 1740 as a result of significant improvements, such as the development of postal services, and the invention of the helm wheel, which dramatically increased rudder control on large ships. The number of trans-Atlantic voyages was doubled in this period and the number of ships that extended or ignored the 'optimum' shipping seasons also increased on several major routes. Average peacetime passages from England to Newfoundland were five weeks, from the eastern Caribbean colonies to England eight, and from Jamaica fourteen.[1]

Trade was central to the colonial economy. External trade accounted for nearly 20 per cent of the total income of the Thirteen Colonies at the end of the colonial era. There was no integrated colonial economy; rather, there were colonial economies linked more closely with London than with each other.[2]

The enormous wealth that colonies did, or could, or were believed, to bring was a major reason for interest in them. They played a steadily greater role in Britain's foreign relations. The period from 1688 until the fall of Napoleon in 1815 saw what has been called the Second Hundred Years War. Britain and France were in active competition in colonial trade and expansion. Some ministries were less enthusiastic than others about colonial confrontation. The Walpole ministry resisted opposition pressure in 1730 to take an aggressive stance over competing claims to St Lucia, while assurances were exchanged over the Gambia in 1772–3. Efforts were made to end North American border disputes in the early 1750s. However, the last failed, and, at the best, only short-term agreements could be negotiated with France.

Successful negotiations of colonial issues tended to be held only at the end of wars, but the hurry that marked most peace congresses, as powers tried to beat their allies in settling their specific interests first, made many peace settlements unsatisfactory. The Peace of Utrecht (1713) left important Anglo-French disputes unresolved in North America and the West Indies, and it was largely the alliance of the two governments in 1713–14 and 1716–31 and their relative lack of interest in colonial matters that prevented more serious disputes in this period. In 1729, Anglo-Spanish and in 1748 Anglo-French disputes in the Americas were referred to commissioners who met without appreciable success.

The sole Anglo-French treaty that solved most colonial disputes for a while was the Peace of Paris of 1763. This was partly because it dealt with British, French, Portuguese and Spanish interests only, while the role of colonial issues in creating tension in the 1750s meant that they occupied the central place in the negotiations. The completeness of British colonial and naval victory in the Seven Years' War, rather than the quality of the peace settlement, deterred the Bourbons from attempting to challenge the terms at once. None the less, they inspired a desire for revenge.

In the Nine Years' War (1689–97) conflict between Britain and France overwhelmingly focused on Europe, but concern about trans-oceanic interests had risen as a result of greater maritime and colonial activity on the part of France. In the Nine Years' War, 'English' military activity in North America, such as the successful attack on Port Royal in 1690 and the unsuccessful attack the same year on Québec, was in fact almost entirely locally generated, with little impact from England. Québec, however, was too formidable for the attacking New England force, and its fortifications were improved in the 1690s. As a consequence, any attack would require more powerful forces, especially artillery. Such forces would likely be regulars, yet the dispatch of regular units raised the issue of priorities in England. In the 1690s, Ireland and the Low Countries definitely came first. Fighting in the Caribbean in 1689–97 was also a matter of local initiatives and occasional interventions by metropolitan forces. Much of the conflict bore many of the characteristics of buccaneering. An expedition sent against Guadeloupe in 1691 failed.

In Europe, William III was successful in conquering Ireland, but far less so in the Low Countries, where he was defeated at Steenkirk (1692) and Neerwinden (1693). The French army was the leading one in Western Europe and was at the peak of its capability. However, the commitment of Anglo-Dutch strength in the war denied Louis XIV decisive victory, and the loss of Namur to William in 1695 shook French prestige.

The British proved capable of supporting a larger, more sustained, and more expensive commitment than any that had been mounted hitherto. Having secured an Act declaring that its consent was necessary for a peacetime standing army, Parliament was willing to pay for a substantial war army. Furthermore, the British played an active role in the great rearming of the 1690s, when pikes were replaced by muskets equipped with socket bayonets, and matchlock muskets were replaced by flintlocks. The Ordnance Office displayed flexibility in this rearming, using the capacity of the Birmingham gunsmiths and thus circumventing the monopoly of their London counterparts.

At sea, the British navy was defeated off Beachy Head (1690), but the French failed to exploit this in order to mount an invasion and in 1692 the French were defeated off Barfleur. This helped lead to a major shift in European naval history, which was accentuated from 1694 when the French concentrated on the army and, at sea, on privateering. The dispatch of a large fleet to the Mediterranean in 1694 was followed by its wintering at the allied port of Cadiz, which aided British power projection in the region. In Britain, naval facilities were expanded at Portsmouth and Plymouth.

The British were better able to take the initiative in colonial operations in the War of the Spanish Succession (1702–13), in part because French naval weakness gave the British greater freedom to mount expeditions. However, this led to more operations in the Mediterranean than in the Caribbean, and attacks on St Augustine, the centre of Spanish-ruled Florida, in 1702 and on Guadeloupe in

1703 both failed. Further north, Port Royal, the leading French base in Acadia (Nova Scotia) resisted an attack by New England forces in 1707, but in 1710, supported by British marines, they were successful.

The British government sent a major force to attack Québec in 1711: 5,300 men escorted by 14 ships of the line, the largest hitherto sent to North America. This was designed to improve Britain's position in negotiations, but also reflected political considerations – the impact of politics in particular conjunctures has repeatedly to be borne in mind because politics affected the perception of circumstances and the response to opportunities. In 1711, the new Tory government wished to distract attention from the Duke of Marlborough and also to vindicate the 'blue water' policies they had advocated in opposition. However, preparations were hasty, the government relied too much upon their own over-optimistic assumptions of logistical support from New England, and the expedition was abandoned after a night-time error in navigation had led to the loss of eight transport ships on rocks in the St Lawrence estuary.

Canada had not fallen. Nevertheless, the Peace of Utrecht of 1713 left Britain with Nova Scotia, Newfoundland and Hudson's Bay. These increased the British stake in North America and weakened the defences of New France, an important advantage as, in each conflict, the British would only have several years campaigning.

In Europe, despite defeats and failure in Spain, the war had offered an impressive display of the effectiveness of the British army (see p. 239), certainly in comparison with that provided by the Nine Years' War. The British were helped by a decline in the fighting quality and size of the French army, and by the ability to create and sustain an effective coalition against France. Nevertheless, even allowing for troops from allies, Marlborough's forces were still outnumbered on many occasions. Yet, this did not prevent him from both engaging and winning: Marlborough understood that generalship entailed the application of resources, not their addition. Both strategically and tactically, he sought to use the forces he controlled with great vigour. Although some campaigns brought only disappointing results, Marlborough never suffered a defeat.

Aside from success in the field, the army also enabled the government to play a major role in what was a period in which the European world altered territorially to a greater extent than at any time in the eighteenth century prior to the French Revolutionary crisis at its close. Both by stopping France and by showing that Britain possessed a land capability, the army ensured that Britain played a major role in this process. Not least, the activities and size of the army, and of the supporting subsidised troops, made it important for France to detach Britain from the opposing alliance in 1713 and, therefore, to accept British views in international relations. Indeed, the Anglo-French alliance of 1716–31 was in part a testimony to the recent strength of Britain's military position.

At sea, Britain's naval strength was barely contested by the French during the war, in large part because their expenditure continued to be dominated by the army. This enabled the British to inhibit French invasion planning, to maintain control of maritime routes to the Low Countries, the crucial axis of the alliance, and to project power, especially into the Mediterranean. But for the British navy, there would have been no war in Iberia.

Between 1713 and 1739, North America was again the major overseas sphere of military activity, although the British presence was by no means restricted to it. Elsewhere, however, there was only limited interest in territorial expansion, especially among ministers in London, although there was concern to maintain the security of possessions. In Jamaica, this led to unsuccessful operations in the 1730s against the Maroons, runaway or, in some cases, freed slaves who controlled much of the interior. The Maroons were finally granted land and autonomy by treaties in 1738 and 1739. The militia suppressed the Stono slave rising in South Carolina in 1739. In India, attacks on coastal forts on the Konkan coast of the Maratha naval commander Kanhoji Angria, who launched piratical attacks on British trade, failed in 1718, 1720 and 1721. The British naval presence increased in Caribbean waters.

Whereas the frontier of British control did not advance in India or West Africa in this period, the situation was very different in North America, where the war with the French in 1702–13 had interacted with tension and conflict with Native Americans, and the population growth of the British colonies exacerbated land hunger. The Tuscaroras were defeated in 1713 by North Carolinian forces helped by Native allies, and in 1716–17 the Yamasee were pushed back after South Carolina had secured Native support. The colonists were helped by the impact of European diseases, especially smallpox, on the Natives. The colonists were disunited and had competing territorial claims west of the Appalachians, but were not in conflict and could provide mutual support. In contrast, the Natives were greatly harmed by their rivalries.

British advance was not solely a matter of conflict. Merchants increasingly traded among Native groups west of the Appalachians. In the 1720s, temporary posts were established on the upper Ohio and in 1725 the Iroquois permitted the Governor of New York to construct a stone fort at Oswego. This was the first British base on the Great Lakes. The expansion of trading networks were a crucial means by which the British and French furthered their interests and influence. British activity was largely a matter of initiatives by colonists. The government in London took little interest in the interior of North America, a situation that was not to change until the 1750s, and was an important aspect of the mid-century changes discussed elsewhere in this book. In contrast, the French followed an active policy of expanding their power in the interior.

Whatever the attitude of home governments, it was difficult to prevent colonial rivalry. Merchants, settlers and many colonial governors proved willing to risk conflict to attain their goals, and they played major roles in pushing Britain and Spain and Britain and France towards war in 1739 and 1754–6 respectively. The commercial concessions in the Spanish empire obtained by the British at Utrecht both compromised Spanish imperial mercantile policies and plans and were exploited, often illegally, in order to further British commercial penetration. Relations were further exacerbated by frontier disputes between Spanish Florida and the new colony of Georgia, and by British subjects cutting logwood on the coast of Honduras. The energy of British colonial and mercantile enterprise threatened Spanish assumptions and interests.

The Anglo-Spanish War of Jenkins' Ear (1739–48) was embarked on with high hopes in Britain, where the Spanish American empire was regarded as vulnerable and ready to rebel. Porto Bello fell in 1739 to Admiral Vernon leading to a wave of jingoism that created high expectations. In the volatile political atmosphere of the closing years of the Walpole ministry, the government felt it necessary to respond, and major resources were committed. A large force was sent to the West Indies in 1741, but the ability of Spain, assisted by tropical diseases, to defend its empire had been underestimated. In 1740–2, the British forces in the West Indies lost over 70 per cent of their strength. In 1762, when they took Havana, they lost a third of their troops to yellow fever and malaria.

The continued ravages of disease, despite some medical advances, indicated that British science and organisation, while capable of charting the Pacific, could not meet the ecological challenge of the Tropics. Though scurvy had been recognised as a problem of diet, little was known about the cause or transmission of the major tropical diseases, and this hindered efforts at prevention or cure. Body lice and a fly-carried bacillus were not recognised as the carriers of typhus and dysentery respectively, while mosquitoes were not seen as the vectors of dysentery and yellow fever. A medical regime of bloodletting was unable to provide cures.

The failure to seize Cartagena (modern Colombia) in 1741 was a cathartic experience, and also greatly harmed the Walpole ministry. Thereafter, as war neared with France, the focus of British attention turned to Europe. Colonial rivalry did not at this point play much part in the drift to war with France, although tension was evident in a number of areas, including North America. French concern in the western hemisphere in the 1730s and early 1740s focused on possible British gains from the Spaniards in the Caribbean, rather than on controlling the lands to the west of the Appalachian mountains. Wealth, not land, was at stake.

British intervention in the War of the Austrian Succession led to conflict with France in 1743, war being declared the next year. Although the British planned an attack on Québec, colonial hostilities with France were restricted substantially to the capture of the major French fortress of Louisbourg on Cape Breton Island in 1745 by New England militia supported by British warships, and the loss of the British East India Company's trading station at Madras in 1746. Both sides focused their military efforts on Europe, and the British were made more cautious both by the Jacobite threat and by the failure to defeat the French fleet until two battles off Cape Finisterre in 1747. However, these two victories were severe blows for the French: their fleet could no longer escort major convoys bound for French colonies, and this destroyed the logic of the French imperial system. The navy ended the war in a rich glow of success that helped to sustain the maritime patriotism that had become increasingly important in the definition of national interests.

The war had shown that the navy was an effective fighting force and administrative body, and this was true not only in European, but, also, in trans-oceanic waters. In the West Indies, the most lucrative area of colonial interests, British failures, as at Cartagena, were not primarily due to administrative deficiencies, although the size of the forces deployed there caused victualling problems. The Admiralty's failure to keep the fleet in the Caribbean adequately manned was a reflection of the degree to which it had not yet solved the problem of manning in general. This was exacerbated by the effects of disease. The sick were given good treatment by the standards of the day, but the nature of the diseases was not understood. The men on the spot were generally able to make good whatever administrative deficiencies were revealed. British warships in the West Indies were able to fulfil their operational role, the decisive test of a naval administration.[3]

A later test of administrative effectiveness was seen in 1779–80 as Sir Charles Middleton, Comptroller of the Navy, pressed forward the copper sheathing of much of the navy, in order to reduce the difficulties caused by barnacles, weeds, and the teredo worm, and the consequent loss of speed. The value of copper sheathing in the conduct of naval operations has since been queried, but the organisational achievement was considerable; the demand for copper also brought great wealth to Wales.[4]

Naval activity was not simply a matter of conflict. The government was also interested in circumnavigating North America by discovering a navigable Northwest Passage to the Pacific. In 1741, the Admiralty sent the *Discovery* and *Furnace* to Hudson Bay under Christopher Middleton. The following year, he sailed further north along the west coast of the Bay than any previous European explorer, but could not find the entrance to a passage. Such government activity is a reminder of the need not to minimise state interest in Britain's global expansion.

Louisbourg and Madras were returned after the Peace of Aix la Chapelle in 1748. It was not inevitable that another war would begin soon after. Britain, France and Spain had not done well enough in the war to encourage them to begin again; they were exhausted and their governments did not seek war. The supposed threat to the European system represented by French victories over Austria had been resolved. The Anglo-French alliance of 1716 had followed hard on the heels of a major conflict and, although there was no reason in 1748 to believe that such an alliance was imminent, there was equally no reason why Anglo-French relations should not have developed towards a close state, as their Anglo-Spanish counterparts did in the early 1750s.

However, territorial disputes in North America were made more serious by the British belief that there was a French plan to weaken fatally their position and that it was necessary to act vigorously in order to show the French that they should abandon this plan. As in 1739, the government's room for manoeuvre was restricted by opposition pressure on a divided government. Border hostilities in 1754 were followed in 1755 by a British attack on a French force sailing to Canada. Although war was not declared until the following year, both powers continued hostile acts.

Anglo-French maritime and colonial conflict was more significant in the Seven Years' War (1756–63) than in the preceding conflict. The early stages of the war were unsuccessful for Britain. Minorca was lost (1756), Hanover overrun (1757), and there were defeats in North America (1755–7). Thereafter, the situation radically altered as British amphibious forces succeeded in capturing most of the major overseas centres of the French empire: Louisbourg and Gorée (1758), Guadeloupe and Québec (1759), Montreal and, with it, New France (1760), Pondicherry and, with it, French India, and Dominica (1761), and Martinique (1762).

The French navy was defeated at Lagos and Quiberon Bay in 1759, ending French invasion plans. The British naval position had been challenged by the Bourbons in 1746–55 as the total displacement tonnage of warships they launched then was nearly three times that launched by the British. Fortunately for Britain, Spain did not join the war until France had been defeated at sea. In 1759, the leading French minister, Choiseul, planned a naval concentration to cover an invasion of Britain, prefiguring the strategy of Napoleon. However, the division of the French navy between the distant bases of Brest and Toulon prevented this concentration, and the British were able to defeat the two fleets separately. British gunnery and seamanship proved superior in battle. Naval superiority gave the British the ability to choose where to direct efforts and enabled the application of strength to achieve a local superiority at crucial points at a time of choosing. The forces sent to Germany in 1758 to help Britain's ally Frederick II, 'the Great', of Prussia, defeated the French at Minden in 1759.

The new king of Spain, Charles III, signed an alliance with France in 1761, but was defeated the following year, with the fall of Havana and Manila. The capture of Manila encouraged British interest in the Pacific. An expeditionary force sent to Portugal helped protect it from a French-supported Spanish invasion in 1762. The British benefited greatly from their considerable and unmatched experience in amphibious operations; by 1762 much of the army and navy had experience of them. As was indicative of a culture in which print played a steadily greater role, experience was distilled in Thomas More Molyneux's *Conjunct Expeditions, or Expeditions that have been carried on jointly by the Fleet and Army* (1759). Success also depended on a more general systemic co-ordination: the ability to mount amphibious operations stemmed from a degree of naval superiority in home waters that both made invasion improbable and could permit the dispatch of fleets to distant waters. The creation of naval bases, providing refitting and repair facilities overseas, Port Royal and Port Antonio on Jamaica, English Bay, Antigua from 1728 and Halifax from 1749, helped considerably. Port Royal was able to careen the larger ships of the line sent there.

British naval success was not due to superior weaponry. Neither the ships nor their equipment were substantially different from those of the Bourbons. Indeed the effective series of two-decker 74-gun warships designed by Sir Thomas Slade, Surveyor of the Navy, 1755–71, was based on Spanish and French warships captured in the 1740s. Instead, the crucial factors were: first, a level of continuous high commitment and expenditure that helped to ensure that a high level of both was regarded as normal and necessary, and that naval strength never collapsed; secondly, the inculcation of an ethos and policy that combined the strategic offensive with tactical aggression; and, thirdly, within the constraints of naval warfare and technology, an effective use of the warships of the period. British naval commanders generally took the initiative and were therefore best placed to obtain propitious circumstances. An experienced admiral, George, Lord Anson, was First Lord of the Admiralty in 1751–62, while admirals such as Boscawen, Hawke, Pocock and Rodney were bold and effective commanders. At a gut level, the British fought to win, not to survive for another day, and this was apparent in the victories that gave them the commanding position in the European world. The French financial system lacked the institutional strength and stability of its British counterpart, and this badly affected French naval finances in 1759. Britain also made a greater commitment of national resources to naval rather than land warfare, a political choice that reflected the major role of trade and the national self-image.

The army was able to cope with the tasks it was set and to campaign successfully in America, Germany, Portugal and the West Indies, but it suffered from the absence of a united military command structure that would be able to devise and sustain coherent peacetime programmes of planning and improvement. This reflected the anti-military ethos of British politics, the difficulties of enforcing discipline and diligence on aristocratic officers who owned their positions, and the more general absence of a bureaucratic ethos. As a consequence, the ability of the army to respond in a united and planned fashion to new developments was limited, and it had only limited success in improving its capability during the years of peace. Nevertheless, a successful wartime expansion helped bring victory in the Seven Years' War.

Under the Peace of Paris of 1763, Guadeloupe, Martinique, St Lucia, and Gorée were returned to France, and Havana and Manila to Spain, but the return of Minorca to Britain, the recognition of Britain's gains of New France (Canada), Senegal, Grenada, Tobago, Dominica and St Vincent, and the acquisition of Florida from Spain, amounted to an impressive British triumph.

Naval and colonial victories brought more of the world within Britain's real and imaginative grasp. Greater interest was not restricted to mercantile and political circles. The commemoration of victories such as Vernon's at Porto Bello in 1739 and Wolfe's at Québec in 1759 can be traced through society. Maritime mastery was increasingly seen as the national destiny, and part of the identity of both state and people. Furthermore, it was not simply that the navy and amphibious operations were more successful in the Seven Years' War than in earlier conflicts, but also that their activities and triumphs could be seen clearly as designed to further what were particularly seen as British objectives, rather than those of allies, as with earlier naval operations in the Mediterranean. Between 1688 and 1763, there was a major shift in naval commitments that reflected diplomatic and strategic exigencies, and, in turn, affected the political context that helped to shape expectations concerning naval power.

The navy had always been helped in its public and political reputation by the minor degree to which it required the support of allies, a marked contrast to the army. The growing weakness of Dutch naval power furthered this process, as the Dutch were allies in the Nine Years' War, and the Spanish and Austrian Succession Wars, although not the Seven Years' War. By the last, the trend was complete, and naval action could be envisaged simply in an Anglo-Bourbon context.

The navy could be seen as truly British, not only in its composition, but also in its objectives.

It is important not to neglect the difficulties that faced Britain during the Seven Years' War. It is often claimed that, thanks to Pitt's strategic vision, the two spheres of the war – in Europe and beyond – were held in productive balance, but this underrates the extent to which Britain's Continental commitments threatened the success of trans-oceanic ambitions. In 1748, Louisbourg had to be returned as part of a settlement in which the French evacuated their conquests in the Low Countries. In 1757, Hanover was overrun by France and in 1762 Spain invaded Britain's ally Portugal. In the event, Britain did not suffer too seriously from the consequences of being allied to the weaker bloc on the Continent, but that was fortuitous, and more so than most commentators allowed. Had France and Spain conquered and retained Hanover and Portugal, then it is difficult to see what Britain could have done to free them other than by returning colonial gains. Furthermore, it is important to note the time it took to conquer the latter. In 1757, there was little to show and in 1758 the main advance in Canada failed. Far from having a clear strategic vision, Pitt's strategy emerged as a consequence of an *ad hoc* process of conflict. The war was extended piecemeal, the coastal raids that were Pitt's most distinctive contribution were unsuccessful in their strategic purpose of diverting French resources from Germany, and Pitt was irresponsible about the unprecedented costs of the war.

These points have to be underlined, because a simplistic, and, in large part, erroneous assessment of Britain's position plays a major role in the literature. In addition, there is still inadequate understanding of the domestic constraints and political contexts that affected policy and its public construction. Chance played a major role. Pitt was helped in his emphasis on naval and colonial warfare by the state of the royal family. It was easier to cut across the monarchical emphasis on conventional campaigning on the Continent when George II was elderly and his second son, William, Duke of Cumberland, was discredited by his failure in Hanover in 1757. Had events been otherwise, then the political arithmetic of faction might well have created pressure for a very different strategic vision.

Chance was also significant in international relations. A settlement of the Franco-Prussian conflict in 1757, as Frederick the Great indeed probed, or, later, of the war between Britain's ally Prussia and her Continental rivals would have left Hanover exposed and the French able to devote more resources to the struggle with Britain. Such scenarios are not simply counterfactual speculations: they were advanced by informed contemporaries less certain than later scholars that Pitt had discovered a successful strategic recipe and rhetoric. Nevertheless, Pitt's clear vision of national greatness, 'projected through the great drama of the struggle against the Bourbons',[5] his determination to confront France in the maritime and colonial sphere, and his conviction that Britain must make substantial territorial gains, were of material importance in global history for it was in his period of power that Britain became the leading power in the world.

This was also a period of major expansion in India. France had been the leading European power there in 1750, but by 1765 the situation had been transformed.

Robert Clive's victory over the Nawab of Bengal at Plassey (1757) was the key battle, but victories at Patna and Buxar in 1764 were also crucial. Tactics varied, but the British benefited from disciplined defensive firepower and from a willingness to advance against much larger forces.

British successes at the expense of hostile Indian rulers led to Bengal, Bihar and Orissa being brought under the control of the East India Company. The Company gained the *diwan*, the right to collect revenue and conduct civil justice, and thus a crucial source of revenues that supported future expansion in India. Bengal was virtually invulnerable to the Marathas and Mysore who fought the Company's other Presidencies, respectively Bombay in 1778–82 and Mysore in 1780–4. Bengal's massive resources were at the disposal of these presidencies. Furthermore, although hostile Indian rulers could threaten Bombay and Madras (and the cavalry of Haidar Ali of Mysore advanced to Madras in 1769), they could not challenge their maritime links, unless in alliance with the French, whose forces in India had been defeated in 1760–1. The British military and political presence ensured India's role in the British imperial economy. This role was seen as crucial to British public finances and foreign trade. In December 1782, Sir John Macpherson wrote to Shelburne, 'India has sent in specie and in goods and in drafts upon foreign nations to England since the year 1757 upwards of 50 millions sterling upon balance of account with Britain'.[6]

Thanks to the despatch of regular forces to North America and India in increased numbers in the 1750s, Britain's trans-oceanic presence increasingly took on an official, military dimension and was more integrated at the governmental level with decision-making in London. This was to have different consequences in India, where it is unlikely that the East India Company would have made much headway territorially without the support of Crown forces, and in North America where the imperial system ceased to be successful in both giving rein to local initiatives and in reconciling them with a measure of central direction.

Company tea was to be dumped into Boston harbour in 1773, a public rejection of the structure and rationale of empire. Over the previous decade, British governmental attempts to impose a new fiscal regime in the North American colonies had clashed with established assumptions, as well as the belief that the levying of taxation for revenue purposes by a Parliament that included no colonial representatives was a dangerous innovation. A sense of shared community with Britain had for long been matched by one of particular interests, shown for example by Maryland and Virginia which tried to encourage local shippers by giving them preferential treatment over the British. Rising hostility reflected increasing democratisation in American society. Equally, successive British governments, under pressure from the size of the national debt, were determined to make America pay the cost of its defence. Between 1763 and 1775, nearly four per cent of the entire British national budget was spent on maintaining the army in North America.

British ministries responded with wavering acts of firmness. The Stamp Act, passed in 1765, was withdrawn the following year. The Revenue Act of 1767 drawn up by Charles Townshend, the Chancellor of the Exchequer, imposed customs duties for the American colonies on a variety of goods, including tea. The Americans responded with a trade boycott and action against customs officials, which led to the dispatch of troops to Boston. In government, William Pitt the Elder, now Earl of Chatham, had failed to give coherence to Britain's American policy, let alone to devise a new policy that would help to repair recent differences and give a new direction, or even advance a vision of empire that would win American support. He turned down the idea of a Secretary of State for American affairs, a suggestion that would have offered not only coherence in the implementation of policy, but also a source of ideas and an agency for links with the colonies. Instead, Chatham showed little interest in America or American views.[7]

The landing of troops in Boston in 1768 helped to increase tension. Policing involved the use of military force. The 'Boston Massacre' of 5 March 1770, in which five Bostonians were killed, was seen by many Americans as demonstrating the militarisation of British authority.

The Boston Tea Party of 16 December 1773 dramatised the problems of law and order and the maintenance of authority. The British government believed these arose from the actions of a small number, rather than from widespread disaffection, and, mistakenly, hoped that tough action against Massachusetts, the so-called Coercive or Intolerable Acts of early 1774, would lead to the restoration of order. The Boston Port Act was designed to protect trade and customs officials from harassment, the Massachusetts Charter Act to strengthen the executive, the Administration of Justice and Quartering Acts to make it easier to enforce order.

These measures were criticised by the opposition in Britain as oppressive, but passed by overwhelming majorities. More troops were sent to Massachusetts. General Thomas Gage, the Commander-in-Chief in America, was appointed Governor of the colony and ordered to use force to restore royal authority.

Eventually, the British government was to adopt the path of conciliation, unsuccessfully in the case of America in 1778, when the Carlisle Commission was sent to try to negotiate a settlement, but successfully in Ireland in 1782–3 when British legislative authority was renounced in favour of the Dublin Parliament. However, although earlier compromises, such as a permanent American legislature to exercise powers of taxation renounced by Westminster, were floated, it would have been difficult to win widespread support in America, and there was no consensus in favour of compromise in Britain. The claims of Congress were seen as an unacceptable challenge to parliamentary sovereignty.

Fighting began on 19 April 1775 when the British tried to seize a cache of arms reported to be at Concord, a town 16 miles from Boston, past the village of Lexington. The troops found about 70 militia at the village drawn up in two lines. Heavily outnumbered, the militia began to disperse, but a shot was fired – it is not clear by whom – and the British opened fire, scattering the militia. The shedding of blood outraged New England, and a substantial force, largely dependent on their own guns, soon encircled Boston. The British suffered heavy casualties from defensive fire when they attacked these men at Bunker Hill on 17 June. Elsewhere in the Thirteen Colonies, British authority collapsed: due to the concentration of troops in Massachusetts, governors elsewhere were defenceless.

Although only a minority of colonists wished for independence at the outbreak of fighting, the strength of separatist feeling within this minority was such that compromise on terms acceptable to the British government and British public opinion appeared increasingly unlikely. The emptiness of the imperial ethos for many was revealed in the paranoia and the symbolic and practical acts of defiance that had led to a spiral of violence. In 1776, a congress of representatives at Philadelphia declared the colonies independent.

In 1776–7, British forces were able to win individual engagements, such as the battles of Long Island (1776) and Brandywine Creek (1777) but not to crush the rebellion, and on 17 October 1777 a British army was forced to surrender at Saratoga. France entered the war on the American side in 1778, Spain following a year later. The list of enemies swelled to include the Dutch in 1780. The French made gains in the West Indies, including Dominica (1778), Grenada (1779), St Vincent (1779), Tobago (1781), and Nevis (1782), while the Spaniards overran West Florida in 1779–81.

The surrender of Lord Cornwallis's besieged and outnumbered army at Yorktown in Virginia on 19 October 1781, with naval relief blocked by a French fleet at the mouth of the Chesapeake, seemed to indicate the end of empire. In the Treaty of Versailles of 3 September 1783, American independence was recognised, and Britain ceded the new state the 'Old North West', the area between the Great Lakes and the Ohio River, while Spain regained Florida and Minorca (captured by a Franco-Spanish force in February 1782), and France Senegal and Tobago.

The war had revealed serious faults in the British military system, including the problems posed by the absence of a large enough army. The forces operating in the field were often quite small and thus especially vulnerable to casualties. The limited forces at their disposal affected the strategic plans and tactical moves of the generals. The initial stages of the war with France had revealed a crisis in naval preparedness, but, by the end of the conflict, the British were outbuilding the French. The need to confront a number of challenges around the world placed considerable burdens on the ability to control and allocate resources and raised issues of strategic understanding and of the accurate assessment of threats, all of which were exacerbated by poor communications. There were also serious problems in co-operation between army and navy, as well as problems in co-ordination in both land and sea operations that raise questions about both the calibre of the military leadership and the ability of the military system to execute plans. Blame has been widely distributed. Some generals, particularly Burgoyne and Cornwallis, have been accused of rashness, and others, especially Howe and Clinton, of excessive caution.

However, the war also showed the resilience of the British system. It had required the combined opposition of the American rebels, France, Spain, and the Dutch to bring Britain low. The French had only attacked after the American rebels had shown an ability to win on the battlefield. Even so, the war was not a complete disaster for Britain: the American attempt to conquer Canada was defeated in 1776; the Franco-Spanish attempt to invade England in 1779 failed (largely due to disease, the weather and poor organisation); Gibraltar resisted a blockade that began in 1779 and a major siege that followed in 1781; British India held on against the Marathas, Mysore and France; in his defeat of the French at the battle of the Saints in 1782, Rodney saved the reputation of British naval power; and the British were able to hold onto New York, Charleston, Savannah and East Florida until the close of hostilities.

Arguably, the task of suppressing the American revolution was anyway too great for the British military. The swift revival of the British empire in the years after the war, which was dramatically shown when British objectives were obtained in the Dutch crisis of 1787 and the Nootka Sound Crisis of 1790, suggests that it would be unwise to underrate the resilience of the British imperial system and its comparative strength. Yet, at the same time, it is necessary to note the precarious character of many of the achievements noted in the previous paragraph. When the Americans invaded Canada in late 1775 they were everywhere successful until they besieged Québec, and eventual British victory was dependent on the arrival of a relief force. Rodney was successful at the Saints, but in 1778 Keppel had failed to defeat the Brest fleet off Ushant. Thereafter, there was no sense that Britain controlled the war at sea. In the summer of 1781 a Franco-Spanish fleet was able to cruise in the Channel approaches without the outnumbered British risking battle.

In India, the British were put under formidable pressure. An advance from Bombay towards the Maratha capital in 1778–9 was poorly conducted and the Marathas were able to surround the British force and press it hard, obliging it on 12 January 1779 to sign a convention at Wadgaon under which the British retreated. On 10 September 1780, an outnumbered British army was destroyed by Haidar Ali of Mysore at Perumbakam; in 1782 his son, Tipu Sultan, was similarly successful just south of the Coleroon River. The British were fortunate that the French were handicapped by the limited military forces they could deploy in India and by the mutual antipathy of Mysore and the Marathas. By the time the 1,400 French reinforcements *en route* for India reached Mauritius in July 1782, 1,032 were ill with scurvy and many others had died. At Cuddalore in June 1783, Bussy had 2,200 French troops, rather than the 10,000 he was supposed to have, and 2,000 sepoys. He still defeated the 12,000 strong British East India Company force.[8] The supporting French squadron under Suffren proved a redoubtable opponent at sea, and forced the British garrison in Trincomalee to capitulate in August 1782. When the war ended, Suffren was planning an attack on Madras. Suffren suffered from the lack of a well-equipped local base and from poor relations with some of his captains, but his battles with Edward Hughes in 1782–3 showed that the British navy was not inherently bound to triumph. On land, the British did not necessarily enjoy an advantage in weaponry and tactics over their Indian opponents, and there was no sense of inevitable success. Instead, the developing sophistication of Indian opponents was noted. The Secret Committee at Fort St George noted of Haidar Ali in the 1781 campaign:

> though he had engaged three times in the late campaign he discontinued the combat on each occasion before any durable impression could be made on his

army, that Sir Eyre Coote always possessing the field of battle had a fair title
to the laurels due to victory but that Haidar suffered few of the disadvantages
of a defeat, that his numerous bodies so far from dispersing as had in general
been the case with Indian armies in contest with our troops were for the most
part as well kept together as before, and did not seem to feel the humiliation
or adopt the fears of the vanquished, that they were driven to no permanent
distress nor did they abandon the territory they had invaded, that the decided
superiority of the British arms in Indostan had been maintained but the solid
purpose of the war to expel the enemy remained to be effected.[9]

Thus, the course of the war suggested that the British position was vulnerable in
areas where control had been maintained. There were fears that the Bourbons
would resume hostilities.[10] Fears were raised about their plans in India, Canada,
the eastern Mediterranean and other areas. India acted as the focus of a sense of
vulnerability bred out of recent defeat and of distrust of France.

Aside from anxieties about military weakness, there was a strong consciousness of diplomatic isolation, and worry about the consequences of domestic instability on Britain's international status. In 1783, Thomas, 2nd Lord Grantham, the
Foreign Secretary in the Shelburne ministry, expressed the hope 'that our civil
revolutions may not destroy all confidence from abroad in our councils', while
Sir Robert Murray Keith, envoy in Vienna, and a former MP, wrote: 'I presume
the parties in Parliament are whetting their knives to assassinate each other at the
opening [of the session] without any regard to the welfare of old England. You
are a set of hardened sinners, and nothing will reclaim you'. He also referred
to an absence of 'steady government'.[11] That summer, John, 2nd Earl of
Buckinghamshire, a former diplomat, took time off from admiring the scantily
clad bathing beauties at Weymouth, to reflect on 'this unhappy disgraced country
surrounded by every species of embarrassment, and without even a distant
prospect of establishing an administration so firm and so respectable as to restore
to England any proportion of her defeated dignity. The state is now circum-
stanced as a human body in the last stage of a decline.'

Like George III, who had been driven to consider abdication, the political
crisis led Buckinghamshire to question his assumptions: 'Whig as I am and sufficiently vain of my descent from Maynard and Hampden [opponents of the
Stuarts], it sometimes occurs to me that something might be obtained by strengthening the hands of the Crown.'[12]

The British political system appeared to have failed. Defeat abroad, the crisis
of the imperial system, was matched by debilitating instability at home. Indeed,
in February and March 1783, Pitt rejected royal invitations to form a government.[13] These domestic weaknesses seemed to guarantee continued imperial vulnerability and diplomatic isolation: who would want to ally with Britain? As the
last section of Chapter 13 makes clear, the crisis was to be resolved and indeed
by the end of 1787 Britain was to be in a far stronger international position, as
French influence in the United Provinces had been overthrown thanks to a
British-instigated Prussian invasion.

Although the crisis of the early 1780s was to be shortlived, it poses important questions about Britain's strength as a world power. All world powers have faced such questions, as, for example, with the USA at the time of its failure in the Vietnam War. However, the loss of Britain's American colonies was a more fundamental challenge. It revealed important deficiencies in the incorporating character of British empire, deficiencies which were to be tested thereafter in relations with Ireland. In addition, the war suggested that the clearcut victory over France (and Spain) in the Seven Years' War was as much the result of the particular circumstances of the conflict as of inherent British strengths. This opens up fundamental questions relating to the respective roles of structure and process, and more specifically to the nature of determinism in military history. Scholars are divided on this point, and it is appropriate to conclude on an open-ended question. It returns us to the uncertainty of the past.

CONCLUSIONS

British military power rested on four fundamental capabilities: the successful suppression of internal revolt (except in America), a small, but highly trained, army that could engage its larger enemies in Europe, naval power, and successful trans-oceanic land warfare. There was nothing inevitable about how these capabilities emerged or inter-related. They were forged by circumstance from experiment and hard fighting. Command decisions and skills were important, not least in explaining why Britain's performance was better in 1702–13 and 1756–63 than in 1689–97 or 1739–48. A thriving market economy and effective public finances were vital aids but wars had to be fought. In turn, these conflicts affected Britain, its economy, society and politics. War led to demand for munitions,[14] and affected many aspects of the economy, not just with short-term disruptions and opportunities, but also in more fundamental ways. The greater prospects created by an imperial economy also influenced domestic suppositions about national goals and thus affected the parameters of politics.

Imperial conquest does not conform to current mores, and there is profound ambivalence, not to say amnesia, towards Britain's imperial past. At the time, however, victories and conquests abroad were deplored by few. Britain was ruled not by pacifist Quakers, but by a political élite determined to pursue national interests and destiny across the world, and this resonated with the aspirations of the wider political nation. Truly a world that is lost, but one that cannot be disentangled from the history of the period.

NOTES

1. I. Steele, *The English Atlantic 1675–1740: An Exploration of Communication and Community* (Oxford, 1986).
2. J.J. McCusker and R.R. Menard, *The Economy of British America 1607–1789* (2nd edn, Chapel Hill, North Carolina, 1991).

3. D. Crewe, *Yellow Jack and the Worm: British Naval Administration in the West Indies, 1739–1748* (Liverpool, 1993).
4. J.E. Talbott, 'Copper, salt, and the worm', *Naval History*, 3 (1989), p. 53. See, more generally, R.J.W. Knight, 'The Royal Navy's recovery after the early phase of the American Revolutionary War', in G.J. Andreopoulos and H.E. Selesky (eds), *The Aftermath of Defeat. Societies, Armed Forces, and the Challenge of Recovery* (New Haven, 1994) pp. 10–25.
5. M. Peters, *The Elder Pitt* (1998), p. 246.
6. Macpherson to Shelburne, 6 Dec. 1782, Bowood, papers of 2nd Earl of Shelburne, Box. 56.
7. P.D.G. Thomas, *The Townshend Duties Crisis. The Second Phase of the American Revolution 1767–1773* (Oxford, 1987).
8. S. Das, *Myths and Realities of French Imperialism in India, 1763–1783* (New York, 1992), p. 193.
9. BL. Add. 22422 fol. 11.
10. Lord North to Charles James Fox, 27 Aug. 1783, BL. Add. 47561 fol. 7.
11. Grantham to Keith, 22 Feb., Keith to his cousin Frances Murray, 10 Oct., 18 Dec. 1783, BL. Add. 35528 fol. 22, HL. HM. 18940 pp. 266, 270–1.
12. Buckinghamshire to Sir Charles Hotham, 12 July 1783, Hull, University Library, DDHo/4/22.
13. Pitt to George III, 25 Mar. 1783, PRO. 30/8/101 fol. 1.
14. D. Crossley and R. Savage (eds), *The Fuller Letters: Guns, Slaves and Finance 1728–1855* (Lewes, 1991).

16

Conclusions

Changes over the last half century have challenged, and even reversed, the major developments of the eighteenth century. The size of the indigenous population has ceased to grow, Britain is no longer at the forefront of technological development or of European economic strength, empire has gone, and the Union with Scotland is under challenge as a result of separatist nationalism and devolution. It is therefore important to turn back to the eighteenth century to survey the early stages of these developments and to probe how far they derived from structural or inherent features in Britain's history and how far from contingent events. In part, there is a problem of distinguishing what is specific to Britain from more general trends. Demographic growth and imperial expansion can be located in the latter, although there are also particular characteristics with the timing or course of these developments in Britain. Thus, for example, the French empire also expanded after 1688, but, eventually, due to defeat, less than that of Britain.

As far as contingencies are concerned, the defining moment was the Jacobite retreat from Derby on 6 December 1745. Had the Jacobites advanced they might have won, ensuring that the new state created in 1688–9 and 1706–7, with its Protestant character and limited government would have been altered. Although Jacobites called for a restoration of liberties, and a balanced constitution, Jacobite victory might have led to a Catholic, conservative, autocratic and pro-French Britain, or, in turn, such a state might have provoked a violent reaction akin to that of the French Revolution.

Instead, thanks to the Duke of Cumberland's victory at Culloden in 1746, the Whig Ascendancy was not to be overcome from outside. In addition, the defeat of Jacobitism helped to overcome or lessen the impact of long-lasting divides in British society, for example between Gaeldom and the world of English in Ireland and Highland Scotland, between English and Scots in Lowland Scotland, between Catholic, Anglican and Presbyterian in Ireland, and between Highland and Lowland and Presbyterian and Episcopalian in Scotland. Instead, there was a process of identification around English norms, as in John Walker's *Pronouncing Dictionary of English* (London, 1774), which provided 'rules to be observed by the natives of Scotland, Ireland and London for avoiding their respective peculiarities'. Culloden ensured that the new British state created in 1707 would continue to be specifically Protestant and with a political tone and agenda set in London and southern England but with the support of the Scottish and Irish Protestant élites.

Thanks to Culloden, as well as to a growing economy, an expanding population, and a powerful world empire, there was a strong feeling of national confidence and superiority. This replaced seventeenth-century anxiety and a marked sense of inferiority vis-à-vis Louis XIV's France. Whig confidence broadened in mid-century into the cultural moulding of the notion and reality of a united and powerful country. It was no coincidence that 'Rule Britannia' was composed in 1740. Cultural nationalism and xenophobia were other aspects of a growing assertiveness that was, in part, a continuation of earlier anti-Popery and, also, involved a hostile response to cosmopolitan influences. This assertiveness was on behalf both of what were presented as traditional liberties, especially the role of Parliament and the rule of law, and also what was seen as the Modern, not least the role of trade, the strength of a vernacular culture, and the political, ideological and constitutional changes stemming from the 'Glorious Revolution'.

Britishness was one response to the need to create a political culture to accompany the new state formed by the Act of Union. Sympathetic Scots made a major contribution. Yet, Britishness was also in many respects a product of English triumphalism and, in part, a vehicle for it. Conceptions of Englishness, not least of the notion of a chosen Protestant nation, and of a law-abiding society, were translated into Britishness. There was a sense of superiority over Scotland, Wales, Ireland and the rest of the world. Although, in the period 1689–1714 many people were angered by the 'Glorious Revolution' and by the burdens of war with France, while, in 1714–45, many thought England was being ruined by the rising national debt and becoming corrupt and weak under the Hanoverians, mid-century victories helped to produce a self-confidence in national identity and destiny.

The English dimension of Britishness is one that for long received insufficient attention, but was highlighted by Scottish and Welsh separatists in the late-twentieth century. They, however, while emphasising the extent to which the creation of Britain rested in large part on military conquest, underplayed the vitality of England as a model. In part, the skill of the concept of Britishness rested on its ability to draw on assessments of Englishness but not to associate them too closely with England. As a result, Britishness could be combined with still vigorous senses of local, provincial and national loyalties.

Englishness/Britishness was contrasted with Continental Europe by contemporary commentators, both British and foreign. It was argued that the English were free, and this contributed to a public myth of uniqueness. The Common Law was seen as a particularly English creation, was contrasted with legal precepts and practice in, above all, France, and enjoyed marked attention. Liberty and property, and freedom under the law were cried up as distinctly English. Foreign commentators observed a lack of deference to the monarch, and also to aristocrats in elections and in the life of the counties, even though, as the century progressed, wealthy aristocrats grew richer and had greater electoral influence. Indeed, in power, the Whigs grew complacent and, to an extent, intellectually bankrupt. They forgot the demand made by the 1st Earl of Shaftesbury and the Exclusion Whigs for a freeholder franchise in all boroughs, and ignored radical suggestions. Instead, Whigs in power defended the status quo they had created, while opposition Whigs once they gained power accepted, and profited from, the situation. A pro-government pamphleteer declared in 1743:

> Miscreants cover their seditious views, with a pretended concern for the welfare of the people, and endeavour to keep them daily alarmed with the danger of slavery from standing armies, and of poverty from the loss of trade, although their liberties have been enjoyed to a greater extent, and the commerce of this nation has been in a more flourishing state during the reign of this royal family, than was ever known in the same period of time before; and indeed the happiness that every honest Briton may securely enjoy in his own vineyard under this government, where the sovereign has made the law of the land the standard and rule of all his actions, is so conspicuous ... [1]

The comparisons of the Whig system with a self-serving criminal group despoiling the public made by critics such as John Gay and Henry Fielding were a biting comment on such claims.

The ideology of liberty and property which the Whigs propagated was not one of unrestrained freedom. Richard Hurd, one of George III's favourite bishops, referred to a sermon preached by Dr John Brown in Cambridge in November 1754:

> He preached a sermon here, which many people commended; it was to prove that tyranny was productive of superstition, and superstition of tyranny; that debauchery was the cause of free-thinking and free-thinking of debauchery. His conclusion was that the only way of keeping us from being a French province was to preserve our constitutional liberties, and the purity of our manners. [2]

Meanwhile, landed society celebrated its position by spending large sums of money on splendid stately houses and on surrounding grounds which increasingly changed from geometric patterns towards a naturalistic parkland style. This was to become part of the visual character of Englishness, a counterpart to the hedgerows of the enclosed worked landscape. Both reflected the power relationships of the period.

This was taken furthest where settlements were moved, as when the medieval Oxfordshire village of Nuneham Courtenay and its church were destroyed to make way for Earl Harcourt's new park in 1759, although Harcourt did provide the displaced villagers with well-built, spacious houses. The village of Shugborough was bought up and demolished by Thomas Anson between 1731 and 1773 in order to create open parkland in front of the house. Villages were also swept aside for stately homes at Kedleston, Stowe and Wimpole. In the *Deserted Village* (1770), Oliver Goldsmith complained about the tyrant that had destroyed 'sweet Auburn' village:

> ... The man of wealth and pride
> Takes up a space that many poor supplied;
> Space for his lake, his park's extended bounds,
> Space for his horses, equipage and hounds.

Power relationships were also reflected in the West End of London, which established the 'classical' style of Georgian town-building and in buildings such as the Bank of England. London was disproportionately important to the character of England, in so far as such a concept can be used. It promoted the interaction of bourgeois/middle-class and aristocratic thinking and values, and also helped secure the influence of commercial considerations upon national policy. Furthermore, London moulded a national economic space, although it is clear that specialisation for the London market was accompanied by the persistence of more local economic patterns.

More generally, the dynamic character of urban life was seen in the number of town histories published – 241 between 1701 and 1820. This was civic pride with a purpose. Town life was presented as the cutting edge of civilisation. Towns were crucial to provincial culture, and to the vitality of the middling part of society, and were also nodes in the expanding transport system. Town and transport improvements both reflected a sense that change was attainable and could be directed. This was also very important to the Industrial Revolution. A belief in its possibility and profitability fired growth; which took the form not only of quantitative expansion but also of changes in the nature of the economy. While it is important not to exaggerate the scale of economic change, it was more extensive in Britain than elsewhere in Europe or the world. In his *Inquiry into the Nature and Causes of the Wealth of Nations* (1776), Adam Smith regretted expenditure on successive wars, but continued:

> though the profusion of government must, undoubtedly, have retarded the natural progress of England towards wealth and improvement, it has not been able to stop it. The annual produce of its land and labour is, undoubtedly, much greater at present than it was either at the Restoration [1660] or at the Revolution [1688]. The capital, therefore, annually employed in cultivating this land, and in maintaining this labour, must likewise be much greater. In the midst of all the exactions of government, this capital has been silently and gradually accumulated by the private frugality and good conduct of individuals, by their universal, continual, and uninterrupted effort to better their own condition. It is this effort, protected by law and allowed by liberty to exert itself in the manner that is most advantageous, which has maintained the progress of England towards opulence and improvement in almost all former times, and which, it is to be hoped, will do so in all future times.[3]

This assessment of economic progress as dependent on freedom, the rule of law and limited government was to be very important to the British conception of national history and development. It failed to give much attention to the social problems arising from economic growth. This growth depended on a number of factors, but one that is too easy to overlook was the growing ability to systematise understandings of cause and effect and to measure, rather than guess. In part, this organisation and application of knowledge can be seen in a number of spheres of national life, although its scope should not be exaggerated. The law, for example, was a matter of accretion through case law, rather than a systematised codification based on clearly ranked written principles.

Applied knowledge was related to commodification, the sense that everything could be traded. Such a description would usually be attributed to the active land market in which land and status could be bought or to the expanding world of goods described in terms of a consumer revolution. Commodification has however wider resonances. It can be ascribed to the treatment of time. Developments such as the accurate measurement of longitude and the growth of regular fast stage coach services made it easier to divide up time and travel into predictable segments. Commodification could also be ascribed to political structures and events. The structures could be understood as machines operating in a scientific fashion. This was very clearly the case with the concept of the balance of power which was extensively employed for both international relations and the operations of the constitution. The 'Address to the Public' at the beginning of the first volume of *The Senator*, a new periodical devoted to reporting parliamentary debates, offered a summary of the established thesis of the British constitution:

> ... that firmness, beauty, and magnificence of our excellent Constitution, founded on the mutual consent of Prince and People; both moving, as it were, in one orb, reciprocally influencing, attracting, and directing each other; whose united power may be compared to a machine for the determining the equality of weights; the sovereign and the representative body counterpoising each other, and the peers preserving the equilibrium.[4]

The use of mechanistic language was appropriate, and reflected the sway of Newtonian physics or at least their role in explaining how things worked and could be made to work. Thus the comparison was to a machine in which separate bodies balanced each other and to a solar system in which reciprocally influencing and directing bodies moved in the same orbit. Such coordination was necessary to prevent disharmony, an ancient theme that drew on astronomical images, but also to prevent disintegration, a thesis that was given new strength by Newton's emphasis on the atomic nature of matter: that God at the creation had formed matter in solid particles. Atoms were seen as possessing 'powers' or forces of attraction and repulsion. These were subject to mathematical analysis,[5] and this encouraged a belief that science could be used for human benefit, a belief that took form in the rising number of patents from the 1750s.

Atomisation was a threat to political harmony, rather as individualism was to society. Stressing what he saw as the depth of the political crisis, Pitt told

Newcastle in 1755, 'that the House of Commons was now an assembly of atoms; that the great wheels of the machine were stopped'.[6] It was unclear to contemporaries how best to, as Pitt phrased it, put the wheels 'in motion'. Machinisation suggested the possibility of establishing a political order that was consistent, predictable and stable, but the threat appeared to come from the fallibility of human ambitions and schemes; just as unwarranted ambition, vice and self-indulgence appeared to challenge the social order and social propriety. This moralistic approach gave too little weight to differences in interests, assumptions and values. Instead, a belief in perfectibility, or at least order, stability and politeness, led to a definition of difference in terms of threat. In political terms, this was seen poignantly in the way in which constitutional, political and financial differences were rapidly overlain on both parts with the paranoid language of tyranny or treason.

Desperate language was also used for disputes within Britain. Indeed, the usual strength of governmental control of Parliament helps explain the readiness with which opposition politicians resorted to such language. In 1778, John, 3rd Earl of Bristol wrote:

> These accumulated evils are really too much, not to feel, and wish to resist in an effectual manner. What is to become of us, are we determined to submit and be tamely sacrificed or not? Do not the real friends of this country wish for such meetings, in order to endeavour to stem the torrent of destruction? ... all the zealous well-wishers of the King and Country, must confront and unite under one great principle of disinterested zeal.[7]

Such concern tended to focus on criticism of allegedly malign ministers, especially on policies that were screened from public view and political scrutiny, but it would be mistaken to underrate interest in constitutional change. First and foremost were the major changes stemming from the 'Glorious Revolution' and the Act of Union with Scotland, but they were not alone. Thus, the Septennial Act of 1716 represented not only an immediate search for party advantage but also a determination to bring more governmental stability by markedly limiting the frequency of the political process. Indeed, a repeated theme in the eighteenth century, a period commonly noted for its constitutional and institutional conservatism, was the willingness of politicians to press for change, although this was often presented as restorative change. There were repeated calls in the 1720s, 1730s and 1740s for legislation designed to alter the conduct and composition of Parliament. Pressure for more frequent elections, for the banning of office-holders from Parliament and for the enforcement and extension of landed qualifications for MPs, reflected a sense that the nature of Parliament was far from fixed. These themes, especially the banning of specific categories of office-holders, recurred in the second half of the century, and led to particular pieces of legislation, such as Crewe's Act (1782) and Clerke's Act (1782).

The loss of America raised and raises questions about the effectiveness of British politics and government, but it was far from easy to govern transoceanic empires in a flexible fashion. It is more instructive to note the essential political stability of Britain in the 1750s–80s. This description may seem surprising, as this was a period noted for constitutional disputes and also for extra-parliamentary agitation, some of it radical, for example the Wilkesite disputes of the 1760s and the Yorkshire Association movement of the early 1780s. Nevertheless, discord was compatible with a stable political system, although a degree of ambivalence towards the notion of a loyal opposition helped to blind many contemporaries to this. Ministries were stable as long as they could avoid unforeseen problems and retain royal confidence.

More generally, government relied on co-operation with the socio-political elite, and lacked the substantial bureaucracy and well-developed bureaucratic ethos that would have been necessary had they sought to operate without such co-operation. This extended to newly prominent social and economic interests. They were incorporated into the state.

The character of the political conflicts and divisions within the British world in 1775–83 was different to that of less than a century earlier. In 1688, as in 1485 when Henry Tudor (VII) had seized the throne from Richard III, England had been successfully invaded. In 1688, the situation had been very different to 1485 for a number of reasons, not least the validating role of Parliament and the need to ensure that Scotland and Ireland were brought in line. Nevertheless, there was also a fundamental continuity between 1485 and 1688 and a corresponding discontinuity with 1775–83. In 1485 and 1688 not only were political issues settled by conflict but, in addition, the dynastic position was crucial: political legitimacy could not be divorced from the sovereign and the succession. These ensure that the elements of modernity suggested by the constitutional products of the 1688 invasion – especially the Bill of Rights of 1689, and the moves towards regular parliaments and elections, and a freer press – have to be qualified by reminders of more traditional features of the political system. The foreign force invading England and the aristocrats rising against the king were reminiscent of the French-supported baronial opposition to King John in 1216 and of Henry VII's French-backed invasion in 1485. It is misleading to present the 'Glorious Revolution' as an unqualified advance on the march to modernity.

A parallel with opposition to John was drawn over the resignation of ministers that in 1746 obliged George II to abandon his attempt to bring Carteret back into the government:

> This was called a factious measure by some, who compared it to the violence offered to their kings by the barons of old; and was universally condemned by all, when it appeared that the public had no concern in the dispute; that instead of obtaining a second Magna Carta to bespeak the favour and good will of the people, they had only made a new provision for themselves and their creatures; and that the same men were employed, and the same measures pursued as before.[8]

The willingness to 'espouse the cause of the people against the oppressions of men in power'[9] and to limit authority was a characteristic of opposition writing throughout the period that became more pronounced from the 1760s. However, the notion of the people and how they should act were both narrowly defined by modern standards, and it would be unwise to stress changes in the attitudes and conduct of those who held office.

By the 1770s, in Britain as well as her American colonies, there was a strongly-argued case for a more inclusive form of politics. There were parallels with the crisis of 1688. The French supported the American Revolution (and the abortive Irish Revolution of 1798), as the Dutch had backed (indeed made possible) opposition to James, but, by the 1770s, politics was affirmed in terms of representation rather than dynastic legitimacy. Clearly the contrast should not be exaggerated. The constitutional elements of the Revolution Settlement were important. Nevertheless, the prospect of a transformation in politics and society made possible by the overthrow of James had been contained by William's sweeping (and in England swift) success. There had been widespread politicisation, but social change was limited.

In the 1770s and early 1780s, demands for a new form of politics cost Britain her American colonies, but did not lead to a political breakdown in the British Isles. The political system was not so rigid that it could not cope with challenges. There was no matching rebellion in England, Ireland or Scotland in 1775–83; although the Irish Volunteer movement posed the threat of power slipping away to an ad hoc, non-governmental organisation. Failure in the War of American Independence did not lead to an insuperable crisis at home. The fundamentals of the mid-eighteenth century British achievement held. This was crucial to the way in which the population and economy expanded without political or social breakdown. The way was open to the Industrial Revolution and to the challenge of coping successfully with over two decades of conflict with Revolutionary and Napoleonic France.

NOTES

1. Anon., *The Interest of Great Britain Steadily Pursued* (1743), pp. 58–9.
2. S. Brewer (ed.), *The Early Letters of Bishop Richard Hurd 1739–1762* (Woodbridge, 1995).
3. Adam Smith, *An Inquiry into the Nature and Causes of the Wealth of Nations*, edited by R.H. Campbell and A.S. Skinner (2 vols, Oxford, 1976), I, 345.
4. *Senator* I (1791), iii.
5. A. Thackray, *Atoms and Powers: An Essay on Newtonian Matter – Theory and the Development of Chemistry* (Cambridge, Mass., 1970).
6. Newcastle to Hardwicke, 3 Sept. 1755, BL. Add. 32857, fols 409–10.
7. Bristol to Earl of Shelburne, 27 Aug. 1778, Bowood, Shelburne papers, Box 36.
8. Anon., *Apology for a Late Resignation* (1747), p. 8.
9. Anon., *A Letter to the Craftsman, upon the Change of Affairs in Europe* (1734), p. 63.

Selected further reading

It is impossible to mention more than a small fraction of the many important works that are available. In this brief section the focus is on recent works. Earlier works can be traced through their bibliographies. It is also important to follow up works cited in the footnotes of this and other books.

1. GENERAL

K.M. Brown, *Kingdom or Province? Scotland and the Regal Union, 1603–1715* (1992).

S.J. Connolly, *Religion, Law and Power: The Making of Protestant Ireland, 1660–1760* (1992).

T.M. Devine and J.R. Young (eds), *Eighteenth Century Scotland: New Perspectives* (1999).

G. Holmes, *The Making of a Great Power. Late Stuart and Early Georgian Britain 1660–1722* (1993).

G. Holmes and D. Szechi, *The Age of Oligarchy. Pre-Industrial Britain 1722–1783* (1993).

J. Hoppit, *A Land of Liberty? England 1689–1727* (2000).

P. Langford, *A Polite and Commercial People: England, 1727–1783* (1989).

T.W. Moody and W.E. Vaughan (eds), *A New History of Ireland, IV. Eighteenth-Century Ireland, 1691–1800* (1986).

A. Murdoch, *British History 1660–1832. National Identity and Local Culture* (1998).

F. O'Gorman, *The Long Eighteenth Century. British Political and Social History 1688–1832* (1997).

W. Prest, *Albion Ascendant. English History 1660–1815* (1998).

R. Price, *British Society 1680–1880* (1999).

T.C. Smout, *A History of the Scottish People, 1560–1830* (1986).

C.A. Whatley, *Scottish Society 1707–1830. Beyond Jacobitism, towards Industrialisation* (2000).

2. LIFE AND DEATH

B. Capp, *Astrology and the Popular Press: English Almanacs, 1550–1800* (1989).

A. Doig *et al.* (eds), *William Cullen and the Eighteenth-Century Medical World* (Edinburgh, 1993).

R.A. Houston, *The Population History of Britain and Ireland, 1500–1750* (1992).

P. Razell, *Essays in English Population History* (1993).

I.D. Whyte, *Migration and Society in Britain 1550–1830* (2000).
E.A. Wrigley and R.S. Schofield, *The Population History of England, 1541–1871: A Reconstruction* (1989).

3. AGRICULTURE

J.V. Beckett, *The Agricultural Revolution* (1990).
M. Overton, *Agricultural Revolution in England: The Transformation of the Agrarian Community, 1500–1850* (1996).
J. Thirsk, *England's Agricultural Regions and Agrarian History, 1500–1750* (1987).

4. INDUSTRY

M. Berg, P. Hudson and M. Sonenscher (eds), *Manufacture in Town and Country before the Factory* (1983).
M. Berg, *The Age of Manufactures, 1700–1820* (1994).
M.J. Daunton, *Progress and Poverty: An Economic and Social History of Britain, 1700–1850* (1995).
J. Langton and R.J. Morris (ed.), *Atlas of Industrializing Britain, 1780–1914* (1986).
J. Mokyr (ed.), *The British Industrial Revolution: An Economic Perspective* (1993).
P. O'Brien and R. Quinault (eds), *The Industrial Revolution and British Society* (Cambridge, 1992).
J. Rule, *The Vital Century: England's Developing Economy, 1714–1815* (1992).

5. THE MEANS OF COMMERCE

W. Albert, *The Turnpike Road System in England, 1663–1840* (1972).
J. Brewer and R. Porter (eds), *Consumption and the World of Goods* (1993).
J.A. Chartres, *Internal Trade in England, 1500–1700* (1997).
R. Davis, *A Commercial Revolution* (1967).
M. Duffy and others (eds), *The New Maritime History of Devon, I. From Early Times to the Late Eighteenth Century* (1992).
B. Lemire, *Fashion's Favourite: The Cotton Trade and the Consumer in Britain, 1660–1800* (1991).
H. and L. Mui, *Shops and Shopkeeping in Eighteenth-Century England* (1989).
C. Shammas, *The Pre-Industrial Consumer in England and America* (1990).
L. Weatherill, *Consumer Behaviour and Material Culture in Britain, 1660–1760* (1988).
C. Wilson, *Mercantilism* (1958).

6. SOCIETY

J. Barry and C.W. Brooks (eds), *The Middling Sort of People: Culture, Society and Politics in England, 1550–1800* (1994).
J.V. Beckett, *The Aristocracy in England, 1660–1914* (1986).
P. Earle, *The Making of the English Middle Class: Business, Society and Family Life in London, 1660–1730* (1989).
A. Fletcher, *Gender, Sex and Subordination in England 1500–1800* (1995).
N. Hans, *New Trends in Education in the Eighteenth Century* (1966).
D. Hay and N. Rogers, *Eighteenth-Century English Society: Shuttles and Swords* (1997).

B. Hill, *Women, Work and Sexual Politics in Eighteenth-Century England* (1989).
T. Hitchcock, *English Sexualities 1700–1800* (1997).
R.A. Houston, *Scottish Literacy and the Scottish Identity* (1985).
R.A. Houston and I. Whyte (eds), *Scottish Society, 1500–1800* (1990).
M.G. Jones, *The Charity School Movement* (1938).
R.W. Malcolmson, *Life and Labour in England, 1700–1780* (1981).
T. Meldrum, *Domestic Service and Gender 1660–1750. Life and Work in the London Household* (2000).
V.E. Neuberg, *Popular Education in Eighteenth-Century England* (1971).
R. Porter, *English Society in the Eighteenth Century* (1990).
J. Rule, *Albion's People: English Society, 1714–1815* (1992).
K.D.M. Snell, *Annals of the Labouring Poor: Social Change and Agrarian England, 1660–1900* (1985).
L. Stone, *The Family, Sex and Marriage in England, 1500–1800* (1977).
L. Stone, *Road to Divorce: England, 1530–1987* (1990).
A. Wilson (ed.), *Rethinking Social History: English Society 1570–1920 and its Interpretation* (Manchester, 1993).

7. TOWNS

P. Borsay, *The English Urban Renaissance: Culture and Society in the Provincial Town, 1660–1770* (1989).
C.W. Chalkin, *The Provincial Towns of Georgian England* (1984).
P. Clark (ed.), *The Cambridge Urban History of Britain, II. 1540–1840* (2000).
P.J. Corfield, *The Impact of English Towns, 1700–1800* (1982).
G.S. de Krey, *A Fractured Society: The Politics of London in the First Age of Party, 1688–1715* (1985).
R.A. Houston, *Social Change in the Age of Enlightenment, Edinburgh 1660–1750* (Oxford, 1994).

8. FAITH AND THE CHURCHES

J.E. Bradley, *Religion, Revolution and English Radicalism: Nonconformity in Eighteenth-Century Politics and Society* (1990).
C.G. Brown, *The Social History of Religion in Scotland since 1730* (1987).
W. Gibson, *Church, State and Society, 1760–1850* (1994).
H.D. Rack, *Reasonable Enthusiast: John Wesley and the Rise of Methodism* (1989).
W. Gibson, *The Church of England 1688–1832* (2000).
W.M. Jacob, *Lay People and Religion in the Early Eighteenth Century* (1996).
E.G. Rupp, *Religion in England, 1688–1791* (1991).
P. Virgin, *The Church in a State of Negligence: Ecclesiastical Structure and Problems of Church Reform, 1700–1840* (1989).
J. Walsh, C. Haydon and S. Taylor (eds), *The Church of England c. 1689–c.1833. From Toleration to Tractarianism* (Cambridge, 1993).
W.R. Ward, *The Protestant Evangelical Awakening* (1992).

9. ENLIGHTENMENT AND SCIENCE

A.C. Chitnis, *The Scottish Enlightenment: A Social History* (1976).
J. Gascoigne, *Joseph Banks and the English Enlightenment* (1994).
M.C. Jacob, *The Newtonians and the English Revolution, 1689–1720* (1976).

R. Porter, *Disease, Medicine and Society in England, 1550–1860* (1987).
S. Shapin, *The Scientific Revolution* (1996).
L. Stewart, *The Rise of Public Science: Rhetoric, Technology, and Natural Philosophy in Newtonian Britain, 1660–1750* (1992).
K. Thomas, *Man and the Natural World: Changing Attitudes in England, 1500–1800* (1983).

10. CULTURE AND THE ARTS

J. Brewer and A. Bermingham (eds), *The Consumption of Culture, 1600–1800: Image, Object, Text* (1995).
M. Dobson, *The Making of the National Poet: Shakespeare, Adaptation, and Authorship, 1660–1769* (1992).
J. Feather, *The Provincial Book Trade in Eighteenth Century England* (1985).
J. Harley, *Music in Purcell's London: The Social Background* (1968).
S. Jones, *The Cambridge Introduction to Art. The Eighteenth Century* (Cambridge, 1985).
R. Leppert, *Music and Image: Domesticity, Ideology and Socio-Cultural Formation in Eighteenth-Century England* (1988).
M. Pointon, *Hanging the Head: Portraiture and Social Formation in Eighteenth-Century England* (1993).
C. Rawson, *Satire and Sentiment 1660–1830* (1994).
J. Sambrook, *The Eighteenth Century: The Intellectual and Cultural Context of English Literature, 1700–1789* (1986).
J. Sutherland, *English Literature of the Late Seventeenth Century* (1969).
D.Underdown, *Start of Play. Cricket and Culture in Eighteenth-Century England* (2000).
W. Weber, *The Rise of Musical Classics in Eighteenth-Century England: A Study in Canon, Ritual, and Ideology* (1992).
S.N. Zwicker (ed.), *The Cambridge Companion to English Literature, 1650–1740* (1998).

11. AUTHORITY, THE STATE AND ADMINISTRATION

J.M. Beattie, *Crime and the Courts in England, 1660–1800* (1986).
M.J. Braddick, *State Formation in Early Modern England, c. 1550–1700* (2001).
J. Brewer and J. Styles (eds), *An Ungovernable People: the English and their Law in the Seventeenth and Eighteenth Centuries* (1980).
A. Fletcher, *Reform in the Provinces: The Government of Stuart England* (1986).
P. King, *Crime, Justice, and Discretion in England 1740–1820* (2000).
G. Lamoine (ed.), *Charges to the Grand Jury 1689–1803* (1992).
M. de Lacy, *Prison Reform in Lancashire, 1700–1850* (1986).
D. Lieberman, *The Province of Legislation Determined: Legal Theory in Eighteenth-Century Britain* (1989).
J. Oldham (ed.), *The Mansfield Manuscripts and the Growth of English Law in the Eighteenth Century* (1992).
J.S. Sharpe, *Crime in Early Modern England, 1550–1750* (1984).

12. POLITICAL WORLDS

H. Barker, *Newspapers, Politics, and Public Opinion in Late Eighteenth-Century England* (1998).
J. Black, *The English Press 1621–1861* (2001).

J. Cannon, *Parliamentary Reform, 1660–1832* (1972).
J. Cannon (ed.), *The Whig Ascendancy: Colloquies on Hanoverian England* (1981).
J. Clark, *The Language of Liberty 1660–1832: Political Discourse and Social Dynamics in the Anglo-American World* (Cambridge, 1993).
I.R. Christie, *Wilkes, Wyvill and Reform* (1962).
E. Cruickshanks and J. Black (eds), *The Jacobite Challenge* (1988).
H.T. Dickinson, *Liberty and Property: Political Ideology in Eighteenth-Century Britain* (1977).
H.T. Dickinson, *The Politics of the People in Eighteenth Century Britain* (1995).
F. O'Gorman, *Voters, Patrons, and Parties: The Unreformed Electoral System in Hanoverian England, 1734–1832* (1989).
T. Harris, *Politics under the Later Stuarts: Party Conflict in a Divided Society, 1660–1715* (1993).
B. Kemp, *King and Commons, 1660–1832* (1957).
J.P. Kenyon, *Revolution Principles: The Politics of Party, 1689–1720* (1977).
C. Roberts, *The Growth of Responsible Government in Stuart England* (1966).

13. POLITICS

R. Beddard (ed.), *The Revolutions of 1688* (1991).
J. Black, *Walpole in Power* (2001).
J. Black, *Pitt the Elder* (2000).
J.E. Bradley, *Religion, Revolution and English Radicalism* (1990).
J. Brewer, *Party Ideology and Popular Politics at the Accession of George III* (1976).
T. Claydon, *William III and the Godly Reformation* (1996).
H.T. Dickinson, *Bolingbroke* (1970).
B.W. Hill, *British Parliamentary Parties, 1742–1832* (1985).
C. Jones (ed.), *Britain in the First Age of Party 1680–1750* (1987).
J.R. Jones (ed.), *Liberty Secured? Britain before and after 1688* (1992).
G.S. de Krey, *A Fractured Society: The Politics of London in the First Age of Party, 1688–1715* (1985).
F.P. Lock, *Edmund Burke, I. 1730–1784* (1999).
M. Peters, *The Elder Pitt* (1998).
N. Rogers, *Whigs and Cities: Popular Politics in the Age of Walpole and Pitt* (1989).
C. Rose, *England in the 1690s: Revolution, Religion, and War* (1999).
L.G. Schwoerer (ed.), *The Revolution of 1688–1689: Changing Perspectives* (1992).
P.D.G. Thomas, *Lord North* (1976).
P.D.G. Thomas, *John Wilkes: A Friend to Liberty* (1996).
K. Wilson, *The Sense of the People: Politics, Culture and Imperialism in England, 1715–1785* (1995).

14. CONTINENTAL COMPARISONS AND LINKS

T. Ertman, *Birth of the Leviathan: Building States and Regimes in Medieval and Early Modern Europe* (1997).
J. Glete, *Nations and Navies: Warships, Navies and State Building in Europe and America, 1500–1860* (Stockholm, 1993).
R.M. Hatton, *George I. Elector and King* (1978).
D. Szechi, *The Jacobites: Britain and Europe 1688–1788* (1994).
R. Szostak, *The Role of Transportation in the Industrial Revolution: A Comparison of England and France* (1991).

15. THE RISE OF A WORLD POWER

J. Black, *A System of Ambition? British Foreign Policy 1660–1793* (2000).

J. Black, *Britain as a Military Power 1689–1815* (1999).

T.O. Lloyd, *The British Empire, 1558–1983* (1989).

P.J. Marshall, *'A Free though Conquering People': Britain and Asia in the Eighteenth Century* (1981).

P.J. Marshall (ed.), *The Oxford History of the Eighteenth Century, II. The Eighteenth Century* (1998).

S. Taylor, R. Connors and C. Jones (eds), *Hanoverian Britain and Empire* (1998).

Chronology

1688 William of Orange lands at Torbay. James II's government collapses.
1689 Bill of Rights. William and Mary become joint sovereigns. Toleration Act. Nine Years' War with France begins.
1690 William defeats James at Battle of the Boyne in Ireland.
1691 Irish Jacobites defeated at Aughrim and capitulate at Limerick.
1694 Triennial Act. Bank of England incorporated. Queen Mary dies. Terrible fire in Warwick.
1695 Licensing Act lapses: end of pre-publication censorship. Bank of Scotland founded.
1697 Treaty of Ryswick ends war with France.
1698 Society for Promoting Christian Knowledge founded.
1700 Play *The Way of the World* by William Congreve.
1701 Act of Settlement.
1702 William III dies. Queen Anne to throne. English joins War of the Spanish Succession.
1704 Duke of Marlborough victorious at Blenheim.
1705 Work starts on Blenheim Palace (finished 1724).
1707 Union between England and Scotland. Bath turnpike trust established.
1709 Abraham Darby smelts iron with coke. French-backed Jacobite invasion of Scotland fails. Whigs dominate government.
1711 *The Spectator* begins.
1712 Handel settles in London. Thomas Newcomen's atmospheric engine.
1713 Treaty of Utrecht.
1714 Schism Act. Anne dies and replaced by George I.
1715 Jacobite rebellion. Publication of first volume of *Vitruvius Britannicus*.
1716 Septennial Act.
1717 Whig Split.
1718 Smallpox inoculation introduced.
1719 Repeal of Occasional Conformity and Schism Acts.
1720 South Sea Bubble. Walpole returns to government.
1721 Walpole First Lord of Treasury. St Martin-in-the-Fields built by James Gibbs.
1722 Daniel Defoe publishes *Moll Flanders*.
1724 Levellers Revolt in Galloway.
1725 Chiswick House built by Lord Burlington and William Kent.
1726 Jonathan Swift publishes *Gulliver's Travels*. John Harrison invents a compensating balance for clocks.
1727 George I succeeded by George II. Avon made fully navigable between Bath and Bristol.

1728 John Gay's *Beggar's Opera* performed.
1729 John Wesley begins Holy Club meetings at Oxford. Royal Infirmary opens in Edinburgh.
1731 Fire devastates Blandford Forum.
1732 Colony of Georgia founded. Covent Garden Theatre opens in London. Vauxhall Gardens opened.
1733 John Kay patents the 'flying shuttle'. Excise Crisis. *Essay on Man* by Alexander Pope. Jethro Tull publishes *Horse-Hoeing Husbandry*. Molasses Act.
1736 Witchcraft Act bans accusations of witchcraft and sorcery. Gin riots.
1737 Stage Licensing Act.
1739 War of Jenkins' Ear against Spain begins. Great North Road turnpiked from Grantham to Stamford.
1740 Samuel Richardson publishes *Pamela*. Thomas Arne composes *Rule Britannia*. Production of crucible steel by Benjamin Huntsman of Sheffield.
1741 Walpole does badly in general election. First performance of Handel's *Messiah*.
1742 Walpole resigns. Henry Fielding's *Joseph Andrews*.
1743 Henry Pelham becomes First Lord of the Treasury. Devon and Exeter Hospital opens.
1744 War with France formally declared. Unsuccessful French invasion attempt.
1745 Charles Edward Stuart lands in Scotland and invades England. Turns back at Derby. New Market-House in Bristol.
1746 Defeat of Jacobites at Culloden.
1747 Pelhams victorious in general election. Heritable Jurisdictions Act. Hogarth's *Industry and Idleness*.
1748 Treaty of Aix-la-Chapelle ends war with France and Spain. *The Adventures of Roderick Random* by novelist Tobias Smollett.
1749 Henry Fielding's *The History of Tom Jones*.
1750 London earthquake.
1751 Frederick, Prince of Wales dies.
1753 Jewish Naturalization Act. Hardwicke's Marriage Act. Salthouse Dock in Liverpool completed.
1754 Henry Pelham succeeded by Duke of Newcastle. General election. Fighting between British and French begins in North America.
1755 Samuel Johnson's *Dictionary of the English Language* published.
1756 Britain and France go to war in the Seven Years' War. Loss of Minorca. Newcastle resigns. Pitt–Devonshire ministry formed.
1757 Pitt–Newcastle ministry formed.
1758 Major strike by check weavers in Lancashire.
1759 British capture Québec and defeat French fleet.
1760 George II succeeded by George III. Surrender of Montreal. *Fragments of Ancient Poetry* by James MacPherson launches Ossian cult.
1761 Surrender of Pondicherry, last French base in India. Pitt resigns. First regular Norwich to London coach service taking less than a day.
1762 Newcastle replaced by Bute.
1763 Peace of Paris ends Seven Years' War. Bute replaced by Grenville. *North Briton* no. 45.
1764 *The Castle of Otranto* by Horace Walpole. James Hargreaves's spinning jenny. Expulsion of Wilkes from House of Commons.
1765 Stamp Act. Grenville replaced by Rockingham. James Watt invents the separate condenser for the steam engine. Irish Road Act.
1766 Rockingham replaced by Chatham. Stamp Act repealed. Food riots. Henry Cavendish discovers hydrogen to be an element.
1767 New Quay in Lancaster completed.
1768 St George's Fields Massacre. Chatham replaced by Grafton. Royal Academy founded. Richard Arkwright invents the water-powered spinning frame. London silk-weavers strike. New bridge across Avon at Bristol.

1769 Josiah Wedgwood opens Etruria pottery. Tees bridged at Stockton and Thames at Blackfriars. Shakespeare Jubilee.
1770 Grafton replaced by North. Falkland Islands crisis. Boston Massacre.
1773 *She Stoops to Conquer* by Oliver Goldsmith. Boston Tea Party. *Encyclopaedia Britannica*.
1774 North succeeds in general election.
1775 American War of Independence begins. New bridge across Severn at Stourport.
1776 American Declaration of Independence. Adam Smith publishes *The Wealth of Nations*.
1777 *The School for Scandal* by Sheridan. Battle of Saratoga.
1778 France joins war against Britain. Catholic Relief Act. *Evelina* by Fanny Burney. First exhibition of paintings by Joseph Wright at Royal Academy.
1779 Completion of iron bridge at Coalbrookdale. Samuel Crompton's mule. Spain enters war.
1780 Gordon 'No Popery' Riots. Association Movement.
1781 Cornwallis surrenders at Yorktown. William Herschel discovers Uranus. Henry Cavendish determines the composition of water.
1782 North resigns, replaced by Rockingham, and, on his death, by Shelburne. Battle of the Saints. James Watt patents innovations that give a comparative uniformity of rotary motion.
1783 Shelburne resigns. Replaced by Fox–North coalition. Peace of Versailles ends War of American Independence. Fall of Fox–North ministry. William Pitt the Younger forms new government. Bank of Ireland established.

Index